A Life of John Keats

BY DOROTHY HEWLETT

Biography: *Elizabeth Barrett Browning*
Novels: *Victorian House*
A Shocking Bad Hat
Better than Figs
The Two Rapps
The Flying Horse

Plays: *The Losing Side*
Illusions
Penny Plain
The Magician
Ozymandias the King

From an early drawing by Joseph Severn in the
Dyce and Forster Collection at the Victoria and
Albert Museum

A Life of John Keats

Dorothy Hewlett

BARNES & NOBLE, Inc.
NEW YORK
PUBLISHERS & BOOKSELLERS SINCE 1873

HUTCHINSON & CO (*Publishers*) LTD
178–202 Great Portland Street, London, W.1

London Melbourne Sydney
Auckland Johannesburg New York

First published by Hurst & Blackett 1937
Third revised edition 1970

Published in the United States of America, 1970
by Barnes & Noble, Inc.

This book has been printed offset litho in Great
Britain by The Camelot Press Ltd.,
London and Southampton
ISBN 389 02041 9

To the dear memory of my cousin,

Florence Terry

. . . till the Future dares
Forget the Past, his fate and fame shall be
An echo and a light unto eternity.

CONTENTS

LIST OF ILLUSTRATIONS

IN THE TEXT

PREFACE

It has been my aim in this book to set Keats against the Georgian background. I have let him speak in his own words as much as possible. I have approached the man from the angle of his life rather than his work (so far as the two can be separated), though I have out of enthusiasm been betrayed into more commentary on the poems than I originally intended. I have, as a part of my scheme of presenlting Keats 'in period,' given more space to the reviews of his books than previous biographers. If these are found not to be of general interest I hope the reader will skip with a clear conscience. The reviews are all concentrated at the end of Chapters VII, XIII and XIX. They are, however, of value to the specialist in assessing the attitude of contemporary critics and readers to the romantic movement.

Now for the agreeable ceremony of thanks. To Mr. Buxton Forman I make my first bow. With sources, with advice and kindly criticism he has removed many briars from my path. Without his help and preliminary encouragement this book would not have *been*. I am indebted also for help, advice and criticism to Dr. Willard B. Pope who has in addition generously put at my disposal unpublished research upon Brown, Haydon, Reynolds and others of Keats's circle. My thanks are due to the officials of the Hampstead Library who have allowed me access to much material in their possession and especially to Mr. Lionel R. McColvin, the Chief Librarian, and to Mr. Fred Edgcumbe, Curator of the Memorial House, the fairy godfather of all good students of Keats. To Dr. Barry L. Garrad, who has given me much of his valuable time, my debt is a peculiar one and of longer standing. I am proud to call myself his pupil. Mr. Edmund Blunden has in his unfailing kindness read two chapters of my book relating to Leigh Hunt and answered various questions out of his wide knowledge of the period. Professor H. W. Garrod has given me a delightful foretaste of his new edition of the poems and allowed me to use information. Dr. E. de Sélincourt has also helped me on some points connected with the poems. The Secretary and Librarian at Guy's Hospital have given me access to records and books. Mrs. Stanley Unwin has allowed me to make use of letters by Severn belonging to her and the Director of the Pierpont Morgan Library has given me permission to quote from letters in their possession. I have endeavoured whenever possible to work direct from sources but I am naturally in some measure indebted to the works of the late Sir Sidney Colvin and Miss Amy

Lowell and must thank Mr. E. V. Lucas, Messrs. Macmillan & Co.,
Ltd., Jonathan Cape, Ltd., and the Houghton Mifflin Co., Boston,
U.S.A., for allowing me to make some quotations from them.

I render also grateful thanks to the following kind people who
have given me information upon special points or aspects: the Duke
of Argyll; Messrs. G. Allen, Clerk to Christ's Hospital; Mr. F. N.
Doubleday of Guy's Hospital; Leonard Jordan of Newport, Isle of
Wight; Miss Naomi Kirk; Dr. T. Wilson Parry; Mr. Francis W.
Robinson, Assistant Curator to Cincinnati Art Museum; the Keeper
of the Scottish National Portrait Gallery; Signorina Vera Signorelli,
Curator of the Keats Shelley Memorial, Rome; Messrs. H. Tapley-
Soper, City Librarian, Exeter; Sotheby and Co.; H. W. Turner,
Teignmouth; Dr. G. C. Williamson and Mr. H. Saxe Wyndham.

DOROTHY HEWLETT.

February 18th, 1937.

In this, my second edition, I have corrected a few errors, presented
new material and thrown fresh light, thanks to the labours of my husband, Norman Kilgour, on the tangled financial affairs of the Keats
family. This subject we hope to pursue further when leisure permits:
we have, however, at least cleared away some of the thorns in the path.

I have, in affection and gratitude, to renew my thanks to Mr.
Maurice Buxton Forman who has so generously allowed me to publish
a new portrait of Keats, to print the 'Amena' letter, and to quote
direct from Haydon's *Journals*. I also owe a considerable debt to
Professor Willard B. Pope, of the University of Vermont who has
very kindly given up much of his valuable time in selecting and
photographing the relevant passages of the *Journals*. For many minor
but precious items of Keatsiana I must thank Mr. Edmund Blunden
who, with his invariable generosity, has put at my disposal the fruits
of years of diligent and inspired search in the byways of literature and
journalism. Mrs. Mina Osborne has graciously given me the privilege
of using family information about her grandfather, Charles Brown.
Mr. J. T. Bailey, Chief Librarian of Hampstead, has again put at my
disposal, with the ever friendly help of Mr. Harold Preston, Assistant
Curator, the treasures in the House and Museum. Mr. J. Ward
Perkins, honorary secretary of the Keats-Shelley Memorial in Rome,
has kindly allowed me to use Severn's death-bed portrait. I have

also to thank Professor Werner W. Beyer and the Oxford University Press, New York, for permission to quote from Professor Beyer's valuable book, *Keats and the Daemon King*; and for advice, help or information on various points, Mr. C. K. Adams, of the National Portrait Gallery; Mr. Harold Baker, Clerk to the Shanklin–Sandown Urban District Council; Professor Beyer; Mr. Harold Busby, Clerk to the Worshipful Society of Apothecaries; Signora Signorelli Cacciatore of the Keats–Shelley Memorial House, Rome; Mr. G. E. Clarke, Borough Librarian, Margate; the late Dr. T. G. Crump; Dr. I. H. Gosset of Salisbury and Mr. Thorold Gosset of Cambridge; Miss Greta Lamb; Mr. T. Bramley Layton, of Guy's Hospital; Rev. J. Ross Macvicar, of Colne, Lancs; Mr. Richard Murry, of the Central School of Arts and Crafts; Mr. W. H. Parker, of Edinburgh; Mr. Neville Rogers; Professor Clara Troisi, of Naples; Miss H. Swann, City of Leicester Information Bureau; the late Dr. Cecil Wall, Senior Warden to the Worshipful Society of Apothecaries; Mr. T. D. Wilson, and Professor F. Wood Jones, Royal College of Surgeons.

As eleven years have elapsed since my first edition too many of those who helped me have now left this 'vale of soul-making'; among them Dr. Barry L. Garrad, a valued friend whose erudition, never-failing patience and kindliness were always at the service of his many pupils.

The loss of Mr. Fred Edgcumbe, that stalwart Man of Keats, was and still is a severe one to scholar and mere enthusiast alike. One who was his friend describes him as 'an inimitable man, who was equally capable of enjoying the finest poetry of Keats and entertaining the modern representatives of Keats's family—learned without calling himself learned, rapid at seizing every opportunity of making the collections at Hampstead more attractive and extensive, and inspired with a sense of the deathlessness of those who had lived and loved in those rooms over a century since.' To this tribute from a poet and scholar all those who knew him will join in reverence.

DOROTHY HEWLETT.

September 17th, 1948.

Since writing the above I have had the privilege, through the kindness of the editor, Professor Hyder Edward Rollins, of revising my proofs in the light of fresh information contained in *The Keats Circle*. I have to thank the Harvard University Press for permission to quote from this valuable publication which should be in the hands of every student and lover of Keats.

D.H.

January 31st, 1949.

In this, a second impression of the edition published last October, I have to thank Messrs. Hurst & Blackett for giving me an opportunity of embodying a few fresh items of information and some small corrections.

February 4th, 1950.   D. H.

As this edition is being issued in offset form I have not been able drastically to revise, but I have tried to embody fresh information either within the text or by appendices. I have, as before, made little or no use of contemporary biographies which I have therefore not listed; though I must acknowledge a debt to Professor Bate's admirable work.

I have to thank my husband, Norman Kilgour, Hon. Secretary of the Keats-Shelley Memorial Association, for his help in the difficult matters of Keats finances and genealogy, both of which he has made his especial study. Mr. John Buxton, Mrs. Christina Gee of Keats House, Hampstead, Mr. R. A. J. Jennings, Mrs. Jean Haines, Mr. P. E. Jones, Deputy Keeper of the City of London Records, Miss Phyllis Mann, Mrs. Mary Moorman. Dr. Fernando Paradinas and Mr. John Rutherford have all assisted me on certain points, for which I am grateful.

D. H.

March, 1970.

CHAPTER I

His Birth, Parentage and Early Childhood

ON the 31st of October, 1795, at the 'Swan and Hoop' Livery Stables, 28 Finsbury Pavement, John Keats was born.

Finsbury Pavement, outside the precincts of the City of London, faced a wide stretch of flat fields, the Moorfields. Within the City narrow streets were thronged with life both commercial and domestic: the majority of City tradesmen still lived over their shops. But London was beginning to spread outwards and the stables were on the fringe of the growing suburb of Finsbury. Near by were the new and stately Square and Circus, now the last remnant of the living green of Moorfields.[1]

With the bustle of the prosperous stables, the ring of hooves on the cobbled yard, the jingle of harness and the shouts of ostlers, it must have been a cheerful and stimulating environment for a lively baby. The legend goes that he was a seven-months' child but there seem to have been none of the characteristic signs of delicacy about him.

Thomas Keats, the poet's father, head ostler to John Jennings, the proprietor of the 'Swan and Hoop', married his master's daughter. In addition to the livery stables John Jennings ran an ale house, also called the 'Swan and Hoop', adjoining. Altogether a man of substance, Keats's grandfather at his death, in March, 1805, left a fortune of over thirteen thousand pounds.

We know little of Keats's mother and still less of his father. One account of him suggests that he was a boorish fellow unduly elevated by his rise in the world, apt to carouse with jolly companions, that 'he did not possess or display any great accomplishments.' The second account gives him as 'a man of remarkably fine common sense and native respectability' with 'a lively energetic countenance'. The first is in the reported words of Richard Abbey, afterwards guardian to the Keats children, and the second that of Charles Cowden Clarke, son of the headmaster of the school at which the boys received their education. Abbey's account of Keats's parentage is, on certain points, of proved inaccuracy.

In 1827, six years after Keats's death, his publisher, John Taylor, intending to write a memoir of the poet, asked Abbey for particulars of his origins and early years. These Taylor wrote down in a letter to his friend, Richard Woodhouse. Abbey, he said, came from the same

[1] *See* Appendix I (i)

village as Keats's grandmother, Colne,[1] at the foot of Pendle Hill in Lancashire. In the absence of a close family connection, Abbey should have been just the man to give Taylor the information he wanted; but the picture he presents of Keats's mother is so black that we can only hope, as it has been proved incorrect in several particulars, that his view of her was distorted and wrongheaded.

After describing Keats's grandfather, John Jennings, as too fond of the pleasures of the table, 'a complete Gourmand' (a statement which has at least a partial support in his death certificate; he died of 'the Gout'), the Abbey memoir continues:

His Daughter in this respect somewhat resembled him, but she was more remarkably the Slave of other appetites, attributable probably to this for their exciting Cause.—At an early Age she told my Informant, Mr. Abby, that she must & would have a Husband; and her passions were so ardent, he said, that it was dangerous to be alone with her.—She was a handsome, little woman.—Her Features were good & regular, with the Exception of her Mouth which was unusually wide. A little Circumstance was mentioned to me as indicative of her Character—She used to go to a Grocers in Bishops-gate Street, opposite the Church, probably out of some Liking for the Owner of the Shop,—but the Man remarked to Mr Abby that Miss Jennings always came in dirty weather, & when she went away, she held up her Clothes very high in crossing the Street, & to be sure, says the Grocer, she has uncommonly handsome Legs.—He was not however fatally wounded by Cupid the Parthian.—

But it was not long before she found a Husband, nor did she go far for him—a Helper in her Father's Stables appeared sufficiently desirable in her Eyes to make her forget the Disparity of their Circumstances, & it was not long before John Keats had the Honor to be united to his Master's Daughter.

The man whom Frances Jennings married on the 9th of October, 1794, was not 'John', but Thomas; nor was he a mere helper in the stable but the head ostler, a position of trust and responsibility. To this couple were born, after John, George in 1797, Tom in 1799, Edward who died in infancy in 1801, and in 1803 their daughter, Frances Mary.

Almost certainly before the birth of the younger children the family moved to Craven Street, City Road, half a mile away from the stables. His parents-in-law having retired to Ponders End, a village in Middle-sex, the management of the business seems now to have fallen entirely into the hands of Thomas Keats.

On April 15th, 1804, at thirty years of age, he met with a fatal accident which was reported in *The Times* for Tuesday, April 17th, as follows:

[1] Her maiden name was Whalley.

On Sunday, Mr. Keats, livery-stable keeper in Moorfield, went to dine at Southgate; he returned at a late hour, and on passing down the City-road, his horse fell with him, when he had the misfortune to fracture his skull. It was about one o'clock in the morning when the watchman found him, he was at that time alive, but speechless; the watchman got assistance, and took him to a house in the neighbourhood, where he died about eight o'clock.

A similar notice appeared in *The Star* for April 19th, and was repeated in *The Gentleman's Magazine* for May. They both agree entirely with the Coroner's findings at the inquest on April 17th.

According to Cowden Clarke, Thomas was returning from a visit to his boys who were at boarding-school at Enfield. Southgate is only a short distance from Enfield; he may well have followed up his visit to the school by dining with a friend there. Richard Abbey is reported to have said in regard to the accident:

He kept a remarkably fine Horse for his own Riding, and on Sundays would go out with others who prided themselves in the like Distinction, to Highgate, Highbury, or some other places of public Entertainment for Man & Horse. —At length one Sunday Night he was returning with some of his jolly Companions from a Carouse at one of these Places, riding very fast, and most probably very much in Liquor, when his Horse leaped upon the Pavement opposite the Methodist Chapel in the City Road, & falling with him against the Iron Railings so dreadfully crushed him that he died as they were carrying him Home.

It is clear from all accounts that Thomas Keats was riding alone.

Frances Keats, at the age of twenty-nine, was now left with three growing boys and a baby girl. There was an adequate income to support them but its source was a livery stable, a difficult business for a woman to manage. As her father died less than a year later, it is possible that he was too ill to give her much assistance. She had a brother, Midgley[1] John Jennings, but he was an officer in the Marines and probably away on service. Within three months, on the 27th of June, 1804, she became the wife of a William Rawlings, marrying him, curiously enough, in the church at which her first marriage had taken place, St. George's, Hanover Square.

It seems odd that Frances chose on both occasions to marry here, out of her own parish, but there do seem to be strong family connections with St. George's. There were several Keatses in the Street Directory at the time of her marriage to Thomas and a considerable number of Keats marriages entered in the church register between 1764 and 1784.

---

[1] In 1756 a John Whalley married Ann Midgley at Adel, near Colne.

Added to this, Jennings is a common name in the district; borne possibly by descendants of the Marlborough family.

Taylor's version of Abbey's account of the second marriage, and of the subsequent career of Frances Rawlings, is as follows:

I think it was not much more than 8 Months after this Event that Mrs Keats again being determined to have a Husband, married Mr Rawlins, a Clerk in Smith Payne & Co's—I know very little of him, further than that he would have had a Salary of 700£ a year eventually had he continued in his Situation.—I suppose therefore that he quitted it on becoming the Proprieter of the Livery Stables by his Marriage with Mrs Keats, but how long the Concern was carried on, or at what period Mr Jennings died, or relinquished it, I did not learn—It is perhaps sufficient to know that Rawlins also died after some little Time, and that his Widow was afterwards living *as* the Wife of a Jew at Enfield, named Abraham.

The statement that Rawlings was a clerk in 'Smith Payne & Co's' (Smith, Payne and Smiths of George Street, Mansion House) is probably correct. In 1886 Fanny Keats de Llanos (Keats's sister) told her lawyer that Rawlings was at one time a bank clerk.

Fanny Keats stated in old age that the children never lived with Rawlings. When next we hear of them they were at Edmonton living with their grandmother. Mrs. Rawlings herself soon left her husband. As to Rawlings, we know no more of him than that he appears in *Holden's Triennial Directory* as stable keeper at the 'Swan and Hoop' from 1805–1808.[1] The Jew, except for a bare fact that there was a J. Abraham at that time owning property in Edmonton, may perhaps be regarded as common City gossip. When a woman leaves her husband the public is apt to assume that she goes to another man.

The Jew named Abraham was not the only irregularity of conduct attributed to poor Frances by Richard Abbey. He said that after Thomas Keats's death she took to 'the Brandy Bottle' and that

the Growth of this degrading Propensity to liquor may account perhaps for the strange Irregularities—or rather Immorality of her after-Life—I should imagine that her children seldom saw her, and would hope that they knew not all her Conduct.

Much of this we know to be untrue. Frances Rawlings was with her mother and children for some years before her death. As there were only six years between that event and her second marriage, during several of which she lay ill, there could not have been much time for protracted 'Irregularities'.

[1] *See* Appendix I (ii)

Of Rawlings' character we know nothing. There must, however have been some cause for the grandmother's drastic action in removing the children. It seems likely that he was a common adventurer. He had, according to Fanny Keats, no property whatever when he married her mother. Before the Married Woman's Property Act there was no lack of needy gentlemen willing to acquire property by marriage with a well-to-do woman. Having taken possession of the 'Swan and Hoop', Rawlings might not be sorry to rid himself of the encumbrance of four children. Soon he was to be free of their mother too. The departure of Frances might have been the result of deliberate action on his part. It was the habit of these men who preyed upon women to make the home so uncomfortable that the wife was glad to leave. Once having left her husband she had no further claim on him for support. He would remain sole master of her property which he had acquired by strictly legal methods.

Frances was an affectionate mother and not likely to let her children go willingly. She would, however, have no say in the matter. By her marriage with Rawlings she made her children his property. If he chose to hand them over to their grandmother she could only protest in vain.

Cowden Clarke had, unfortunately, only met with Keats's mother when she visited her boys at school. His description of her, however, gives a very different impression from that of the Abbey memoir. He says she was tall (against Abbey's 'little woman'), 'of good figure, with large oval face, and sensible deportment'. Indeed, to her own sons Abbey himself gave a very different account of their mother. According to George, he 'used to say he never saw a woman of the talents and sense of my grandmother, except my mother.' Of the direct opinion of the children we have only George's. John Keats was devoted to his mother, but we have no word of his about her. Although he was thirteen when she died, George does not seem to have remembered her well, but this might be accounted for by a long illness and by the absence of the boys for the greater part of the year at boarding-school. He described her as 'a most excellent and affectionate parent and as I thought a woman of uncommon talents'. She was, according to him, ambitious for her boys intending, had their father lived, to send them to Harrow. 'She was confined to her bed many years before her death by a rheumatism and at last died of a Consumption.'

As John attended her in her last illness and she was bedridden for many years before, it seems fairly safe to assume that when Frances left Rawlings, or soon after, she went to her mother.

It is a popular and perhaps well-founded belief that the mother of a man of genius transmits more to her child than the father. Even discounting Abbey's report of Frances' strong physical passion, the evidence of her hasty second marriage would suggest her as a woman of impulse, of feeling rather than prudence; feeling sublimated to a fine sensibility in the son. Abbey's description of her to George as of 'talents and sense', together with Cowden Clarke's 'sensible deportment', does not, however, suggest a creature of mere impulse. With regard to the father, whom Keats resembled in shortness of stature and hazel eyes, again the accounts differ widely, though Clarke's attribute of a 'remarkably fine common sense' and a 'lively energetic countenance' would seem to imply a mental heritage from Thomas Keats.

The maternal grandmother, too, was a woman of character. Abbey has nothing but good to say of Alice Jennings 'She was a very different kind of woman' (different from her daughter) '& when left to herself appears to have acted the part of a discreet Parent to the Children.' However it may be, somehow from those obscure folk there sprang a genius. But genius is, perhaps, the fine flower of a whole generation rather than of a family.

Of the baby Keats we have only information at third hand through B. R. Haydon, the painter, somehow reaching him from Mrs. Grafty who lived next door to the family in Craven Street. When learning to speak he did not, as most babies do, merely echo what was said but would give a rime to the last word and then laugh. His mother was indulgent to her children and especially to her first-born whom, his brother said, she 'humoured in every whim, of which he had not a few.' Another story runs that at one time when his mother was ill and absolute quiet was ordered, he kept guard at her door with an old sword and allowed no one to enter. Haydon in his journal coloured up this, or a similar story, into:

He was when an infant a most violent and ungovernable child—at five years of age or there abouts he got hold of a naked sword and shutting the door swore nobody should go out—his mother wanted to go out—but he threatened her so furiously that she burst into tears, and was obliged to wait until somebody through the window saw her situation, came, & released her.[1]

The sword may have been, in sober fact, a little iron one, this being a favourite toy far into the nineteenth century. However, the first of these stories of John's belligerent conduct demonstrates his undoubted devotion to his mother, and both can remind us that he was born in wartime.

In 1795 we had been at war with France for nearly two years. In

---

[1] *The Diary of Benjamin Robert Haydon*, II, 1.107.

1797 Great Britain was the sole antagonist by land and sea of a vigorous, militant Republic. The war at sea was indeed of vivid and peculiar interest to the young Keatses: their uncle, Captain Midgley John Jennings, then Lieutenant (born 24th October, 1777) was a Royal Marine serving from January, 1797 to September, 1800 in H.M.S. *Russell* (seventy-four guns, commanded by Captain Trollope). During the Battle of Camperdown in 1797 Midgley was in temporary command on board of the Marine detachment.[1] Charles Cowden Clarke tells us that he was a hero to his nephews; and, no doubt, at the Enfield school which Midgley had himself attended when a boy, John, George and Tom boasted loudly about their uncle at sea.

In the early years of the new century England herself was threatened with invasion. Naughty children were subdued by the name of 'Boney' who in 1804 crowned himself Emperor of the French. The South Coast was ringed with Martello towers and many people who lived by the sea were afraid to undress at night for fear of a landing, of swift, sudden attack under cover of darkness. London was astir with preparations for home defence. Little boys were whipped into military ardour, both by tales of valour from abroad and drillings and marchings within their midst. Large bodies of Volunteers were raised. The Swan and Hoop stables were close to the ground of the Honourable Artillery Company. The exercising ground of the Clerkenwell Volunteers was on the south side of Corporation Lane; their regular field days were held in Tub Field adjoining Claremont Square near to the Craven Street home of the Keatses. The Clerkenwell cavalry was composed of the richer tradesmen (was Thomas Keats among them?) who wore 'leathern breeches and boots and bearskin helmet cap, plumed with a white feather'. Did they ride on their fine, curvetting horses in and out of the Swan and Hoop? At the Grand Muster in Hyde Park in 1803 the London Volunteers were twenty-seven thousand strong.

In or about 1803 the two elder boys were sent to school at Enfield, a village within easy reach of their grandfather's house in Ponders End. They were 'not yet out of child's dress'; probably still wearing frocks. Little boys were breeched late in those days. Their lives were yet unshadowed, but soon the father's death came as the first of a series of domestic losses to darken their youth.

When they were taken from their mother the children must have gone to Ponders End, but on the death of their grandfather in 1805 Mrs. Jennings moved to Edmonton. There John spent his holidays as an ordinary, happy little boy, playing, quarrelling, scuffling with his brothers and showing no extraordinary mental powers. He rambled about joyfully in the lanes and meadows and along the lovely Pymmes

[1] From information given by the National Maritime Museum.

brook as it ran to join the River Lea. He had the natural boy's thought-
less love of catching and meddling with the creatures of the wild. . . .
'Goldfinches, Tomtits, Minnows, Mice, Ticklebacks, Dace, Cock
salmons and all the whole tribe of the Bushes and the Brooks.' Reviving
these childish memories in a letter to his sister in 1819 Keats added,
'but verily they are better in the Trees and the water . . .' He wrote
in some delightful rimes to her:

> There was a naughty boy
>   And a naughty boy was he
> He kept little fishes
>   In washing tubs three
>   In spite
>   Of the might
>   Of the Maid
>   Nor affraid
>   Of his Granny-good—
>   He often would
>   Hurly burly
>   Get up early
>   And go
>   By hook or crook
>   To the brook
>   And bring home
>   Miller's thumb
>   Tittle bat
>   Not over fat
>   Minnows small
>   As the stall
>   Of a glove
>   Not above
>   The size
>   Of a nice
>   Little Baby's
>   Little finger—
>   O he made
>   'Twas his trade
> Of Fish a pretty Kettle
>   A Kettle—A Kettle
> Of Fish a pretty Kettle
>   A Kettle!

Fanny Keats herself wrote when she was nearly eighty: 'I well remember . . . our pleasure in keeping little fish (called minnows I
think) and his love of birds, especially a favorite Tom Tit.' The little
sister was not excluded from boyish pleasures. John, George and Tom
were devoted to one another but even more devoted to their little sister,
whose favour each tried, by artful schemes for her amusement, to gain
for himself.

From some lines in *Endymion* it would appear that Keats liked to make little ships to float upon the brook:

> Of moulted feathers, touchwood, alder chips,
> With leave stuck in them! and the Neptune be
> Of their petty ocean.

To these poetic clues to Keats's boyhood life there may perhaps be added a third. Craven Street was conveniently near to Sadler's Wells Theatre. Mrs. Keats was, we are told, fond of amusement. At Easter in 1804 there was inaugurated in the theatre a form of entertainment which was to survive into the 'twenties, the Aquatic Theatre. Water was brought in from the New River and, at the first performance upon it, 'real ships of 100, 74 and 60 guns built rigged and manœuvred in the most correct manner' fired their broadsides. The play was *The Siege of Gibraltar* in which 'the gallant Sir Roger Curtis appeared in his boat to save the drowning Spaniards, the British Tars for that purpose plunging into the water'. This exciting entertainment was, if he were taken to see it, one which must have impressed Keats's imagination. The name of it was *Naumachia* and it may have led to his use of the Greek word in that curious sonnet: 'Before he went to feed with owls and bats.' Nebuchadnezzar's 'ugly dream' was

> Worse than an Hus'if's when she thinks her cream
> Made a Naumachia for mice and rats,

The word *Naumachia*, however, occurs in Bailey's Dictionary which Keats was in the habit of using.

In the July following her daughter's death in March, 1810, Mrs. Jennings, now seventy-four, chose two guardians for her grand-children. As her son, Captain Midgley Jennings, had died late in 1808 or early in 1809 there was apparently no near relative to whom she could confide them. The only other known relations of the Keats are Mary Sweetingburgh (of Old Street, City of London), great-aunt, who died on 4th November, 1813, and her children Charles, Betsy Cousins (of Lothbury, City of London) and Sarah Boswell (of Wal-worth, Surrey); Mrs. Midgley Jennings (*née* Margaret Peacock), aunt by marriage, and (born between 1806 and 1808 or 1809) three[1] cousins: Margaret Alice (later the wife of Canon Melvill), Midgley John and Meriam (Marian or Mary Anne?). It is possible there were some Keats connections (see p. 272) in business in the City, and in 1858 a Brighton bookseller named Keats claimed, B. W. Procter reported to

---

[1] There was actually a fourth cousin, William, but he died in infancy.

Leigh Hunt, to be a second cousin of the poet. This Keats mentioned as a mutual relation a 'Mr. Sheriff Keats.'

The men Mrs. Jennings chose were John Nowland Sandell and Richard Abbey, tea-dealer. 'In consideration of the love and affection which she had for them' she at once made over by indenture the money derived from her late husband, about £8,000, to be held in trust for the benefit of the boys until they came of age and in the case of their sister as a life settlement. Out of John Jennings' fortune of £13,000 capital sufficient to produce £200 a year went to his wife, £3,900 to Midgley for life (enough to produce £117 a year), £50 annuity to his daughter, Frances Rawlings (capital £1,600, later to be divided among her children), and £1,000 to be divided among the Keats grandchildren as each came of age.

The will,[1] being badly drafted, was submitted to the Court of Chancery, which settled the controversial points with laudable speed; also deciding what should be done with a surplus undisposed. For some reason unexplained the money from Mrs. Rawlings' annuity and the direct legacy lay unclaimed in Chancery until long after Keats's death, so that all that he had in life, so far as we know, was represented by the money left to him by his grandmother, about £2,000. From his father he inherited nothing: the small sum Thomas Keats left unwilled, under £2,000, was either spent by Frances or appropriated by Rawlings.

When Mrs. Jennings died in 1814 her trustees omitted to prove the will: it was not until 1817, a year after Sandell's death, that Abbey registered it, as sole trustee, stating that she 'died this year.' So the trusteeship started with irregularity.

Within a short space of ten years the Keats children were deprived of the love and care of parents, grandparents and uncle. After Sandell's death they came into the sole charge[2] of Richard Abbey, a guardian whom, in spite of a recent attempt to clear him, it is difficult to regard as an honest man.

---

[1] *See* Appendix I.

[2] Dilke speaks of a trustee who 'fled to Holland' who, until the publication of Norman Kilgour's article 'Mrs. Jennings' Will' K-S.M. *Bulletin XIII*, was thought to be Sandell. There are suggestions in the *Letters* of another trustee on the Continent, but no tangible evidence. The Mrs. Sandell mentioned on p. 111 was probably a sister.

CHAPTER II

Schooldays and Apprenticeship (1803-1815)

MATTHEW ARNOLD, referring to Keats's own statement, 'I think I shall be among the English poets after my death,' added, 'he is—he is with Shakespeare.'

In the preparation for his high destiny Keats was with Shakespeare. They both had the limited education of a middle-class boy and, to complete it, ranged freely among the English writers and moved among men. They sounded the depths of the heart's suffering and rose to the heights of creative imagination; both with a quick capacious intellect, a love of life and of their fellow-beings and the humour which enables a man to see in true perspective. *Julius Cæsar*, with its anachronisms, is more Roman in feeling than the scholarly plays of Ben Jonson: Keats (though it is true that later he felt the gaps in his knowledge, setting himself to fill them up with an intensity beyond a failing strength) had no Greek to balance the 'little Latin' of Shakespeare, but came nearer to the Greek spirit than any other English writer. The intuitive spirit of genius carries a man far. Perhaps he had better not be bound too tightly in chains in his boyhood.

Mrs. Keats is credited with a desire to send her sons to Harrow; a Harrow still in the grip of the classics, where the boys spent their days in construing. The greatest gain to Keats might have been a fine library, but he managed to obtain, mainly by borrowing, enough books to quicken his imagination into life and to produce within four short years poetry that will live through the ages.

In reality Keats was singularly fortunate in his school. At a tender age he came under the influence of John Clarke, 'a man of nobly liberal opinions, of refined taste in literature . . . as gentle-hearted as he was wise, and as wise as he was gentle-hearted.' Clarke must, too, have been a man of considerable courage: while Leigh Hunt was under sentence for his attack in *The Examiner* on the Prince Regent, he sent his son to the prison in Horsemonger Lane every week with baskets of vegetables and eggs. Although the Prince was unpopular and Liberal opinion was with the Hunt brothers, headmasters cannot usually afford to go against the established order of things. There must have been among the tradesmen fathers of his pupils many staunch 'Bible-crown-and-Constitution' men who would look askance at an acknowledgment of sympathy with a notorious Radical and rebel.

As a schoolmaster Clarke was years ahead of his time, relying not on the cane to stimulate his scholars, but upon kindness and a system of marks and awards. Each boy had an account book into which was put a mark against each task achieved. Prizes were given for voluntary work done out of school hours. His humanity and the results he obtained filled the school. We do not know whether the curriculum was freer and wider than that of the typical school of that day, but there was certainly at one period a native French master, an *émigré*.

So John Keats escaped the monotony and the brutality of the contemporary Public School and his young spirit was given room to grow. The direct influence on him of such a man as John Clarke can only be surmised, but we are on firmer ground with his son, Charles Cowden Clarke, who was an usher in the school, and at the age of only fourteen or fifteen gave Keats his first lessons. 'Ever-young' Cowden Clarke was a healthy-minded, intelligent man with a buoyant spirit, tolerably well-read in the classics and feeling strongly that revived interest in the Elizabethan writers fostered by Coleridge, Lamb and later by Hazlitt. He nursed the mental growth of the young poet with affectionate care.

The school was at Enfield, a village about ten miles from London, in a country of beautiful elm-bordered fields, rose-hedgerowed lanes, meadows and wooded estates. It stood opposite to a bend in the New River in which the boys used to bathe. Disdaining the use of towels, they would dry themselves by running about the fields. Further up the road from the schoolhouse, visible from one window, was a small, wooded slope, a remnant of the old Enfield Chase which, as a boy, Cowden Clarke used to imagine 'a forest peopled with dragons, lions, ladies, knights, dwarfs and giants.' The road led on to, and terminated in, Ponders End, where Keats's grandparents lived until the death of John Jennings in 1805.

The schoolhouse was a fine building, erected, it was said, by a West India merchant, and bore the date 1717. It was almost certainly the birthplace of Isaac Disraeli in 1766. In 1849 it was bought by the Eastern Counties Railway, became the station-house for the branch brought from the Ware and Cambridge line to Enfield, and was pulled down in 1872, but the top part of the old front was preserved and re-erected in the Victoria and Albert Museum. It is classic in feeling. Two foliated capitals support a pediment. Between the pilasters are two niches and in the arches of these are winged cherubs' heads in moulded brick. Above each niche is a garland of flowers and pomegranates in the same medium. The workmanship is beautiful. The bricks, small and of a rich rose colour, have been ground down to a perfect face and joined, not with lime and mortar but beeswax and

resin, so that the whole front is a solid block. The niches and orna-
mental work were cut out with a chisel. Between the central pillars
was a window with a lead flat beneath on which a curious boy could
creep surreptitiously to examine the decoration he had heard praised
by his elders. Cowden Clarke made this little adventure once when he
was put to sleep in the room between the niches during some
childish illness. He gave in his old age a charming description of the
school:

The house, airy, roomy, and substantial . . . was especially fitted for a school.
"The eight-bedded room," "the six-bedded room," as they were called, give
some idea of the dimensions of the apartments. The school-room, which
occupied the site where formerly had been the coach-house and stabling,
was forty feet long; and the playground was a spacious courtyard between
the school-room and the house. In this play-ground there flourished a goodly
baking-pear tree; and it was made a point of honour with "the boys" that
if they forebore from touching the fruit until fit for gathering, they would
have it in due time for supper regales, properly baked or stewed.

From the playground stretched a garden one hundred yards in length,
where in one corner were some small plots set aside for certain boys fond of
having a garden of their own . . . and farther on was a sweep of greensward,
beyond which existed a pond, sometimes dignified as "The Lake" . . . Round
this pond sloped strawberry-beds, the privilege of watering which was
awarded to "assiduous boys" on summer evenings, with the due understanding that they would have their just share of the juicy red berries when
fully ripe. At the far end of the pond . . . beneath the iron railings which
divided our premises from the meadow beyond, whence the song of the
nightingales in May would reach us in the stillness of night, there stood a
rustic arbour, where John Keats and I used to sit and read Spenser's "Faery
Queene" together, when he had left school, and used to come over from
Edmonton, where he was apprenticed to Thomas Hammond the surgeon.
On the other side of the house lay a small enclosure which we called "the
drying-ground," and where was a magnificent morello cherry-tree . . .
Beyond this, a gate led into a small field, or paddock, of two acres,—the
pasture-ground of two cows that supplied the establishment with fresh and
abundant milk.

Not far from the house there was a rookery. The boys used to see
the birds flying home to roost in the evening and, as they watched
the long, black train, they would cry: 'Lag, lag, laglast!'

In his old age Cowden Clarke wrote his reminiscences of Keats's
schooldays. Looking back over the long years he tried to recollect
the little boy who came to Enfield dressed in a child's frock with his
brother in 1803; but he could not 'from a corporation of seventy or
eighty youngsters' distinguish him very clearly. He remembered that

the boy, who had 'a brisk, winning face,' was a favourite with all, and particularly with Mrs. Clarke, his mother.

The boys were visited from time to time by their parents, coming from the City in a gig driven by Thomas Keats whom Mr. and Mrs. Clarke liked and respected; he was of 'so remarkably fine a common-sense and native respectability; a man utterly free from vulgarity.' But Thomas Keats was not long to visit his boys. In 1804 came the tragedy of his sudden death.

As a little boy Keats showed no sign of exceptional powers. He worked well and was 'a most orderly scholar' but, like the average healthy boy, liked playing better than working, and fighting best of all; it was 'meat and drink to him.' Although small for his age, he was strong and athletic, had the courage of a lion, and 'would fight anyone —morning, noon or night.' All three brothers (later Tom entered the school) felt they had, as the nephews of Lieutenant Midgley Jennings, a family reputation for valour to keep up. George, although the strongest and tallest, was the least belligerent.

Edward Holmes, a schoolfellow, said of Keats: '. . . He was a boy whom anyone from his extraordinary vivacity and personal beauty might easily fancy would become great—but rather in some military capacity than in literature . . . in all active exercises he excelled.' Holmes had a great admiration for the generous-hearted, daring boy and, being some years his junior, had to woo his friendship by doing battle. He speaks of his 'violence and vehemence,' saying that his moods were 'always in extremes,' and that he would often be either in 'passions of tears or fits of outrageous laughter.' 'Associated as they were with an extraordinary beauty of person and expression these qualities captivated the boys, and no one was more popular.'

He made few close friends; his brothers were so dear to him that probably they were all he needed. 'The favourites of John,' said Holmes, 'were few; after they were known to fight readily he seemed to prefer them for a sort of grotesque and buffoon humour. I recollect at this moment his delight at the extraordinary gesticulations and pranks of a boy named Wade who was celebrated for this.'

He was, although apparently far from being the conventional 'good boy,' a favourite with the masters too. No doubt they felt him, with his daring, his 'terrier courage and great charm,' to be an influence in the school, and, with 'his high-mindedness, his utter unconsciousness of a mean motive, his placability, his generosity,' a good influence. He was, however, too much the natural human boy to become a prig. It was fortunate, perhaps, that his younger brother, being taller and stronger, could administer effective and salutary chastisement. Keats's temper was fiery: when he was in a rage his more placid brother would hold him down by main force, laughing as John roared and tried to beat him. But John's temper never lasted long; it was a 'wisp-of-straw conflagration.' The struggle generally ended in affectionate laughter on both sides.

Perhaps this early pugnacity was in some measure an outlet for a crude creative power already within him. Cowden Clarke says that his fighting temper when roused 'was one of the most picturesque exhibitions—off the stage—I ever saw. One of the transports of that marvellous actor Edmund Kean—whom, by the way, he idolized—was its nearest resemblance; and the two were not very dissimilar in face and figure.' This was not the mere blind hitting out of a furious child but something controlled; a natural acting. One of his small gestures had a minor splendour. One day his little brother Tom was rude to an usher and had his ears boxed. 'John rushed up, put himself in the received position of offence, and, it was said, struck the usher—who could, so to say, have put him into his pocket.'

It was not until his fifteenth year that Keats turned passionately to books and study. Up to that time he had read little with profound attention. Among his early reading Holmes remembered *Robinson Crusoe* and 'something about Montezuma and the Incas of Peru.' He thought that Keats must have read Shakespeare early; he remembered him saying: 'No one would care to read *Macbeth* alone in a house at two o'clock in the morning.' It is possible, however, that Keats was familiar with the story in Lamb's *Tales*, published in 1806, when he was ten.

Most children of higher mental powers than the average have known that sudden flowering of the spirit in adolescence; when school subjects begin to fall into place in a scheme and learning acquires a meaning and a vitality. To Keats in the richness of his nature this must have been an astounding revelation: with his usual impetuosity and passionate self-devotion he turned whole-heartedly to books. Now the 'active exercises,' the running, jumping, fighting and swimming were forgotten. He had to be driven away from study into the open air by the masters. Even then he would be found walking with a book in his hand. 'The quantity he read was surprising.'

He soon exhausted the school library, books of voyages and travel, Mavor's collection and his *Universal History*, Robertson's histories of Scotland, America and Charles the Fifth, and the stories, including Miss Edgeworth's, thought fit for youth in the early days of the nineteenth century. *Pilgrim's Progress* would have been in the library and probably a few volumes of natural history, perhaps among them Goldsmith's delightful book with its spirited woodcuts. He steeped himself in classical mythology, constantly poring over Spence's *Polymetis*, Tooke's *Pantheon*, Fénelon and Lemprière's *Classical Dictionary*,

'which he appeared to learn.' He also studied, either now or in his
apprenticeship days, Sandys' translation of Ovid's *Metamorphoses*.
'His amount of classical attainment extended no farther than the
Æneid with which epic, indeed, he was so fascinated that before leaving
school he had *voluntarily* translated in writing a considerable portion.'

Every minute snatched from his lessons or enforced exercise was
devoted to reading, even at meals. His studies were not entirely in the
past, for Clarke says:

. . . in my 'mind's eye' I now see him at supper (we had our meals in the
schoolroom), sitting back on the form, from the table, holding the folio
volume of Burnet's "History of his Own Time" between himself and the
table, eating his meal from beyond it. This work, and Leigh Hunt's *Examiner*
—which my father took in, and I used to lend to Keats—no doubt laid the
foundation of his love of civil and religious liberty.

At each half-year Keats won the prize given by John Clarke for the
greatest amount of voluntary work, and won it easily, the work he had
done far exceeding that of any other boy. In 1809 he was awarded
Kauffman's *Dictionary of Merchandise*, and in 1811 John Bonnycastle's
new edition of his *Introduction to Astronomy*.

The *Introduction to Astronomy* is a lively, well-written book. The
subject is handled with imagination. The vastness of the firmament is
conveyed with a perception of its essential beauty as revealing the
primal power of the Creator. Quotations from the poets are introduced
'as an agreeable relief to minds unaccustomed to the regular deduction
of facts.' Most of the quotations are from Milton; others from translations of the classics, from Thomson, Pope, Young and Samuel Butler
and all are finely chosen. It seems likely that Keats read this book with
attention: he certainly valued it enough to make a present of it to
George on his departure from England in 1818. Bonnycastle's account
of the discovery of Uranus or Georgium Sidus by Herschel may have
helped to produce those ringing lines:

> Then felt I like some watcher of the skies
> When a new planet swims into his ken;

There is, too, on page 6 of the book, a reference to 'Lapland witches,
who pretend to regulate the course of the winds by tying knots in a
string.' These fantastic witches may have sunk deep down into his
mind to come to the surface years later in a detail of his word-picture
of the Enchanted Castle in the Epistle to John Hamilton Reynolds:

> Then there's a little wing, far from the Sun,
> Built by a Lapland Witch turn'd maudlin Nun.

Keats's happy absorption in books and study was, in or before 1810, broken by anxiety over his mother. She had developed tuberculosis.

During a period of her last illness (probably in the Christmas holidays of 1809) Keats, then a boy of fourteen, 'sat up whole nights in a great chair, would suffer nobody to give her medicine but himself, or even cook her food—he did all, and read novels to her in her intervals of ease.' He went back to school apparently lulled into a false security, for when news of her death came in March the blow was all the more severe because it was unexpected. He was heart-broken; giving way, said Holmes, 'to such impassioned and prolonged grief (hiding himself under the master's desk) as awakened the liveliest pity and sympathy in all who saw him.'

John and George both left school at the end of the summer of 1811; George to enter Mr. Abbey's counting-house and John to be bound apprentice for five years to Thomas Hammond, surgeon and apothecary. This choice of a profession has been a continued source of astonishment to posterity. Cowden Clarke implies that it was chosen for him by his guardian as a means of livelihood. It seems, however, unlikely that a boy of Keats's spirit would submit tamely to enter a profession he hated. During his apprenticeship Cowden Clarke, only eight years older than Keats, was his intimate friend: if Keats had felt discontent he would surely have murmured it to Clarke. He did not and it was, according to Clarke, only when he was on the eve of abandoning medicine that he expressed a dislike for it. It seems probable that Keats had a genuine wish to become a doctor, and that it was not until he knew himself to be a poet that he decided to abandon the profession.

It is barely possible that an ambition to be a doctor may have originated in very early childhood. Finsbury Square and its environs were the headquarters of the City physicians and surgeons, some of whom would almost certainly keep their horses in the nearby stables. The bright-eyed, quick-witted boy may have drawn their notice, and attention from them roused in his small breast an ambition to become a doctor too.

Hammond's house, 'Wilston,' at Edmonton, remained in the occupation of a doctor until it was pulled down in 1931. In the garden was a small building, consisting of a surgery and a room above, reached by an outside staircase, known locally as Keats's Cottage. Here, traditionally, he worked and lived.

There were two Edmonton boys, about Tom's age, and probably playmates of his, who took a strong interest in Keats; Richard Henry Horne and Charles Jeremiah Wells, a precocious red-headed lad, brimming over with animal spirits, whom later Keats made his friend. Both

Wells and Horne were in after life ardent admirers of Keats's poetry, but now it was his reputation as a fighter which drew them.

Richard Horne attended an Edmonton school kept by the Rev. W. Williams.[1] One cold winter's day while his master was on professional attendance within, Keats was waiting outside in a gig, his thoughts far away from a little group of admiring lads gaping at the 'old boy' with such a formidable reputation as a 'bruiser.' Horne was dared to snowball him. He accepted the challenge and hit Keats full in the back, but even before Keats could attach the reins in order to come in pursuit of him he took the precaution of instant flight.

Beyond the 'Keats Cottage' tradition and stories of day-dreaming in the gig we have no information about Keats's work with Hammond except that his duties were not arduous. A fellow-apprentice described him as 'an idle loafing fellow, always quoting poetry.' The known integrity of his character does not, however, suggest a neglect of duties. Perhaps Hammond, like many men who were glad to take the fees of apprentices, did not make full use of Keats. It is evident from the Abbey memoir quoted in Chapter I that his guardian was dissatisfied with Hammond's treatment of him. Or, alternatively, this accusation may be purely the jealous view of an ignorant lad who came in at the usual apprenticeship fee of forty pounds and had his time more fully occupied in menial tasks. George mentions a much larger sum, two hundred guineas, as the fee for Keats's apprenticeship.

Keats himself seems to have felt some antagonism towards Hammond: he wrote in 1819 of having seven years before clenched his fist at him. It seems more than likely that there were occasional brushes between the proud high-spirited boy and his master.

Whether he neglected his duties or no, Keats certainly had time for reading and study. He finished his translation of the Æneid into prose and eagerly devoured Cowden Clarke's library of books. At least five times a month he would walk over the two miles of field-path to Enfield, book in hand, to revel in poetry with his friend.

The two young men, children of their age, although able to appreciate intellectually 'the sharp, the rapier-pointed epigram,' could see no beauty in the typical poets of the last century,

> . . . closely wed
> To musty laws lined out with wretched rule
> And compass vile . . .

with their formal didacticism. They turned with passionate attention to the older poets. Shakespeare was already familiar, and now Clarke,

---

[1] See H. Buxton Forman, pp. 237 and 291, *Literary Anecdotes of the Nineteenth Century*. It seems highly probable that Wells also attended this school.

reading to Keats in the little arbour in the school garden, aroused his enthusiasm for other great Elizabethans and Jacobeans, including Milton in his earlier romantic poetry and, above all, Edmund Spenser.

Through Spenser 'at the touch of Archimago's wand' Keats entered into an entire new world; a world enchanting to a romantic boy. Here were the familiar knights and ladies of a child's tale transmuted in a light that never was on sea or land. The gallant boy who had squared up to the usher twice his size went adventuring with gentle Una and her milk-white lamb in strange and monstrous woods. One day Cowden Clarke read the 'Epithalamium' aloud to him and 'as he listened his features and exclamations were ecstatic.' The tender bright beauty of the poem lit up his young mind. The passage to 'Cinthia' may well have sown the seed of the long-pondered *Endymion*:

> O! fayrest goddesse, do not thou envy
> My love with me to spy:
> For thou likewise didst love, though now unthought,
> And for a fleece of wooll, which privily
> The Latmian shepherd once unto thee brought,
> His pleasures with thee wrought.

'That night he took away with him a volume of the *Faerie Queene*, and he went through it as a young horse through a spring meadow—ramping!' Spenser was like 'a clear sunrise' to his mind and the craftsman already awake in him savoured 'Spenserian vowels that elope with ease.'

No doubt in soberer moments the two young men talked of the Liberal question; of the need for drastic reform in government and the misery of the common people; of the imprisonment of 'the lov'd Libertas,' Leigh Hunt and of Cowden Clarke's visits to him.

Keats had always a great love for pianoforte music: sometimes Cowden Clarke would play to him. There was an old school memory of Cowden Clarke's music-making, heard intermittently from below as he lay in bed, which later he put into stanza xxix of 'The Eve of St. Agnes':

> The boisterous, midnight, festive clarion,
> The kettle-drum, and far-heard clarinet,
> Affray his ears, though but in dying tone:—
> *The hall door shuts again, and all the noise is gone.*

In another way Clarke must have been a stimulating influence. Keats in his letters often deplores his 'horrid morbidity of temperament': the sanguine Cowden Clarke with the hearty manner and rather loud voice was the antithesis of him. Adolescence has its natural glooms, deeper in a hypersensitive boy smarting under the loss of his mother. Contact with the older man would bring a salutary bracing of the spirit.

The influence of home, of the sensible Mrs. Jennings, was not wanting either: his grandmother lived in the same road only a short distance from 'Wilston.'

In December, 1814, the strongest family link was snapped with the death of Mrs. Jennings. The Edmonton home was broken up. George, and probably Tom, had already gone into Abbey's counting-house in the City and now the little sister went away into the unsympathetic care of Mr. and Mrs. Abbey.

Keats felt acutely the death of his grandmother, to whom he was tenderly attached. A few days after the event he wrote a sonnet (the earliest known to us) and, with characteristic reticence, did not disclose even to his brothers the circumstance of its composition. It was not until 1819, when grief was long past, that in answer to a direct question he told Richard Woodhouse how it came to be written.

> As from the darkening gloom a silver dove
>   Upsoars, and darts into the Eastern light,
>   On pinions that naught moves but pure delight,
> So fled thy soul into the realms above,
> Regions of peace and everlasting love;
>   Where happy spirits, crown'd with circlets bright
>   Of starry beam, and gloriously bedight,
> Taste the high joy none but the blest can prove.
> There thou or joinest the immortal quire
>   In melodies that even Heaven fair
> Fill with superior bliss, or, at desire
>   Of the omnipotent Father, cleavest the air
> On holy message sent—What pleasures higher?
>   Wherefore does any grief our joy impair?

It is probable that Keats was now discontented and lonely at Edmonton. Even if Hammond were not the careless master Abbey suspected him to be, his apprentice would, with his quick intellect, have learned from him all he had to offer in a far shorter time than the average boy. The clenching of his fist at his master has been held to suggest that the breaking of the apprenticeship in 1815 was caused by an open breach between Keats and Hammond. This may have been so, but it was not, however, uncommon for an apprenticeship to a surgeon to be broken. This fact is made clear in the evidence given before a Select Committee on Medical Education in 1834, only nineteen years later.

On October 1st, 1815, Keats, bearing with him the necessary certificate of good behaviour, entered Hammond's own old hospital, Guy's in the Borough, to train as an apothecary in the joint medical school of Guy's and St. Thomas's.

CHAPTER III

A Medical Student (1815-1816)

FROM his lodgings near to Guy's Hospital Keats wrote to Cowden Clarke in October, 1816:

Although the Borough is a beastly place in dirt, turnings and windings; yet No 8 Dean Street is not difficult to find; and if you would run the Gauntlet over London Bridge, take the first turning to the left and then the first to the right and moreover knock at my door which is nearly opposite a Meeting you would do one a Charity . . .

Cowden Clarke, then living in Clerkenwell (with his married sister, Mrs. Isabella Towers), might in crossing the ancient narrow Bridge 'run the Gauntlet' of the long whips of carters driving waggons drawn by six or eight horses to and from the market gardens of Kent and Surrey: as there were only three London bridges over the Thames at that time other traffic would be thick too.

On the other side Clarke would come upon 'a jumbled mass of murky buildings'; gloomy hop-warehouses and a tangle of mean streets swarming with people in the extreme of poverty, many of them Irish living in unspeakable squalor. Those immediately round the hospitals of Guy's and St. Thomas's were of a better type and in them the students lodged. As the average course was only one year lectures and demonstrations were spread over the day so as not to overlap, the first being at eight o'clock in the morning and the last at eight o'clock at night: it was therefore necessary for the students to live very near the hospitals. What is left of Dean Street is now Stainer Street. The house Keats lodged in disappeared, together with St. Thomas's Hospital, when London Bridge Station was built.

On October 1st, 1815 (a Sunday), Keats was entered in the Register of Surgeon's Pupils as 'No. 57, 6 Mo' and paid an office fee of one pound, two shillings. For the next day this entry appears: 'John Keats, (Mr. L) 12 Mo. £25. 4.' At the side is written in, probably later, '6 Mo.' There are two possible explanations of this, one being that, in view of the fact that he soon became a dresser, six months' fee (£6. 6s.) was returned to him. On October 29th there is a further entry in the Registers recording the return of the six guineas to John Keats, 'he becoming a dresser.' None of the other pupils entered in the same quarter became dresser in so short a time. This might argue an unusual proficiency in Hammond's late apprentice, or may merely indicate that he decided to change his method of training from that of surgeon's pupil to the more active one of dresser. On March 3rd, 1816, Keats appears under 'Dressers to the Surgeons' with the entry '12 Mo. £1. 1.'

It has been suggested that if Keats had been attached to the skilful and charming Astley Cooper (who by his knighthood in future years raised surgery from a trade to a profession) he might have been inspired to do great things in Medicine. This we cannot know, but it is certain that 'Mr. L' was neither skilful nor charming. Although Lucas was 'good-natured and easy and liked by everyone' he was

a tall ungainly, awkward man, with stooping shoulders and a shuffling walk, as deaf as a post, not overburdened with brains . . . His surgical acquirements were very small, his operations generally badly performed, and accompanied with much bungling, if not worse.

Apart from the above entries in the registers of Guy's we have little detail at first hand of Keats as medical student. As, however, nearly five years of his brief life were spent in the service of Medicine it seems worth while to try to reconstruct life in the hospital from contemporary accounts and from others not far removed in date.

The surgeon was responsible for the first few dressings after an operation and went round the ward twice a week accompanied by four dressers, each of whom carried a 'tin plaister box,' in shape not unlike a knife-box and 'considered a mark of distinction as shewing their official position.' All wore their hats. They were accompanied by students 'in shoals, if the surgeon was a favourite,' who

pushed and jostled, and ran and crowded round the beds, quite regardless of the patient's feelings and condition . . . The whole business was concluded in an hour and a half. Certainly not much was to be learned at these 'goings round'; they were mostly occupied with chattering and playing, and making extra-hospital arrangements.

Pupils who were keen to learn, however, seem to have had the freedom of the wards to study and care for the patients. They were allowed to assist the dressers to carry out the surgeon's orders.

Guy's and St. Thomas's stood opposite to one another. Friday was operation day in both hospitals. Operations were performed at noon in Guy's and at one o'clock at St. Thomas's. The students would attend at Guy's and then rush over in an unseemly, struggling mass to get good seats at St. Thomas's where the operating theatre was small. 'The rush and scuffle there to get a place was not unlike that for a seat in the pit or gallery of a dramatic theatre, and the crowding and squeezing was oftentimes unbearable.' John Flint South, from whose 'Memorials' much of this material is taken, says:

The pupils were packed like herrings in a barrel, but not so quiet, as those behind were continually pressing on those before, often so severely that several could not bear the pressure, and were continually struggling to relieve themselves of it, and had not infrequently to be got out exhausted. There was also a continual cry of 'Heads, heads', to those about the table whose heads interfered with the sight-seers, with various appellatives, in a small way resembling the calls at the Sheldonian Theatre during Commemoration. . . . I have often known the floor so crowded that the surgeon could not operate till it had been partially cleared.[1]

The feelings of the patient, strapped down on a dirty, bloodstained table, can be imagined, especially as he had to undergo the operation without anæsthetic. South says:

So long as the patient did not make much noise, I got on very well, but if the cries were great, and especially if they came from a child, I was quickly upset, had to leave the theatre and not infrequently fainted . . . the atmosphere was stifling.

It is recorded that once when a little child patient was brought to him and smiled up from her grandfather's arms, Sir Astley Cooper, tried and skilful operator though he was, burst into tears. As the surgery to be performed by most of these pupils in the future would be of a minor character, attendance at many of the operations seems to have been cruelly unnecessary. Minor surgery, such as venesection (bloodletting) was learnt in the wards.

Keats had to attend lectures on Anatomy and Surgery, the practice of Medicine, chemistry, midwifery, and other kindred subjects; also *Materia Medica*, botanical work being done on this subject, under the superintendence of the lecturer, in the Herb Garden at Chelsea and in the country around London. Away from the macabre surroundings of pain, sickness and suffering, this must have been a joyful interlude in the poet's working day.

Much of his time would be spent in the dead-house in practical anatomy. Conditions here might, after the preliminary initiation (accompanied in some hospitals apparently, according to an unwritten law, by the standing of two pots of beer by the novice) to some extent have hardened the student to the horrible conditions of the operating theatre. There was a total lack of reverence for the dead. The dissecting-room seems to have been used as a species of common-room by the

---

[1] One of the operating theatres has survived—*see* Appendix II.

students 'amidst a heterogeneous assemblage of pipkins, subjects (bodies), deal coffins, sawdust, inflated stomachs, syringes, macerating tubs and dried preparations.' Here, and in the dissecting-room, they drank, 'broiled sprats and herrings on the fire-shovel,' and the brighter spirits indulged in horse-play to the detriment of fittings and furniture.[1]

The lectures of Astley Cooper, a brilliant and amusing man, were always well attended. There is in the Museum at Hampstead a little leather-covered book of Keats's which, in the opinion of Sir William Hale-White, contains notes of lectures delivered by the great surgeon. Amid the serious and scientfic entries there is one delightful and human touch: 'In disease medical men guess, if they cannot ascertain a disease they call it nervous.'

On one page there are some delightful drawings of flowers. As it was the custom then to repeat each statement three times it is strange that there are not more of these idyllic interludes in the note-taking: but Astley Cooper was an exceptional man and demanded close attention. Some of the other lectures must have been intolerably tedious to a man of Keats's rapidity of mind; those of Henry Cline, Junior, for instance, who 'went on in a quiet, monotonous tone, and very slowly,' always prolonging the lecture by half or three-quarters of an hour. Many of the students wisely abstained from attendance.

Of this course of lectures we have in the library at Guy's three thick volumes of notes written out fair, in close detail, by Joshua Waddington, a fellow-student: compared with Waddington's laborious work Keats's notes are sketchy and intermittent. Those of the earlier lectures are taken with the most care.

As the place of the modern house-surgeon was then taken by the dressers Keats had to shoulder a good deal of responsibility. A week at a time each dresser took charge in the ward, living in the hospital at his own expense. Theoretically, he spent his whole time there but in practice he took some hours off away from the hospital, spending the night within its walls and always within call in case of need. Thursdays was 'taking-in' day for the surgical cases and every day he attended to all accidents. He 'dressed hosts of out-patients, drew innumerable teeth, and performed countless venesections, till two or three o'clock . . . till the surgery was empty.' The dresser in charge had to use his judgement in discriminating from among the out-patients those cases he considered should be brought to the notice of a surgeon.

Work in the wards must have been gruesome enough in those rough-and-ready days when, the germ theory being unformed, rigid cleanliness was not considered a necessity. A dark hint of the physical

---

[1] The details to the end of the paragraph are taken from 'The Medical Student', *Punch*, 1841, by Albert Smith, a medical student twenty years later.

conditions is given in the old registers by the entry of an annual salary of forty pounds to the bug-catcher. The nurses and night-watchers were of the 'Mrs. Gamp' variety. Wounds, with no aseptic precaution, became infected and many patients died.

But more gruesome still, grotesque and macabre, were those extraordinary muffled figures which came under cover of night with their ghastly burdens. This was the era of the 'resurrection-men,' the 'sack-em-up gentlemen' on whom the surgeons were forced to rely for supplies to the Anatomical Schools. Wild, abandoned, drink-sodden, they were capable of any audacity in their search for their unlawful prey. In the ridiculous state of the law body-snatching was a misdemeanour but the taking of the shroud a crime: the bodies, therefore, were brought stark naked in sacks. The price paid varied as to size, four guineas being the maximum. The notorious gang of Ben Crouch's, son of the carpenter at Guy's, supplied the hospital. It is more than likely that Keats had dealings with these ruffians.

In Keats's medical training he ran the gamut of human nature from the low to the high. He saw in men like Astley Cooper an inspired devotion to duty in a painful profession: from body-snatcher to surgeon; from pain to the joy of recovery; from the misery of the sick to the cheerful companionship of the young men around him; from arduous duty to the high delights of poetry; these were magnificent preparations for the master dramatist he might have been, and the great poet he was. They were magnificent preparations but at the cost of strain in mind and spirit: a deeply conscientious man, he knew his heart was not in his work.

Keats was not happy living by himself. His frequent depressions of spirit were aggravated by loneliness and the creative activity of his mind, if uninterrupted by the calls of cheerful human society, obliged him to be 'in a continual burning of thought.' In his lone condition he wrote the sonnet beginning:

> O Solitude! if I must with thee dwell,
> Let it not be among the jumbled heap
> Of murky buildings. . . .

To the country-bred boy the Borough must have seemed a noisome desolation.

His brothers were not far away, working for Richard Abbey in Pancras Lane, and he had a friend, a 'kindred spirit,' George Felton Mathew; but their companionship was not always at hand.

He was, too, almost certainly paying visits to a happy household which must painfully have reminded him of a home lost; that of 'the witty Isabella' Towers (Cowden Clarke's sister in Warner Street,

Clerkenwell), as famous later to her sister-in-law, Mary Cowden Clarke, for 'her home-made jams and other dulcet preparations as for her books and verses.' She wrote for children. John, her husband, besides being an apothecary of some repute, the maker of 'Towers' Patent Pills' and other advertised medicines, was an enthusiastic lover of music and a good pianoforte player. Probably not least in comfort to the lonely affectionate young visitor was their baby son, Charles Towers, to whom in a boy's book, *Adam the Gardener*, dedicated to his nephew, Cowden Clarke was to refer to Keats as 'the kind playfellow of his infancy.' But Keats could have had little leisure to spend with his friends in Clerkenwell.

Astley Cooper took an especial interest in Keats and, perhaps seeing that the boy was not happy, recommended him to the care of his dresser and young relation, George Cooper. Keats went to live with Cooper and a friend in rooms over the shop of one Markham, a tallow-chandler in St. Thomas's Street. George Cooper and his friend, Frederick Tyrrell, were, however, near the end of their course and soon Keats was sharing lodgings with George Wilson Mackereth and Henry Stephens.[1]

Stephens, afterwards a surgeon of good repute, had literary leanings and wrote a tragedy, *Edwy and Elgiva*. He is known to the modern world as the inventor of a famous ink.[2] In later life he gave his impressions of 'little Keats' in a letter to Lord Houghton, Keat's first biographer:

... His passion ... for Poetry was soon manifested. He attended lectures and went through the usual routine, but he had no desire to excel in that pursuit. ... In a room, he was always at the window, peering into space, so that the window-seat was spoken of by his comrades as Keats's place. . . . In the lecture room he seemed to sit apart and to be absorbed in something else, as if the subject suggested thoughts to him which were not practically connected with it. He was often in the subject and out of it, in a dreamy way.

He never attached much consequence to his own studies in medicine, and indeed looked upon the medical career as the career by which to live in a workaday world, without being certain that he could keep up the strain of it. He nevertheless had a consciousness of his own powers, and even of his own greatness, though it might never be recognized. . . . Poetry was to his mind the zenith of all his Aspirations: the only thing worth the attention of superior minds: so he thought: all other pursuits were mean and tame. . . . The greatest men in the world were the poets and to rank among them was the chief object of his ambition. It may readily be imagined that this feeling

[1] These two continued friends. Stephens' eldest son married Mackereth's daughter Agnes.
[2] He made a fortune and lived at Avenue House, Finchley, which his son bequeathed to the borough in 1918.

was accompanied with a good deal of pride and conceit, and that amongst mere medical students he would walk and talk as one of the Gods might be supposed to do when mingling with mortals. This pride had exposed him, as may be readily imagined, to occasional ridicule, and some mortification.

We learn that Keats, in his poetic ambition, dressed the part, having 'his neck nearly bare à la Byron' with a turned down collar and a ribbon. 'He also let his mustachios grow occasionally,' with startling effect in that clean-shaven age.

Having a taste and liking for Poetry myself, though at that time but little cultivated, he regarded me as something a little superior to the rest, and would gratify himself frequently, by showing me some lines of his writing, or some new idea which he had struck out. We had frequent conversation on the merits of particular poets, but our tastes did not agree.

Stephens was an adherent to the old order of things, whereas Keats asserted, with the splendid arrogance of youth, that Pope was 'no poet, but a mere versifier.' Apparently both Spenser and Byron were outside the range of young Stephens' sympathies. It is no wonder then that when he showed his first attempts in verse to the young Romantic they were 'condemned.' Poor Stephens adds 'he seemed to think it presumption in me to attempt to tread along the same pathway as himself at however humble a distance.' The clumsy prose style of his memoir would suggest that Stephens was by nature more suited to invent ink than to employ it. But we have all had misguided ambitions and Keats wounded him.

He had two Brothers who visited him frequently, and they worshipped him. They seemed to think their brother John was to be exalted, and to exalt the family name.

This hero-worship must have annoyed the irritated Stephens but he enjoyed a vicarious revenge:

I remember a Student from St. Bartholomew's Hospital who came often to see him, as they had formerly been intimate, but though old friends they did not cordially agree. Newmarsh, or Newmarch (I forget which was his name) was a Classical Scholar, as was Keats, and therefore they scanned freely the respective merits of the Poets of Greece and Rome. Whenever Keats shewed Newmarch any of his poetry it was sure to be ridiculed, and severely handled.

Stephens has made a slip here. Keats had no Greek. Newmarch

he described as 'a light-hearted and merry fellow' . . . 'rather too fond of mortifying Keats,' and teasing his brothers for their hero-worship.

To his fellow-students Keats never mentioned his origins though it was generally known that he was the son of a livery-stable keeper. As the majority of the students were of the tradesman class his reticence was thought to show an improper pride. This may have been so, but on the other hand Keats was not likely to want to dwell upon early memories, the father's sudden death and his mother's hasty and disastrous marriage.

Stephens says that, instead of taking notes, Keats would scribble doggerel rimes (a specimen of which is given below), preferably in another man's note-book; but in this he was apparently doing what nearly every other student did—it was an established jest.

> Give me women, wine and snuff
> Until I cry out, "hold! enough!"
> You may do so, sans objection;
> Till the day of resurrection;
> For bless my beard they aye shall be
> My beloved Trinity.

Stephens thought him

gentlemanly in his manners and when he condescended to talk upon other subjects he was agreeable and intelligent. He was quick and apt at learning, when he chose to give his attention to any subject. He was a steady quiet and well behaved person, never inclined to pursuits of a low or vicious character.

There is also a prose fragment said to have been scribbled during a lecture, the 'Alexander Fragment,' given in the appendix of Colvin's 'Life,' and in H. Buxton Forman's 1901 edition, together with a description of Keats in a 'deep poetic dream' in the lecture theatre by 'another fellow student.' This student was Walter Cooper Dendy who, as he left St. Thomas's medical school before Keats's arrival at Guy's, was not actually a contemporary. He probably remained in connection with the hospital as a junior demonstrator under Cline, and so would have met Keats. Dendy was the author of a little book *On the Phenomena of Dreams* (1832) and also a work, half fact, half fiction, called *The Philosophy of Mystery* in which occur the two passages; the description of Keats with his mind 'on Parnassus with the Muses' and the 'Alexander Fragment.'

Other friends of Keats at this time were Charles Butler, Frederick Leffler, son of a music-master, living at Hercules Buildings on the

Surrey side of the river, apprentice to an apothecary in Soho Square, Charles Severn[1] and Daniel Gosset, fellow-students with whom he was said to be on intimate terms. As Daniel Gosset[2] came of a family living at Langhedge Hall, Tanner's Inn, Edmonton, it is possible the friend-ship, or acquaintance, dated from earlier days. Another passing friend recently come to light was John Spurgin who, after he left St. Thomas' for Cambridge, wrote Keats a letter (now in the Houghton Library, Harvard) full of ardent Swedenborgian arguments obviously pre-viously discussed.

Among fellow-students were Thomas Wakly and John White Webster from Boston, North America; both famous in after years, though one was distinguished and the other notorious. Thomas Wakly was the dauntless founder, proprietor and first editor of *The Lancet*, Coroner for Middlesex, and John Webster, a professor at Harvard, committed a brutal murder in 1850, an account of which can be read in *Famous Trials*.

On July 25th, 1816, Keats, Butler and Mackereth went up to Apothecaries' Hall for examination. Keats (examined by Mr. Brande) was 'granted a Certificate to practise as an Apothecary in the Country' (i.e. in the United Kingdom).[3] Mackereth failed. The examination was oral and probably not too searching. Albert Smith, writing in 1841, calls it 'the jalap and rhubarb botheration.' Successful examinees were at once informed they had passed and were given a tea by the Worshipful Masters.

Keats's name appears in *The London Medical Repository* for the half-year ending December, 1816, in a list of certified Apothecaries. Repro-ductions of this list, of his two certificates and of the pages of Guy's Registers on which his name appears are in the Keats Memorial House at Hampstead. On the Apothecaries' Certificate Keats is described as of full age, whereas according to the Baptismal Register he was not twenty-one until October.

After his examination Keats went away to Margate and there he wrote his rimed epistle to George. In it he spoke of the joys of poetry, of dreams of chivalry linked with the living beauty of the sea, of the 'coy Moon' (always his dear love); of 'the living pleasures of the Bard':

> But richer, far, Posterity's award . . .
> "What, though I leave this dull, and earthly mould,
> "Yet shall my spirit lofty converse hold
> "With after times. . . ."

[1] Apprenticed at Harlow, Essex. Was he related to Joseph Severn?
[2] See *Music and Friends*, Wm. Gardiner, 1838, p. 428, and *D. N. B.* under Gosset, Montague. Montague, a distinguished London surgeon, was a brother.
[3] One of the first under the Apothecaries Act for Examining and Licensing apothecaries to practise throughout England and Wales.

He had already spoken to Cowden Clarke of a feeling of unfitness for medicine. 'The other day,' he said, 'during the lecture, there came a sunbeam into the room, and with it a whole troop of creatures floating in the ray: and I was off with them to Oberon and fairy-land.' And in moments of greater responsibility his imagination seized and mocked him. 'My last operation was the opening of a man's temporal artery. I did it with the utmost nicety, but reflecting on what passed through my mind at the time, my dexterity seemed a miracle, and I never took up the lancet again.'

He wrote in the poetic epistle to George:

> Full many a dreary hour have I past,
> My Brain bewildered, and my Mind o'ercast
> With Heaviness; in seasons, when I've thought
> No spherey strains, by me, could 'er be caught
> From the blue Dome. . . .
> That I should never hear Apollo's song,
> Though feathery clouds were floating all along
> The purple West, and two bright Streaks between,
> The golden Lyre itself were faintly seen . . .

Keats was not yet certain of his high destiny. Later he could write with calm and certainty, 'I think I shall be among the English poets after my death,' but now he was young and his powers untried. He was unhappy; torn in two by poetic ambition and the dictates of a sterling common sense:

> Could I, at once, my mad Ambition smother
> For tasting Joys like these; sure I should be
> Happier, and dearer to Society.

His hesitation certainly lasted until the October of that year when we find Cowden Clarke visiting him in the Dean Street lodging: it may even have extended until the March of 1817. Two entries in the Guy's registers tend to suggest that Keats remained on there until March 3rd, a date roughly corresponding with the publication of his first volume of poems; the second mentioned (on p. 35), of which there is an alternative interpretation to that given, and the last dated March 3rd.

But, however long he may have continued to study, or practise medicine, Keats's mind was concentrating on his true vocation. To paraphrase the words of Sir George Newman, the apothecary was soon to become the superb alchemist.

CHAPTER IV

Early Friends

THE closest of Keats's friends were his two brothers, both young men of intelligence with similar tastes to his own. George was Keats's complement, sanguine and cheerful where he was pessimistic and moody, more practical than his greater brother who was careless in worldly affairs. Of Tom's character we know little beyond that he too was of a sanguine nature and had 'an exquisite love of life.' There was no one who understood John so well as Tom. All three brothers shared in a love of Shakespeare.

When George and Tom left school they both entered Abbey's tea warehouse[1] at 4 Pancras Lane. George we know lived at one time over the business and probably both brothers lived in the Abbey household in winter when their guardian, like most City tradesmen, moved in from Walthamstow with his family. They would therefore be for some months of the year with their little sister, Fanny.

Tom, tall, thin and narrow-chested, soon to become an invalid, did not remain long in the warehouse. To us but a shadowy figure, we know little of his movements. There is a bare record of a visit to Lyons. As Abbey had an interest in a hatter's in the Poultry and Lyons was a centre for hatmaking, Tom may have been sent there to gain some knowledge of the trade. But Tom was not fitted for the battle of life. His illness, combined with the cost of maintaining Keats at Guy's, was a heavy drain on the estate. Money difficulties were early to dog the steps of these unfortunate boys.

On Tom's seventeenth birthday, November 18th, 1816, John wrote a tender sonnet into which he put his love, the friendship between the brothers, their mutual delight in Shakespeare and a wish, pitiful to the reader, that they may long be together:

> Small, busy flames play through the fresh laid coals,
>   And their faint cracklings o'er our silence creep
>   Like whispers of the household gods that keep
> A gentle empire o'er fraternal souls.
> And while, for rhymes, I search around the poles,
>   Your eyes are fix'd, as in poetic sleep,
>   Upon the lore so voluble and deep,
> That aye at fall of night our care condoles.

[1] Mason's, the oldest tea-shop in the City, stood on this site before it was destroyed by enemy action.

> This is your birth-day Tom, and I rejoice
> That thus it passes smoothly, quietly.
> Many such eves of gently whisp'ring noise
> May we together pass, and calmly try
> What are this world's true joys,—ere the great voice,
> From its fair face, shall bid our spirits fly.

There is a holograph of this sonnet in Emma Isola's album. Perhaps it was a favourite of Charles Lamb's.

Keats had for other men an exceptional charm and never needed to exert himself to make friends. Most of the early acquaintances came to him through his brothers. Of his fellow students Charles Butler was, so far as we know, the only one he cared to visit outside the hospital.

Among his earliest friends was one to be so tenderly associated with him in his last days, Joseph Severn. Through Severn the brothers came to know William Haslam, the true and steady, 'our oak friend.' We know little about Haslam except that in time of need he was unwearying in his kindness.

Joseph Severn is a clear, bright figure. It is to his writings that we owe much of our knowledge of Keats. He was a struggling painter whose ambition, like that of many of the painters of his time, was to cover large canvases with historical scenes. It was perhaps a loss to a charming and intimate art that Severn had this ambition. His miniatures and especially those works of love, the portraits of his friend Keats, are lifelike and delicate. His finest piece, a group on ivory of his family painted not long before he went to Italy in 1820, now in the Museum at Hampstead, is, in the words of Dr. G. C. Williamson, 'a work of high accomplishment and an important example of skill on the part of an artist who has not always been highly appreciated.'

Severn was not intellectually well informed: the closest link between the friends was 'a mutual love of nature.' Visual memory was strong in Keats and the faculty of observation had been more highly developed by his medical training. He could see a landscape with the painter's eye. There was a further bond between the two young men in a love of music of which Severn had a fair knowledge. He played on the pianoforte.

Severn was two years older than Keats but had for him the worship of a younger man. He speaks of Keats's 'generous bestowal of his mental richness, and the free imparting of his poetical gifts, as well as his taste in the arts, his knowledge of history, and his most fascinating power in the communicating of these.' Keats opened a new world to Severn who was 'raised from the mechanical drudgery' of his art 'to the hope of brighter and more elevated courses.'

He was the eldest son of a music-master who had strongly opposed his son's desire to be a painter on the grounds that there was no money in it: as a compromise he apprenticed him for seven or eight years to an engraver. But Severn was unhappy and dissatisfied. To the end of his long days (he lived to be 86) he deplored the time wasted and a lack of equipment for his chosen art, painting in oils. He attended art classes at night and in his leisure, when he was not 'stabbing copper' or walking to and from his father's house in Hoxton, made small water-colour portraits at ten-and-sixpence in order to buy colours for his painting. Occupied as he was with little free time to devote to his friends, it was probably not until 1816 or 1817 that Severn had more than an occasional hour or so to spend with Keats. By this time he had developed in a small way quite a prosperous business in miniature-painting.

The Keats boys had not long been in the City before they came to know a number of young people who were interested in literature. Keats's particular friend in this group was George Felton Mathew whose father, a mercer in Oxford Street, had a house in the new Regent's Park. In after years Mathew gave to Lord Houghton a pleasant picture of the young poet:

Keats and I, though about the same age, and both inclined to literature, were in many respects as different as two individuals could be. He enjoyed good health—a fine flow of animal spirits—was fond of company—could amuse himself admirably with the frivolities of life—and had great confidence in himself. I on the other hand was languid and melancholy—fond of repose —thoughtful beyond my years—and diffident to the last degree.

Mathew added rather smugly that he 'always delighted in adminis-tering to the happiness of others.' It pleased him very much to see John and George enjoying themselves at little 'domestic concerts and dances'; entering into the cheerful life of a large family. Mathew 'loved the institutions of my country' and had no sympathy with the 'sceptical and republican' views of Keats whom he found to be 'a fault-finder with everything established.' He bore with him, however, because his views were sincere and he 'would often express regret on finding that he had given pain and annoyance by opposing with ridicule or asperity the opinions of others.'

There was a sister Mary and two cousins, Caroline and Anne Mathew, with whom Keats was friendly. We know little of Mary except that in her album she wrote down some of Keats's early poems.

Once when Anne and Caroline were on holiday at Hastings he sent them some quaint verses, breathing eighteenth century, deploring that he could not 'their light, mazy footsteps attend':

'Tis morn, and the flowers with dew are yet drooping,
   I see you are treading the verge of the sea:
And now! ah, I see it—you just now are stooping
   To pick up the keep-sake intended for me.

The keepsake which the 'fair nymphs' picked up was a beautiful dome-shaped shell and he prizes it:

For, indeed, 'tis a sweet and peculiar pleasure,
   (And blissful is he who such happiness finds),
To possess but a span of the hour of leisure,
   In elegant, pure, and aerial minds.

These elegant, pure and aerial minds hardened later in a sour evangelical mould: the Mathews, feeling their early association with Keats to have been part of a mere juvenile frivolity, destroyed writings and poems of his. They seem, with their cousin, to have been in their lighter-minded days young people of the rather morbid sensibility then in fashion. Mathew, himself a writer and poetiser, thought a low trembling voice a suitable vehicle for poetry. He accused Keats of a lack of emotion in reading aloud.

Keats followed up these verses with more of a distinctly inferior quality, 'On Receiving a Curious Shell, and a Copy of Verses, from the same Ladies' and addressed them to Mathew under the pseudonym of 'Eric.' The poem sent was Tom Moore's 'Golden Chain' in the same pretty jingle. Keats's verses end prophetically:

Adieu, valiant Eric! with joy thou art crown'd;
   Full many the glories that brighten thy youth,
I too have my blisses, which richly abound
   In magical powers, to bless and to sooth.

They were in reply to an even more complimentary set addressed to him by Mathew. Jane Austen has said that though poetry is the food of love one good sonnet is enough to starve entirely away 'a slight, thin sort of inclination.' Perhaps a dose of poetry can have the same effect on a failing friendship. Keats was soon to grow beyond Mathew and his kind, to make friends of a finer mental calibre and more congenial views.

It seems odd that Keats with his strong sense of humour could have been intimate with these young sentimentalists, especially after the society of Cowden Clarke; but sensibility was the fashion. His liking for Dr. Beattie and Mrs. Tighe, poets in the third or fourth class, was also in period. To us, glancing through dusty volumes of these once fashionable writers, it seems strange that, after swallowing the heady draughts of the robust Elizabethans, he could sip their thin potations with any measure of delight. But genius has strange bedfellows. Often the young poet can learn more from the second-rate because the skeleton of their work is not so well clothed. Experiments in versification, imagery and development are more apparent as the whole is not forged into an ultimate perfection. He can see more clearly how the wheels go round. Both Mrs. Tighe and Beattie abound in the new, natural imagery and make use of what Beattie called the 'Gothic stanza' of Spenser; the stanza Keats was to employ so skilfully in 'The Eve of St. Agnes.' He read both poets with the young Mathews and perhaps, both in the case of the poets and the youthful sentimentalists, refined away the dross in the alembic of his own mind. Having seized the gold he passed on.

In the light of recent research, however, the transient Mathew has acquired new interest. It will be remembered (see p. 44) how Keats during a lecture at Guy's lost himself with Oberon in fairyland. This Oberon we now know almost certainly to have been not Shakespeare's but a greater spirit in essence, the powerful dæmonic King of the sylphs and fays in Wieland's *Oberon*. Keats's verses to Mathew quoted above, together with *To Some Ladies*, written to the Mathew girls, and some complimentary lines by Mathew to Keats, 'To a Poetical Friend' in *The European Magazine*, October, 1816,[1] are full of allusions to that poem which influenced the whole romantic movement. In Coleridge, who read the German original, *Oberon* with its dæmonic lore and power touched to life an eerie vein of poetry which gave us the dark depth, the primal magic of 'Christabel' and 'The Ancient Mariner.' Keats could read *Oberon* only in Sotheby's popular translation but even in an alien dress the poem had a strong influence upon him, going deeper as his mind and art developed. For a close and detailed study of *Oberon* in relation to Keats Mr. Beyer's book must be read.[2]

There was a girl in the Mathew group who was apparently a centre of interest for the young men. Her name was Mary Frogley. She was reputed in later life to have been 'an old flame' of Keats and it is said that many of his early verses were addressed to her. The verses headed 'To * * * *' beginning 'Hadst thou liv'd in days of old,' in the *Poems*, 1817, were certainly to Mary. These lines were shortened by Keats and sent to her as a valentine by George in 1816. Mathew also addressed verses to her.

Mary Frogley was a pretty girl with dark curly hair and dimples in a 'lively countenance.' Keats admired vivacious women. She took an interest in his work: it is to her and to another early friend, Kirkman,[3] a

[1] *See* PMLA XI, 1930, also *Studies in Keats*, J. Middleton Murry.
[2] *Keats and the Daemon King*, Werner W. Beyer.
[3] *See* Appendix III.

cousin of Mathew's, that we are indebted for the preservation of many early verses. Mary seems in his later career and after his death to have kept up an interest in him. In 1838 we hear of her, as Mrs. Neville, being in possession of one early and two late sketches of Keats made by Severn. Mary was cousin to Richard Woodhouse, the young lawyer who 'boswellized' Keats and his work for the benefit of posterity. If one of Woodhouse's notebooks of Keatsiana had not been destroyed in a fire[1] we might know considerably more about Keats's early life.

There was another girl with whom the Keatses were certainly acquainted in the December of 1816 and perhaps earlier, Georgiana Augusta Wylie, the daughter of James Wylie, Adjutant of the Fifeshire Regiment of Fencible Infantry, and afterwards the wife of George Keats. To her Keats addressed the sonnet beginning:

> Nymph of the downward smile and sidelong glance,
> In what diviner moments of the day
> Art thou most lovely?

For Georgiana Wylie, a girl of eighteen, Keats had not only a strong affection but a high regard. He called her 'disinterested'; a word which he applied to no others but Socrates and Christ. By 'disinterested' he meant something more positive than unselfish; an ability to stand apart, to work for the common good in a spirit wholly divorced from self. But her detachment did not make Georgiana austere. She was a lively girl with a strong sense of fun. If Georgiana had not been taken so early from him (she went with George to America in the summer of 1818) she might have given Keats that sisterly companionship he lacked and helped him to an understanding of women.

In the summer of 1816 Keats was on friendly terms with young Charles Wells, Tom's schoolfellow: in June we find him addressing a sonnet to Wells thanking him for some garden roses:

> Soft voices had they, that with tender plea
> Whisper'd of peace, and truth, and friendliness unquell'd.

Wells (later the author of *Stories after Nature* and *Joseph and his Brethren*, a poetic drama which had a vogue among the Pre-Raphaelites) was a singular character with a streak of cruelty in him: even while professing, or implying, 'friendliness unquell'd' he was playing a practical joke on Keats's delicate younger brother, his school friend, writing him a series of letters supposed to be from a woman, and even

---

[1] As Woodhouse was at Eton with Shelley we may also have lost information about a second poet.

(according to Wells's brother-in-law, William Smith Williams), inducing him 'to go to France in the idea of meeting his correspondent.' Tom, a boy of sixteen perhaps already in the grip of a fatal disease, was strongly affected by these letters, stupid as they appear to have been from the specimen we have, and apparently kept the correspondence, at least for a while, a secret. The surviving letter,[1] written in August, 1816, and addressed to 'Post Office, Margate' is in a neat small hand on four crowded quarto pages. If composed by Wells himself, who was even younger than Tom, it shows an extraordinary and unpleasant precocity, but Keats, when he came to read them, thought there had been a confederate. The letter must have taken a long time to concoct and set down, but this was an age when those addicted to practical joking would take immense trouble. A wearisome farrago, half amorous, half literary with chivalric and Spenserian echoes, it is the only one surviving and was passed on by Keats to Thomas Richards[2], brother of Charles who printed *Poems, 1817*. 'Disappointing stuff, indeed,' M. Buxton Forman commented, 'to come from the pen of a man who a few years later was to produce *Stories after Nature* and *Joseph and his Brethren.*'

But Keats, entering the literary world as a poet of promise, was to grow away from certain of these early friends: in the late autumn of 1816 or the spring of 1817 he came to a momentous decision. Mr. Abbey, who had plans for the future of his eldest ward, was soon to be affronted by his announcement of an intention to abandon medicine for poetry.

---

[1] For text *see* M. Buxton Forman's *Letters*, 1952.
[2] Thomas Richards was the son of a livery stable keeper in Oxford Street and at 1, Bayswater and great-grandfather to Grant Richards.

CHAPTER V

Keats's Personality, his World and an Experience

RICHARD ABBEY was a man of affairs, one who had practical interests beyond his business of tea-broking. He was a churchwarden at St. Stephen's, Walbrook, twice Master of a City Company (the Pattenmakers'), and in 1820 we find him recorded in *The Times* as one of the Stewards for the Annual Examination of the City of London National Schools in the Egyptian Hall, Mansion House ('dinner at 5 o'clock precisely').

In appearance Abbey was, according to John Taylor, 'a large stout goodnatured looking man with a great Piece of Benevolence standing out on the Top of his Forehead.' If the benevolence were there it did not overflow in his dealings with the Keats children. At least on one count, however, Richard Abbey deserves our sympathy: the eldest was a genius, and geniuses are unpredictable kittle cattle to handle. He was old-fashioned; up to 1827 still wearing the dress of his youth, 'white Cotton Stockings & Breeches & half Boots,—when for a long Time there had been no other Man on the Exchange in that Dress, & he was become so conspicuous for it as to be an object of attention in the Streets.'[1]

To an elderly man with set ideas the care of four lively young people could not have been an easy one. He must have felt some relief that soon he would be quit of his eldest ward, John, now on the eve of his majority and fitted, by the expenditure of more than his share of the family money, for a prosperous career. Little Fanny was in the charge of his wife and the two younger boys under his eye in the countinghouse at 4 Pancras Lane.

Partly to spite Hammond at Edmonton, and partly because the late Mrs. Jennings had been known and respected in the district, Abbey had determined that John should start a practice in the nearby village of Tottenham. 'He communicated his Plans to his Ward but his Surprize was not moderate to hear in Reply, that he did not intend to be a Surgeon.'

Taylor's report of Richard Abbey's words dramatizes the encounter between ward and guardian. The fat tradesman, secure in his authority and probably seated comfortably in a familiar armchair, and the vivid, beautiful boy standing before him.

"Not intend to be a Surgeon! Why, what do you mean to be?"

[1] *See also* 'New Light on Mr. Abbey'. Joanna Richardson, K-S. M. *Bulletin*, V 1953.

"I mean to rely on my abilities as a poet."

"John, you are either mad, or a fool to talk in so absurd a manner."

"My mind is made up," John said very quietly. He added that he knew he possessed abilities greater than most men, and he meant to get his living by exercising them. 'Abbey called him a Silly Boy, & prophesied a speedy Termination to his inconsiderate Enterprise.'

Knowing Keats's hot temper, it is possible that high words followed. With head thrown back, chin out and lip quivering, the boy would seem to rise in stature and his wine-dark eyes flash. The pursy old Abbey might scoff: he went home to his brothers secure in their approval and proudly conscious of his high destiny. 'I think I shall be among the English poets after my death.'

Keats, though very short, was of good figure, broad-shouldered and well-proportioned. He had inherited from his father a West Country russet colouring. His bodily appearance, but the mere shell of the protean spirit within, changed considerably, and to each of his friends and in varying but characteristic moods he appeared differently. The familiar portraits by Severn, Brown and Haydon all present the particular aspect of himself he was in the habit of turning to these very dissimilar friends. In Severn's likenesses he is all beautiful sensibility; one can almost see the wide mouth quiver. Brown draws a strong, intellectual man, and Haydon depicts a creature of high poetic fire.[1]

Similarly, in the descriptions given of him details vary. Cowden Clarke speaks of his eyes as light hazel; Severn adds 'like the hazel eyes of a wild gipsy-maid in colour, set in the face of a young god.' In another place Severn speaks of 'the wine-like lustre of Keats's eyes, just like those of certain birds which habitually front the sun.' Leigh Hunt describes them as 'large, dark and sensitive,' and Mrs. George Keats as 'dark brown.' The colour of his hair is also variously described, Cowden Clarke giving it as lightish brown, Mrs. George Keats a golden red, and Leigh Hunt, who possessed a lock, as brown with reddish or golden tints, according to how it was held up to the light. The last was the true colour so far as we can judge from a lock in the Keats Museum formerly belonging to the Llanos family (descendants of Fanny Keats) which had been carefully wrapped away in an envelope; a colour which probably varied, as reddish hair is apt to do, with the condition of health and age of its owner. Worn long at this period, after the fashion of the young romantics, it grew gracefully: according to his friend Bailey, 'if you placed your hand upon his head, the silken curls felt like the rich plumage of a bird.'

[1] The sketch, however, done from memory in 1831 (facing page 193), shows a calm, thoughtful face.

His features are known to us by the life mask, though the upper lip was more curled and so shortened in effect: in the mask the weight of the clay has lengthened it. His expression was as mutable as the face of the sea; dimpling with gay life in the light of the sun and strongly sombre under cloud. He had 'a peculiar sweetness of expression' in the company of friends. His face was darkly pathetic in moments of brooding and when lit up by inspiration 'his eye had an inward look, perfectly divine, like a Delphian priestess who saw visions.'[1]

In building up a portrait of Keats we must not forget, as many of his romantic friends did in their descriptions of him, his gaiety and strong sense of humour. This is abundantly clear in his earlier letters, which are full of an odd fun inclined to richly ridiculous hyperbole, and sprinkled with occasional verse as cheerful as daisies on a green lawn.

This rare creature, gifted with a sensibility beyond that even of most poets, now stepped out of uncongenial bondage into a freer world; into a feverish, post-war world in which violently opposed forces could be palpably felt. He stood with one foot in the old world and one in the new. Around him were the old narrow City streets and courts, evil-smelling and dark, lit by feeble oil-lamps which served only to make 'darkness visible': but in the West End and in the East beyond the borders of the old crowded City, were new roads and those spacious, bright squares, the beautiful gift to London of late eighteenth-century architecture. Already in Westminster and Finsbury there were the new-fangled gas-lamps, a rich illumination which had penetrated even into the houses of the more progressive Londoners. Although the old-fashioned cesspool was still noisomely evident there was already a sewer constructed in the Strand.

The streets were patrolled by old and inefficient watchmen, but the Bow Street Runners, heralding the modern police, had been embodied. Although the long-distance services out of London were efficient and swift, the suburban coaches were slow and uncomfortable. The traveller was still not entirely safe from highwaymen. In a guide book for 1815 the visitor is warned to travel into London from the Surrey side well before sundown in case of attack. The railway engine was already in being. As early as 1808 Robert Trevithick's engine, 'Catch-me-who-can,' was running on a circular track near Euston giving 'joy-rides' for a shilling a head at a speed of eighteen miles an hour. On the sea tall-masted ships made long, uncertain and uncomfortable journeys, sped by the winds as they blew, but at least four noisy, jolting steam-boats were already carrying passengers on the Thames.

A new humanitarian spirit was abroad but animals were still

[1] Haydon.

callously treated; badgers, bulls and bears were baited for man's amusement. Men and women were hanged and transported for theft, put in the pillory or flogged. A few gibbets, with their hideous, blackened, white-ribbed burdens, still clanked and swung on the public roads. Although there was agitation among the Evangelicals for the abolition of slavery abroad, here in England little children under six toiled all day in stifling cotton mills. Many people thought it a good thing that the poor should be thus early introduced to habits of industry.

The Prince Regent and an aristocracy grown rich and powerful in land during the wars spent lavishly on building, on mistresses, gambling, heavy eating and hard drinking: the middle classes were in many areas sinking into dire poverty and the poor were destitute. There were demands for drastic reform in Parliamentary election, in government, and the widespread misery of the people led to riots and attacks on property. The Tory Government, bolstered up by land, wealth and the prevalence of rotten boroughs, in no way representing the country, was out of touch with new movements and modern thought.

Agriculture was still the staple industry of Great Britain but the new machines in the North were already imprisoning human beings in smoky, crowded cities and throwing the handworkers out of employment. Bad harvests and the aftermath of the ancient evil of war were pauperizing the small farmer and his labourer. Starvation walked gaunt and rattling through the land. The Government's reply to agricultural distress was the passing of the stupid and drastic Corn Laws. When the hungry men of the North demonstrated with violence, and rioted in desperation, it passed the oppressive Six Acts, taking away liberty of thought and action. The panacea for widespread misery was the raising of a few private subscriptions: public relief was left to financially crippled local government.

To the young Liberals, roused by the weekly fulminations of Hunt's *Examiner* and of *The Political Register* published by that stout and fearless old yeoman, William Cobbett, the burden of this misery was a heavy one, but there must have been much that we look back upon with shame which they, children of their generation, accepted as a part of the order of things. We know, and the knowledge gives us a distinct shock, that Keats in boyhood was present at a bear-baiting which he afterwards described for Cowden Clarke with vivacity. He imitated the antics of the bear and made his old usher laugh. 'His perception of humour,' said Clarke, 'was both vivid and irresistibly amusing.' But human injustice always aroused in Keats a swift anger. 'The form of his visage was changed,' and drawing himself up so that he appeared to grow immensely in stature he would shout: "Why is there not a human dustbin in which to tumble such fellows?" He was to write later: 'Health and Spirits can only belong unalloyed to the selfish Man—the Man who thinks much of his fellows can never be in Spirits.'

In the autumn of 1816 Keats was, so far as we know, living with his brothers, probably at first in Poultry and later certainly at 76 Cheapside in rooms over the archway[1] leading into Bird-in-Hand Court and the Queen's Arms Tavern, later Simpson's which was partially destroyed by enemy action in the 1939 war and is now totally obliterated.

Keats developed rapidly. Most of what he wrote, though not in the first rank of poetry, was crammed with the luxuriant fancy of a young genius and grew steadily in power, culminating that year in the great sonnet, 'On first looking into Chapman's Homer.'

The story of the poem is among the most interesting in the annals of English literature. Cowden Clarke tells us that now he and Keats were not living far apart, they had resumed their old habit of meeting to read and talk about books. The Elizabethans, their darlings, were hard to come by in those days; there were few reprints and when, in October, a Mr. Alsager lent Clarke the folio edition, 1616, of Chapman's translation of Homer, they hung over it till daybreak.

It was, says Clarke, 'a memorable night . . . in my life's career . . . to work we went, turning to some of the "famousest" passages, as we had scrappily known them in Pope's version. . . . One scene I could not fail to introduce to him—the shipwreck of Ulysses . . . and I had the reward of one of his delightful stares, upon reading the following lines:

> Then forth he came, his both knees faltring; both
> His strong hands hanging downe; and all in froth
> His cheeks and nosthrils flowing. Voice and breath
> Spent all to vse; and downe he sunke to Death.
> *The sea had soakt his heart through:* all his vaines
> His toiles had rackt, t'a labouring woman's paines.
> Dead weary was he.

'The sea had soakt his heart through.' The magnificent conception, the direct expression, must delight the common reader and how much more the poet. Here was the antique world, which Keats had only known till now through mythologies, a few Latin authors, Fénelon and polite eighteenth-century translations, echoing down to him through the voice of old Chapman roaring through the polter's measure. Clarke later drew Keats's attention to Pope's rendering of that line. It must have been pleasant to hear his shout of laughter:

---

[1] Here Severn made the drawing of Keats given as frontispiece to this book.

From mouth to nose the briney torrent ran,
And *lost in lassitude lay all the man.*

To Keats the rough letters of this old book were 'spiritual hiero-glyphics': he read, though he knew it not, the stuff of life, of his own poetic life. This robust verse, opening up a vista into a world so old and yet living, wrought a miracle in his brain. Much that was before un-related, cohered; within a few months he could state in 'Sleep and Poetry' his creed, that orderly progression of poetic growth to which he adhered steadily throughout his short life. In his *Studies in Keats* Middleton Murry made a masterly analysis of the evidence which goes to show that this reading in old Chapman was momentous, and the sonnet which sprang from it a landmark.

When at length Keats tore himself away he walked in the rising of the late October sun back to the City. Through the short two miles he was composing at fever heat. By ten o'clock that morning there was on Clarke's breakfast table a letter. Clarke must have wondered to see his friend's handwriting when they had parted so soon before. Wonder mounted into high amazement when he broke the seal and found within 'On first looking into Chapman's Homer.' The sonnet was not in the final version; 'eagle eyes' was not there and 'Yet did I never breathe its pure serene' had in its place a poorer, though more self-revelatory line. This is probably how the poem stood as Cowden Clarke read it:

Much have I travell'd in the Realms of Gold,
  And many goodly States and Kingdoms seen;
  Round many Western Islands have I been,
Which Bards in fealty to Apollo hold.
Oft of one wide expanse had I been told,
  Which deep brow'd Homer ruled as his Demesne;
  Yet never could I tell what men could mean,
Till I heard Chapman speak out loud, and bold.
Then felt I like some Watcher of the Skies
  When a new Planet swims into his Ken,
Or like stout Cortez, when with wond'ring eyes
  He star'd at the Pacific, and all his Men
Look'd at each other with a wild surmise—
  Silent upon a Peak in Darien.

CHAPTER VI

Haydon and the Elgin Marbles; Leigh Hunt
(October, 1816—January, 1817)

CHARLES COWDEN CLARKE had fostered the early poetic growth of his pupil and it was appropriately he who first drew him into the liberal and artistic circle, prominent members of which were Leigh Hunt, poet, graceful prose-writer and editor of the rebel journal *The Examiner*, and Haydon the painter.

Some time in 1816 Cowden Clarke, in a glow of anticipation, took to Leigh Hunt some of the young Keats's poems. Knowing that there was merit in them he anticipated some measure of praise, but, he said, 'my partial spirit was not prepared for the unhesitating and prompt admiration which broke forth before he had read twenty lines of the first poem.' Hunt himself wrote: 'I shall never forget the impression made upon me by the exuberant specimens of genuine though young poetry that were laid before me.'

The praise of a man recognized by the younger generation as one of its most sensitive and discriminating critics was gratifying enough but, to Cowden Clarke's delight, it was endorsed by the harder-headed Horace Smith, wit and man of letters, who happened to be present. Among the poems was a sonnet written on the day Hunt left prison (February 3rd, 1815) beginning: 'How many bards gild the lapses of time.' Hunt read the sonnet aloud and in reference to the thirteenth line, 'That distance of recognisance bereaves,' Smith exclaimed: 'What a well-condensed expression for a youth so young!' Horace Smith's opinion was soon to be echoed by William Godwin, Basil Montagu and Hazlitt, to whom Hunt introduced the poems as they dined with him.

On May 5th Hunt had published in *The Examiner* the first poem of Keats's to be printed, the sonnet, 'O Solitude! if I must with thee dwell.' This, he stated, had been published 'without knowing more of him than any other anonymous correspondent'; it would therefore appear that it was after this date that Cowden Clarke took the sheaf of poems to him. The evidence as to when Keats first met Hunt is conflicting. Mr. Blunden considers that it was not until late in 1816; but from a rimed invitation to visit him at No. 7 Pond Street, Hampstead (where he spent a fortnight or more in October), sent by Haydon to John Hamilton Reynolds,[1] it would appear as if Keats met Haydon,

---

[1] See *The Keats Circle*, p. 4, ed. H. E. Rollins, Harvard University Press, 1948.

Reynolds, and possibly Leigh Hunt too, earlier than we had thought. Though in verse admitted by the writer to be far from expert ('For Painting I am much more fit') and which may distort sense for sound, one may fairly deduce from the invitation to come

> Next Sunday to Hampstead Town
> To meet John Keats, who soon will shine
> The greatest, of this Splendid time
> That e'er has woo'ed the Muses nine.

that Keats was by October well acquainted with Haydon, and already acclaimed in the Hampstead circle. On the other hand, on the last day of October, 1816, Keats wrote to Cowden Clarke:

> My daintie Davie,
>   I will be as punctual as the Bee to the Clover. Very glad am I at the thoughts of seeing so soon this glorious Haydon and all his creation. . . .

From the tone of this we might assume Keats was looking forward to a first meeting with Haydon: perhaps he had been unable to accept an invitation to meet his young fellow-poet, Reynolds, at Hampstead, and perhaps it was Cowden Clarke who introduced Keats to Haydon in the studio at 41 Great Marlborough Street, that small room blocked on one side by an enormous canvas on which Haydon had already been working more than a year. It was his 'Christ's Entry into Jerusalem,' a picture that, in Haydon's own vapourish imagination, was to lift British art to the heights of the Old Masters. On this picture he worked for seven years. Art to him was apparently great in proportion to its size, and although he knew that large canvases could not easily find a place in the homes of his patrons, he persisted in painting larger and larger. Haydon was an extraordinary man with the mind of a genius, the capacity of genius for hard, unremitting toil, but with neither the skill of a born painter, nor the eyesight to put his ideas accurately into execution. His tragedy was that in his headstrong youth he had seized hold of the wrong tool: the brush instead of the pen. He was a born writer. His letters, and the journals from which I have the privilege of quoting,[1] are vivid, enthusiastic, compelling in interest. In self-revelation he comes near to Rousseau and, like the French egoist, although a shrewd observer, saw the world largely as an appanage to himself. He, the great artist, the heaven-born genius with the brush, had a right to be supported while he achieved his mighty work; even to the extent of borrowing money from impecunious friends. It was less degrading to borrow than to prostitute his divine art by painting portraits or saleable pictures. Here is an extract from his diary:

[1] *The Diary of Benjamin Robert Haydon*, ed. by Willard Bissell Pope.

April 29, 1815. This week has really been a week of great delight. Never have I had such irresistible, perpetual continued urgings of future greatness. I have been like a man with air balloons under his arm pits, and ether in his soul. While I was painting or walking, or thinking, these beaming flashes of energy followed and impressed me! O God, grant they may not be presumptuous feelings. Grant they may be the fiery anticipations of a great Soul born to realize them. They came over me, & shot across me, & shook me, & inspired me to such a degree of intensity, that I lifted up my heart, & thanked God.

Haydon was constantly thanking God, or exhorting God to support him against his enemies and his creditors. He felt himself to be under the divine protection but was constantly reminding Him of His duty.

To us, looking back, Haydon is both a tragic and a comic figure, but in his own age the great and abounding personality of the man, his exalted power of mind, so impressed his friends, many of them men of true genius, strong talent or marked common sense, that they too, sometimes against the evidence of their own eyes, believed him to be a remarkable painter. Haydon himself with perhaps, keen critic as he was, a personal private doubt of his ultimate artistic value, unwittingly comments on this phenomenon: 'The interest I excite among the genius of the Country, is certainly very singular—there must be something in me too'—(*Journal*, March 17, 1817.)

It was not only among the 'genius of the Country' that Haydon excited interest: his self-enthusiasm, his energy, the choice of religious subjects and the size of his canvases not only hypnotized his friends into lending him money, but even influenced Coutts, the banker, to advance a large sum. The rent he owed to an admiring landlord ran into hundreds and once he dazzled his wine merchant into making him a present of a dozen bottles.

If this man, strong-willed, bull-necked and abounding in physical energy,[1] could charm the minds of sober, middle-aged folk, what was his effect on that young, untried enthusiast, John Keats? After an evening spent with Haydon (probably this first exciting occasion) he wrote:

My dear Sir—
    Last Evening wrought me up, and I cannot forbear sending you the following—

Yours unfeignedly
John Keats.

---

[1] His laughs, said Hunt, 'sound like the trumpets of Jericho and threaten to have the same effect.'

He enclosed the sonnet, with its grave and beautiful movement, 'Great Spirits now on earth are sojourning.'

With characteristic precipitation Haydon answered immediately. He was enthusiastic about the sonnet and told Keats he would like to send it to his friend Wordsworth. Keats, like all the young men of his time, looked with admiration towards the North, up to that craggy landmark of the new poetry. He wrote to Haydon the next day, enclosing a carefully written copy of the sonnet:

Your Letter has filld me with a proud pleasure and shall be kept by me as a stimulus to exertion—I begin to fix my eye upon one horizon. . . . The Idea of your sending it to Wordsworth put me out of breath—you know with what Reverence I would send my Wellwishes to him—

Keats, of whom the impetuous Haydon immediately made a close friend, was soon a frequent visitor to the studio. Often he sat quietly watching the painter at work, but sometimes Haydon would talk; glorious, half-mad, inspired talk, strengthening the young poet in a faith in his own genius, or uttering violent but often sound criticism on art and literature. It was probably he who started Keats off on that voyage of discovery which ended in the bourn, tranquil and sublime, of the 'Ode on a Grecian Urn,' with its triumphant ending:

> Beauty is Truth, Truth Beauty.—That is all
> Ye know on Earth, and all ye need to know.

for we read in Haydon's journal, under the date January, 1813 (over three years before he met Keats):

You say 'After all beauty is the thing.' No, it is not the chief thing; intellect, the feelings of the heart, are the chief things. The more beautiful the garb that expression is dressed in, the better, but if you dress expression so beautifully as to overwhelm it, the object is not attained.

Beauty of form is but the vehicle of conveying Ideas, but truth of conveyance is the first object . . . beauty is but a means. . . . Perfect beauty can only belong to beings not agitated by passion, such as Angels.

With the pregnant mythology of Ancient Greece Keats was already familiar, but it was reserved for Haydon, in practical illustration of the theory suggested above, to introduce him to a solid reality, a more tangible evidence of that old and abiding power, the Elgin Marbles. Haydon had made himself their champion and, after long and bitter warfare with the Academy and the Government, he secured recognition

of their authentic beauty, and saw them housed in the British Museum.
To Keats they were a superb revelation. Their influence on him, in
fixing his æsthetic aim and strengthening his determination, is perhaps
incalculable. They stimulated him to write two sonnets, one of which
was addressed to Haydon. The sonnets are not among his best, but
the second, 'On seeing the Elgin Marbles,' is of strong autobiographical
interest, and has at least a magnificent conclusion:

> My spirit is too weak—mortality
> Weighs heavily on me like unwilling sleep,
> And each imagin'd pinnacle and steep
> Of godlike hardship, tells me I must die
> Like a sick Eagle looking at the sky.
> Yet 'tis a gentle luxury to weep
> That I have not the cloudy winds to keep,
> Fresh for the opening of the morning's eye.
> Such dim-conceived glories of the brain
> Bring round the heart an undescribable feud;
> So do these wonders a most dizzy pain,
> That mingles Grecian grandeur with the rude
> Wasting of old Time—with a billowy main—
> A sun—a shadow of a magnitude.

To most artists these great fragments are overwhelming in their
dazzling light and power and for some they are a draught too potent.
In the first vision Keats felt the weight of their perfection too heavy for
him. Afterwards he spent many hours with them, sometimes in the
company of Severn but more often alone. Once his friend came upon
him in rapt contemplation before them, his face glowing with inward
vision. Respecting this happy absorption Severn went quietly away.
Another time when Keats was alone there a foppish acquaintance
joined him and viewed the Marbles condescendingly through a quizzing-
glass. After teasing the poet for some time with vapid remarks he left
him with the words: "Yes, I believe, Mr. Keats, we may admire
these works safely."

Another 'realm of gold' opened up to Keats by Haydon was the
cartoons of Raphael which, on Haydon's instigation, were brought
from Hampton Court to London and exhibited. These cartoons,
lauded by Haydon and his set, were almost as much a subject of
controversy as the Elgin Marbles. One of them, 'The Sacrifice at
Lystra,' was to contribute directly to the subject matter of the 'Ode on a
Grecian Urn': in the spring of 1819 it was on view at the British
Gallery, and in May, when the Ode was almost certainly being
composed, Haydon published an article upon it in *The Examiner*.[1]

[1] *See* Letter, *Times Literary Supplement*, July 9th, 1938, by Mr. J. R. MacGillivray of University College, Toronto.

Haydon's picture, finely hung at Saint Gregory Seminary, Ohio, shews Christ riding on the ass and closely surrounded by a throng of people. In imitation of the Old Masters he put in figures of modern historical personages and also of living men. Voltaire, the hero of the Liberal free-thinkers and the devil of the orthodox, Haydon depicted as a smiling scoffer; Newton as a believer; Hazlitt as a detached observer; Wordsworth with bowed head as a devout man; Charles Lamb in characteristic pose; and Keats, a bright amazed face in the background. For this purpose Haydon took casts and it is to that fortunate accident we owe the life mask at the Keats Memorial House.

Haydon was surrounded at this time by a group of ardent young men, his pupils, to whom he was generous, choosing them less for what they might pay him than for their own individual merit. Among them were William Bewick, the Landseers, George Lance and William Mayor. Beyond their acquaintance Keats was introduced through Haydon or Severn to other painters, including David Wilkie, William Hilton and Peter de Wint, the great water-colourist.

Haydon's friend, James Henry Leigh Hunt, was a man of thirty-two; an idealist after a different fashion and perhaps in a lesser degree. Thrown into the arena of dusty polemics at an early age through relationship to a sterner brother, John Hunt, his character had been strengthened by the combat; but his sufferings in mind and in pocket through heavy fines and imprisonment had driven him, paradoxically, further from reality than his vivid nature warranted.

He had made of his prison room in Horsemonger Lane (at an expense he could ill afford) a bower lined with rosy trellised wallpaper and ceiled with a painting of a skyscape: the little courtyard allotted to him for exercise he turned into a flower garden. Public indignation and the resolution of friends, added to 'monstrous *douceurs*' amounting to several hundred pounds out of the prisoner's own pocket, had exacted these privileges from a turnkey already under the influence of Hunt's personal charm. Here he studied the fifty volumes of the *Parnaso Italiano*, resulting in what was perhaps his finest literary work, a graceful translation into verse of Italian poets unknown to nineteenth-century England. In this and in the direction of other writers' attention to the Italians, Hunt rendered service to the cause of literature, but the study accentuated in himself a flowery, exotic quality not suited to our harsher northern tongue. The artificially created bower had become his refuge in prison, and now he was to find (although he still continued, but less vehemently, to wage warfare on both political and literary tyranny) a refuge in 'leafy luxury,' in poetical unrealities, in classical and romantic book-dreams. His son, Thornton, wrote of him:

. . . his *indoles*—which we imperfectly call taste, genius, or natural bent,
led him to the lighter "humanities." A devoted idealist, he actually lived
in the world of poetry, painting, and music; coming into the real world only
to play his part, confessedly with very elementary knowledge, in the stern,
unprofitable business of constitutional politics; and mingling in the business
of common life only to treat his affairs on bookish principles and to invest his
personal friends with ideal attributes. . . . He seldom viewed anything as it
really was, but as it looked under the atmosphere of poetry, by the light of
classic illustrations.

It was Hunt's misfortune that he had to scramble for money and
too often feel the want of it when, in Hazlitt's words, he 'ought to have
been a gentleman born, and to have patronized men of letters. He
might then have played, and sung and laughed and talked his life
away; have written manly prose, elegant verse; and his *Story of Rimini*
would have been praised by Mr. Blackwood.'

In person Hunt was handsome, dark and vivid, with the exotic
flavour of Creole descent. He made graceful verses, wrote lively
prose, and savoured life in an elegant way. His mind had a delicate
'vinous quality.' He talked amusingly on many subjects, he criticized
acutely and was that rarity, a good listener. He would discuss orthodox
religion, which he repudiated, with that earnest soul, Haydon. When
argument became too fierce for his liking he would turn gracefully
away to his pianoforte and, in a charming tenor, break into an Italian
aria. Mrs. Carlyle dubbed him 'the talking nightingale'; he had something of the apparent inconsequence of a lightly flitting bird.

This charming man lived poetically in the Vale of Health in
Hampstead, surrounded by a wife, Marianne, as unpractical and with
a taste for modelling, a sister-in-law, Bessy Kent, a keen botanist,
and several lively, dark-eyed young children. Carlyle, knowing him
in later days in Cheyne Walk, when times were harder, his wife more
slatternly and debased by secret drinking, and the children more
numerous, called his household a 'poetical Tinkerdom' . . . 'yet
the noble Hunt received you in his Tinkerdom in the spirit of a
King.'

On December 1st, 1816, Hunt published in *The Examiner* an
unsigned article, 'Young Poets.' It began with some remarks on the
rise of the new school of poetry, pointing out that the term 'new' was
incorrect, for it looked back to 'the finer times of the English Muse . . .
its only object being to restore the same love of nature, and of *thinking*
instead of mere *talking*, which formerly rendered us real poets, and
not mere versifying wits, and bead-rollers of couplets.' The object of
his article was 'merely to notice three young writers, who appear to
us to promise a considerable addition of strength to the new school.'

George Keats
From a miniature by
Joseph Severn in the
Keats-Shelley Memorial
House, Rome

Tom Keats
From a drawing by
Joseph Severn in the
Keats-Shelley Memorial
House, Rome

Joseph Severn
From a self-portrait in the possession of the late M. Buxton
Forman, Esq.

The three writers were Keats, Shelley and John Hamilton Reynolds. Reynolds had recently published his *The Naiad*, showing a promise he was not to fulfil. Hunt was not alone in expecting great things of Reynolds; Hazlitt in his lecture on 'The Living Poets,' at the Surrey Institution in 1818, gave his sonnet on Sherwood Forest the honour of quotation.

Hunt did not enlarge upon Shelley's work as he had none of his poems beside him. He called him 'a striking and original thinker.' Quoting from *The Naiad*, after criticizing Reynolds for a certain artificiality and for too much detail, he continued:

The last of these young aspirants whom we have met with, and who promise to help the new school to revive Nature and

> "To put a spirit of youth in everything,"

is, we believe, the youngest of them all, and just of age. His name is John Keats. He has not yet published anything except in a newspaper; but a set of his manuscripts was handed to us the other day, and fairly surprised us with the truth of their ambition, and ardent grappling with Nature. In the following Sonnet there is one incorrect rhyme, which might be easily altered, but which shall serve in the mean time as a peace-offering to the rhyming critics. The rest of the composition, with the exception of a little vagueness in calling the regions of poetry "the realms of gold," we do not hesitate to pronounce excellent, especially the last six lines. The word *swims* is complete; and the whole conclusion is equally powerful and quiet:

He then quoted 'On first looking into Chapman's Homer.' The incorrect rime was, of course, the 'mean' and 'demesne' of the first version. Keats took this criticism to heart and altered the line to 'Yet could I never breathe its pure serene.' 'Pure serene' he might have got from Cary's translation of the Divine Comedy, though there is no evidence that he had yet seen it. Compounds of this type are common enough in eighteenth-century verse; 'pure serene' occurs more than once. Coleridge used it in his second version[1] of 'Hymn before Sunrise' and Thomson in 'To the Memory of the Right Honourable the Lord Talbot.'

On the Sunday the article appeared Keats went up to Hampstead with Cowden Clarke. This praise of him, his first public recognition as a poet, was enough to exalt a young man even without the anticipation of meeting with the valiant editor of *The Examiner* and author of *The Story of Rimini*. Cowden Clarke records the pilgrimage:

The character and expression of Keats's features would arrest even the

---

[1] *The Friend,* October, 1809—reprinted in collected form, 1812, in London.

casual passenger in the street; but now they were wrought to a tone of animation that I could not but watch with interest, knowing what was in store for him. . . . As we approached the Heath, there was a rising and accelerated step, with a gradual subsidence of all talk.

In prison Hunt had thought yearningly of 'dear Hampstead': now he had realized his dream of living there in a pretty white house, styled a cottage in the fashionable spirit of urban rusticity.

> It was a poet's house who keeps the keys
> Of pleasure's temple.

We can imagine Hunt, his large dark eyes bright with anticipation, awaiting the two young men in that poet's bower, in which

> Round about were hung
> The glorious features of the bards who sung
> In other ages—cold and sacred busts
> Smiled at each other.

There were warm and mannered pictures of the domesticated nymphs and satyrs of the elegant century, and a touch of the heroic in images of 'great Alfred'

> . . . with anxious, pitying eyes,
> As if he always listened to the sighs
> Of the goaded world; and Kosciusko's worn
> By horrid suffrance—mightily forlorn.

There was the beloved pianoforte at which Hunt would sit and play lightly, singing Italian airs in a voice of remarkable range and sweetness. It should have been summer when Keats first came here so that Hunt might be poetically embowered in blossoms; but the flowers and foliage were there symbolically.

The delight in the meeting was mutual. Clarke's rosy face beamed with pleasure. 'The interview, which stretched into "three morning-calls," was the prelude to many after-scenes and saunterings about Caen Wood and its neighbourhood; for Keats was suddenly made a familiar of the household, and was always welcomed.'

It was Hunt's custom to commemorate an occasion in a sonnet. The same day he wrote one to Keats which I give in full because it is not well known and is so characteristic of the man:

'Tis well you think me truly one of those
  Whose sense discerns the loveliness of things;
  For surely as I feel the bird that sings
Behind the leaves, or dawn as it up grows,
Or the rich bee rejoicing as he goes,
  Or the glad issue of emerging springs,
  Or overhead the glide of a dove's wings,
Or turf, or trees, or midst of all, repose:

And surely as I feel things lovelier still,
  The human look, and the harmonious form
Containing woman, and the smile in ill,
  And such a heart as Charles's, wise and warm,—
As surely as all this, I see, ev'n now,
Young Keats, a flowering laurel on your brow.

Though not in the first rank of poetry there is a warmth in these lines
and a quiet beauty. 'The harmonious form containing woman' is a
nasty drop, and characteristic. Keats's early work has similar common-
place lines and a luxuriousness common to Hunt, but we cannot lay the
blame wholly at the elder poet's door: an over-lushness of expression
was inevitable in the young poetry of a man so acutely sensuous. The
dropping into flat commonplace, a prominent weakness of Wordsworth's
poetry, was perhaps inevitable too in early romantic work because
of the studied avoidance of the conventional language of verse. There
are also, as Sir Sidney Colvin pointed out, examples of 'chatty' lines
among the Elizabethans, the staple reading of the romantics; we
find them even in the august Milton's early work. He compared
Keats's

    The silence when some rhymes are coming out;
    And when they're come, a very pleasant rout;

with Milton, in the 'Vacation Exercise':

    I have some lively thoughts that rove about,
    And loudly knock to have their passage out.

But though Hunt wrote many graceful lines and some fine ones, and
on one occasion a sonnet superior to those produced by Keats and
Shelley, he never cured himself of occasional banality. In *The Story of
Rimini*, at an emotional point in the story, he perpetrated what is,
perhaps, the worst couplet in the language:

The two divinest things this world has got,[1]
A lovely woman in a rural spot.

which, wickedly and deliciously, Patmore parodied as:

The two divinest things this world can grab,
A handsome woman in a hansom cab.

Keats was soon to refine away the dross in his own work. In the
1820 volume there is only one example of the 'cheap' line and this, to
be fair to Hunt, is almost as dreadful as his couplet:

Of the sweets of Faeries, Peris, Goddesses,
There is not such a treat among them all,
Haunters of cavern, lake, and waterfall,
As a real woman . . .

though in defence of Keats it must be borne in mind that, although
'treat' was used colloquially as early as 1808, it had not so strong a
slang connotation as it has to-day.

On December 30th the three friends were together again. They
were talking of crickets, 'the cheerful little grasshopper of the fireside,'
and Hunt challenged Keats to a poetical contest; each to write in a
given time a sonnet 'On the Grasshopper and Cricket.' Perhaps there
leapt into Keats's mind a memory of hospital days[2] when, sitting on
lonely evening vigil as a dresser on duty, a chirping cricket reminded
him in those dismal surroundings of the open countryside. If Keats
made this mental connection it is probable he did not mention it.
He disliked talking of his medical years.

Cowden Clarke sat by on the sofa while the poets 'set to.' 'I cannot,'
he says, 'say how long the trial lasted. . . . The time, however, was short
for such a performance, and Keats won as to time.' That the younger
man won also as to merit Hunt immediately and generously acknowledged when they exchanged manuscripts.

On the way home, however, Keats told Cowden Clarke that he
preferred Hunt's poem; a tinkling performance but pretty enough.
He invocates the cricket as

.. . you, warm little housekeeper, who class
With those who think the candles come too soon,
Loving the fire, and with your tricksome tune
Nick the glad silent moments as they pass.

The young Keats's poem is a miracle of improvisation:

[1] Deleted by Hunt in later versions.
[2] Almost within living memory crickets chirped on the ancient hearths of the surgical wards.

The poetry of earth is never dead:
When all the birds are faint with the hot sun,
And hide in cooling trees, a voice will run
From hedge to hedge about the new-mown mead;
That is the Grasshopper's—he takes the lead
In summer luxury,—he has never done
With his delights; for when tired out with fun
He rests at ease beneath some pleasant weed.
The poetry of earth is ceasing never;
On a lone winter evening, when the frost
Has wrought a silence, from the stove there shrills
The Cricket's song, in warmth increasing ever,
And seems to one in drowsiness half lost,
The Grasshopper's among some grassy hills.[1]

It is a characteristically romantic poem. Could any classic writer have spoken of 'the poetry of earth'? The flexibility of the sonnet is also typically romantic. Although it is constructed on a rigid rime scheme, the rimes are not insistent to the ear and the lines flow into one another. In it nature and poetry are at one; poetry coming from him, as he wished it should come, 'as naturally as the leaves of a tree.'

Keats was a man of deep affections and naturally domestic; it was a quiet joy to be made one of the happy household rendered felicitous by the witchery of an enchanting man who in his person embodied, somewhat self-consciously it is true, the new romantic spirit. He would stay very late with Hunt in sweet converse. On one solitary walk through the night back to Cheapside he composed:

Keen, fitful gusts are whisp'ring here and there
Among the bushes half leafless, and dry;
The stars look very cold about the sky,
And I have many miles on foot to fare.
Yet feel I little of the cool bleak air,
Or of the dead leaves rustling drearily,
Or of those silver lamps that burn on high,
Or of the distance from home's pleasant lair:
For I am brimfull of the friendliness
That in a little cottage I have found;
Of fair-hair'd Milton's eloquent distress,
And all his love for gentle Lycid drown'd;
Of lovely Laura in her light green dress,
And faithful Petrarch gloriously crown'd.

Sometimes Keats would stay the night at Hunt's cottage, spending it on an impromptu bed in the sitting-room. Once, excited by his surroundings and the spirit of his poetical host, he could not get to

[1] The sonnets were printed together in *The Examiner*, September 21st, 1817, and in the *Monthly Repository of Theology and General Literature* (the Unitarian organ) in October, 1817.

sleep. His brain clarified, as it had done during that walk back from Clerkenwell in October. There came to him a clear consciousness of his poetic creed and the gradual approach to attainment he had mapped out for himself. He had a vision of a flying charioteer; the god of high poesy. He lay awake all night, or thought he did (the sleep of youth is as natural as breathing, and can be as unaware) but was happy in living poetry,

> ... so that the morning light
> Surprised me even from a sleepless night;
> And up I rose refresh'd, and glad, and gay,
> Resolving to begin that very day
> These lines; ...

The lines were 'Sleep and Poetry,' that momentous utterance which not only defined Keats's own poetic aim, but in one passage roared defiance of the old school of poetry. It is the last poem in that unequal but exciting book, the 1817 volume.

CHAPTER VII

Shelley and the 1817 Volume

In 1819 Keats wrote in one of his journal letters to George and Georgiana in America:

A Man's life of any worth is a continual allegory—and very few eyes can see the Mystery of his life—a life like the scriptures, figurative. . . . Lord Byron cuts a figure—but he is not figurative—Shakspeare led a life of Allegory: his works are the comments on it—

The exact meaning of this passage is hard to comprehend, but its application to Keats's own life is not difficult. Endowed as we are with the rich collection of his letters in addition to his poems, we can see the pattern, the shape of his life more clearly than in the case of most writers. The shape suggests an emblem, an allegory, and the beginning and the end of his poetic life is arched over by a misty rainbow; by a rare and beautiful emanation, by that other young poet, Shelley.

Keats probably first met Shelley at Hunt's house in December, 1816. The two poets had already been associated by Hunt on paper in that first public recognition of them in *The Examiner* of December 1st. Shelley took a strong liking for Keats but Keats did not return it in anything like the same degree.

Sensitive as he was to outside influences and to personalities, the positive force of Shelley's ardent mind must have impinged strongly on his. Genius is not perhaps often profoundly influenced by contemporary genius: the mutual stimulation of the young Coleridge and Wordsworth is possibly a notable exception. The creative mind has to work out its own salvation: another creative mind as strong and of a different texture can more easily interfere with the natural course than guide it. Great men often learn more readily from lesser, from men of pure intellect rather than from the formative spirit of another genius. The creative spirit, fluid as it is, needs harder, more concrete minds to rub against, from which to acquire strength. The minds of Keats and Shelley were poles apart: Keats, when he came to control his imagination, felt he had changed, contrary to the process of nature, from a butterfly into a chrysalis 'having two little loopholes, whence I may look out into the stage of the world. . . . ' He had moulted, 'not for fresh feathers and wings: they are gone, and in their stead I hope to have a pair of patient sublunary legs.' He wrote later to Shelley, saying that an artist must have ' "self-concentration," selfishness, perhaps.' . . . 'The thought of such discipline must fall like cold chains upon you, who perhaps never sat with your wings furl'd for six Months together.'

Keats, with his intuitive knowledge of character, has suggested the difference between himself and Shelley. He was, and always would have been, true flesh-and-blood with his feet firmly fixed on the ground however high his head might rise into the clouds, whereas Shelley was ethereal, soaring like a butterfly or bird above mankind; seeing much, wise in his own way, but seeing from his own individual skyey angle. Shelley lived more among men; against men, bruising the delicate fabric of his being in violent contacts with their stupidities, their brutalities, but Keats, living among them, was like his master Shakespeare, a man apart, above mankind, and yet in them. He had more dramatic power than Shelley; that power which enables a man to feel himself another.

On the side of mere intellect the two differed profoundly. Keats felt strongly the evils of his own time but he realized the inherent imperfections of mankind and knew that no 'Godwin-perfectibility' panaceas could reform: he was the more modern man in outlook. Shelley had the late eighteenth-century notions firmly in his head, and at this period talked long and loud about them in his harsh, shrill voice. He says himself that he loved argument and argued with everyone he met. This would have tired Keats. Also, and this is always important in human intercourse, Keats had a strong sense of humour and Shelley but an odd sense of fun. A sense of humour enables a man to see in truer proportions. A reformer, necessarily a fanatic, rarely has this sense of proportion. Keats, young as he was, would realize how impotent an unknown writer would be against the established forces of tradition, money and natural reaction from the violence of the French Revolution: Shelley, in the blindness of his enthusiasm threw away with both hands, by the dissemination of his ideas in fugitive pamphlets and in immature verse, his reserve of strength to serve mankind.

Hunt and Haydon both stated that Keats's reserve with Shelley was partly the outcome of class-antagonism. The reactionary Government was in the hands of powerful aristocratic Tories: Keats probably shared with Leigh Hunt a suspicion of lords, and may have had at this early date a very natural feeling of ill-ease in the company of 'his betters.' We know that he kept silence about his origins. It is, however, unlikely that he could feel any degree of patronage in the manners of the democratic Shelley. It is possible that Keats, who, after all, was very young, may have felt a subconscious jealousy of Shelley in relation to Leigh Hunt, who instantly adored the new planet which had rushed into his orbit and felt strongly the influence of Shelley to the end of his days.

However, remote as Keats might feel himself from the strange, excitable young genius, Shelley was to be bound up with him inevitably in the minds of posterity. When Keats died in Italy (the alien land in which Shelley was then living) he wrote one of his finest poems in elegiac lament over that untimely end, and in that remarkable last stanza of 'Adonais,' foreshadowed his own death:

> . . . my spirit's bark is driven,
> Far from the shore, far from the trembling throng
> Whose sails were never to the tempest given;
> The massy earth and spherèd skies are riven!
> I am borne darkly, fearfully, afar;
> Whilst, burning through the inmost veil of Heaven,
> The soul of Adonais, like a star,
> Beacons from the abode where the Eternal are.

When his shipwrecked body was cast up on the shore a copy of Keats's last volume of poems was in his pocket, doubled back as if he had been reading it at the very moment disaster overtook him: the pitiful, sea-wracked volume was flung on to the funeral pyre and went up in odorous essence in the pure, spice-laden flames. The Fates, cruel to these two young men, ended their story in a splendid gesture.

Their fame, too, slight enough when they died, was linked and gathered strength together throughout the nineteenth century. In 1829, while in London a few stray volumes of their poems languished in the fourpenny boxes of booksellers, the Galignanis of Paris, those 'pirates' of vision and imagination, made a collection of their work and published it (together with poems by that other pure romantic, Coleridge) with a memoir of each young poet.[1]

It was but fitting then, and it falls into the pattern or allegory of Keats's life, that the publication of his first book should be associated with Shelley. Keats's brothers and his friends, now including the enthusiastic Woodhouse and the clever, understanding Reynolds, urged publication, but Shelley, wiser perhaps than they, advised against rendering up to the unfeeling eye of the public the poet's 'first-blights.' Keats, however, relying on the admired and more mature judgment of Leigh Hunt and Haydon, held to his determination.

---

[1] An American edition was published by John Grigg, Philadelphia, 1831, 1832 and by Thomas, Cowperthwait & Co., 1838 and others followed. *See* Appendix XII.

Although Shelley had protested, it may have been he who introduced Keats to the Olliers, his own publishers: he certainly visited Charles Richards, the Olliers' printer, in regard to the printing of the volume. Richards said he had never had so strange a visitor. 'He was gaunt, and had peculiar starts and gestures, and a way of fixing his eyes and whole attitude for a good while, like the abstracted apathy of a musing madman.' This impression of Shelley serves to remind us that he was not in his intercourse with Keats at his social best; but in a nervous condition, worried about domestic affairs and financial difficulties. His elopement with Mary Godwin had further embittered his father, antagonized Godwin, helped to cause his wife's suicide and lost him his children.

The book came out in early March. 'The first volume of Keats's muse,' says Cowden Clarke, 'was launched amid the cheers and fond anticipation of all his circle. Everyone of us expected (and not un-reasonably) that it would create a sensation in the literary world; for such a first production (and a considerable portion of it from a minor) has rarely occurred.'

There is necessarily a lack of restraint and power in the volume, and many echoes of the Elizabethans and of Wordsworth, the father of the romantic school. The acute sensibility of the young man had to be schooled and his wide reading among the elder poets more fully digested. It is difficult with the knowledge of his ultimate achievement fresh in the mind to assess the value of the book, and perhaps with a fear of partiality it has been too much condemned by some critics. Swinburne wrote of 'so singular an example of a stork among the cranes as the famous sonnet on Chapman's Homer . . . the value of such golden grain amid a garish harvest of tares. . . .' But tares have their own wild, luxuriant beauty, and a child will seek them out among the corn. The 1817 volume, immature though it is, has already the fluidity, the loveli-ness of diction characteristic of Keats and linking him with Shakespeare. Is there a line which can be picked out as definitely ugly, as unpleasing to the ear? Admitting that this young poetry is too sensuous, too little pruned; that often we cannot see the wood for the trees in the riot of 'leafy luxury,' the poems have a wild, natural beauty.

Here is a poet employing his five senses more actively than any other, perhaps, except Shakespeare, Spenser and Coleridge. In youth the senses are acuter and more tyrannous than in maturity, and it is to youth that the early Keats can bring rich delight. The boy or girl opens a volume of Keats at the first page and reads:

> I stood tip-toe upon a little hill,
> The air was cooling, and so very still,
> That the sweet buds which with a modest pride
> Pull droopingly, in slanting curve aside,
> Their scantly leav'd, and finely tapering stems,
> Had not yet lost those starry diadems
> Caught from the early sobbing of the morn.
> The clouds were pure and white as flocks new shorn,
> And fresh from the clear brook; sweetly they slept
> On the blue fields of heaven, and then there crept
> A little noiseless noise among the leaves,
> Born of the very sigh that silence heaves: . . .

He is too young to analyse his sensation, but the breath is sharply caught. He reads on:

> Open afresh your round of starry folds,
> Ye ardent marigolds!
> Dry up the moisture from your golden lids,
> For great Apollo bids
> That in these days your praises should be sung
> On many harps, which he has lately strung. . . .
>
> Here are sweet peas, on tip-toe for a flight:
> With wings of gentle flush o'er delicate white,
> And taper fingers catching at all things,
> To bind them all about with tiny rings.

Here are the beauties of field and garden of which we are so rapturously aware at this age crystallized, made tangible. Our own individual vague feelings of a new delight in nature are shared by a poet and expressed by him in beautiful poetry: and, far from discouraging us in our own callow attempts at the making of verse, he seems to help us, to stimulate self-expression.

Here, too, in the first volume lovely myths are touched upon; the proper food of youth, the clear, bright stories of the childhood of the world. Here is the tale of Eros and Psyche condensed with a rare dramatic power into eight lines:

> And how they kist each other's tremulous eyes:
> The silver lamp,—the ravishment,—the wonder—
> The darkness,—loneliness,—the fearful thunder;

Later there is a self-consciously austere period when the early Keats cloys the palate; we taste poetry rather than swallow it with the avidity of a child. When maturity comes, with its hoarding of loved beauty, we can return to the earlier work, not only recapturing some of the ecstasy of youth, but reading with a literary background, a feeling for period, and, above all, a knowledge of the brief, sad life of the man. It is dear to us as the dewy wide-eyed song of the poet before the shadows had closed round his heart.

The book is also of strong autobiographical value as a part of the pattern, or allegory of his life. His poetic growth can be watched, starting from the callow imitation of Spenser and ·the 'square-toed' eighteenth-century lines to Hope; through the fragment 'Calidore,' with its boyish memories of knights and ladies, and the echoes of the fashionable Tom Moore in verses addressed to the Mathews; through the Epistles and sonnets to his brothers and friends revealing his young joys and interests, to the great 'Chapman's Homer' sonnet and the finer lines of the last poem in the volume, 'Sleep and Poetry,' stating the poetic creed to which he adhered throughout his life.

The choice of sonnets for the volume seems at first glance to be an arbitrary one: among those rejected there are at least four more worthy of printing than, say, 'Had I a man's fair form.' The two sonnets to Haydon 'on seeing the Elgin Marbles' may have been omitted in view of acceptance for publication in *The Examiner* early in March. 'After dark vapours,' charming in its slow, gentle movement, had the approval of Leigh Hunt who printed it in a February *Examiner*. It is possible that Keats discarded it because of the colloquial use in the sixth line of 'feel, as a substantive; though, as Colvin pointed out in connection with Keats's use of it in the first draft of 'In a Drear-nighted December,' 'feel, which after all was good enough for Horace Walpole and Fanny Burney, was to Keats and the Leigh Hunt circle no vulgarism at all, it was a thing of everyday usage both in verse and prose.' The sonnet beginning, 'This pleasant tale is like a little copse,' with its happy epithet 'the tender-legged linnet' and its lovely line

Oh! what a power hath white simplicity!

is charming and was written under happy associations; Keats wrote it at the end of 'The Floure and the Lefe' in a volume of Cowden Clarke's Chaucer when he came home one day and found his friend asleep on the sofa with the volume beside him. Clarke claims it as 'an extempore effusion and written without the alteration of a single word.' Keats may have omitted it because in the last two lines he rimes 'sobbings' and 'robins.' This was a correct ear-rime and had the authority of Wordsworth, for sobbing was pronounced 'sobbin' far into the nineteenth century. It was not, however, an eye-rime, and it would seem as if in serious poetry the eye-rime was preserved, though in lighter pieces it was often dispensed with. Even the correct Pope could write:

This gallery's contrived for walking,
The window to retire and talk in.

Cowden Clarke tells us that the dedication sonnet to Leigh Hunt was also extempore, and this time he was fully awake to vouch for it. It was written 'on the evening when the last proof-sheet was brought from the printer.' The bearer of the proof, probably Charles Ollier himself, said that if Keats wished to print a dedication he must have it at once. There were several friends in the room, and 'in the buzz of a mixed conversation' Keats quietly withdrew to a side table and wrote the poem without the alteration of a single word.

The book did not sell. 'It was read,' said Keats, 'by some dozen of my friends who lik'd it; and some dozen whom I was unacquainted with, who did not.' Among the 'dozen' admirers was Haydon, who wrote in his customary extravagant style, 'I have read your "Sleep and Poetry"—it is a flash of lightening that will round men from their occupations and keep them trembling for the crash of thunder that *will* follow,' and in his Journal under March, 1817, 'Keats has published his first Poems—and great things indeed they promise—he is a sound young man and will be a great one—There are parts in his "Sleep and Poetry" equal to anything in English poetry—never was a truer call!' Other friends, including Charles Ollier, sent flattering sonnets.

Cowden Clarke laments, 'Alas! the book might have emerged in Timbuctoo with far stronger chance of fame and approbation.' He attributed its failure entirely to Keats's avowed discipleship of Leigh Hunt, 'A Radical and a dubbed partizan of the first Napoleon; because when alluding to him, Hunt did not always subjoin the fashionable cognomen of Corsican Monster.' But Cowden Clarke in his partiality is exaggerating the neglect of the book; there are six known reviews of it, and in every one Keats was recognized as a poet of promise.

Three, it is true, were written by friends, but the independent ones were in solid journals, Constable's *Edinburgh and Scots Magazine*, *The Eclectic Review*, an important nonconformist organ, and *The Monthly Magazine*, a non-party journal on the side of reform. In the *Eclectic* he shared the honour of notice with the fashionable Lord Byron for his *Lament of Tasso* and in the *Edinburgh* with the elder poet Coleridge for *Sybilline Leaves*.

From the literary point of view Hunt's notice in *The Examiner* is the most important, coming from a man whom we acknowledge to be a fine critic; but from a historical aspect the three impartial reviews are of value in showing, not only contemporary and varying attitudes to this new poet, but to poetry in general. The two long ones are heavy reading, written in the ponderous, involved style then in fashion among the older journals, but they show a vivid interest in the new poetry and the way it was to develop.

Only the born critics, Hazlitt, Lamb, Hunt, Coleridge, with their clearer vision, could know that the romantic movement was an entire change of outlook, of heart: these professional reviewers cannot be blamed if they were near-sighted and cautious in assuming romantic poetry to be merely a new mode of presentation, a new set of mannerisms. They were still inclined to demand that poetry shall be improving, didactic in the full eighteenth-century manner, or the vehicle for simple sentiment in the later vogue. They were uneasy about the trend of the new poetry and inclined to suspect as licentious the attitude presented in Keats's motto to his book from Spenser's 'Muiopotmos':

> What more felicity can fall to creature,
> Than to enjoy delight with liberty.

and they still found it difficult to free their ears from the tyranny of the balanced antithesis of the Popean couplet.

Constable's *Edinburgh Magazine* (October, 1817) gave three and three-quarter pages, with long quotations. In his opening paragraph the critic said:

(Mr. Keats) is said to be a very young man and a particular friend of Messrs Hunt, the editors of the Examiner, and of Mr. Hazlitt. His youth accounts well enough for some injudicious luxuriancies and other faults in his poems; and his intimacy with two of the wittiest writers of their day, sufficiently vouches for his intellect and taste. Going altogether out of the road of high raised passion and romantic enterprise, in which many ordinary versifiers have been drawn after the example of the famous poets of our time, he has attached himself to a model more pure than some of these, we imagine; and at the same time, as poetical as the best of them. "Sage serious *Spencer*," (sic), the most melodious and mildly fanciful of our old English poets, is Mr. Keats's favourite. . . .

He found in the poems, in addition to 'abundant *Spencerianisms*,' 'a great deal of that *picturesqueness* of fancy and licentious brilliancy of epithet which distinguishes the early Italian Novelists and amorous poets . . . the careless, sketchy, capricious and yet archly-thoughtful manner of *Pulci* and *Ariosto*.' After quoting freely from 'I stood tip-toe' and the Epistles in a tone of praise, he added:

These specimens will be enough to shew that Mr. K. has ventured on ground dangerous for a young poet;—calculated, we think, to fatigue his ingenuity, and try his resources of fancy, without producing any permanent effect adequate to the expenditure of either.

He then criticized the supposed models of Keats, Leigh Hunt and Hazlitt. They were

. . . vivacious, smart, witty, changeful, sparkling, and learned—full of bright points and flashy expressions that strike and even seem to please by a sudden boldness of novelty,—rather abounding in familiarities of conception and oddnesses of manner which shew ingenuity, even though they be perverse, or common, or contemptuous . . . they appear to be too full of conceits and sparkling points, ever to excite any thing more than a cold approbation at the long-run—and too fond, even in their favourite descriptions of nature, of a reference to the factitious resemblances of society, ever to touch the heart. Their verses are straggling and uneven, without the lengthened flow of blank verse, or the pointed connection of couplets.

He spoke of the danger to this school of 'the inlets of vulgarity.' These poets forget 'the appalling doom which awaits the faults of mannerism or the ambition of a sickly refinement.'

If Mr. Keats does not forthwith cast off the uncleannesses of this school, he will never make his way to the truest strain of poetry in which, taking him by himself, it appears he might succeed.

Extolling the simple poetry of the heart, he quoted 'O Solitude' and 'To one who has been long in city pent,' in which the poet expressed his love of nature 'so touchingly' and, quoting the sonnet to Haydon, 'Highmindedness, a jealousy for good,' said it had 'the veritable air of Milton.' He added:

We are sorry that we can quote no more of these sweet verses which have in them so deep a tone of moral energy, and such a zest of the pathos of genius. We are loth to part with this poet of promise, and are vexed that critical justice requires us to mention some passages of considerable affectation, and marks of offensive haste. . . . "Leafy luxury," "jaunty streams," "lawny slope," "the moon-beamy air," "a sun-beamy tale," these, if not namby-pamby, are at least the "holiday and lady terms" of these poor affected creatures who write verses "in spite of nature and their stars."

With a word or two more of criticism, he ended by quoting the 'glorious and Virgilian conception'

> . . . the moon lifting her silver rim
> Above a cloud, and with a gradual swim
> Coming into the blue with all her light.

and compared it to

Ipse Pater, mediâ nimborum in nocte *coruscâ*
Fulmina molitur dextra.

The *Eclectic* review (September, 1817), almost certainly by the owner-editor, Josiah Conder,[1] was rather more severe but, on the whole, just. In the opening remarks upon modern poetry, the writer said:

... Wordsworth is by far the deepest thinker of our modern poets, yet he has been sometimes misled by a false theory, to adopt a puerile style of composition; ... Scott, of all our leading poets, though the most exquisite artist, occupies the lowest rank in respect of the intellectual quality of his productions. ... To Mr. Hunt's poetical genius we have repeatedly borne testimony, but the affectation which vitiates his style must needs be aggravated to a ridiculous excess in the copyist.

He then quoted as an example of the aping of Leigh Hunt the opening sixty lines of 'I stood tip-toe,' adding this comment:

There is certainly considerable taste and sprightliness in some parts of this description, and the whole poem has a sort of summer's day glow diffused over it, but it shuts up in mist and obscurity.

This is, perhaps, though grudging, a fair criticism of the poem. We know the young poet's head was full of Greek legend, of Cynthia and Endymion, but the reviewer of 1817 could not foresee the poem yet to be born.

He considered the sonnets to be the best things in the volume and quoted 'To My Brother George.' 'Sleep and Poetry' he called a 'strange assay,' and if 'it is to be taken as the result of the Author's latest efforts, would seem to show that he was indeed far gone, beyond the reach of the efficacy either of praise or censure in affectation and absurdity.' It was natural that the personal outburst of Keats ending:

> ... yet there ever rolls
> A vast idea before me, and I glean
> Therefrom my liberty; thence too I've seen
> The end and aim of Poesy

would seem extravagant to the sober-minded reviewer, who comments:

We must be allowed, however, to express a doubt whether its (poetry's) nature has been as clearly perceived by the author, or he surely would never

---

[1] The London Library's copy of *The Eclectic Review* is marked, in ink brown with age, with the initials of contributors. At the end of this article is 'J.C.'

have been able to impose even on himself as poetry the precious nonsense which he has here decked out in rhyme. Mr. Keats speaks of

> The silence when some rhymes are coming out;
> And when they've come, a very pleasant rout:

and to the dangerous fascination of this employment must be attributed this half-awake rhapsody.

Having scored this neat point, he indicated some defective rimes, including, strangely, *livers* and *rivers*. He then scored again with:

Mr. Keats has satirized certain *pseudo* poets, who,

> With a puling infant's force
> Sway'd about upon a rocking horse
> And thought it Pegasus.

Satire is a two-edged weapon: the lines brought irresistibly to our imagination the Author of these poems in the very attitude he describes.

He regretted that 'a young man of vivid imagination and fine talents should have . . . been flattered into the resolution to publish verses, of which a few years hence he will be glad to escape the remembrance. . . . To have committed oneself in the character of a versifier, is often a formidable obstacle to be surmounted in after-life.' A man should build up a reputation in some 'useful sphere of exertion' before he seeks the fame of a poet!

In summing up he hinted that he might have been mistaken in his estimate of this young man's powers (though 'the lash of a critic is the thing the least to be dreaded'), for 'brilliant exceptions . . . make the critic's task of peculiar delicacy.' He then quoted 'Happy is England' as 'simple and pleasing.'

The short notice in *The Monthly Magazine* for April 1st is almost wholly favourable:

A small volume of poems, by Mr. KEATS, has appeared; and it well deserves the notice it has attracted, by the sweetness and beauty of the compositions. For the model of his style, the author has had recourse to the age of Elizabeth; and if he has not wholly avoided the quaintness that characterizes the writings of that period, it must be allowed by every candid reader that the fertile fancy and beautiful diction of our old poets, is not unfrequently rivaled by Mr. Keats. There is in his poems a rapturous glow and intoxication of the fancy—an air of careless and profuse magnificence in his diction—a revelry of the imagination and tenderness of feeling, that forcibly impress themselves on the reader.

The notices in *The Champion* (March 9th, 1817), now thought to be written by Reynolds, or in *The European Magazine* (May, 1817), by George Felton Mathew, are printed in full by Middleton Murry in his *Studies in Keats*. *The Champion* review interpreted Keats's mind and poetic aims as, perhaps, only a close friend could do at this early stage and, quoting extensively, concluded with an earnest recommendation of the book to readers, giving, for further knowledge of this new poet, the two sonnets to Haydon on seeing the Elgin Marbles. The claims made for Keats in the opening paragraph are not extravagant to us but must have appeared so to contemporaries:

At a time when nothing is talked of but the power and the passion of Lord Byron, and the playful and elegant fancy of Moore, and the correctness of Rogers, and the sublimity and pathos of Campbell (these terms we should conceive are kept ready composed in the Edinburgh Review-shop) a young man starts suddenly before us, with a genius that is likely to eclipse them all.

Mathew in *The European Magazine* (in a piece of writing joyous to the modern reader, for he throws tremendous images about with the puny skill of an inexpert juggler) objected to this bold statement, thus:

. . . we cannot, as another critic has injudiciously attempted, roll the name of Byron, Moore, Campbell and Rogers, into the milky way of literature, because Keats is pouring out his splendours in the Orient. We do not imagine that the fame of one poet, depends upon the fall of another, or that our morning and our evening stars necessarily eclipse the constellations of the meridian.

He admitted the beauty of the poems, though criticizing the 'slovenly independence of his versification,' adding:

But if the gay colours and the sweet fragrance of bursting blossoms be the promise of future treasures, then we may prophesy boldly of the future eminence of our young poet, for we have no where found them so early or so beautifully displayed as in the pages of the volume before us.

He deplored the evidences of 'the foppery and affectation of Leigh Hunt' in the poems. He thought the attack in 'Sleep and Poetry' on Pope and the old school futile and likely to rebound against the author.

The Champion reviewer had regretted the inclusion of the earlier poems in the middle of the volume. To this Mathew, with a tender and perhaps rather sore feeling of old and broken association, took exception, saying they were 'of superior versification.' He quoted, as 'spirited and powerful,' the juvenile verses to Woman:

> Ah! who can e'er forget so fair a being?
> Who can forget her half retiring sweets?
> God! she is like a milk-white lamb that bleats
> For man's protection.

It is a bitter reflection of the position of women a hundred and fifty years ago that apparently no contemporary found anything comic in these lines.

The review ended with a rich 'period' passage on the high moral aims a poet should have, with a side-hit, perhaps, at the friend now grown cold to him and whose advanced ideas had been so repugnant to his young-elderly mind.

> But remember that there is a sublimer height to which the spirit of the muse may soar; and that her arm is able to uphold the adamantine shield of virtue, and guard the soul from those insinuating sentiments, so fatally inculcated by many of the most popular writers of the day, equally repugnant to reason and religion, which, if they touch us with their poisoned points, will contaminate our purity, inoculate us with degeneracy and corruption, and overthrow among us the dominion of domestic peace and public liberty.

After fifteen more lines in this lofty strain he ended, more generously in a sublimely ridiculous metaphor:

> These observations might be considered impertinent, were they applied to . . . one who could not soar to the heights of poesy,—and ultimately hope to bind his brows with the glorious sunbeams of immortality.

Leigh Hunt's review in *The Examiner* (June 1st, July 6th and 13th) given in full by Mr. Blunden in his *Leigh Hunt's "Examiner" Examined*, opens with a friendly reference to Keats, 'a young poet indeed,' a friend of the writer's and already known to readers, and then gives a rapid and brilliant survey of the growth of poetry from Dryden to the new poets, ending:

> Poetry, like Plenty, should be represented with a cornucopia, but it should be a real one; not swelled out and insidiously *optimized* at the top, like Mr. Southey's stale strawberry baskets, but fine and full to the depth, like a heap from the vintage. Yet from the time of Milton till lately, scarcely a tree had been planted that could be called a poet's own. People got shoots from France, that ended in nothing but a little barren wood, from which they made flutes for young gentlemen and fan-sticks for ladies.

Keats's poetry is genuine stuff. 'The very faults indeed of Mr. Keats arise from a passion for beauties, and a young impatience to vindicate them.' Hunt criticizes the profusion of detail, a lack of selection, and the strain for variety of versification 'without a due consideration of its principles.' His criticism with regard to the handling and selection of images is genuinely constructive. He then picked out fine lines, putting them under subject headings:

A STARRY SKY

The dark silent blue
With all its diamonds trembling through and through,

or,

SOUND OF A PIPE

And with some are hearing eagerly the wild
Thrilling liquidity of dewy piping.

He included the 'little noiseless noise' passage and the description of the rising of the moon so highly praised in Constable's *Edinburgh Magazine*.

Hunt has a characteristically playful and personal touch in his remarks, reflecting the general love for that warm-hearted man, on the Epistle to Cowden Clarke:

"Life's very toys
"With him," said I, "will take a pleasant charm;
"It cannot be that ought will work him harm."

And we can only add, without disrespect to the graver warmth of our young poet, that if Ought attempted it, Ought would find he had stout work to do with more than one person.

He then quotes again, generally under subject headings (THE OCEAN, AN ASPIRATION AFTER POETRY, etc.), and ends with this acute summing up of the book as a whole: 'It is a little luxuriant heap of

Such sights as youthful poets dream
On summer eves by haunted stream.'

Not only is this article a brilliant piece of criticism but it is also a skilful piece of special pleading. Although hinting at the young poet's faults, it picks out and presents in tiny exquisite pictures many of the outstanding beauties of the book. It is strange, however, that neither Hunt, nor any other reviewer, singled out for praise that lovely passage

which anticipated the early maturity of thought and style to which
Keats was to attain:

> Stop and consider! life is but a day;
> A fragile dew-drop on its perilous way
> From a tree's summit; a poor Indian's sleep
> While his boat hastens to the monstrous steep
> Of Montmorenci. Why so sad a moan?
> Life is the rose's hope while yet unblown;
> The reading of an ever-changing tale;
> The light uplifting of a maiden's veil;
> A pigeon tumbling in clear summer air;
> A laughing school-boy, without grief or care,
> Riding the springy branches of an elm.

In spite of these reviews, not one of them damning and one in
the widely read and powerful *Examiner*, the book did not sell. Haydon
blamed the Leigh Hunt set who, he said, cried up each other so
consistently that they injured their own reputations. George, boy-like,
blamed the publishers and wrote a hasty letter to them, bringing back
a tart reply:

By far the greater number of Persons who have purchased it from us have
found fault with it in such plain terms, that we have in many cases offer'd to
take it back rather than be annoyed with the ridicule which has, time after
time, been shower'd on it. In fact it was only on Saturday last that we were
under the mortification of having our own opinion of its merites flatly
contradicted by a Gentleman who told us he considered it 'no better than
a take in.'

Keats was, after all, only sharing the fate of those other poets, now
placed so much higher than the fashionable Southey, Campbell, Scott,
Moore and Rogers, who were, during the whole or greater part of their
lifetime, ignored or scoffed at by the general public. Wordsworth
(with the *Lyrical Ballads* published as far back as 1798) only sold very
sparingly until well into the thirties of the nineteenth century.

There was one critic of the volume whose opinion as such was
negligible, but who unfortunately had that power over Keats which
the control of the purse-strings can give. Let us go forward to 1827
and hear Richard Abbey talking to John Taylor over their wine. Let
us visualize him stout, red-faced, complacent, stretching his white
cotton-stockinged legs out comfortably before him. He has just told
Taylor how, when John told him he was determined to gain his living
by writing poetry, he 'called him a Silly Boy, and prophesied a speedy
Termination to his inconsiderate Enterprise.'

'He brought me,' he went on, 'not long after a little book which he had got printed. I took it and said I would look at it because it was his writing, otherwise I should not have troubled my head with any such thing. When we next met I said: "Well, John, I have read your book, and it reminds me of the Quaker's horse which was hard to catch, and good for nothing when he was caught—so your book is hard to understand and good for nothing when it is understood." '

The worthy Abbey must, since he laboured it so heavily, have appreciated his own jest; perhaps looking sharply at Taylor to see if he too were amused. No doubt Taylor, ever a cautious man and anxious to get more information out of Keats's guardian for the memoir he was contemplating, smiled a little wider and filled up the old man's glass. Abbey spoke again:

"Do you know, I don't think he ever forgave me for uttering this opinion, which, however, was the truth."

CHAPTER VIII

New Friendships; Reynolds, Rice and Bailey. (December, 1816—March, 1817)

THE winter and early spring of 1817 was a period of new contacts and experiences. The mind of Keats, fixed to the rock of his own character and individuality, was reaching out its tentacles and grasping food for new poetry and thought.

He must have spent many hours in Leigh Hunt's booklined study and in Haydon's crowded painting-room. Although public association with Hunt did damage to Keats's reputation, and although Hunt perhaps encouraged him unduly in his native luxuriance of sentiment and expression, his influence was a fruitful one. Hunt was a fine and a constructive critic (his reputation as a critic has been overshadowed in that age so rich in criticism by Hazlitt, Coleridge and Lamb) and, though as a writer of poetry his taste was faulty, it was fastidious, epicurean in his reading of it. Later in *Imagination and Fancy* he shewed how swiftly he was able to get at the heart of a poet.

Hunt could bring Keats not only into closer acquaintance with the Elizabethans, but into early touch with that wealth of poetry from which the Elizabethans drew their early inspiration, the Italian. Keats could not yet read the language, but he had a fair knowledge of Latin and he would hear its beautiful cadences as Leigh Hunt read aloud to him. We know that Hunt's reading of poetry was a joy to his friends. Keats could not fail, with his keen ear, to catch something of the liquid and lovely movement. Colvin pointed out that the opening of the sonnet, 'On a Picture of Leander' (now considered to have been written in 1817):

> Come hither all sweet maidens soberly,
>> Down-looking aye, and with a chastened light,
>> Hid in the fringes of your eyelids white,
>> And meekly let your fair hands joined be . . .

has a feeling of:

> [1]Voi, che portate la sembianza umile,
>> Cogli occhi bassi mostrando dolore,
>> Onde venite, chè'l vostro colore
>> Par divenuto di pietà simile?

[1] Ye that bear a lowly mien, with eyes downcast betraying grief, whence come ye, for your hue seems grown to pity's semblance.—(THOMAS OKEY's translation.)

This is the invocation by Dante in *La Vita Nuova* to the ladies who wept over Beatrice's grief for her dead father.

The movement of the rest of the sonnet seems to me to have strongly the feeling of 'Hero and Leander,' and it is possible that Hunt directed or re-directed Keats's attention to Marlowe, whom he placed high. 'If ever there was a born poet,' he wrote, 'Marlowe was one . . . Marlowe and Spenser are the first of our poets who perceived the beauty of words . . . as receiving and reflecting beauty through the feeling of the ideas.'

Haydon encouraged and strengthened Keats's ambition illuminating by flashes of his electric mind the ardent spirit groping after an ultimate beauty. Crowded in by his huge canvas and the casts of the new and wonderful Elgin Marbles he read Shakespeare with his friend. 'Except the blind forces of Nature, nothing lives in this world which is not Greek in origin,' and here were the old and the new, a heady wine to ferment in the head of this young arch-romantic. Shakespeare must have come to Keats with a stronger reality, a subtler fragrance in the midst of these mighty fragments of the ancient, basic civilization. There were evenings of pure delight. Haydon wrote: 'I have enjoyed Shakespeare more with Keats than with any other Human creature.'

But there is a degree of fruitful intimacy in youth which can only be enjoyed with others of the same age. These men were older; mature men to be looked up to. Haydon was thirty-one and Leigh Hunt a year older. Keats was modest and well aware of his own deficiencies, both on the score of youth and a lack of background. The new friends he made within the Hunt-Haydon circle were to bring him intellectual and social intercourse with younger folk.

There was living at 19 Lamb's Conduit Street, within easy calling-distance of Cheapside, a cheerful, clever family of Shropshire origin. The parents, George and Charlotte Reynolds, were lively people with literary interests, friendly with Lamb, Leigh Hunt, Haydon and Hazlitt. George Reynolds had been appointed writing-master at Christ's Hospital (the Blue Coat School), then in Little Britain, and was waiting to move into one of the masters' houses in its precincts. His wife wrote album verses and later published a novel which was admired by Charles Lamb. Mr. and Mrs. Reynolds had four daughters and one son, John Hamilton, who soon became an intimate friend of Keats.

With the two elder daughters, Jane and Marianne, the relations of both George and John Keats were easy and pleasant. Marianne was George's favourite but, if we can judge from his letters to her, John seems to have been more friendly with Jane. The two earlier letters to Jane are among his most delightful. She, and indeed all the family, shared his interest in Shakespeare. Marianne had musical tastes as well as literary. Though apparently more gifted than Jane, she was the rather cold type of woman not attractive to Keats. Charles Dilke, a friend of the family, said of her: 'She was a very beautiful girl—somewhat cold and saturnine, and though always admired not generally liked.'

The third daughter, Eliza, was still in her teens. Keats's only known connection with her is that, one day in the February of 1818, he gave her a copy of his sonnet to Spenser.

John Reynolds, only a year older than Keats, had achieved a precocious literary reputation. Before *The Naiad*, quoted and praised by Leigh Hunt in *The Examiner* article on December 1st, 1816, he had already published three books. *Safie, an Eastern Tale* (1814) was dedicated to Byron and praised by him. Reynolds was fairly generally regarded as a young poet of great promise; a promise he was not to fulfil. Some time before April, 1816, he was a clerk in the Amicable Insurance Company, now absorbed into the Norwich Union. He worked for *The Champion*, a Sunday paper under the editorship of John Scott, writing dramatic and other criticisms. It will be remembered that the friendly review of *Poems*, 1817 in that journal is attributed to him.

Reynolds was wit as well as poet. This was an age of good sayings. The eighteenth century art of conversation had not yet died though it was fast degenerating into the punning so skilfully used by Lamb. Reynolds was a constant entertainment to his companions. He played artfully upon words and had a knack of making Shakespearean puns. Asked once if the beef he was eating was good, he replied: 'It would be if damned custom had not *braised*[1] it.' John Clare, the poet, has given us a lively portrait of him in 1823:

He was the most good-natured fellow I ever met with. His face was three-in-one of fun, wit and punning personified. He would punch you with his puns very keenly without ever hurting your feelings, for if you looked in his face you could not be offended; and you might retort as you pleased—nothing could put him out of humour, either with himself or others. . . . He sits as a careless listener at table, looking on with a quiet knapping sort of eye, then turns towards you as quick as lightning when he has a pun, joke or story to give you . . . flashes of the moment and mostly happy. He is a slim sort of make, something . . . of an unpretending sort of fashionable fellow without the desire of being one. . . . He is quite at home with content.

Clare describes him as having 'a plump round face, and nose

[1] *See Hamlet* iii, iv, 37.

something prigish, and a forehead that betrays more of fun than poetry. . . . He is a man of genius, and if his talent was properly employed he would do something. . . . Himself is his only hindrance at present.' Reynolds wrote of himself as early as 1816: 'I am one of those unfortunate youths to whom the Muses have glanced a sparkling of her light—one of those who pant for distinction but have not within them that immortal power to command it.'

It is probable that much of his ease and fun was a mask to conceal, not only a smouldering but fruitless ambition after the highest, but a certain diffidence in company. He wrote in an unpublished poem:

> Those whom my heart hath chosen for its own
> Are crown'd with all my feelings—and they take
> Their seat upon my thought, as on a throne,—
> And there repose for ever,—Doubts ne'er shake
> My fair allegiance to the friends I make
> My trusted ones;—But I am slow to woo
> A Stranger's fellowship,—Reserve doth break
> My course from that warm path which crowds pursue
> But well my heart doth hallow its selected few!

Among the 'selected few' before he met Keats were James Rice, a young solicitor, and Benjamin Bailey, an undergraduate at Oxford. The tastes of Reynolds, Rice and Bailey, a trio of friendship, can be gathered from a set of commonplace books[1] kept by three girls, daughters of a Unitarian family of Slade in Devon, the Misses Leigh. The three young men were on terms of sentimental friendship with them and used frequently to visit them between 1814 and 1816. In their circle was Eliza Powell Drewe, the future wife of Reynolds.

In ·these commonplace books, elegant little volumes filled with fine, sloping handwriting, are extracts from writers, supplied or suggested by the young men, together with original poems by Reynolds and Bailey and a few by Rice. There is a long passage by Reynolds in praise of 'The Excursion,' indicating the proper frame of mind in which to approach that sober poem, which is important as shewing in what degree he shared with Keats, not only an adoration of Shakespeare, but an admiration for the living poet. He had also a love for Spenser whom he placed next to Shakespeare.

These young people, like the young Keats and Mathew circle, had their admirations for those fashionable writers now long forgotten: there is from Reynolds a graceful little tribute in verse to Mrs. Tighe. The poems by him show, on the whole, little distinction and, curiously enough, no wit. Their chief subjects are nature and friendship and

[1] In the Keats Museum.

their style is the fashionable Byronic, with lugubrious references to death and disappointments in life. There are wan apostrophizings of a romantic moon. The verses by Bailey are weaker and even more lugubrious. The moon, a melancholy moon, is his goddess, and he writes by her light, alone at the midnight hour. Of those written by Rice, one is so pleasant, and we know so little about that lovable man,[1] that it seems worth while to quote it in full:

> Your nice Definers tell you that a Glutton
> In quantity not quality delights
> Equal to him is Ven'son, beef or Mutton
> Nought comes amiss to his good appetites.
>
> Gluttons in love Coquettes most surely are
> Equal to them the Coxcomb or the wise
> For Tom, Dick, Jack or Will they little care
> 'Tis not the men but Lover's that they prize
>
> But when your Lover or your Dish you'd chuse
> Do you dear Girl steer clear of either vice
> Shun crowding fops, and Surfeiting Ragouts
> And stick to honest hearts, and humble
>
> *Rice*

The verses are given above as written in Rice's own firm handwriting.

Rice was probably a little older than the other two but we do not know his age. Tantalizingly, there is in the commonplace books a birthday-poem from Reynolds to Rice, dated August 18th, 1815, so that we can gather from it the day and the month of his birth but not the year. Keats wrote of Rice, he 'is the most sensible and even wise man I know. He has a few John Bull prejudices, but they improve him.' Reynolds said: 'He was a quiet true wit—extremely well read— had great taste and sound judgment. For every quality that makes the sensible companion—the valuable friend—the gentleman, and the Man—I have known no one to surpass him.' He had poor health but good spirits and fine powers of recovery. 'Master Jemmy . . . always comes on his Legs like a Cat.' It was through one of Rice's frequent illnesses that he and his friends had met the Misses Leigh. He had in 1814 been down at Sidmouth for his health.

Keats was to pass many of his most carefree hours with Rice. Though a 'most sensible and even wise man' he was far from being a prig. Through him Keats got 'initiated into a little band—they call drinking deep dying scarlet . . . they call good Wine a pretty tipple, and call getting a Child knocking out an apple, stopping at a Tavern

[1] *See* Appendix IV.

they call hanging out.' These men played cards at one another's houses, drank and gambled after the fashion of the age. After one all-night sitting Keats was left with only a sixpence to his name. In letters to Reynolds he reveals his poetic life but in the serious letters to Rice (there are only four in all) he is more purely psychological, telling Rice of morbid feelings and odd states of mind often shared, apparently, by Rice himself.

Benjamin Bailey, four years older than Keats, was the 'man of principle,' more correct than these other two, addicted to moralizings and extracts from the more serious writers. His favourite poet was Milton. He was studying for orders and in later life became Archdeacon of Colombo. In the spring of 1817 he was up at Oxford and did not become acquainted with Keats until later in the year, but his interest was already aroused by the 1817 volume and by the glowing references to him in Reynolds' letters. Although a man of rather self-conscious rectitude, Bailey seems to have had one very human weakness, a strong but fickle affection for what I am sure he called 'the fair sex.' At one time he was paying court to Thomasine, or Tamsine Leigh at Slade. Bailey seems to have been not without humour. There is in the common-place books an impromptu by him 'On a Parson with a weak voice and weaker understanding':

> So small his voice—so puny in his mind
> That like a reed he whistles to the wind.

He was a close student and ardent reader. 'I should not,' Keats wrote to him, 'like to be Pages in your way when you are in a tolerably hungry mood you have no Mercy. Your teeth are like the Rock Tarpeian down which you capsize Epic Poems like Mad—I would not for 40 Shillings be Coleridge's Lay's [Lay Sermons] in your way.'

In the Reynolds household there was one other daughter, Charlotte, who although barely fifteen and rather young to be on equal terms with Keats, was able to give her new friend a great deal of pleasure: she would play to him for hours on the pianoforte. That charming fugitive piece 'Hush! hush! tread softly! hush, hush, my dear!' with its thistledown tiptoe movement, was composed to a Spanish air Charlotte played to him. The tender 'I had a dove and the sweet dove died' was also written 'to some Music as it was playing.' Probably she, or Marianne, sang: there are several other sets of words for music written about this time, some of which ('Hither, hither, love' for example) are so true to the weaker popular songs of the period that they read like subtle parodies. It was Charlotte who gave Keats the Tassie gem which inspired the sonnet on Leander quoted above.

These 'gems' were small coloured paste reproductions of engraved gems in classical subjects. They were sold in numbers by an enterprising Scot in Leicester Square and used as letter seals.

One other member of the Reynolds family must not be forgotten, the old cat, a doughty fighter, whom Keats has immortalized in a delightful sonnet, Miltonian in form, with a full-bodied epic flavour:

> CAT! who hast pass'd thy grand climacteric,
> How many mice and rats hast in thy days
> Destroy'd?—How many tit bits stolen? Gaze
> With those bright languid segments green, and prick
> Those velvet ears—but pr'ythee do not stick
> Thy latent talons in me—and upraise
> Thy gentle mew—and tell me all thy frays
> Of fish and mice, and rats and tender chick.
> Nay, look not down, nor lick thy dainty wrists—
> For all the wheezy asthma,—and for all
> Thy tail's tip is nick'd off—and though the fists
> Of many a maid have given thee many a maul,
> Still is that fur as soft as when the lists
> In youth thou enter'dst on glass bottled wall.

There was another house in London, this time further afield, where Keats could hear music, and of a more professional standard than within the family circle at Lamb's Conduit Street. Vincent Novello, 'the golden-hearted musician,' beloved of Lamb and Hunt, lived at 240 Oxford Street, at the end of the Town by the Tyburn toll-gate. He was the first man in England to edit Mozart in popular form, and the father of Alfred Novello, the founder of the famous firm of music publishers. He had a chamber-organ and at his evening parties (in the words of Charles Lamb) converted 'his drawing-room into a chapel, his week days into Sunday, and these latter into minor heaven . . . till the coming in of the friendly supper-tray . . . and a draught of the true Lutheran beer.'

The musical atmosphere was not, however, always religious. Novello and his friends enjoyed the music from the Italian operas then so fashionable. Leigh Hunt would sing arias in his voice of a remarkable range and sweetness. Here Keats could hear Haydn, Mozart, Bach, Purcell, and probably, for the Novellos had a lively interest in contemporary music, some early Beethoven. A little daughter, Mary Victoria, was listening in a quiet corner, and, although too young to join in, she looked with the awe of an intelligent child on these distinguished people: musicians, poets, writers, actors, and the artists, among them Varley, Copley Wood, Havell and Cristall, whose watercolours hung round on the delicately-tinted pink wallpaper. 'I have even now,' she wrote in her old age, 'full recollection of the reverent look with which I regarded John Keats as he leaned against the side of the organ, listening with rapt attention to my father's music. Keats's favourite position—one foot raised on his other knee—still remains imprinted on my memory.'

The Novellos, 'the most catholic of Catholics, for their spirit embraced the whole world,' were not only musicians, but people of culture and breadth of mind: when the supper-tray put an end to music their conversation ranged over world affairs, literature, painting, and the stage. There was plenty of fun, too, and punning, especially when Lamb was there.

Apart from his connection with the Leigh Hunt circle, Keats had a personal link with the Novellos; Edward Holmes, his old schoolfellow, was a pupil of Vincent's and at one time lived with the family. It was Cowden Clarke who, as he had fostered the spirit of poetry in Keats, trained and encouraged young Holmes in music and introduced him to his old friends. The house in Oxford Street was a second home to Clarke and Leigh Hunt records how, when there was music, he 'groaned a hundred times of an evening in the fullness of his satisfaction,' so that one could hear 'the benevolent grind of his epiglottis.' When she was husband-high, Mary Victoria became his wife. Mrs. Cowden Clarke has, apart from her connection with the famous group of friends, a distinction of her own; she gave us our first Shakespeare concordance.

We know nothing of the movements of Tom at this period, or whether he ever accompanied Keats on his visits to Leigh Hunt, Haydon, to the Novellos or to Lamb's Conduit Street. It is possible that at some time after September, 1816, he was living in France, at Lyons. At the end of March, 1817, he was, however, with his brothers, and probably failing in health, for by March 26th they had moved out to Hampstead, perhaps in search of purer air for him.

CHAPTER IX

Hampstead, the Isle of Wight, and Oxford (March—November, 1817).

A steeple issuing from a leafy rise,
  With farmy fields in front, and sloping green,
  Dear Hampstead, is thy southern face serene,
Silently smiling on approaching eyes.
Within, thine ever-shifting looks surprise,—
  Streets, hills, and dells, trees overhead now seem,
  Now down below, with smoking roofs between,—
A village revelling in varieties.

(LEIGH HUNT.)

THE modern suburb of Hampstead still retains much of the flavour of that old village, though it and the houses, farms and scattered hamlets to be seen from its church-crowned height are now all joined up into long arms of bricks and mortar embracing the Heath which, happily, no builder can touch.

The Heath itself is but a pale shadow of the Heath Leigh Hunt loved. In the midst of open fields and meadows and as yet undrained, it was wild, natural country. There were stretches of marsh and bog. Buck bean, kingcups, anemones, crowsfoot, marsh and dog violets, ragged robin, stitchwort, wild geraniums and vetches grew in a sweet abundance; and bryony, pennywort, speedwell, nightshade and yellow loosestrife. There are a few hawthorns left of its ancient spring glory, and a little gorse, but in 1817 there were wild cherries, pears, crabs and bullace plums. A myriad of small life crept and scrambled in the tangled grass and bushes; red admirals, brimstone and yellow butterflies fluttered in the sight.

All this country quiet and loveliness was within easy walking distance of London (as distances were judged in those walking days) and a fare to the Bank was only one shilling outside the coach and one and sixpence in.

Keats and his brothers took lodgings in Well Walk, a wide, pleasant road on the height, leading on to the Heath and bordered with ancient limes. The Walk is now sleepily restful in its old age, but once it was gay and bustling with leisured life, for there was a mineral spring there and the Hampstead Spa was a rival to Tunbridge Wells. In 1817 its heyday was over. The flying coaches were carrying people in summer to a newer attraction, the sea: to Hastings, Weymouth, South End,

Margate and Brighton with their Assembly Rooms, their balls and their card-tables.

But although Hampstead was no longer a fashionable spa it was near enough for a rural jaunt and a pleasant place for Londoners to retire to: the Assembly Rooms, at this time on Holly Bush Hill, had the added attraction to girls and matchmaking mothers, of red-coated officers come up from St. Johns Wood Barracks. These were post-war days when the men returned from battle were eager for pleasure, for dancing and flirting. With the slackening of etiquette brought about by war and revolution; a licence in the higher ranks of society which descended as a wider freedom to the middle classes; with the comparatively new and seductive waltz as a symbol of this new order of things, there was gaiety on the Hill.

But Keats would take little or no part in these festivities. The brothers were not well off and although Keats loved his friends, the society of acquaintances never attracted him. He did not dance. The quiet beauty of the Heath, fit home for a poet, was there as a background for his dreams of Endymion.

The brothers lodged in a tall narrow house next to 'The Green Man' (now the Wells Hotel) which was pulled down when the inn was rebuilt and extended. Mrs. Bentley, their landlady, wife of the village postman, was a motherly soul kind to young men. The only drawback to their lodging was the noisy presence of her red-headed boys ('the young Carrots') who further offended by the smell of their coarse worsted stockings. But perhaps in regard to noise Mrs. Bentley had herself at times cause for complaint: her lodgers and their friends were in the habit of holding a 'concert' in their rooms, imitating instruments with their voices. Once they kept it up from four o'clock in the afternoon until ten at night. Keats himself seems to have favoured the bassoon.

Keats had only to walk down a short slope of the Heath to Hunt's cottage in the Vale of Health. The two men must have spent many hours of good talk together. Hunt was writing 'The Nymphs' and, Keats wrote, was saying in it 'a number of beautiful things.' Keats was not alone in admiring Hunt's work; Hazlitt, Lamb, Moore, Rogers and Byron all enjoyed and praised it. Haydon said of *The Story of Rimini* it is 'the sweetest thing of the time . . . it will establish your genius.' Unequal as that poem is, it has a flexibility of style and a freedom in the use of language new to its first readers, and (to quote Mr. Blunden) 'brought into the Northern air a welcome Southern warmth and vinous brilliance, urging the senses of poets to triumph over a bleak environment and to irradiate it with the sunshine and

James Henry Leigh Hunt
From a painting by Samuel Lawrence in the National Portrait
Gallery

Benjamin Robert Haydon
From the print of a portrait by George H. Harlow in the Keats
Memorial House

azure of Ariosto's country.' This was no mean gift to the poet who was presently to write 'The Eve of St. Agnes.'

The poem was moderately popular among general readers and became a mild fashion. Samuel Rogers, the banker-poet, quoted it at his breakfasts and women shed tears over the sad story of Paolo and Francesca. Hunt had a gift for narrative: when the exuberance of a long-protracted youth had been sobered away he gave us his one perfect poem, a story in little, 'Abou Ben Adhem.' This, the lyric 'Jenny kiss'd me,' and that popular Victorian recitation, 'The Glove and the Lions' are the only works by which he is popularly known as a poet to-day. Towards the end of his life Hunt wrote with regret of *The Story of Rimini*, wishing he had not enlarged upon Dante's famous episode 'which had been treated with exquisite sufficiency, and to his immortal renown, by a great master.' With his fine ear for good lines in other poets he must have regretted that he had dulled the perfection of *la bocca mi baciò tutto tremante* into 'And kiss'd her, mouth to mouth, all in a tremble.'

Keats, re-reading *The Story of Rimini* in the freshness of the spring of 1817, wrote a sonnet on it, commencing:

> Who loves to peer up at the morning sun,
>   With half-shut eyes and comfortable cheek,
>   Let him, with this sweet tale, full often seek
> For meadows where the little rivers run.

Alas, for the meadows where the little rivers ran in a network of 'little brooks unknown to all but the eyes of their lovers'; the massy elms and the rose-hedgerowed lanes . . . they are gone for ever. Where are now Kilburn, Cricklewood, West Hampstead and Marylebone they lay spread out, a wide and lovely prospect, to the south and south-west of the Hampstead heights; in one direction the dome of St. Paul's glittering above the smoke pall of London and in the other the church-crowned bosky hill of Harrow. London had been expanding rapidly since the beginning of the century. This was an era of feverish building, but it had not yet destroyed more than a few miles of the country north of the Edgware Road.

On March 27th Keats went with Hunt to Novello's house by the Tyburn Gate to hear performed, or to carry thither, a hymn for four voices 'To the Spirit great and good,' the words and music of which were composed by Hunt. It is more than likely that they walked there, going through open country until they reached Seymour Place. If they started from Well Walk they would go down Field Place and follow a footpath across the Conduit Fields (now covered by Fitzjohn's Avenue). They would pass Shepherd's Well, the main water supply for Hampstead, and might see there a patient crowd of poor people waiting their turn with pitchers, and men with yoked buckets to carry water to those willing to pay twopence or threepence a pail for it. The spring, under a low brick arch, would sometimes fail, so heavily was it taxed by those who had not pumps or wells, and then the tired folk would wait until it bubbled up again.

The two men would walk across fields passing St. John's Wood Farm, the Chapel and the cricket ground soon to become Lord's, across the new Regent's Canal and down the arcadian Lisson Grove.

Haydon who, from the Journals, appears to have alternately hated and loved his friend Hunt, now resented and suspected an intimacy necessarily closer because Keats and Hunt lived near to one another: Hunt's free-thinking would damage the morals of his new friend and undo Haydon's own attempt to bring back Keats to orthodox belief. In March he wrote him a strange rhodomontade,[1] telling how the mighty spirits of the immortal dead crowded his room and shook their hands at him 'in awful encouragement':

My dear Keats, the Friends who surrounded me were sensible to what talent I had,—but no one reflected my enthusiasm with that burning ripeness of soul, my heart yearned for sympathy,—believe me from my Soul in you I have found one,—you add fire, when I am exhausted, & excite fury afresh —I offer my heart & intellect & experience—at first I feared your ardor might lead you to disregard the accumulated wisdom of ages in moral points —but the feelings put forth lately have delighted my soul. . . .

Keats was in a mood to be influenced against Hunt, familiarity with whom was breeding some measure of contempt. Poetry was to Keats the stuff of life, not a bookish abstraction: Hunt's refuge from reality in books and riming could not be for long a congenial home to a mind so robust and universal. Hunt had at this time an exaggerated opinion of his own powers. This, sound critic that he was, he realized in later years and admitted in his autobiography. The young are never tolerant of pretensions and Keats had by now estimated him at something like his true value as a poet. Hunt was, too, more than a little fantastic in his romanticism; his flowery little celebrations of occasions and of anniversaries with sonnets and garlandings were boyish gambols for the greater Keats.

There had been one absurd evening when Hunt and Keats over their after-dinner wine crowned each other with laurels and ivy 'after the manner of the elder bards' and wrote sonnets. Some lady visitors came in: Hunt snatched off his crown and suggested to Keats that he should do so, but Keats 'in his enthusiastic way declared he would not

[1] Given in full in *Letters of John Keats.*

take off his crown for any human being.' He kept it on without any explanation during the ladies' call. This unusual headgear must have excited some astonishment in their minds, and probably Keats enjoyed their bewilderment. He was, however, afterwards ashamed of the prank and in a half-humorous hymn to Apollo he asked,

> Where—where slept thine ire,
> When like a blank idiot I put on thy wreath,
> Thy laurel, thy glory,
> The light of thy story,
> Or was I a worm—too low crawling, for death?
> O Delphic Apollo!

This was not the first time he had felt the illustrious leaves upon his brow; in 1815 some ladies (the Misses Mathew?) sent him a laurel crown.

There is a second version of this story in which Thomas Love Peacock is involved. The first evidence that we have of a meeting between Keats and the poet and satirist is a year later, in the spring of 1818, but it is unlikely that Keats would have taken part in this poetic prank at that time, especially as he was then out of sympathy with Leigh Hunt in regard to poetry. It is easy in recollection to slip a year and it seems likely that it was on this occasion that Peacock made his entry. If Keats insisted on retaining his crown of leaves under Peacock's withering eye he must have been a youth of almost superhuman courage. The incident as reported in *Fraser's Magazine* for August, 1831, is worth quoting:

Some time ago it entered the imagination of Hunt and Keats and some other of that coterie, to crown themselves with laurel and to take off their cravats. This was the jaunty thing and quite poetical. While the coronated and uncravated company were sitting thus one day "with their singing robes about them" Peacock came in. "Do" said the lady who officiated as coronet manufacturer "do, dear Mr. Peacock, let me weave you a chaplet, and put it on your head; then you will all sit as poets together." "No ma'am" said Peacock, wiping his head, "no, ma'am; you may make a fool of your own husband, but there is no need of your making a fool of me."

There was another of the younger generation who was impatient with Hunt, one who now had a considerable influence with Keats, John Reynolds. Three years later we find Reynolds writing to John Taylor of 'the vain and heartless eternity of Mr. Leigh Hunt's indecent discoursings . . . that Feeble Man. . . .'

On March 17th Keats wrote to Reynolds:

My Brothers are anxious that I should go by myself into the country—they have always been extremely fond of me, and now that Haydon has pointed out how necessary it is that I should be alone to improve myself, they give up the temporary pleasure of living with me continually for a great good which I hope will follow.

Perhaps it was with an idea of weaning him from Hunt that Haydon urged this retreat.

Haydon, who had known him for ten years, admired Hunt for 'his poetry, his taste, his good humour,' for his charm which no one could long resist, but the two men were diametrically opposed in outlook. Haydon took nothing lightly, accepted a fixed code, an orthodox belief where Hunt doubted and questioned. 'I really love him to my heart, and only feel panged at his liability to delusive principles,' Haydon wrote in his journal on the very day Keats was writing to Reynolds. These delusive principles were, Haydon considered, influencing Keats. Whenever Hunt and Haydon met there were arguments about religion. Haydon remarks in the same entry that his 'resolution to put Voltaire's head into my Picture seems to have brought up all Hunt's bile and morbidity boiling with froth into his acrid and gloomy imagination, for Hunt's imagination is naturally and inherently gloomy' for all 'his leafy bowers, and clipsome waists, and balmy luxuries.' This view of Hunt as 'inherently gloomy' is interesting, though perhaps of little value from a man who could see in Keats 'no decision of character.'

Probably at this time—for the head of Voltaire was already painted or at least sketched in—Keats aggravated Haydon's suspicion that Hunt 'was the great unhinger of his best dispositions' by a deliberate gesture, or jest; placing his hand on his heart before the head of Voltaire and saying: 'There is the being I will bow to!'

But Haydon, who sincerely loved Keats, may have had a simpler reason for urging him to leave Town; a conviction that he needed rest and change. The winter had been a busy one. Friends, new and exciting friends, had made many demands upon the time and energy of one whose mind was ever creatively active to a feverish degree. There had been the worry of a first essay at proof-reading, the anxiety over the reception of his book, while that mind, so long haunted by the old bright tale of Endymion and the Moon-goddess, strained at the leash. Now his old work was behind him, fixed in print, he would go forward to a new trial of strength. The long poem from which Hunt, perhaps wisely, had tried to dissuade him, was to be both a test of his power and a means of growth.

It was natural that the story of Endymion should haunt Keats, strongly influenced as he was by the Elizabethans and by Shakespeare. The romantics, whether of the sixteenth or the nineteenth century, were bathed in the cold, bright beauty of the moon; she governed the restless tides of their minds. The theme of Endymion was a favourite one. As far back as 1815 Keats had already written the first lines of his poem. Henry Stephens tells us that one evening in the twilight the two students were sitting together, Stephens working and Keats wrapped in thought. Suddenly Keats interrupted Stephens with a line of poetry, 'A thing of beauty is a constant joy.'

"What think you of that, Stephens?"

"It has the true ring, but is wanting in some way," Stephens answered, going on with his work.

There was silence, broken only perhaps by the ticking of a clock, or the scratching of Stephens' quill. Then on the quiet air there broke the sound of those words which were to go echoing through the centuries:

A thing of beauty is a joy for ever

"What think you of that, Stephens?"

"That will live for ever."

Stephens' reply is a little too apt to have the ring of authenticity, but it is a dramatic touch that may well be forgiven in an elderly man who had looked upon genius in his youth.

Curiously enough the fine opening was abandoned by Keats in 'I stood tip-toe,' at first entitled 'Endymion,' but now he returned to it. It was taken with him, either in his head or on a shabby scrap of manuscript, when he set out in April for the Isle of Wight. He also took seven precious pocket volumes of an edition of Shakespeare, edited by Dr. Johnson and George Steevens, which he had apparently just purchased, for in the two first volumes he has written 'April, 1817.'

Keats probably took coach at 'The Bell and Crown' in Holborn at four o'clock in the afternoon. The coach roads were well kept in 1817: when they bowled off with a crack of the whip and a shrill of the horn the going would be good and exhilarating in the cool spring air. He would pass up Oxford Street and out of London through the toll-gate at Hyde Park Corner. There was little building beyond Knightsbridge: he would soon be out on the open road, leaving the smoking town behind.

As it was early in the season the coach was not full. After three stages Keats began to feel cold and went inside. Here is his own picture of the journey sent in a letter to his brothers from Southampton:

I did not know the Names of any of the Towns I passed through all I can tell you is that sometimes I saw dusty Hedges sometimes Ponds—then nothing—then a little Wood with trees look you like Launce's Sister "as white as a Lilly and as small as a Wand"—then came houses which died away into a few straggling Barns then came hedge trees aforesaid again. As the Lamp light crept along the following things were discovered. "long heath brown furze"—Hurdles here and there half a Mile—Park palings when the Windows of a House were always discovered by reflection—One Nympth of Fountain *N.B. Stone*—lopped Trees—Cow ruminating—ditto Donkey—Man and Woman going gingerly along—William seeing his Sisters over the Heath—John waiting with a Lanthen for his Mistress— Barbers Pole—Docter's Shop—However after having had my fill of these I popped my Head out just as it began to Dawn—*N.B. this tuesday Morn saw the Sun rise*—of which I shall say nothing at present . . . from dawn to half past six I went through a most delightful Country—some open Down but for the most part thickly wooded. What surprised me most was an immense quantity of blooming Furze on each side the road cutting a most rural dash. . . .

That morning at breakfast in the inn at Southampton Keats felt lonely, so 'went and unboxed a Shakespeare.' It was probably *The Tempest* (the first play in Volume I) that he read over a solitary meal for he wrote to his brothers, 'Here's my Comfort.' Shakespeare was ever his warming draught, his pleasure and a source of spiritual strength; his letters are full of Shakespearean quotations and allusions. After breakfast he went down to Southampton Water to inquire about the boat to the Island. As the water was low the boat could not sail until the afternoon; he wrote to his brothers, telling them:

. . . it will go at 3 so shall I after having taken a Chop . . . You Haydon, Reynolds &c have been pushing each other out of my Brain by turns—I have conned over every Head in Haydon's Picture—you must warn them not to be afraid should my Ghost visit them on Wednesday—tell Haydon to Kiss his Hand at Betty over the Way for me yea and to spy at her for me—

He sent his love to the Misses Reynolds and to Fanny Keats, 'who I hope you will soon see. Write to me soon about them all—'

The crossing of the sixteen miles to Cowes would depend on the winds. Sometimes it took a mere two hours, sometimes a good part of the day. In a diary of the period one hour and three minutes is given as a triumphant record for the crossing. This is only three minutes over the scheduled time for the modern paddle-wheel steamers. He went to Newport and stayed the night there. The next day, from Carisbrooke in the centre of the Island, he wrote to Reynolds:

On the road from Cowes to Newport I saw some extensive Barracks which disgusted me extremely with Government for placing such a Nest of Debauchery in so beautiful a place—I asked a man on the coach about this—and he said that the people had been spoiled—In the room where I slept at Newport I found this on the Window "O Isle spoilt by the Mil*a*tory!" I must in honesty however confess that I did not feel very sorry at the idea of the Women being a little profligate—

The barracks had been built there during the wars as a depot for recruits. They had previously been at Chatham, but the poor wretches, pressed or snared into the Army, had escaped up to London and hidden themselves in the narrow lanes and courts of the City.

'I did not feel very sorry at the idea of the Women being a little profligate. . . .' These were the coarse, full-blooded times of the Georges when men were expected before marriage to 'sow their wild oats.' Although we have among Keats's fugitive verses a few erotic poems, such as 'Unfelt, unheard, unseen' and 'Sharing Eve's Apple,' we have no evidence that he favoured the company of loose women. This expression of a prevalent attitude to working women may have been boyish bravado, an attempt to appear man-of-the-worldish in the eyes of Reynolds, but 'Sharing Eve's Apple,' though so delicately licentious as not to be offensive, certainly has an authentic ring as if it were the outcome of sexual experience. This we can accept, and with it a certain Georgian coarseness of expression: for the rest we can only wish his memory had been spared a recent denigration.

He was drawn by the beauty of Shanklin, by the sea and the wild wooded grandeur of the Chine; but Shanklin was a more expensive place. It was becoming the fashion among the rich and idle to 'hunt,' said Keats, 'after the picturesque like beagles' and to admire rhapsodically 'romantic' scenery.

In comparing Keats with other travellers of the period it is noticeable how reticent he is in description of scenery. He makes no use of the catchword 'romantic.' The beauty of nature was too close to his heart for easy expression; truth in his inmost being which could only be blended into poetry. It was so with him in all things; where feeling was strong he could not speak directly. In his letters the little sister he loved is seldom mentioned or, later, the loss of his brothers. When he came to fall in love so deeply, the sweet and poignant grief was a secret to be jealously guarded.

Carisbrooke was a convenient centre for walking over the Island and near to Newport, where was the post office. Keats settled there at a Mrs. Cook's, now Canterbury House, in the New Village, on the Castle Road, probably occupying a bedroom and the drawing-room on the first floor, from which he had a fine view of the ancient Keep of Carisbrooke Castle. He wrote to Reynolds:

... from here I can see your continent—from a little hill close by, the whole north Angle of the Isle of Wight, with the water between us. . . . I see Carisbrooke Castle from my window, and have found several delightful wood-alleys, and copses, and quick freshes. As for Primroses—the island ought to be called Primrose Island: that is, if the nation of Cowslips agree thereto, of which there are diverse Clans just beginning to lift up their heads. . . . I intend to walk over the Island east—West—North South—I have not seen many specimens of Ruins—I dont think however I shall ever see one to surpass Carisbrooke Castle. The trench is o'ergrown with the smoothest turf, and the Walls with ivy—The Keep within side is one Bower of ivy— a Colony of Jackdaws have been there many years. I dare say I have seen many a descendant of some old cawer who peeped through the Bars at Charles the first, when he was there in Confinement.

Keats, still thinking yearningly of his brothers and friends, demanded 'a sketch of you and Tom and George in ink which Haydon will do if you tell him how I want them.' That morning he had tried to make a solitary lodging more home-like, arranging his books and pinning up 'Haydon—Mary Queen (of) Scotts, and Milton with his daughters in a row.' A print of Shakespeare found hanging in the passage he moved to above his books 'having first discarded a French Ambassador.' Not having been sleeping well he felt 'rather narvus,' but the next day wrote a sonnet which, he said, 'did me some good.' This sonnet he copied in his letter to Reynolds, prefacing it with 'the passage from Lear—"Do you not hear the sea?"—has haunted me intensely':

On the Sea

It keeps eternal Whisperings around
   Desolate shores, and with its mighty swell
   Gluts twice ten thousand Caverns; till the spell
Of Hecate leaves them their old shadowy sound.
Often 'tis in such gentle temper found
   That scarcely will the very smallest shell
   Be moved for days from whence it sometime fell
When last the winds of Heaven were unbound.
O ye who have your eyeballs vext and tir'd
   Feast them upon the wideness of the Sea
O ye whose Ears are dinned with uproar rude
   Or fed too much with cloying melody—
Sit ye near some old Cavern's Mouth and brood
   Until ye start as if the Sea Nymphs quired—

Perhaps at Luccombe near Shanklin he had entered the great cave and, from its dark depths, seen the vast ocean anew, a rock-framed picture, an immensity brought down to an epitome within man's comprehension. It is possible too that the very line itself, the haunting line from *King Lear*, 'Do you not hear the sea?' had come to him, consciously or subconsciously, from an Island experience. Shakespeare's description of the high Dover cliff and

> . . . half way down
> Hangs one that gathers samphire, dreadful trade!

occur only a few lines from 'Do you not hear the sea?' Samphire was until about sixty years ago brought regularly into Newport market from the southern parts of the Island. If Keats walked along the shore to the Culver he might have shuddered to watch, half-way down the precipitous chalk cliff, a swaying, hunched figure. Men hazarded their lives for a miserable pittance in the 'dreadful trade,' or trades, of gathering samphire and capturing nesting sea-birds for the down-feathers by sitting astride a piece of wood suspended by a rope which they manipulated themselves, letting it slip over an iron crowbar driven in at the summit. Less than a month later we find Keats at Margate, where again the white cliffs rear, writing to Haydon: 'I am "one that gathers Samphire dreadful trade," the Cliff of Poesy Towers above me—'

He was now reading Shakespeare in his loneliness with passionate attention: ' 'twould be a parlous good thing' if he were to receive a letter from Reynolds and from his brothers on Shakespeare's birthday.

Whenever you write a line say a Word or two on some Passage in Shakespeare that may have come rather new to you; which must be continually happening, notwithstanding that we read the same Play forty times—for instance, the following, from the Tempest, never struck me so forcibly as at present,

> "Urchins
> *Shall, for that vast of Night that they may work,*
> All exercise on thee—"

How can I help bringing to your mind the Line—

> *In the dark backward and abysm of time.*

I find I cannot exist without poetry—without eternal poetry—half the day will not do—the whole of it—I began with a little, but habit has made me a Leviathan—I had become all in a Tremble from not having written any thing of late—the Sonnet over leaf did me some good. I slept the better last night for it—this Morning, however, I am nearly as bad again—Just now I opened Spencer, and the first lines I saw were these—

> "The noble Heart that harbors virtuous thought,
> And is with Child of glorious great intent,
> Can never rest, until it forth have brought
> Th' eternal Brood of Glory excellent—"

Solitude on the lovely island, with a weight of beauty and poesy a heavy though a sweet burden, was not long to be borne. Keats had been expecting that Reynolds would join him later: perhaps it was an intimation that this was not possible added to a conviction, or fancy, that he could not get wholesome food on the island which made him finally decide to leave for Margate where he would meet Tom.

Mrs. Cook, the landlady, must have been a good-natured woman. She does not seem to have resented either the displacement of her pictures or the sudden departure of her lodger after a stay of only a week; even presenting him with the portrait of Shakespeare he had hung up over his books which came, he said, 'nearer to my idea of him than any I have seen.' This delighted Keats. He felt it to be a good omen.

It seems highly probable that Keats travelled to Margate on board one of the many small trading vessels circling the coast at that time: otherwise, unless he went by chaise, a far too expensive mode of conveyance, he would have a tedious and tiresome disjointed journey by coach or stage wagon.

The change from the lush, hilly Island to the flat cliffs of Thanet was drastic, but Margate, 'that treeless affair,' is at its best in May or early June and the breezes blow keen and healthful. There was his old love, the sea; a grayer turbulent sea but with the sun rising and setting over its heaving surfaces and the moon making a long glistening white track across it at night. And he was no longer 'obliged to be in a continual burning of thought,' of solitary thought, for Tom was now with him; Tom who understood him best. Keats had come from his island sojourn in a mood very like despair, asking himself

why I should be a Poet more than other Men,—seeing how great a thing it is. . . . What a thing to be in the Mouth of Fame—that at last the Idea has grown so monstrously beyond my seeming Power of attainment that the other day I nearly consented with myself to drop into a Phaeton—yet 'tis a disgrace to fail even in a huge attempt, and at this moment I drive the thought from me. . . . These last two days . . . I have felt more confident.

He is reading and writing most of the day in a mood humble yet splendidly arrogant. 'I am "one that gathers Samphire dreadful trade" the Cliff of Poesy Towers above me—yet when Tom who meets with some of Pope's Homer in Plutarch's Lives reads some of those to me they seem like Mice to mine.'

On May 11th Haydon wrote warning him against Hunt:

I love you like my own Brother, beware for God's sake of the delusions and sophistications that is ripping up the talent and respectability of our Friend —he will go out of the World the victim of his own weakness & the dupe of his own self delusions—with the contempt of his enemies and sorrow of his Friends—the cause he undertook to support injured by his own neglect of character—his family disordered, his children neglected, himself, petted & his prospects ruined!

Keats should preserve this letter for one day he would see the prophecy fulfilled. The passage is magnificently ironic; Hunt, though he had a chequered and difficult life, lived to an honoured old age, whereas poor Haydon at sixty, in debt and ultimately a failure, committed suicide.

In Keats's reply he admitted Hunt's self-delusions and agreed that he must come to a sad end. 'There is no greater Sin after the 7 deadly than to flatter oneself into an idea of being a great Poet—'

Haydon had in his letter exhorted Keats in the moods of doubt and depression arising out of his (self-styled) 'horrid morbidity of temperament' to 'Trust to God' and to pray to Him for strength. Keats does not reply to this directly but says: 'I never quite despair and I read Shakespeare—indeed I shall I think never read any other Book much—I am very near Agreeing with Hazlit that Shakespeare is enough for us— . .' He tells Haydon of an experience:

. . . you had notions of a good Genius presiding over you. I have of late had the same thought—for things which I do half at Random are afterwards confirmed by my judgment in a dozen features of Propriety. Is it too daring to Fancy Shakspeare this Presidor?

The subconscious mind works for the artist, absorbing and making in its own mysterious depths. Most creative writers have the astonishment of this experience and it has at times a strong feeling of inspiration, of an outside influence.

Keats had heard from George that 'Money Troubles are to follow us up for some time to come perhaps for always—these vexations are a great hindrance to one,' a minor but irritating annoyance, 'rather like a nettle leaf or two in your bed.'

The cause of this financial worry is not evident: between them, leaving out the sums lying untouched in Chancery, the brothers had inherited a capital of about four thousand, five hundred pounds, an amount sufficient in those days on which to live modestly; although the cost of John's medical training and Tom's ill-health had almost certainly diminished it.[1] Added to this capital, Tom probably, and George certainly, had been working in Abbey's counting-house; though George may by now, perhaps through a dislike of the junior partner, Hodgkinson, have left his guardian's employment. That he was living at Hampstead, however, is no proof of this: the daily coach fare of two shillings would be beyond a slender purse, but no wage-earner of that period would have considered the walk to Pancras Lane unduly long. When John Taylor, the publisher, was temporarily living at the Spaniard's Inn he walked regularly between Hampstead and Fleet Street.

Whatever the cause of a shortage of money, we find Keats glad to receive an advance of twenty pounds from his publishers and, early in June, asking reluctantly, and in a falsely jocular tone, for more to settle up with a 'Couple of Duns.'

It was not to the Olliers that Keats wrote but to John Taylor and James Augustus Hessey of 93 Fleet Street. These men were young publishers of vision, ready to welcome new talent and willing to risk their limited capital on works of originality. There are several men who might have introduced Keats to Taylor and Hessey; Woodhouse, reader probably in an unofficial capacity to the firm, or Reynolds for whom they had published, are the most likely.

Taylor was the moving spirit; a dabbler in poetry himself and a writer of pamphlets. He lived over the premises, keeping in close touch with literary men who had, after the pleasant manner of the time, the freedom of the place. Hessey seems to have been responsible for the routine of the business, handling the ledger-books and running the retail side. Publishing and bookselling were not yet distinct trades; most publishers sold books, old and new. Taylor and Hessey's shop was a pleasant haunt.[2]

Taylor's first contact with Keats both astonished and amused him. The young poet at this time affected 'a singular style of dress.' Unfortunately we have no detail of his costume though we know that he wore long hair and the collar 'à la Byron'. Reynell, the printer, however, who met Keats in or about 1817, thought he was wearing 'some sort of sailor costume.' Perhaps Keats came to interview his prospective publisher in loose, light trousers and jacket similar to those worn by many of the common seamen of the time. This would have looked

---

[1] Later Charles Brown—admittedly prejudiced however—accused George of extravagant expenditure, especially on dress.

[2] There are fine portraits of the two partners in Mr. Blunden's book on Taylor, *Keats's Publisher*.

singular enough in the days of tight clothes and swallow-tailed coats. Later Keats's commonsense led him to drop an eccentricity in dress and to cut his hair.

Taylor was no whit discouraged by the failure of the 1817 volume. He wrote to his father on the very day that Keats arrived in the Isle of Wight, 'I cannot think he will fail to become a great Poet, though I agree with you in finding much fault with the Dedication etc. These are not likely to appear in any other of his Productions.'

On May 16th Keats with his brother moved across to Canterbury, 'having got tired of Margate—I was not right in my head when I came.' Keats hoped the move would stimulate him to further exertion. He had been feeling stale, 'all the effects of a Mental Debauch—lowness of Spirits.' At Canterbury the remembrance of Chaucer was to set him forward 'like a Billiard-ball.' This lively image is perhaps strengthened by a statement of his recorded by Woodhouse that he could conceive that a billiard-ball 'may have a sense of delight from its own roundness, smoothness and volubility and the rapidity of its motion.' As he had 'some idea of seeing the Continent some time in the Summer,' Keats could only have considered the hampering shortness of money a temporary one.

From Canterbury he went on alone to Hastings, staying at the village of Bo-Peep (now St. Leonard's) but probably joining in some of the frivolities of the fashionable watering-place: we know he flirted with a lady whom later he was to meet again in London. By September he was at Oxford with Benjamin Bailey who, charmed with Keats when he had met him in Town, had given an invitation.

From Oxford on the 5th Keats wrote to Jane and Marianne Reynolds at Littlehampton one of his wildest letters, a piece of inconsequent, ridiculous hyperbole I should like to give in full, but it is not possible to quote all the delightful letters Keats wrote. An excerpt from it would spoil the humour and the shape of the whole: in a minor way it is as genuinely a work of art as a wrought poem.

With Bailey he was tranquilly happy in an atmosphere of peaceful tradition and of books. His friend was putting in hours of close study for his examination. Keats, undisturbed by his presence, would sit near, at work upon the third book of *Endymion*. Bailey was astonished at the ease with which he wrote about fifty lines a day. 'Sometimes he fell short of his allotted task—but not often: and he would make it up another day. But he never forced himself.' He usually read aloud what he had written to his friend and then quietly turned to a book or wrote letters until Bailey was ready to go out. September was a beautiful month that year and the river, the delight of running water, was there for Keats. On the 21st he wrote to Reynolds:

For these last five or six days, we have had regularly a Boat on the Isis, and explored all the streams about, which are more in number than your eye lashes. We sometimes skim into a Bed of rushes, and there become naturalized riverfolks,—there is one particularly nice nest which we have christened "Reynolds's Cove," in which we have read Wordsworth and talked as may be.

Bailey was a devout admirer of Wordsworth with whom he had some little personal acquaintance. They 'often talked of that noble passage in the lines on "Tintern Abbey":

> That blessed mood
> In which *the burthen of the mystery,*
> In which the heavy and the weary weight
> Of all this unintelligible world,
> Is lightened:'

'Tintern Abbey' was to the young romantics of 1817, together with passages in 'The Excursion,' an expression of a prevailing mood or attitude to life. It was a poem as vital and important as *The Waste Land* to another post-war generation.

They talked of Chatterton, whom Keats ardently admired, and to the memory of whom he dedicated *Endymion*. Bailey records that the line 'Come with acorn cup and thorn' possessed a great charm for Keats. On these golden September afternoons amid the bird-haunted reeds and rushes they filled their minds with poetry. After a consideration of a fine passage, especially in one of the older poets, Keats would say in gentle undertone 'It's *nice*.' He expressed particular admiration for the lines given to Ulysses in Act III of *Troilus and Cressida*:

> Time hath, my lord, a wallet at his back
> Wherein he puts alms for oblivion,
> A great-sized monster of ingratitudes:
> Those scraps are good deeds past, which are devour'd
> As fast as they are made, forgot as soon
> As done:

'It was,' he thought, 'pregnant with practical wisdom, such as Shake-speare alone could produce.' Of Keats himself Bailey said, 'his common sense was a conspicuous part of his character.'

They discussed melody in poetry and Keats expounded to Bailey his theory as to the proper arrangement of open and closed vowels; the theory he put so magnificently into practice. 'No one else,' said Matthew Arnold, 'save Shakespeare, has in expression quite the fascinating felicity of Keats, his perfection of loveliness.' In this con-nection it is interesting to record that Keats was acutely sensitive to harmony in music. Charlotte Reynolds has recorded that, although he had no knowledge, practical or theoretical, when a wrong note was played in a public performance, he had been known to say that he would like to 'go down into the orchestra and smash all the fiddles.' Unfortunately the standard of performance was in his time deplorably low. Keats himself felt that, if he had studied music, he could have shewn as much originality as in poetry.

He wrote on September 14th to Jane Reynolds in praise of Bailey:

Poor Bailey scarcely ever well has gone to bed very so so, and pleased that I am writing to you. To your Brother John (whom henceforth I shall consider as mine) and to you my dear friends Marriann and Jane I shall ever feel grateful for having made known to me so real a fellow as Bailey. He delights me in the Selfish and (please God) the disinterrested part of my disposition. If the old Poets have any pleasure in looking down at the Enjoyers of their Works, their eyes must bend with double satisfaction upon him—I sit as at a feast when he is over them and pray that if after my death any of my Labours whould be worthy saving, they may have as "honest a Chronicler" as Bailey. Out of this his Enthusiasm in his own pursuit and for all good things is of an exalted kind—worthy a more healthful frame and an untorn Spirit. He must have happy years to come—he shall not die by God—

'Endymion and I,' he told her, 'are at the bottom of the Sea.'

From Oxford Keats wrote the first of the delightful letters to his sister, Frances Mary, kept very strictly by the Abbeys at Walthamstow. She was now fourteen. When over eighty she wrote to H. Buxton Forman:

I seldom saw my Brothers more than for short visits three or four times a year, I was frequently invited during the vacations, by the Dilke's, Reynolds, Wylie's and other friends of my brothers; but my guardian Mr. Abbey was *too* careful of me, and always kept me a complete prisoner having no other acquaintances than my books, birds and flowers . . . my holydays were spent between the two houses of my Guardians.

From one visit to John Sandell, her second guardian, Fanny came home with a curious little document (now in the Keats Museum):

This is to Certify to whom it may concern, that Frances Mary Keats during the time she was on a Visit to Mrs Sandell, was a very good Girl.
                                        J.S. 14 Jany. 1816.

If this were not a mere joke between the Abbeys and the Sandells it would suggest that Fanny was held in with the severity only too common in those days. We know that she was not happy at Walthamstow.

It is, however, only fair to the Abbeys to say that they may have felt themselves morally obliged to keep Fanny away from her brothers and their friends. Abbey was probably a staunch old Tory, as were most of the older and more prosperous business men who, remembering the horrors and the loss of property in the French Revolution, felt that the reformers were advocating the overthrow of a stable Government for possible anarchy. Keats had publicly avowed himself to be a friend of that dangerous Jacobinical editor of *The Examiner*. The Tories were only too ready to ascribe a looseness of moral and social conduct to the Radicals: Fanny's brothers and their associates might be doubtful company for a young girl.

Keats's letters to his sister are written with loving care and with a laudable restraint on his natural eccentricities of spelling. Tentatively, since he knew so little of her, he tried to interest her and to share in her young life. The first letter we have is dated September 10th:

> My dear Fanny,
>   Let us now begin a regular question and answer—a little pro and con; letting it interfere as a pleasant method of my coming at your favorite little wants and enjoyments, that I may meet them in a way befitting a brother.
> We have been so little together since you have been able to reflect on things that I know not whether you prefer the History of King Pepin to Bunyan's Pilgrims Progress—or Cinderella and her glass slipper to Moor's Almanack. However in a few Letters I hope I shall be able to come at that and adapt my scribblings to your Pleasure. You must tell me about all you read if it be only six Pages in a Week—and this transmitted to me every now and then will procure you full sheets of Writing from me pretty frequently —This I feel as a necessity: for we ought to become intimately acquainted, in order that I may not only, as you grow up love you as my only Sister, but confide in you as my dearest friend.

He told her in brief the story of Endymion, adding:

> but I dare say you have read this and all the other beautiful Tales which have come down from the ancient times of that beautiful Greece. If you have not let me know and I will tell you more at large of others quite as delightful.

He talked of Oxford and of Paris, where George and Tom were on holiday, and, referring to 'those pleasant little things the Original Poems' (*Original Poems for Infant Minds* by Jane and Ann Taylor), asked Fanny if she also liked the Taylors' *Essays in Rhyme on Morals and Manners*, the second edition of which, published by them, he had probably seen in that favourite haunt of his, Taylor and Hessey's bookshop: later he sent her a copy of the *Essays*.

After a lively disparagement of the French tongue in favour of the Italian—'full of real Poetry and Romance of a kind more fitted for the pleasure of Ladies than perhaps our own'—Keats ended his letter with:

Now Fanny you must write soon—and write all you think about, never mind what—only let me have a good deal of your writing—You need not do it all at once—be two or three or four days about it, and let it be a diary of your little Life. You will preserve all my Letters and I will secure yours—and thus in the course of time we shall each of us have a good Bundle—which, here-after, when things may have strangely altered and god knows what happened, we may read over together and look with pleasure on times past—that now are to come. Give my Respects to the Ladies—and so my dear Fanny I am ever

Your most affectionate Brother
John.

This letter was addressed to Miss Caley's school where she lived during term-time.

In her solitude among uncongenial strangers Fanny cherished an adoration for her eldest brother. She kept his letters, as he had directed, to the end of her long life, carrying them with her wherever she went. In 1877 she wrote: 'My enthusiasm and admiration of my dear brother are so strong in me at this moment, as when the blood of youth flowed in my veins.'

On September 17th Haydon wrote asking Keats to make some enquiries about a young man whom on a recent visit to Oxford he had found copying the altar-piece at Magdalen and whom, if he showed promise, Haydon was willing, provided his fare to London was paid and his support guaranteed for a year, to instruct for nothing. Haydon was a born teacher and would do much for love of a genuine artist. Keats found the young man, Charles Cripps,[1] and reported to Haydon that he had 'a great idea that he will be a tolerable neat brush.' Bailey and he thought the money side could be managed, although Cripps himself 'does not possess the Philosophers stone—nor Fortunatus' purse, nor Gyges' ring.'

After making this offer Haydon seems to have been rather more obstructive than helpful in the matter. Keats on his return to London made an effort to collect the money but found it both tiresome and difficult. As Cripps is not among the known pupils of Haydon it seems likely that he was not successful. Bailey, whose sympathy Haydon had enlisted, wrote to him about Cripps and received a rude reply on which Keats commented:

[1] Cripps is an Oxford name to this day.

To a Man of your nature such a Letter as Haydon's must have been extremely cutting. . . . As soon as I had known Haydon three days I had got enough of his character not to have been surprised at such a Letter as he has hurt you with. Nor when I knew it was it a principle with me to drop his acquaintance although with you it would have been an imperious feeling.

It was this intuitive knowledge of character, added to generosity of mind and a sense of humour, that enabled Keats to continue until his death on peaceful terms with his many friends, although they themselves were at times far from harmonious. Indeed, it seems as if Keats were a soothing power among them, a pleasant link. It is noticeable that when he went out of London they began to disagree. This too was painfully evident after his death.

On October 2nd he went with Bailey to Stratford-on-Avon for the day. This visit gave him an immense pleasure, although he was repelled by the commercialization of Shakespeare's birthplace.

Back at Hampstead, Keats wrote to Bailey on October 8th:

—every Body seems at Loggerheads. There's Hunt infatuated—there's Haydon's picture in statu quo. There's Hunt walks up and down his painting room criticizing every head most unmercifully. There's Horace Smith tired of Hunt. The web of our Life is of mingled Yarn." . . . I am quite disgusted with literary Men—and will never know another except Wordsworth—no not even Byron. Here is an instance of the friendships of such. Haydon and Hunt have known each other many years—now they live pour ainsi dire jealous Neighbours. Haydon says to me Keats dont show your Lines to Hunt on any account or he will have done half for you—so it appears Hunt wishes it to be thought.

Hunt and Haydon were now living near one another in Lisson Grove.

Keats was himself feeling irritated with Hunt who, meeting Reynolds at the theatre and hearing that Keats had nearly completed the four thousand lines he had set himself for the length of *Endymion*, said: "Ah, had it not been for me they would have been seven thousand!" This was probably a light remark which would have been better not repeated, but we know that Reynolds did not like Hunt. Keats was not too well and the remark rankled. He wrote:

You see Bailey how independant my writing has been—Hunts dissuasion (not to write a long poem) was of no avail—I refused to visit Shelley, that I might have my own unfetterd Scope—and after all I shall have the Reputation of Hunt's elevé. His corrections and amptuations will by the knowing ones be traced in the Poem. This is to be sure the vexation of a day —nor would I say so many Words about it to any but those whom I know to have my wellfare and Reputation at Heart—

Keats was regretting the lovely peace of Magdalen Hall in vacation: 'Mrs. Bentley's children are making a horrid row.'

Towards the end of the month he wrote again to congratulate Bailey on having obtained a curacy, tilting in the letter at Bailey's 'shocking bad hand.' 'Rome you know was not built in a day—I shall be able, by a little perseverance to read your Letters off hand.' On November 3rd he was condoling with Bailey; there was some difficulty about his ordination in time to take up the curacy. The blame for the delay was apparently put upon the Bishop of Lincoln and Keats wrote with a truly Radical pen some pungent lines about the 'barefaced oppression and impertinence' of those high in office:

There is something so nauseous in self-willed yawning impudence in the shape of conscience—it sinks the Bishop of Lincoln into a smashed frog putrifying: that a rebel against common decency should escape the Pillory! That a mitre should cover a Man guilty of the most coxcombical, tyrannical and indolent impertinence!

In this letter he mentioned the famous, or infamous attack on Hunt in Blackwood's *Edinburgh Magazine*, 'On the Cockney School of Poetry, No. 1.' From a reference in it Keats concluded that 'No. 2' would deal with himself, though he hoped that any further attack on the 'Cockneys' might be prevented by a note John Hunt had put in *The Examiner* inviting 'Z', the writer of the article, to send his address to the printer of *The Examiner* 'in order that justice may be executed on the proper person.'

By November 22nd Keats has gone into Surrey near Leatherhead in order to enjoy solitude and quiet in which to finish the last book of *Endymion*.

CHAPTER X

At Burford Bridge (November—December, 1817)

AT Burford Bridge Keats lodged at the Fox and Hounds (now the Burford Bridge Hotel), a quiet retreat probably recommended to him by Hazlitt whom he had met fairly frequently at Hunt's, Haydon's or the Reynoldses. For that singular man, whose views strongly influenced his own, Keats had a great respect and admiration, though he does not seem ever to have become intimate with him. In the *Philosophy of Mystery* by Walter Cooper Dendy, there is an improbable conversation between Hazlitt and Keats which takes place on the top of Box Hill, but we have no proof that the two men ever did walk together there.

The hotel stands in a garden of two acres at the foot of the Hill, on the steep side of which the evergreens, firs, box and yews make a background darkly green and restful to look upon. In Keats's day the box and yews invaded the garden half-way across the lawn to the house. The bedroom shown as his looks out on to this lawn on which are fine trees he must have admired; a beech and a Scotch cedar which was even then full grown. Near the window is a tall pine which may have delighted him in its tender youth. The garden was covered in a shrubbery, a tangle of nooks and 'Gothick' arbours that lured to the inn many newly married lovers.

The inn, lying on the old Portsmouth Road, has housed many famous people. Nelson made it a temporary home for a while after the battle of Copenhagen. That Keats had the room next to the one he occupied must have both pleased and interested him. He had retained his boyhood's interest in the hero. At Teignmouth a few months later we find him taking a copy of a letter written by Nelson.

In his marginal notes to *Paradise Lost*, against Book 1, lines 318–21, Keats wrote:

There is a cool pleasure in the very sound of vale. The English word is of the happiest chance. Milton has put vales in heaven and hell with the very utter affection and yearning of a great Poet. It is a sort of Delphic Abstraction— a beautiful thing made more beautiful by being reflected and put in a Mist. . . .

Was the valley of Mickleham at the back of his mind when he wrote this? There is a dream-like feeling about this vale of Avalon where the trees, unharried by winter winds, grow tall and shapely. Their interlacing twigs and boughs make gracious patterns against the dove-grey sky. The horizon is hid by the steeply sloping hills clothed darkly in evergreens and veiled in lingering mists. '. . . a beautiful thing made more beautiful by being reflected and put in a Mist. . . .'

Through the valley there runs, slow and silent, the Mole, choked by weeds and overflowing into the rich meadow in winter so that the trees are reflected long and shadowy in the dark water.

'I like this place very much,' wrote Keats. 'There is Hill & Dale and a little River—I went up Box hill this Evening after the Moon—you a' seen the Moon—came down—and wrote some lines.'

At Burford Bridge he was happy in busy solitude. Had he wished for talk he could have had it in plenty; living not far away was 'Conversation' Sharp, a man who attracted to the district men of thought and intellect, both Whig and Tory. Sharp was accustomed to meet his friends at the inn. No doubt such a skilled and inveterate talker would not have despised the company of a young man of intellect in winter when visitors would be rarer. Hazlitt, in describing the inn to Keats, could hardly have omitted a reference to 'Conversation' Sharp.

Alone in Surrey Keats does not appear to have suffered from that yearning for family and friends he had felt in the Isle of Wight. His mind was fast maturing; he could more happily and with greater profit work, dream and think in solitude. His letters now gain both in richness of thought and expression.

He had taken only three books with him and one of them was Shakespeare's Poems. Keats was merging himself in Shakespeare; feeling the beauty, the strength and the rightness of Shakespeare's perfect expression on his pulses. 'Shakespeare,' he said, 'has left nothing to say about nothing or anything. . . .' He decided to take

a poet's rage
And stretched metre of an antique song

as the motto for *Endymion*.

Very few letters written to Keats have survived: we must assume that he destroyed the greater number of them either on receipt or before he went to Italy. It is a matter of regret that we do not possess the other side of the correspondence with Reynolds and with Bailey during this rich middle period. Reynolds's keen mind would seem to have acted as a whetstone to Keats's more universal one, and Bailey, as 'man of feeling' and of principle, aroused in him a desire to explain, to defend his intuitions about life and poetry: so that in the letters to these two friends we see further into the workings of the poet's mind than in any others. It is, by the way, noticeable to a reader sensitive to the general feeling, the trend of a piece of writing, that to each of his friends Keats writes in a subtly different mood. With Reynolds he is intellectual, poetic but robust; with Bailey still intellectual but more emotional, more concerned with 'the holiness of the heart's affections'; with Haydon in the early period he is exalted, at once humble and arrogant with an occasional touch of something rather like hysteria; with Hunt, in the only two letters we have, he is lighter, more self-consciously whimsical.

But, happy as he was in his lovely solitude, Keats had taken anxieties with him. The first was Tom's ill-health, the danger of which he must, with his knowledge of medicine, have fully realized. The second was the minor worry of Cripps' future. But he was determined to be philosophical and wrote to Reynolds, who had worries of his own: 'Why don't you, as I do, look unconcernedly at what may be called more particularly Heart-vexations? They never surprise me— lord! a man should have the fine point of his soul taken off to become fit for this world.'

A letter written to Bailey on November 22nd is a rich one and must be largely quoted. After the passage given in the last chapter about Haydon's character and the necessity of Bailey as 'man of principle' dropping him if he were his friend, Keats indirectly defended or explained his own tolerant attitude to Haydon and expounded certain of his views on poetry and life. These views must have been sufficiently startling to the young clergyman who we know, although he admired Wordsworth and much of the new poetry, disapproved of the new freedom of thought. In 1820 he wrote to Taylor:

(Keats) has good dispositions and noble qualities of heart; but, I think, we shall accord in one conclusion that he has not kept the best society for one of his character and constitution. Many of his moral principles are consequently loose; his moral conduct not very exact; and the Phantom of Honour is substituted for the truth and substance of Religion.

In the light of our knowledge of Keats, his uprightness of soul and his delicacy of conduct, these statements look like mere slander. There was, perhaps, an element of spite in them, for soon the trio of friendship, Reynolds, Rice and Bailey, was to be rudely split and Keats was afterwards reserved with him; but in the main Bailey was only voicing the opinions of the majority of the old school about the dangerous reformers and radicals.

The new school of poetry was in itself felt to be harmful error. In the eighteenth century there was a long struggle in the minds of the philosophers to reconcile poetry with Christianity, and it was laid down that this end could only be achieved by the predominance of reason, the maintenance both in poetry and in the conduct of life of 'decorum', of adherence to a definite code. The philosophers divorced imagination or 'fancy' from reason, or judgment, placing it in the heart and not in the head. 'Fancy leaps and frisks, and away she's gone; whilst reason rattles the chain and follows after.' In a pamphlet published as late as 1805 John Foster asserted that a man's imagination will run away with his judgment or reason unless he has the aid of divine grace. Divine grace was to be sought within the Established Church, and the Church was so bound up with the State that the demands for reform from the new school of writers were held to be immoral.

In the following passage quoted from Keats's letter to Bailey it must be borne in mind that imagination was held to be an attribute of the heart:

I wish you knew all that I think about Genius and the Heart—and yet I think you are thoroughly acquainted with my innermost breast in that respect, or you could not have known me even thus long and still hold me worthy to be your dear friend. In passing however I must say of one thing that has pressed upon me lately and encreased my Humility and capability of submission and that is this truth—Men of Genius are great as certain ethereal Chemicals operating on the Mass of neutral intellect—but they have not any individuality, any determined Character—I would call the top and head of those who have a proper self Men of Power—

This would indeed be to one read in the eighteenth century philosophers and divines a subversive doctrine. The Popean man of genius was not to transform or disturb the tried notions of men of intellect but, as 'Man of Power,' to refine on and to interpret them. He was to attain to 'the grandeur of generality,' but not the generality, the universality in the truly classic sense but in the limited neo-classic meaning of the expression or clarification of the accepted views of a limited cultured class,

What oft is thought, but ne'er so well expressed.

Bailey as a young man familiar with the early romantics, an admirer of Wordsworth, would not entirely accept this neat but unnatural theory (about which, indeed, many of the philosophers themselves were uneasy) but he had evidently been making some defence of it. Keats added:

O I wish I was as certain of the end of all your troubles as that of your momentary start about the authenticity of the Imagination. I am certain of nothing but of the holiness of the Heart's affections and the truth of Imagination—What the imagination seizes as Beauty must be truth—whether it existed before or not—for I have the same Idea of all our Passions as of Love they are all in their sublime, creative of essential Beauty. . . . The Imagination may be compared to Adam's dream—he awoke and found it truth. I am the more zealous in this affair, because I have never yet been able to perceive how any thing can be known for truth by consequitive reasoning—and yet it must be. Can it be that even the greatest Philosopher ever arrived at his goal without putting aside numerous objections. However it may be, O for a Life of Sensations rather than of Thoughts! It is 'a Vision in the form of Youth' a Shadow of reality to come—and this consideration has further convinced me for it has come as auxiliary to another favorite Speculation of mine, that we shall enjoy ourselves here after by having what we called happiness on Earth repeated in a finer tone and so repeated. And yet such a fate can only befall those who delight in Sensation rather than hunger as you do after Truth. Adam's dream will do here and seems to be a conviction that Imagination and its empyreal reflection is the same as human Life and its Spiritual repetition. But as I was saying—the simple imaginative Mind may have its rewards in the repetition of its own silent Working coming continually on the Spirit with a fine Suddenness—to compare great things with small—have you never by being Surprised with an old Melody—in a delicious place—by a delicious voice, felt over again your very Speculations and Surmises at the time it first operated on your Soul—do you not remember forming to yourself the singer's face more beautiful than it was possible and yet with the elevation of the Moment you did not think so—even then you were mounted on the Wings of Imagination so high—that the Prototype must be here after—that delicious face you will see. What a time! I am continually running away from the subject—sure this cannot be exactly the case with a complex Mind—one that is imaginative and at the same time careful of its fruits—who would exist partly on Sensation partly on thought— to whom it is necessary that years should bring the philosophic Mind—such a one I consider your's and therefore it is necessary to your eternal Happiness that you not only drink this old Wine of Heaven, which I shall call the redigestion of our most ethereal Musings on Earth; but also increase in knowledge and know all things.

This is indeed heresy to neo-classicism. His young intuition in its early romanticism, by a swing of the pendulum, claimed too much for unrestrained imagination, but now he was groping after the true classicism, the highest poetry, as a fusion of thought and imagination: that poetry which is the highest philosophy, or love, or God-guided wisdom.

It is only fair to Bailey to add that, although in 1820 he stated that many of Keats's moral principles were loose and 'the Phantom of

Honour is substituted for the truth and substance of Religion,' in 1849, writing to Lord Houghton, he said: 'he had a soul of utter integrity.' Bailey was probably by then a wiser because an older and more experienced man, and had learned to distinguish true character from the expression of opinions or 'principles', which are, after all, largely a matter of fashion and of period. Also by 1849 the world had changed, and changed in the direction of much that was dear to Keats and his friends.

There follows in Keats's letter a passage which, combined with a reference in a previous letter dated October 8th to the taking of mercury, led William Rossetti to the definite conclusion that Keats had contracted syphilis:

. . . but the world is full of troubles and I have not much reason to think myself pestered with many—I think Jane or Marianne has a better opinion of me than I deserve—for really and truly I do not think my Brothers illness connected with mine—you know more of the real Cause than they do nor have I any chance of being rack'd as you have been—

As Miss Lowell pointed out, in the first third of the nineteenth century the doctors were mercury-mad and prescribed mercury for all manner of diseases, including tuberculosis. It may be that Keats had a momentary fear that he, too, was developing the disease from which his mother died. But, the suggestion of syphilis once raised, this passage cannot be explained away by merely negative evidence. There is, I consider, a strong proof that Rossetti's assertion was unjustified: when Lord Houghton was collecting data from friends of Keats for the 'Life' Bailey sent him the letters of October 8th and November 22nd, and with permission to quote from them. Indeed, he suggested that Lord Houghton should make full use of the second letter. An examination of the passage given above makes it clear that if Keats had contracted syphilis so had Bailey: it seems highly improbable that Bailey, then Archdeacon of Colombo and the author of books upon religion, would risk such a revelation. Even though the fact might be only indirectly referred to, it is likely that he would, if he had suffered from that foul disease in his youth, have been self-conscious about the passage.[1]

Keats then gave in his letter a piece of self-revelation not only interesting with regard to himself but also as to the artist temperament:

I scarcely remember counting upon any Happiness—I look not for it if it be not in the present hour—nothing startles me beyond the Moment. The setting Sun will always set me to rights—or if a Sparrow come before my Window I take part in its existence and pick about the Gravel.

[1] See also 'Keats and Mercury' by C. T. Andrews, M.D., F.R.C.P. K-S M. Bulletin XX, 1969.

This is an illustration of his dictum that 'Men of Genius . . . have not any individuality, any determined Character.' The power of the projection of the mind into other minds or extraneous objects, a projection which is strongly physical in feeling, is at once the joy and the penalty of the creative mind; the penalty because it is exhausting, and the joy because it enables the artist to live more happily in the moment than is possible to the ordinary man. Keats wrote:

Too many tears for lovers have been shed

Perhaps 'poets' or 'writers' could be substituted for lovers. Because the writer is vocal, because he can express himself he gives his sorrows to the world and we mourn with him; but the inarticulate man in whom all emotion, all grief is bottled up is the more to be pitied. In giving voice to his grief or his worries the artist in some measure rids himself of them.

But the process of assimilation and creation is in itself physically tiring, and Keats was not well. There had come upon him an exhaustion of spirit. There are distressing periods when the artist feels himself as dry as a sucked orange. Keats at the moment was experiencing this profitless mood:

The first thing that strikes me on hearing a Misfortune having befalled another is this. 'Well it cannot be helped—he will have the pleasure of trying the resources of his spirit'—and I beg now my dear Bailey that hereafter should you observe any thing cold in me not to put it to the account of heartlessness but abstraction—for I assure you I sometimes feel not the influence of a Passion or affection during a whole week—and so long this sometimes continues I begin to suspect myself and the genuineness of my feelings at other times—thinking them a few barren Tragedy-tears—

Yet morally distressing as these dry periods are, there are moods in which a negation of feeling may seem by comparison a happy state. Before Keats left Burford Bridge, in a country winter-bound, he wrote:

In drear-nighted December,
    Too happy happy Tree,
Thy branches ne'er remember
    Their green felicity:
The north cannot undo them,
With a sleety whistle through them;
Nor frozen thawings glue them
    From budding at the prime.

In drear-nighted December,
   Too happy, happy Brook,
Thy bubblings ne'er remember
   Apollo's summer look;
But with a sweet forgetting,
They stay their crystal fretting,
Never, never petting
   About the frozen time.

Ah! would 'twere so with many
   A gentle Girl and Boy!
But were there ever any
   Writh'd not at passed joy?
The feel of not to feel it
When there is none to heal it,
Nor numbed sense to steel it,
   Was never said in rhyme.

This poem was published after his death in varying versions; the above is the one we have in his own handwriting. The model of the versification comes from a song in the *Spanish Fryar* and from this we know that Keats was already reading with attention Dryden's vigorous racy English.

He finished *Endymion* on November 28th, writing the date opposite the last line. The four thousand and fifty lines were composed in less than six months, only exceeding his estimate of time by a month. He had said:

> . . . let Autumn bold,
> With universal tinge of sober gold,
> Be all about me when I make an end.

But perhaps it was fitting that the poem should end in winter, for in contemplation of it Keats felt discontent and, with the cold eye of self-criticism, ranked it as 'a feverish attempt, rather than a deed accomplished.' By September 28th, when the third book was finished, he had marked it down as a failure to Haydon:

My Ideas with respect to it I assure you are very low—and I would write the subject thoroughly again—but I am tired of it and think the time would be better spent in writing a new Romance which I have in my eye for next Summer—Rome was not built in a Day—and all the good I expect from my employment this summer is the fruit of Experience which I hope to gather in my next Poem.

CHAPTER XI

Theatrical Criticism; Brown, Dilke and New Friends; the Immortal Dinner (December, 1817—May, 1818)

BEFORE December 15th Keats was back at Hampstead and alone in Well Walk. George had taken Tom out of the rigour of a London winter to Teignmouth in Devon. Reynolds, who was now courting Eliza Powell Drewe, was bound for Devon also. Keats agreed to take his place for a few weeks over the Christmas holidays as dramatic critic on *The Champion*.

The theatre was an old love and, although he professed a strong dislike for journalism, Keats must have enjoyed and welcomed the new experience, especially as Edmund Kean, then at the height of his powers, had now returned to Drury Lane after an absence of some weeks. On December 15th Keats saw him in his finest part, Richard III.

On the 18th Kean played Luke in a weak play called *Riches*. Keats was present in his official capacity but could muster up no interest in the play, and on Sunday, the 21st, there appeared in his journal, not a report of *Riches*, but a panegyric on Kean as Shakespearean actor. The performance of *Riches* was dismissed in a sentence: 'On Thursday evening he acted Luke in "Riches," as far as the stage will admit, to perfection.'

The article is a fine piece of writing and interesting both as a contemporary view of a young enthusiast for the splendid herald of the new naturalistic school of acting and as a piece of self-revealing and imaginative prose. The style is perhaps too reminiscent of the admired Hazlitt and has not the ease and simplicity of the letters, but the sentences are clear, balanced and rhythmic. They are in the true rhythm of prose and not in the transferred poetic rhythm so often found in the prose of young poets. The article, printed by H. Buxton Forman in the *Complete Works*, is accessible, together with the other *Champion* dramatic criticisms, in the small five-volume edition. I give one of the most striking passages of 'Kean as Shakespearean Actor':

Amid his numerous excellencies, the one which at this moment most weighs upon us, is the elegance, gracefulness, and music of elocution. A melodious passage in poetry is full of pleasures both sensual and spiritual. The spiritual is felt when the very letters and points of charactered language show like the hieroglyphics of beauty; the mysterious signs of our immortal freemasonry! "A thing to dream of, not to tell!" The sensual life of verse springs warm from the lips of Kean, and to one learned in Shakespearian hieroglyphics—learned in the spiritual portion of those lines to which Kean adds a sensual grandeur; his tongue must seem to have robbed the Hybla bees and left them honeyless! There is an indescribable *gusto* in his voice, by which we feel that the utterer is thinking of the past and future while speaking of the instant. When he says in Othello "Put up your bright swords, for the dew will rust them," we feel that his throat had commanded where swords were as thick as reeds. From eternal risk, he speaks as though his body were unassailable. Again, his exclamation of "blood, blood, blood!" is direful and slaughterous to the deepest degree; the very words appear stained and gory. His nature hangs over them, making a prophetic repast. The voice is loosed on them, like the wild dog on the savage relics of an eastern conflict; and we can distinctly hear it "gorging and growling o'er carcase and limb." In Richard, "Be stirring with the lark to-morrow, gentle Norfolk!" comes from him, as through the morning atmosphere, towards which he yearns.

The next week he saw Kean in a curious hash called *Richard Duke of York*, a compilation from the three parts of *King Henry VI*. The mangling of Shakespeare was a common practice: Kean, perhaps the finest 'King Lear' of our stage, always played the tragedy with a happy ending. Keats's opinion was that[1]

the play, as it is compressed, is most interesting, clear and vigorous. It bears us from the beginning to the middle of that tremendous struggle, and very properly stops at the death of the first of the Richards. . . . Perhaps the faults of the compilation are these:—First, the characters are too hastily introduced and despatched, and their language clipped too closely. . . . We see nothing of Talbot, and missing him is like walking among the Elgin Marbles and seeing an empty place where the Theseus had reclined. In the next place the poetry is too much *modernized*. . . . The present play appears to go on by fits and starts, and to be made up too much of unmatchable events. It is inlaid with facts[2] of different colour, and we can see the cracks which the joiner's hand could not help leaving.

But on the whole the compilation deserved praise. 'Great ingenuity is displayed . . . the workings of Richard's mind are brought out as it were by the hand of the anatomist, and all the useless parts are cut away and laid aside.' He thought that Kean 'had a hand in it.' Actually Kean was responsible for a good deal of the compilation, if not for all. This Keats probably knew as a bit of theatre gossip; through Reynolds and others he was in a position to be tolerably acquainted with the back-stage life of the two patent theatres. He continued: 'But with all we fear the public will not take the obligation as it is meant, and as it ought to be received. The English people do not care one fig about Shakespeare,—only as he flatters their pride and their prejudices.'

[1] & [2] *See* Appendix V.

The writing of this critique is, apart from some passages on Kean himself, pedestrian, though there are a few fine phrases, such as 'pelican strife' for the Wars of the Roses. The historical plays of Shakespeare are, he said:

> . . . written with infinite vigour, but their regularity tied the hand of Shakespeare. Particular facts kept him in the high road, and would not suffer him to turn down leafy and winding lanes, or to break wildly and at once into the breathing fields. The poetry is for the most part ironed and manacled with a chain of facts, and cannot get free. . . . The poetry of Shakespeare is generally free as is the wind—a perfect thing of the elements, winged and sweetly coloured. Poetry must be free! It is of the air, not of the earth; and the higher it soars the nearer it gets to its home.

He spoke of the poetry of *Romeo and Juliet*, of *Hamlet* and *Macbeth* as remaining . . . in all men's hearts a perpetual and golden dream. The poetry of "Lear," "Othello," "Cymbeline" &c., is the poetry of human passions and affections, made almost etherial by the power of the poet. . . .' The poetry of the historical dramas is 'often times poetry wandering on the London Road.' But Keats, attacking an idol, felt uneasy. He threw down his pen and opened his Shakespeare. Coming at length back to the manuscript he continued: 'On going into the three parts of "Henry the Sixth" for themselves, we retract all dispraise and accusation, and declare them to be perfect works . . . we live again in the olden time. The Duke of York plucks the pale rose before our eyes.' He gave himself the pleasure of quoting twenty lines of Warwick's fifth speech in Act III, scene 2 of the second part, beginning, 'Oft have I seen a corse from whence a ghost.' Then, with a glance up, perhaps, at his treasured portrait of Shakespeare, he wrote, 'we feel that criticism has no right to purse its little brow in the presence of Shakespeare.' He again praised the depth and feeling of Kean's acting especially in the death scene:

> His death was very great. But Kean always "dies as erring men do die." The bodily functions wither up, and the mental faculties hold out till they crack. It is an extinguishment, not a decay. The hand is agonized with death; the lip trembles with the last breath, as we see the autumn leaf thrill in the cold wind of evening. The very eye-lid dies. The acting of Kean is Shakespearian—he will fully understand what we mean.

On January 1st Keats was at Covent Garden to see a new tragedy by John Dillon, *Retribution or the Chieftain's Daughter*. The play, he says, was 'most wretched; an unpardonable offence, so *sans pareilly*, so inferior to Mrs. Radcliffe, so germain to a play-bill at a fair, that we will say no more about it for fear prejudice and indignation should carry us butt

against the main body of the work to try whose skull is hardest.'
The expression *sans pareilly* was apparently to his own coinage: the
Sans Pareil was a minor theatre not licensed to play legitimate drama
and afterwards called the Adelphi; a house in which rough stuff in the
form of melodrama (at first literally melo-drama to avoid by the
introduction of songs and music infringement of the rights of the two
patent theatres) survived well into the twentieth century. Towards the
end of the critique there is a characteristically kind note:

If the author is young and has a wide chasm to fill up with achievement, and
at the same time gives up writing such common-place as we find in this his
first trial, he need not care what is said for or against in the public prints.

Keats may have been told that the author was very young. This
play was Dillon's first and last essay in the theatre. He soon afterwards
embarked with more advantage to his pocket on a commercial career.

In the same number of *The Champion* there appeared an article by
Keats based on the Drury Lane pantomime, *Don Giovanni*, which he
probably saw on Boxing Night. He told his brothers it was 'a very nice
one but badly acted.' In the article he made little more direct reference
to the show itself than: 'As to the pantomime, be it good or bad, a child
should write a critique upon it. We were pleased knowing how much
better it ought to be—a child's is a eulogy—and that is not merely in
pantomimes.' Don Juan does not seem a promising hero for a child's
entertainment, but he was Harlequin: probably the story itself was
only of the slightest. The pantomime of that period was primarily a
harlequinade with clown and pantaloon as leading characters; the
harlequinade which, in the pantomimes enjoyed by children now
elderly, had sadly dwindled down to a short epilogue.

Keats began his article by saying that for many years the subject
of Don Juan had been done to death, 'wiredrawn' in the theatres,
'made a pet of at the Surrey, and fiddled away to hell at the Italian
Opera.' It had now 'found its way into the Drury Lane pantomime.'
Interest in the Don was characteristic of one aspect of the new movement in literature: the gross libertine was romanticized into a dark,
sad soul in search of the ideal woman. That he should even appear,
as ancient traditional harlequin, in a frivolous and purely popular
pantomime is evidence of the wisdom of Byron in choosing him as
putative hero of his poem.

Keats's article, though not in his happiest style, is amusing and of
period interest. After dilating on the minute interest taken in the
Don's private life he continues: 'In the course of the pantomime Punch
and Judy with their family were introduced: an illustrious house, of

which the pranks and witty squeaking are more popular than Giovanni himself.' Punch and Judy's family? Was there then a legitimate addition to the historic Baby, or was Drury Lane tampering with tradition?

He then makes a solemn enquiry into the phenomenon of the greater popularity of the puppet hero:

In the first place if the Don is well made, Punch is ill made; if the Rake has a dozen mistresses, Punch has his Judy, who has the charms of a dozen in her summed up—if the former has a confident stamp, the latter has the neatest jerk of the left leg; if the former has his quizzing glass the latter has his ladle.

The ladle has now dwindled back into plain stick. Mr. Punch's ladle appears to have been a temporary fashion linking him with the beverage so frequently spooned out hot in Georgian parlours.

Keats now invented a few criticisms of Punch attributing them in thinly disguised names to well-known Shakespearean commentators. His gibes at the pretentions of these gentlemen were driven home by, 'to have a doubt of their vanity would be to take a hawk for a handsaw.' Curiously enough he does not include Dr. Johnson, although his written comments on his notes in the Johnson and Steevens edition of Shakespeare are trenchant, and there are few comments on the notes by Steevens, whom he here pillories as 'Stephanio.'

The modern critic sits in the orchestra stalls; so most probably did Keats, but in a more literal sense. The orchestra-well of those days extended in an oval shape far into the auditorium, and the press, together with friends of the management, often had seats within it. Let us hope that Keats's sensitive ear was not too sharply affronted by the orchestra at such uncomfortably close quarters. Behind him would be the pit which extended right up to the orchestra-well; row upon row of fidgety people upon hard, narrow benches, consuming quantities of food and drink and considerably more vocal than a modern audience.

Comments on the play and upon the actors were not kept back for quiet airing during the intervals or after the performance. To 'get the bird' was a phrase with a more literal meaning to the stage of that day. There is a simile in *Hyperion* (Book I, line 253) which recalls these noisy evenings in the theatre:

> For as in theatres of crowded men
> Hubbub increases more they call out "Hush!"
> So at Hyperion's words the Phantoms pale
> Bestirr'd themselves, thrice horrible and cold;

It is from Keats's letters to his brothers that we know he wrote these articles in *The Champion*. He sent them the articles as they appeared, remarking of the one on *Retribution* that it was 'so badly punctuated

John Hamilton Reynolds
From a painting by Joseph
Severn

James Rice
From a drawing in the Keats
Memorial House

John Keats
From a miniature by Joseph Severn in the Keats Memorial
House

that, as you perceive, I am determined never to write more without some care in that particular.' He also sent them on December 21st *The Examiner*, containing an account of the three days' trial of William Hone, the free-thinking publisher, for publishing 'impious, profane and scandalous libels.' Hone's acquittal was hailed with triumph in Liberal circles. 'His *Not Guilty*,' wrote Keats, 'is a thing, which not to have been, would have dulled still more Liberty's Emblazoning.'

He tells them in the same letter of 'two very pleasant evenings with Dilke' and that 'Brown and Dilke walked with me and back from the Christmas pantomime.' Keats had been acquainted with Charles Wentworth Dilke for some time through the Reynoldses.

Dilke, a clerk in the Navy Pay Office, although only seven years older than Keats, was already an established man of letters and the careful editor of some volumes supplementary to Dodsley's *Collection of Old Plays*. He and Charles Brown, a friend from school days, had built themselves a double house, Wentworth Place, on the edge of Hampstead Heath to the south side. Dilke, a married man with a child, occupied the larger portion and Brown, a bachelor, lived in the smaller.

Although a man of considerable mental powers, Dilke was curiously limited both in sympathies and intellect. Charles Lamb said there was a particular kind of blockhead, 'a *Dilkish* blockhead.' Although of advanced Liberal ideas Dilke kept those ideas in a neat set of mental pigeon-holes for tidy application to illogical humanity. He was, in Keats's own phrase, a 'Godwin-perfectability man,' one who saw through the eyes of the social theorist, William Godwin, human progress as an orderly advance towards an ultimate purity of mind and motive.

In practical affairs, by virtue of his very inelasticity, Dilke had a bull-dog grip on the matter in hand. Later, when Fanny Keats's affairs were being either hopelessly muddled or dishonestly dealt with by Abbey, he managed to wrest them from him, and himself became her trustee. But on Fanny's marriage complications arose: her husband, Señor Llanos, wanted to secure her money to finance a patent bridle-bit of his invention, and Fanny supported his demand. Dilke very wisely refused. There were also complications with the firm of Rice and Reynolds, his friends and Fanny's solicitors, in which he did not wish to involve himself: Reynolds, now the active partner, so dilatory he should not perhaps be called 'active', had not behaved well by her. Dilke was surely right in giving Fanny and her unbusinesslike husband the full protection of an unflexible trusteeship; but he appears to have done it abruptly, and with some tactless plain speaking about the cherished invention. 'What was still more galling to me,' she told H. Buxton Forman, in giving as an old woman her version of the repudiation of the trust, 'and never to be forgotten, his sneering observations on the nervous irritability of my poor brother produced by ill-health, and a thousand unfortunate circumstances.' These unkindnesses to the girl would seem to have been the outcome of lack of imagination rather than of malice. There is no evidence that Keats was ever on anything but good terms with him, although towards the end he felt some irritation over his political views and was always a trifle annoyed at Dilke's over-fondness for his only child, Charley, who was that pest of visiting friends, a spoiled child.

As Keats walked back to Hampstead from the Christmas pantomime with Dilke and Brown he

had not a dispute but a disquisition, with Dilke on various subjects; several things dove-tailed in my mind, and at once it struck me what quality went to form a Man of Achievement, especially in Literature, and which Shakespeare possessed so enormously—I mean *Negative Capability*, that is, when a man is capable of being in uncertainties, mysteries, doubts, without any irritable reaching after fact and reason—

One can imagine Dilke laying down the law in no uncertain tones and the young Keats eagerly questioning his dicta. We do not hear what Brown said: perhaps that cautious man kept his own counsel.

Charles Brown was to become the closest friend of Keats, to take the place in intimacy of his brothers when they were no longer beside him. Brown was both Highland and Welsh by descent. Although to most men he was a good companion, his Celtic blood made him at times difficult for an Englishman to comprehend. He would take odd and unexplained dislikes and was a fierce hater. He was both mean and generous. In the words of Dilke, his friend, 'He was the most scrupulously honest man I ever knew—but wanted nobleness to lift this honesty out of the commercial kennel. . . . His sense of justice led him at times to do acts of generosity—at others of meanness—the latter was always noticed, the former overlooked—therefore among his early companions he had a character for anything rather than liberality —but he was liberal.'

Brown's early circumstances, which were remarkable, had probably accentuated in him that carefulness in the spending of money not always understood by the more lavish Englishman: he had gone out to work at an early age, and by the time he was eighteen had known both responsibility and prosperity. His brother John, having made him a partner in his business, he managed a branch in St. Petersburg. In 1807 the Treaty of Tilsit, in which Russia secretly undertook to aid France in her commercial war against England, brought disaster to the firm. Brown returned to England ruined. For years he made a precarious living by journalism and was at one time so poor that he was forced to dine at a fourpenny 'ordinary' where the knives and forks were chained to the table. In 1814 he had a mild success in the theatre, with the libretto of a serio-comic opera *Narensky, or the Road to Yaroslaf*, produced at Drury Lane with music by Braham and Reeve. Although it ran only for a few nights the opera brought him three hundred pounds and free admission to the theatre for life. Later his brother James died in the service of the East India Company and left him enough income to live upon with care. He still wrote but was freer to follow his own bent, which was the writing of tales of wonder and Shakespearean commentary. His enthusiasm for Shakespeare made a mental bond with Keats.

True to his blood, Brown was fiercely loyal in friendship. His deep love for Keats is manifest in surviving letters long after the poet's death. In appearance and largely in nature he was strong, solid and mundane, but had enough imagination and humour to leaven these earthy qualities and to make him perhaps an ideal friend for Keats, both sympathetic and restful. Brown was thirty-one when he met Keats, but already bald and set in appearance.

The company of Dilke, his pleasant wife and Brown was doubly welcome to Keats living in solitary lodgings; he had only to walk down the hill from Well Walk to reach their homes. No doubt their well-stored bookshelves, the volumes of literature and of old plays, were an additional attraction. He spent more and more of his time with Dilke, sometimes taking his work with him, that of correcting and copying *Endymion* for the press. Tom down at Teignmouth was 'licking his chops' at the thought of early publication, but Keats warned him not to expect to see the volume too soon.

On December 19th he went to Town to see the aged Benjamin West's picture 'Death on a Pale Horse.'

It is a wonderful picture, when West's age is considered; But there is nothing to be intense upon; no women one feels mad to kiss, no face swelling into reality—The excellence of every art is its intensity, capable of making all disagreeables evaporate, from their being in close relationship with Beauty and Truth. Examine 'King Lear', and you will find this exemplified throughout; but in this picture we have unpleasantness without any momentous depth of speculation excited, in which to bury its repulsiveness—

He was reading *King Lear* with close attention at this time in an 1808 reprint of the Folio. This book is now one of the treasures of the Keats Museum and in it *King Lear* is heavily underlined throughout. Keats's intellect was rapidly maturing; he was passing from a state of passiveness, a simple response to natural beauties, to a stronger grip on reality. In the seven little volumes taken with him to the Isle of Wight *The Tempest, A Midsummer Night's Dream, Measure for Measure* and *Antony and Cleopatra* are the most heavily scored. *Hamlet* is a good deal underlined, but *King Lear, Romeo and Juliet* and *Othello* are unmarked. He was now turning to the great tragedies, sagas of the human spirit, and in particular to the 'bitter-sweet' of *Lear*. On January 23rd he wrote to his brothers:

I think a little change has taken place in my intellect lately—I cannot bear to be uninterested or unemployed, I, who for so long a time have been addicted to passiveness. Nothing is finer for the purposes of great productions than a very gradual ripening of the intellectual powers. As an instance of this—observe—I sat down yesterday to read "King Lear" once again the thing appeared to demand the prologue of a Sonnet, I wrote it and began to read—(I know you would like to see it.)

He then copied out for them in its first version 'On sitting down to read King Lear once again.' The sixth line stood as 'Betwixt Hell torment and impassion'd Clay.' His final version (here reproduced) was written down in his folio on the blank space at the end of *Hamlet* facing the opening of *King Lear*.

> On sitting down to read King Lear once again.
>
> O Golden-tongued Romance, with serene Lute!
>   Fair plumed Syren, Queen of far-away!
>   Leave melodizing on this wintry day
> Shut up thine olden Pages, and be mute.
> Adieu! for, once again, the fierce dispute,
>   Betwixt Damnation and impassion'd clay
>   Must I burn through; once more humbly assay
> The bitter-sweet of this Shaksperean fruit.
> Chief Poet! and ye Clouds of Albion,
>   Begetters of our deep eternal theme!
> When through the old oak forest I am gone,
>   Let me not wander in a barren dream:
> But when I am consumed in the fire,
>   Give me new Phoenix Wings to fly at my desire.
>   Jany. 22. 1818

The first line has a boldness and a subtlety of rhythm. It would have been easier and appeared safer to a second-rate poet to write the smoother line: 'O golden-tongued Romance with Lute serene.' And how rich is the melody of the four opening lines:

> O Golden-tongued Romance, with serene Lute!
> Fair plumed Syren, Queen of far-away!
> Leave melodizing on this wintry day
> Shut up thine olden Pages, and be mute.

To most lovers of Shakespeare reading in folio is a joyous revelation; to Keats with a poet's mind and supersensitive ear it yielded an even greater measure of delight. Apart from a new enjoyment of the work of his master, brought nearer by reading in an edition so close to his own time, Keats submitted the text to a strong critical attention. Comparing old and modern editions he suggested certain valuable emendations and questioned others. *King Lear* in folio is heavily marked and all Lear's speeches are underscored. To Act I, scene 1, Goneril's speech at line 291: 'You see how full of changes his age is,' there is a comment which Dr. Caroline Spurgeon rightly terms 'a short prose poem':

How finely is the brief of Lear's character sketched in this conference—from this point does Shakespeare spur him out to the mighty grapple—"the seeded pride that hath to this maturity blowne up" Shakspeare doth scatter abroad on the winds of Passion, where the germs take buoyant root in stormy Air, suck lightning sap, and become voiced dragons—self-will and pride and wrath are taken at a rebound by his giant hand and mounted to the Clouds—there to remain and thunder evermore.

A note and underlinings to what Keats called 'bye-writing' (the lines which are not high poetry but serve to carry forward the action of the play) show that he was already keenly interested in play-construction. To this period Lord Houghton assigned the extracts from an opera and that tantalizing fragment of 'The Castle Builder' with its Browningesque opening:

> To-night I'll have my friar—let me think
> About my room,—I'll have it in the pink;
> It should be rich and sombre, and the moon,
> Just in its mid-life in the midst of June,
> Should look thro' four large windows and display
> Clear, but for gold-fish vases in the way,
> Their glassy diamonding on Turkish floor;
> The tapers keep aside, an hour and more,
> To see what else the moon alone can show;
> While the night-breeze doth softly let us know
> My terrace is well bower'd with oranges.

After a minute and pre-Raphaelitish description of the room ('It is a gorgeous room, but somewhat sad'), the fragment ends:

> My wine—O good! 'tis here at my desire,
> And I must sit to supper with my friar.

An ominous atmosphere is maintained throughout the speech. It is full of dark vowels and blunt consonants with a hint of thunder and fateful lighting in the lines:

> And opposite the stedfast eye doth meet
> A spacious looking-glass, upon whose face,
> In letters raven-sombre, you may trace
> Old "Mene, Mene, Tekel Upharsin."

A few more speeches from the projected play have come to light. The Castle Builder is telling 'Bernadine' (presumably a monk or friar) that if he has got wisdom from 'Convent libraries' he himself has

> . . . been carding
> A longer skein of wit in Convent Garden.

Bernadine shows an eager interest and the Castle Builder goes on:

> Sir, Convent Garden is a monstrous beast
> From morning, four o'clock, to twelve at noon,
> It swallows cabbages without a spoon.
> And then, from twelve to two, this Eden made is
> A promenade for cooks and ancient ladies;
> And then for supper, 'stead of soup and poaches,
> It swallows chairmen, damns, and Hackney coaches.
> In short, Sir, 'tis a very place for monks,
> For it containeth twenty thousand punks,
> Which any man may number for his sport,
> By following fat elbows up a court.

This is eighteenth-century Covent Garden in a nutshell. Keats had already achieved that essential in the art of a dramatist, the power of condensation. The description is clear, succinct, and calls up a complete and immediate picture in the mind of the hearer.

Almost certainly in the February of this year he wrote that sonnet which is more than Shakespearean; an echo of Shakespeare's own voice, 'To a Lady seen for a few Moments at Vauxhall.'

Time's sea hath been five years at its slow ebb,
  Long hours have to and fro let creep the sand,
Since I was tangled in thy beauty's web,
  And snared by the ungloving of thine hand.
And yet I never look on midnight sky,
  But I behold thine eye's well memory'd light;
I cannot look upon the rose's dye,
  But to thy cheek my soul doth take its flight.
I cannot look on any budding flower,
  But my fond ear, in fancy at thy lips
And hearkening for a love-sound, doth devour
  Its sweets in the wrong sense;—Thou dost eclipse
Every delight with sweet remembering,
And grief unto my darling joys dost bring.

Woodhouse put February 4th against this poem. Copies of the poems
in Keats's own handwriting often bear, not the date of composition,
but that of a fair copying, but if the 4th were the date of composition
on this day he wrote two sonnets. He told his brothers that 'The
Wednesday before last' (February 4th) 'Shelley, Hunt and I wrote each
a Sonnet on the River Nile. . . .' The three poems survived and in the
contest clearly the slighter poet won, though he had to sit up half the
night to complete his verses.

   February 19th was a warm sunny morning, a harbinger of spring.
On a black winter bough a thrush was singing. The poet was shaken
from his new activity, tempted by the halcyon day to idleness; but his
idleness was fruitful. His mind strayed from nature to books, from books
to nature and then turned in upon itself. The result of his meditation
was a remarkable letter to Reynolds. At a risk of being overlengthy in
quotation I give it in full: it is such a masterly shadowing-forth of a
mood of the creative mind at once a source of strength and a snare.

I had an idea that a Man might pass a very pleasant life in this manner—let
him on a certain day read a certain Page of full Poesy or distilled Prose,
and let him wander with it, and muse upon it, and reflect upon it, and bring
home to it, and prophesy upon it, and dream upon it, until it becomes stale
—but when will it do so? Never. When Man has arrived at a certain ripeness
in intellect any one grand and spiritual passage serves him as a starting-post
towards all "the two-and-thirty Palaces". How happy is such a voyage of
conception, what delicious diligent Indolence! A doze upon a sofa does not
hinder it, and a nap upon Clover engenders etherial finger-pointings—the
prattle of a child gives it wings, and the converse of middle-age a strength to
beat them—a strain of music conducts to "an odd angle of the Isle", and
when the leaves whisper it puts a girdle round the earth. Nor will this
sparing touch of noble Books be any irreverence to their Writers—for perhaps
the honors paid by Man to Man are trifles in comparison to the Benefit done

by great Works to the Spirit and pulse of good by their mere passive existence. Memory should not be called knowledge.

Many have original minds who do not think it—they are led away by Custom. Now it appears to me that almost any Man may like the spider spin from his own inwards his own airy Citadel—the points of leaves and twigs on which the spider begins her work are few, and she fills the air with a beautiful circuiting. Man should be content with as few points to tip with the fine Web of his Soul, and weave a tapestry empyrean full of symbols for his spiritual eye, of softness for his spiritual touch, of space for his wandering, of distinctness for his luxury. But the Minds of Mortals are so different and bent on such diverse journeys that it may at first appear impossible for any common taste and fellowship to exist between two or three under these suppositions. It is however quite the contrary. Minds would leave each other in contrary directions, traverse each other in numberless points, and at last greet each other at the journey's end. An old Man and a child would talk together and the old Man be led on his path and the child left thinking.

Man should not dispute or assert but whisper results to his neighbour and thus by every germ of spirit sucking the sap from mould etherial every human might become great, and Humanity instead of being a wide heath of Furze and Briars with here and there a remote Oak or Pine, would become a grand democracy of Forest Trees!

It has been an old comparison for our urging on—the Beehive; however, it seems to me that we should rather be the flower than the Bee—for it is a false notion that more is gained by receiving than giving—no, the receiver and the giver are equal in their benefits. The flower, I doubt not, receives a fair guerdon from the Bee—its leaves blush deeper in the next spring—and who shall say between Man and Woman which is the most delighted? Now it is more noble to sit like Jove than to fly like Mercury—let us not therefore go hurrying about and collecting honey, bee-like buzzing here and there impatiently from a knowledge of what is to be aimed at; but let us open our leaves like a flower and be passive and receptive—budding patiently under the eye of Apollo and taking hints from every noble insect that favours us with a visit—sap will be given us for meat and dew for drink.

I was led into these thoughts, my dear Reynolds, by the beauty of the morning operating on a sense of Idleness—I have not read any Books—the Morning said I was right—I have no idea but of the morning, and the thrush said I was right—seeming to say,

> O thou whose face hath felt the Winter's wind,
> Whose eye has seen the snow-clouds hung in mist,
> And the black elm-tops 'mong the freezing stars,
> To thee the Spring will be a harvest-time.
> O thou, whose only book has been the light
> Of supreme darkness which thou feddest on
> Night after night when Phœbus was away,
> To thee the Spring shall be a triple morn.
> O fret not after knowledge—I have none

> And yet my song comes native with the warmth.
> O fret not after knowledge—I have none,
> And yet the Evening listens. He who saddens
> At thought of idleness cannot be idle,
> And he's awake who thinks himself asleep.

Now I am sensible all this is mere sophistication (however it may neighbour to any truths), to excuse my own indolence—so I will not deceive myself that Man should be equal with Jove—but think himself very well off as a sort of scullion-Mercury, or even a humble Bee. It is no matter whether I am right or wrong, either one way or another, if there is sufficient to lift a little time from your shoulders.

The last phrase is probably a sly dig at his friend who was unlikely to be finding time heavy or slow down at Exeter.

H. Buxton Forman comments on the Thrush poem: 'Keats seems to have been really writing in a kind of spiritual parallelism with the thrush's song; it will be noted that line 5 repeats the form of line 1, line 8 of line 4, while lines 11 and 12 are a still closer repetition of lines 9 and 10: so that the poem follows in a sense the thrush's method of repetition ... I think it hardly fantastic to suppose that he consciously translated the wild melody of the thrush into an unrhymed sonnet-structure.'

To this period, so rich in sonnets, there belongs the fine one to Homer:

> Standing aloof in giant ignorance,
>   Of thee I hear and of the Cyclades,
> As one who sits ashore and longs perchance
>   To visit dolphin-coral in deep seas.
> So thou wast blind;—but then the veil was rent,
>   For Jove uncurtain'd Heaven to let thee live,
> And Neptune made for thee a spumy tent,
>   And Pan made sing for thee his forest-hive;
> Aye on the shores of darkness there is light,
>   And precipices show untrodden green,
> There is a budding morrow in midnight,
>   There is a triple sight in blindness keen;
> Such seeing hadst thou, as it once befel
> To Dian, Queen of Earth, and Heaven, and Hell.

Rossetti considered the eleventh line to be one of the finest in all poetry. In 'There is a triple sight in blindness keen' Keats may have had not only Homer, but Milton, in mind. He was reading Milton with Dilke who was an enthusiast, and lately had been startled into a new consciousness of him by seeing at Hunt's a lock of his bright hair. In his Milton Keats has appended the following note to Book I, lines

53 to 75 of *Paradise Lost*, where Satan in Hell rouses from his torpor and discovers the 'sights of woe' in 'darkness visible':

One of the most mysterious of semi-speculations is, one would suppose, that of one Mind's imagining into another. Things may be described by a Man's self in parts so as to make a grand whole which that Man himself would scarcely inform to its excess. A Poet can seldom have justice done to his imagination—for men are as distinct in their conceptions of material shadowings as they are in matters of spiritual understanding: it can scarcely be conceived how Milton's Blindness might here aid the magnitude of his conceptions as a bat in a large gothic vault.

Incidentally, and showing Keats's dramatic perception, he comments on 'round he throws his baleful eyes,' 'nothing can be more impressive and shaded than the commencement of the action here—'

Keats was probably made more consciously critical at this time by hearing Hazlitt lecture on the English poets at the Surrey Institution. These lectures, gripping and stimulating to a reader, must have been doubly so when the sublime sense and brilliant paradox came winged from the man himself. He read in a strong level voice, his dark hair falling forward over his high, white forehead. From time to time he would fix the audience with his large eyes, mazed and defiant, to drive a point home.

Hazlitt employed the keen edge of paradox to pierce the tough husk of the minds of his hearers, the majority of whom were Dissenters who agreed with him in his hatred of the existing Government, Quakers who approved of his advocacy of social reforms, and homely folk who came to improve their minds; people to whom much of the matter he dealt with was either godless or unfamiliar—or both. To a large number of more receptive ears his modernity must have been both bewildering and offensive. One hearer more open to new voices, Crabb Robinson, he affronted by his attacks on Wordsworth. Some who were open enemies of this truculent man came to sneer: a few friends and admirers listened with rapt attention, applauded and agreed. Keats himself placed Hazlitt's 'depth of taste,' together with 'The Excursion' and Haydon's pictures, as 'the three great things to rejoice at in the Age.' He was stimulated and amused by the fiery spirit of the man. 'He is your only good damner and if ever I am damn'd—damn me if I shoul'nt like him to damn me.'

Keats could not accept Hazlitt's estimate of Chatterton, that figure of ill-starred fate so romantic to the early nineteenth century, in whom Hazlitt saw little evidence of anything more than an extraordinary precocity. Probably Keats's disappointment at his treatment of Chatterton was conveyed to Hazlitt, either in person or at second hand, for he prefaced his next lecture by 'I am sorry that what I said . . . should have given dissatisfaction to some persons, with whom I would willingly agree in all such matters.' He then enlarged on his previous statement that the boy Chatterton had shown no definite promise of future greatness but quoted in full the poem he considered the best, the Minstrel's song in Ælla, including Keats's favourite verse beginning: 'Comme, wythe acorne-coppe and thorne.'

It was a sign of his growing reputation that Hazlitt, although he did not really value Keats's poetry till after his death, should pay him the compliment of explaining his attitude in regard to Chatterton. But Keats's fame was growing not only within the Hazlitt–Hunt–Haydon circle but in a wider and more prosperous one. In his own words:

I am in the highway of being introduced to a squad of people, Peter Pindar, Mrs Opie . . . Mr Robinson, a great friend of Coleridge's, called on me—Richards tells me my Poems are known in the West Country, and that he saw a very clever copy of verses, headed with a Motto from my Sonnet to George—Honors rush so thickly upon me that I shall not be able to bear up against them.

'Peter Pindar' was Dr. Wolcot, the political satirist, Mrs. Opie, fashionable novelist, wife of John Opie the painter and a cousin of Woodhouse, Crabb Robinson the diarist and assiduous cultivator of literary men.

Keats was no social climber, nor had he any regard for worldly reputation as a poet or he might long ago have improved acquaintance with an early admirer, Horace Smith, whom he visited, Haydon records, with Hunt and Shelley as early as January, 1817. In 1812 the brothers James and Horace Smith, upon making the Town laugh with their famous *Rejected Addresses*, had, although they were City men, found all the fashionable drawing-rooms thrown open to them. Keats now told George and Tom:

I dined . . . with Horace Smith, and met his two Brothers, with Hill and Kingston, and one Du Bois. They only served to convince me, how superior humour is to wit in respect to enjoyment—These men say things which make one start, without making one feel; they are all alike; their manners are alike; they all know fashionables; they have a mannerism in their very eating and drinking, in their mere handling a Decanter—They talked of Kean and his low company—Would I were with that Company instead of yours, said I to myself! I know such like acquaintance will never do for me.

James and Horace Smith and Edward Dubois, the editor of *The Monthly Mirror*, were all modish wits. They threw with the dexterity of practice a glittering ball of conversation : since wit must have a target the ball might hit someone on a tender spot, but this was part of the game. The Smiths, kindly, thoughtful men, might have suited their conversation to the earnest young romantic, but Dubois was dull in serious discourse and preferred to shine in a darting virtuosity of light malice.

These men had before them that evening a perpetual subject of jest, an insensitive butt, Thomas Hill, the 'literary drysalter' who never took offence so long as he might be among these brilliant men of letters. Hill was a fat, florid, excitable little man, like an elderly cupid, who told richly improbable stories, ending a ridiculous hyperbole with 'Sir, I affirm it with all the solemnity of a death-bed utterance. Sir, I happen to *know* it.' His age was a matter of mirthful speculation. No skill in questioning could draw it from him. 'The fact is, Hill,' said James Smith, 'that the register of your birth was destroyed in the great fire of London, and you take advantage of that to conceal your real age.' Theodore Hook said he might originally have been one of the little Hills recorded as skipping in the Psalms. Perhaps on this occasion he did not skip much, for Keats does not seem to have got any amusement out of him.

It seems difficult to include among these men who were 'all alike' 'the thing Kingston' who was almost certainly that Comptroller of the Stamp Office with his 'mild namby pamby opinions,' who asked Wordsworth silly questions on the night of Haydon's 'immortal dinner.' Of the third Smith brother, Leonard, we know nothing except that he was a prosperous business man.

Looking back on the records of these last wits of the eighteenth century one cannot help feeling a certain amount of sympathy with Keats. One gets weary of their good sayings, even on paper; there were so many of them. One wishes they would be humanly dull for a grateful breathing-space. Keats's attitude to them is interesting as indicative of a change in humour in the two generations; a change which was transforming the bitter personal invective of a Gillray through the kindlier ridicule of Cruikshank to the typical English impersonal humour of the *Punch* artists later in the century.

It was perhaps unfortunate for Keats from a worldly point of view that he was not happy in the company of these men who were all successful and influential; perhaps he might have been spared in some measure the attacks on him in the Tory press if he had moved habitually among them. But Keats would not have been John Keats if he had been worldly-minded.

On December 28th Haydon gave in his painting room what is known to us as 'the immortal dinner.' Of it Keats wrote:

there was Wordsworth, Lamb, Monkhouse, Landseer, Kingston and your humble Sarvant. Lamb got tipsey and blew up Kingston—proceeding so far as to take the Candle across the Room hold it to his face and show us wh-a-at-sort-fello-he-waas I astonished Kingston at supper with a pertinacity in favour of drinking—keeping my two glasses at work in a knowing way—

Hunt was not there. Haydon had now quarrelled openly with him. His antagonism had come to a head over a trivial matter. Mrs. Hunt, a feckless housekeeper, was in the habit of borrowing silver from Haydon. On this occasion Haydon asked for his property back by a certain date: it was not returned so he sent for it. 'Hunt went to expostulate on the indelicacy &c.—they got to words and parted for ever,' wrote Keats. 'All I hope is at some time to bring them all together again.'

Haydon's account in his journal of the dinner is, though not perhaps so highly a work of art as Tom Taylor's version,[1] vivid and amusing:

Dec. 28—Wordsworth dined with me. Keats & Lamb with a Friend made up the dinner party and a very pleasant party we had—Wordsworth was in fine and powerful cue—we had a glorious set to on Homer, Shakespeare, Milton & Virgil—Lamb got excessively merry and witty—and his fun in the intervals of Wordsworth's deep & solemn intonations of oratory, was the fun & wit of the fool in the intervals of Lear's passion—Lamb soon gets tipsey—and tipsey he got very shortly—to our infinite amusement. "Now you rascally Lake Poet" said Lamb "you call Voltaire a dull fellow"—We all agreed there was a state of mind when he would appear so—And "Well let us drink his health" said Lamb—"Here's Voltaire 'the Messiah of the French nation,' and a very fit one"—He then attacked me for putting in Newton—"a Fellow who believed nothing unless it was as clear as the three sides of a triangle." Then he & Keats agreed he had destroyed all the Poetry of the rainbow, by reducing it to a prism! It was impossible to resist them, and we drank Newton's health and "confusion to mathematics!" It was delightful to see the good Humour of Wordsworth in giving in to all our frolics without affectation and laughing as heartily as the best of us—by this time other visitors began to drop in—& a Mr Ritchie who is going to penetrate into the interior of Africa—I introduced him to Wordsworth, as such—& the conversation got into a new train. After some time Lamb who had seemingly [been] paying no attention to any one—suddenly opened his eyes and amid alluding to the danger of penetrating into the interior of Africa—"and pray who is the Gentleman we are going *to lose*"—here was a roar of laughter the

[1] *Diary*, vol. II, p.173.

Victim Ritchie joining with us—we now retired to Tea, and among other Friends a Gentleman who was *comptroller of the Stamp Office* came, he had been peculiarly anxious to know and see Wordsworth—the moment he was introduced he let Wordsworth know who he officially was. This was an exquisite touch of human nature . . Tho' Wordsworth of course would not have suffered him to speak indecently, or impiously without reproof—yet he had a visible effect on Wordsworth—I felt pain at the slavery of office— In command men are despotic, and those who are dependent on others who have despotic controul must & do feel affected by their presence—the Comptroller was a very mild & nice fellow but rather weak & very fond of talking—he got into conversation with Wordsworth on Poetry and just after he had been putting forth some of his silly stuff[1]—Lamb who had been dozing, as usual suddenly opened his mouth and said—"What did you say 'Sir' "? "Why Sir" said the Comptroller in his milk & water insipidity, "I was saying" etc etc etc—"Do you say so Sir?"—Yes Sir was the reply—"Why then Sir, I say"—hiccup—"You are—you are a silly fellow." This operated like thunder!—the Comptroller knew nothing of his previous tipsiness & looked at him like a man bewildered. The venerable anxiety of Wordsworth to prevent the Comptroller being angry, and his expostulations with Lamb, who had sunk back again into his doze, as insensible to the confusion he had produced as a being above it—the astonishment of Landseer the Engraver who was totally deaf & with his hand to his ear & his eyes was trying to catch the meaning of the gestures he saw, & the agonizing attempts of Keats, Ritchie & I to suppress our laughter, and the smiling struggle of the Comptroller to take all in good part, without losing his dignity made up a story of comic expressions totally unrivalled in Nature—I felt pain that such a Poet as Wordsworth should be under the supervisorship of such a being as the Comptroller—the People of England have a horror of Office—and instinct against it—they are right—a man's liberty is gone the moment he becomes official—he is the Slave of Superiors, and makes others slaves to him—the Comptroller went on making his profound remarks—and when any thing very *deep* came forth Lamb roared out,

> Diddle iddle don
> My son John
> Went to bed with his breeches on
> One Stocking off & one Stocking on
> My son John—

the Comptroller laughed as if he mocked it & went on. Every remark Lamb chorussed with

> Went to bed with his breeches on
> Diddle iddle on—

There is no describing this scene adequately—there was not the restraint

[1] Here Haydon interpolated in 1823 '(Such as "Pray, Sir, don't you think Milton a very *great genius?*" This I really recollect.)'

of refined company, nor the vulgar freedom of low—but a frank natural license, such as one sees in an act of Shakespeare, every man expressing his natural emotions without fear. Into this company a little heated with wine, a Comptroller of the Stamp Office walked frilled, dressed, & official, with a due awe of the powers above him, and a due contempt of those beneath him—his astonishment at finding where he was come cannot be conceived, and in the midst of his mild namby pamby opinions, Lamb's address deadened his views. When they separated, Wordsworth softened his feelings, but Lamb kept saying in the Painting [room] "Who is that fellow? let me go and hold the candle once more to his face—

> My Son John
> Went to bed with his breeches on

and these were the last words of C. Lamb. The door was closed upon him.

There was something interesting in seeing Wordsworth sitting, & Keats & Lamb, & my Picture of Christ's entry towering up behind them occasionally brightened by the gleams of flame that sparkled from the fire, & hearing the voice of Wordsworth repeating Milton with an intonation like the funeral bell of St. Paul's, & the music of Handel mingled—and then Lamb's wit came sparkling in between & Keats's rich fancy of Satyrs & Fauns & doves, & white clouds, wound up the stream of conversation—I never passed a more delightful day—& I am convinced that nothing in Boswell is equal to what came out from these Poets—indeed there were no such Poets in his time—it was an evening worthy of the Elizabethan age—and will long flash upon "that inward eye" which is the bliss of Solitude——

Hail & farewell!

Since writing this, poor Ritchie is dead! he died on this rout, 1819—Lamb's feeling was prophetic!

Keats too is gone! how one ought to treasure such evenings when life gives us so few of them—1823 Nov—

Lamb is gone too!—

Monkhouse, the other Friend, is gone. Wordsworth & I alone remain of the party. If the Comptroller lives I know not. Jany 24—1837.

We find the Comptroller of the Stamp Office later inviting both Wordsworth and Keats to dinner but, said Keats, 'not liking that place I sent my excuse.' He hated too to see Wordsworth, once so strong a Liberal, bowing to established authority and going to dine in a stiff collar.

Keats was, however, naturally flattered, when Wordsworth, whom he met frequently during his stay in Town, called and invited him to dinner. Now he met the poet's 'beautiful wife and enchanting sister.' The 'sister' was in fact Wordsworth's sister-in-law, Sara Hutchinson.

On the whole Keats was disappointed in Wordsworth and perhaps to a certain extent this was inevitable: Wordsworth emerged so seldom from his northern 'shell' that he was a half-legendary figure to the young men. Leigh Hunt said of him at this time: 'I never beheld eyes that looked so inspired or supernatural. They were like fires half burning, half smouldering, with a sort of acrid fixture of regard. . . . One might imagine Ezekiel or Isaiah to have had such eyes. . . .' It was impossible that Keats at the outset should not have felt the power of the man. But Hunt added to the above: 'He had a habit of keeping his left hand in the bosom of his waistcoat; and in this attitude, except when he turned round to take one of the subjects of his criticism from the shelves, he was dealing forth his eloquent but hardly catholic judgments.' The poet who had expressed so simply and finely both the new delight in nature and man's joys and sorrows was now, in his forty-eighth year, fast dwindling down into a humourless, didactic egoist who cared for no contemporary poetry but his own.

During one visit to Wordsworth the sage was making some weighty pronouncements to Keats upon poetry. Keats, in full agreement with what he was saying, was about to make an assenting remark. He had scarcely opened his mouth before Mrs. Wordsworth, that sedulous acolyte, had put her hand upon his arm, saying: "Mr. Wordsworth is never interrupted."

Keats wrote in some irritation to Reynolds:

. . . for the sake of a few fine imaginative or domestic passages, are we to be bullied into a certain Philosophy engendered in the whims of an Egotist— Every man has his speculations, but every man does not brood and peacock over them till he makes a false coinage and deceives himself. Many a man can travel to the very bourne of Heaven, and yet want confidence to put down his half-seeing. . . . We hate poetry that has a palpable design upon us—and if we do not agree, seems to put its hand in its breeches pocket. Poetry should be great and unobtrusive, a thing which enters into one's soul, and does not startle it or amaze it with itself, but with its subject. . . . Modern poets differ from the Elizabethans in this. Each of the moderns like an Elector of Hanover governs his petty state, and knows how many straws are swept daily from the Causeways in all his dominions and has a continual itching that all the Housewives should have their coppers well scoured. . . . I will have no more of Wordsworth or Hunt in particular—

There had been one galling experience. At the first meeting Keats, at Haydon's request, had recited his hymn to Pan from *Endymion*, that great passage so directly inspired by Wordsworth. The result was unexpected. I quote Haydon's own account:

Wordsworth received him kindly, & after a few minutes, asked him what he had been lately doing. I said he had just finished an exquisite ode to Pan—and as he had not a copy I begged Keats to repeat it—which he did in his usual half chant, (most touching) walking up & down the room—when he had done I felt really, as if I had heard a young Apollo—Wordsworth dryly said

"a Very pretty piece of Paganism."

This was unfeeling & unworthy of his high Genius to a young worshipper like Keats—& Keats felt it *deeply*. This apparently cold-blooded comment struck the company dumb and broke up the party.

The young Wordsworth, that ardent spirit hailing the French Revolution and toiling in poverty at poetry so near to nature and to the heart of man, was hardening into the elderly pontifical and conservative versifier. His best work was behind him. But once he had written:

> —Great God! I'd rather be
> A pagan suckled in a creed outworn;
> So might I, standing on this pleasant lea,
> Have glimpses that would make me less forlorn;
> Have sight of Proteus rising from the sea;
> Or hear old Triton blow his wreathed horn.

In defence of Wordsworth it must be said that, although Severn considered that Keats read the hymn well, there were others who thought that, as most poets do, he read his own verse badly. Also it is likely that Haydon had been filling Wordsworth's ear with stories of the young man's unorthodox ideas and deploring the influence of Hunt who was present on this occasion. It may be that the 'pretty piece of paganism' was in part an improving and reproving remark.[1]

Throughout Keats's letters we catch pleasant glimpses of his early friend, Severn, whom he introduced into his literary circle and tried to interest in Haydon. But in regard to Haydon, Severn was sharper-eyed than Keats who, though he was revolted by Wordsworth's large claims, accepted on less sure grounds Haydon's bid for greatness. Severn, although interested in Haydon's work, was almost frightened by 'his excessive vanity and presumption.'

Severn enjoyed meeting Keats's friends but he enjoyed still more his solitary company. On Sundays, the only day on which Severn was free from toilsome miniature-painting, more ambitious attempts in oils and art-classes, they would take long walks in the country.

Even to the artist trained to use his eyes Keats's power of observation was an abiding marvel. The song of a bird, the rustle of small creatures in the hedges, the changing light and shadow with their shifting colours, the swaying of a leaf, a branch, the shivering of tall grasses,

---

[1] Further, Mrs. Moorman, Wordsworth's biographer, points out to me that he often talked of 'very pretty verses etc. meaning that he liked them.'

the slow pageant of the clouds; nothing escaped him. He was aware, too, of the human beings they met; the creeping animalism of the many tramps in that starving, workless age, a woman's bright hair, the smile of a rosy child. The sea was never far from his mind. When a wind arose and went, as he said, 'billowing through a tree' or he heard it springing up from afar across a dark-hued woodland he would shout 'The tide, the tide!' and leap up on to a stile or a low bough and await its coming, listening with breath held and cheeks a-glow, 'like a young fawn waiting for some cry from the forest-depths.' Then he would watch intent for the wind to sweep in a gusting wave across the corn or the young tender grasses beneath him.

The rustle of this 'inland sea' was the only thing that could rouse him from certain heavy moods in which he was liable to fall. His eyes veiled in a profound shadow, he would shrink into himself, only answering his companion coldly and absently. From fields of oats or barley with their white shivering response to every breeze it was difficult to move him. The sea or an image of the sea could always bring him back to happy calm.

To the sea he was very soon to go now, to Teignmouth to take George's place beside his ailing brother Tom. On March 4th he set out by night from 'The Bull and Mouth', Holborn, in a terrific storm during which several mail and stage coaches were overturned with injury to passengers. Keats, however, as he wrote later, though travelling outside, 'escaped being blown over and blown under & trees & houses being toppled on me.'

CHAPTER XII

At Teignmouth (March—May, 1818)

TEIGNMOUTH in South Devon would seem to-day an odd choice for Tom, but a mild climate was held to be essential to the cure of consumption far into the nineteenth century. On his brother's arrival Tom was certainly rather better in health; and had a great fancy to his medical attendant, a Dr. William Turton, M.D., F.L.S., who had made a special study of his disease.[1]

The cheerful bustle of a busy port too must have been welcome to the sick boy. He might go down to the harbour at the mouth of the Teign and see the ships being loaded for Liverpool with the pipe and potter's clay from the pits at Kingsteignton, the fishing vessels bound for the Mediterranean markets, or the big seines being dragged out of the water by women. The fishing women were picturesquely dressed 'à la Hollandaise' and an old guide-book says, in recommending this as a sight of the town, 'the mingled air of satisfaction at the expectation of a large draught of fishes, and the chagrin and disappointment pictured on their sunburnt countenances, when a few crabs make their appearance, would not be an unfit subject for the pencil of a Rowlandson.' Tom would have arrived too late in the year to see the Newfoundland fishing fleet sail for their long sojourn in the West. If he were well enough for a walk he might take an easy stroll along the Teign to neighbouring villages or saunter in the sheltered lanes where the deep hedgerows never lose their hint of spring. For George there were steep climbs over Haldon and towards Dawlish along fine sloping cliffs with the sea below.

The town was then divided into two by a stream, the Tame, which now runs below Wellington and Bank Streets. The pleasantly irregular streets were well-paved. In the Public Rooms there were an Assembly, a reading and a billiard room: there was a theatre, Croydon's Library, pleasure boats on the Teign and the sea and bathing machines 'upwards of twelve in number' which 'may justly boast a superiority over those of any other part of the kingdom.' If you took a machine you were ducked with ceremony by a bathing man or woman and in winter it cost you a shilling; double what was charged in summer. This was probably a survival of the uncomfortable old notion that bathing was only beneficial in winter when the pores of the skin were not so open

---

[1] Author of medical and other scientific works, including a Conchological Dictionary.

and you were less likely to take a cold. Keats apparently bathed but he probably did it in a less gentlemanly and more active style in the early morning from the shore.

At No. 20, the Strand, there is a granite plate on the face of the old white Georgian house to the effect that John Keats lived here in 1818. This, by no means a certainty, rests on the memory of one old man in 1901 who said that his father, William Rufus Jordan, a solicitor in the town, had told him that Keats had dined with him one evening and informed him he was lodging in either 21, or 22, the Strand. H. Buxton Forman was able to narrow this down to what is now No. 20. We know that there was opposite Keats's lodging a bonnet-shop—he used to talk to the girls employed there—but reference to old directories failed to track down a bonnet-shop in the Strand at that date. There was one, however, in the thirties, at No. 35, at the corner of Queen Street nearly opposite to No. 20 the Strand which may already have been there in 1818.

If Keats did lodge at No. 20 he had opposite to him a warehouse for the Newfoundland fishery, and perhaps, writing in the window, he looked up at the gaunt outlines of the warehouse and was reminded of the misty regions of the west when he wrote to Reynolds on March 14th:

Write to me . . . or by the holy Beaucœur—which I suppose is the virgin Mary, or the repented Magdalen, (beautiful name, that Magdalen) I'll take to my Wings and fly away to any where but old or Nova Scotia—

The Strand leads to the Den, a ridge of hard sandbank by the sea now levelled and planted with grass and flower-beds. This was the centre of the seaside life and was referred to by Keats in a letter to the Misses Jeffrey written after his departure:

You might praise it (Teignmouth) . . . in the manner of a grammatical exercise—*The* trees *are* full—*the* den *is* crowded—*the* boats *are* sailing—*the* musick *is* playing.

'*The* musick,' a lively orchestra, still plays in summer on the Den.

In March visitors to Teignmouth could not have been numerous enough to crowd the Den: the friends the Keatses made there were residents of the town. They became intimate with a family named Jeffrey, a widow and four daughters, Marian, Sarah, Fanny and a young one with long hair and 'a hard brown fist.' Keats's mention of the hard brown fist suggests that the brothers were on scuffling terms with the younger ones; with the elder girls their relations were equally lively.

There was flirting among the young people but at least one of the daughters, 'the steady quiet' Marian, was intelligent beyond the average and a fit companion for Keats. There was a tradition in the town that he was in love with her; a tradition founded probably on a love-poem in a volume of verse published by Marian as Mrs. I. S. Prowse after her marriage. The verses are in a musical and thoughtful style, with distinct references to the death of Keats and echoes of lines in 'Lamia' and 'Hyperion.' While Keats was in Devon he acquired a black-letter Chaucer which he may have enjoyed with Marian: she employed in certain of these poems the Chaucerian stanza so little in use at the time.

When Lord Houghton was collecting material for his life of Keats, Sarah, the second daughter, wrote offering information. but received no reply to her letter. From her he might have gathered much that would illuminate Keats's life at this period. It is possible that she was 'one of the girls in the bonnet-shop over the way.' We know that in later life she made bonnets for a Lady Tonkin. If this were so, friendship with the family may have ripened from casual chat between the young lodgers at No. 20 and 'the laughing, thoughtless Sarah.'

The effect of John upon the Jeffrey girls was eagerly debated by his admiring brothers. After George had returned to Town and John had taken his place he wrote to the Misses Jeffrey:

How do you like John? Is he not very original? he does not look by any means as handsome as four months ago, but is he not handsome? I am sure you must like him very much, but don't forget *me*. I suppose Tom gets more lively as his health improves. Tell me what you think of John.

George and John were together at Hampstead for a few days. There must have been anxious discussion of ways and means. George had been out of employment for some time. He was now engaged to Miss Wylie and wanted to secure a future for himself.

Keats left London for Teignmouth on March 4th in a heavy storm, on the outside of the coach. His long journey was made the more tiresome by a change: the coach only ran, through Salisbury, Dorchester, Bridport and Honiton, to Exeter. There he could take either the *Royal Express Coach* or the *Diligence* which was slower but cheaper. Even if he took the faster vehicle the last lap of the journey would take him three hours. He would arrive at Teignmouth about seven o'clock in the evening.

His first three days at Teignmouth were a disappointment. The weather was vile. It rained, that heavy, hopeless Devonshire rain which blots out the view except when the wind, tearing aside the thick wet fog of moisture, reveals a green and lovely landscape. 'The hills,' Keats wrote, 'are very beautiful, when you get a sight of 'em . . . the Cliffs are of a fine deep Colour, but then the Clouds are continually vieing with them.' In a jaundiced frame of mind due to fatigue, the weather, and enforced inactivity he dubbed, on very short acquaintance indeed, the men of Devon

the poorest creatures in England—because Government never have thought it worth while to send a recruiting party among them. When I think of Wordsworth's Sonnet 'Vanguard of Liberty! ye Men of Kent!' the degenerated race about me are Pulvis Ipecac. Simplex[1]—a strong dose. Were I a Corsair I'd make a descent on the South Coast of Devon, if I did not run the chance of having Cowardice imputed to me: as for the Men they'd run away into the methodist meeting houses, and the Women would be glad of it. Had England been a large devonshire we should not have won the Battle of Waterloo . . . there are vallies of femminine Climate but there are no thews and Sinews. . . . I fancy the very Air of a deteriorating quality—I fancy the flowers, all precocious, have an Acrasian spell about them—I feel able to beat off the devonshire waves like soap froth.

Keats revealed in the reference to the Methodist meeting-houses his lack of knowledge of the place: there were at this time few Methodists in Teignmouth. Perhaps he had heard his brother or his landlady speak of the 'neat Dissenting Chapel' which had just been erected; the first in the town. Also in abusing the men of Devon Keats probably did not know that most of the able-bodied farm-labourers went off with the Newfoundland fleet, after the harvest had been gathered in, to gut and cure the fish. Of the Teignmouth women Keats said: 'The Women are like your London people in a sort of negative way.' Later he said he admired the beauty of the Devonshire women especially 'the middle-sized delicate Devonshire girls of about 15.'

The passage above, quoted from a letter to Bailey on March 13th, is followed by this fervent expression of feeling:

I like I love England. I like its strong Men. Give me a long brown plain for my Morning so I may meet with some of Edmond Ironside's descendants. Give me a barren mould so I may meet with some Shadowing of Alfred in the Shape of a Gipsey, a Huntsman or a Shepherd. Scenery is fine—but human nature is finer.

Here is the change in outlook which had made him turn from Shakespeare's fairy-tale comedies to *King Lear* and the tragedies; a deepening of the human spirit within him. His contempt at the moment for the

---

[1] An emetic.

men of Devon seems almost an obsession: 'I wonder I meet with no
born Monsters—O Devonshire, last night I thought the Moon had
dwindled in heaven.'

This letter to Bailey began whimsically with an apology for not
having written before and a reply to, or an anticipation of, some
friendly reproaches:

Why did I not stop at Oxford in my Way?—How can you ask such a
Question? Why did I not promise to do so? Did I not in a Letter to you
make a promise to do so? Then how can you be so unreasonable as to ask me
why I did not? This is the thing—(for I have been rubbing up my invention;
trying several sleights—I first polish'd a cold, felt it in my fingers tried it on
the table, but could not pocket it: I tried Chilblains, Rheumatism, Gout,
tight Boots, nothing of that sort would do, so this is, as I was going to say,
the thing.—I had a Letter from Tom saying how much better he had got,
and thinking he had better stop—I went down to prevent his coming up.
Will not this do? Turn it which way you like—it is selvaged all round.

There was a tactful and warm-hearted reference to a printed sermon
of Bailey's,

I have never had your Sermon from Wordsworth but Mrs Dilke lent it to
me. You know my ideas about Religion. I do not think myself more in the
right than other people, and that nothing in this world is proveable. I wish
I could enter into all your feelings on the subject merely for one short
10 Minutes and give you a Page or two to your liking. I am sometimes so
very sceptical as to think Poetry itself a mere Jack a lanthen to amuse who-
ever may chance to be struck with its brilliance. As Tradesmen say every
thing is worth what it will fetch, so probably every mental pursuit takes its
reality and worth from the ardour of the pursuer—being in itself a nothing.

Then followed a richly Keatsian passage,

Etherial things may at least be thus real, divided under three heads—Things
real—things semireal—and no things. Things real—such as existences of
Sun Moon & Stars and passages of Shakspeare. Things semi-real such as
Love, the Clouds &c which require a greeting of the Spirit to make them
wholly exist—and Nothings which are made Great and dignified by an
ardent pursuit—which by the by stamps the burgundy mark on the bottles
of our Minds, insomuch as they are able to "*consecrate whate'er they look upon.*"

This quotation is from Shelley's 'Hymn to Intellectual Beauty' and
one of the few references to contemporary poetry, other than Wordsworth's, in Keats's letters. The Hymn had been published in *The
Examiner* in the previous January. Keats then wrote out for Bailey a

sonnet of his own 'of a somewhat collateral nature,' 'Four seasons fill the measure of the year.' A comparison of the two poems, both for subject-matter and the handling of it, will reveal the essential differences between the two young poets.

He continued his letter in a vein which, although typically romantic, is startlingly modern:

. . . it is an old maxim of mine and of course must be well known that every point of thought is the centre of an intellectual world—the two uppermost thoughts in a Man's mind are the two poles of his World he revolves on them and everything is southward or northward to him through their means. We take but three steps from feathers to iron.

Then, feeling perhaps that this was a little beyond the scope of the young clergyman and might even draw down upon his head a rebuke, he added with bubbling humour:

Now my dear fellow I must once for all tell you I have not one Idea of the truth of any of my speculations—I shall never be a Reasoner because I care not to be in the right, when retired from bickering and in a proper philosophical temper. So you must not stare if in any future letter I endeavour to prove that Apollo as he had cat gut strings to his Lyre used a cats paw as a Pecten—and further from said Pecten's reiterated and continual teasing came the term Hen peck'd.

At the end he gave bad news. Tom had just had a spitting of blood.

Apart from his love for Tom, Keats was physically affected by illness: perhaps it was this sympathy, so strong that it might be called empathy, which made him take up medicine and surely would have made him, if he had not felt the stronger call of poetry, a great healer. Now, when he was not putting his mind and full strength into the battle with disease; working positively to combat it, this intense sympathy was a burden, a pain, especially with those he loved. To Reynolds, at home and seriously ill with a rheumatic fever, he wrote:

. . . I hope by this you stand on your right foot—If you are not—that's all,—I intend to cut all sick people if they do not make up their minds to cut sickness—a fellow to whom I have a complete aversion, and who strange to say is harboured and countenanced in several houses where I visit—he is sitting now quite impudent between me and Tom—He insults me at poor Jem Rice's—and you have seated him before now between us at the Theatre —when I thought he look'd with a longing eye at poor Kean. I shall say, once for all, to my friends generally, and severally, cut that fellow, or I cut you.

There was so close a link between them that Keats could be sure that Reynolds would read this seemingly callous outburst in the right spirit.

It is symptomatic of his mood of depression, shadowed over as he was by Tom's illness and by the dark, wet weather, that he did not speak of poetry to Reynolds and could not even think of 'a little innocent bit of metaphysic,' for

a favorite tune is hardest to be remembered when one wants it most and you, I know have long ere this taken it for granted that I never have any speculations without associating you in them, where they are of a pleasant nature, and you know enough of me to tell the places where I haunt most, so that if you think for five minutes after having read this you will find it a long letter, and see written in the Air above you,

Your most affectionate friend,
John Keats.

Although the weather continued uncertain there were some fine periods in which he explored vigorously the country round. On March 23rd he sent to Haydon those delightful impromptu lines, 'here all the summer could I stay':

> For there's Bishop's teign
> And King's teign
> And Coomb at the clear teign head.
> Where close by the Stream
> You may have your cream
> All spread upon barley bread.

with its rejoicing over the rich spring blossoming of the West:

> And O, and O
> The Daisies blow
> And the Primroses are waken'd
> And the violet white
> Sits in silver plight
> And the green bud's as long as the spike end.

and ending:

> Then who would go
> Into dark Soho
> And chatter with dack'd hair'd critics
> When he can stay
> For the new mown hay
> And startle the dappled Prickets.

White violets, though not very common about Teignmouth, are

abundant at Bishop's Teignton. 'Close by the stream' are the Coombe Cellars, still a refreshment house, where cockles are fished up from the mud below and served with cream. Keats could not now get his barley bread though he still could see on the cliffland rustling fields of barley to delight him.

His rising spirits not only overflowed into this 'doggrel' but in a 'B——hrell' as he called it, 'Where be ye going you Devon maid' with its second verse,

> I love your Meads and I love your flowers
> And I love your junkets mainly
> But 'hind the door, I love kissing more
> O look not so disdainly!

This may have been a dig at Haydon who was fond of flirtation with a pretty girl. Once, in Paris, he found a pretty chamber-maid, went out on the stairs to flirt a little, but found, to his mortification, that a hussar officer 'all in a rattle of chains and spurs' had got there before him.

The verses end in a lovely movement:

> I'll put your Basket all safe in a nook
> And your shawl I hang up on this willow
> And we will sigh in the daisy's eye
> And Kiss on a grass green pillow.

Keats had in his letter attacked the weather once more and Haydon, good Devonian, asserted in his reply that he did not think Devonshire more rainy than any other county and that anyhow it had rained almost incessantly in town ever since Keats's departure. If there were rain in Devonshire he must have taken it with him.

On the 24th Keats wrote a light-hearted letter to Rice in the old spirit of hyperbole, saying:

I have seen every thing but the wind—and that they say becomes visible by taking a dose of Acorns or sleeping one night in a hog trough with your tail to the Sow Sow West. . . . I went yesterday to dawlish fair—

> Over the hill and over the dale,
> And over the bourn to Dawlish—
> Where Gingerbread Wives have a scanty sale
> And gingerbred nuts are smallish.

There followed in the next four verses 'B——hrell' rather more frank than that sent to Haydon.

A letter written to Reynolds the next day is not only of vital interest in the poetic life of Keats but, following as it does the amusing letter to Rice, shows how swiftly his protean spirit changed in mood and how with an exquisite tact he was able to adapt himself to his highly individual friends. Here is no 'B——hrell' suited to the lively Rice, but a rimed epistle illuminated with thought and beauty. The verse itself is direct and easy: it is interesting to compare it both for subject-matter and technical advance with the epistle to George written less than two years before. The luxuriant quality has gone; the pictures conveyed are simple in outline, touched with a surer hand. In the early epistle the rimes of the couplets are obtrusive, but in this letter, as in the major part of *Endymion*, they are imbedded in the fabric of the poem. It begins:

> Dear Reynolds, as last night I lay in bed,
> There came before my eyes that wonted thread
> Of Shapes, and Shadows and Remembrances,
> That every other minute vex and please:
> Things all disjointed come from North and south. . . .

There follows a fantastic group of disconnected images, and then:

> Few are there who escape these visitings—
> Perhaps one or two, whose lives have patent wings;
> And through whose curtains peeps no hellish nose,
> No wild boar tushes, and no Mermaid's toes:
> But flowers bursting out with lusty pride;
> And young Æolian harps personified,
> Some, Titian colours touch'd into real life.—
> The sacrifice goes on; the pontif knife
> Gleams in the sun, the milk-white heifer lows,
> The pipes go shrilly, the libation flows:
> A white sail shews above the green-head cliff
> Moves round the point, and throws her anchor stiff.
> The Mariners join hymn with those on land.—

Without wishing to detract from the quality of the last six lines I would call it near-poetry. In the 'Ode on a Grecian Urn,' written at a period when his aim was 'to load every rift with ore,' the picture is simplified, made more pregnant as,

> Who are these coming to the sacrifice?
> To what green altar, O mysterious priest,
> Lead'st thou that heifer lowing at the skies,
> And all her silken flanks with garlands drest?
> What little town by river or sea shore,
> Or mountain-built with peaceful citadel,
>   Is emptied of this folk, this pious morn?

The painting of which Keats gave a memory in the epistle was not a Titian but a Claude, 'Sacrifice to Apollo.' The confusion of names was natural enough; he had seen the picture hung beside a Titian at the British Institution in 1816. Probably a subconscious doubt about the painter's name led him on to a memory of another picture by Claude, the 'Enchanted Castle.' Of this he had probably only seen an engraving, though the original was within twenty-five miles of London, at Redleaf near Sevenoaks, Kent, in the collection of William Wells.

> You know the Enchanted Castle it doth stand
> Upon a Rock on the Border of a Lake
> Nested in Trees, which all do seem to shake
> From some old Magic like Urganda's sword.
> O Phœbus that I had thy sacred word
> To shew this Castle in fair dreaming wise
> Unto my friend, while sick and ill he lies.
>   You know it well enough, where it doth seem
> A mossy place, a Merlin's Hall, a dream.
> You know the clear Lake, and the little Isles,
> The Mountains blue, and cold near neighbour rills—
> All which elsewhere are but half animate
> Here do they look alive to love and hate;
> To smiles and frowns; they seem a lifted mound
> Above some giant, pulsing underground. . . .
>
> . . . The doors all look as if they oped themselves,
> The windows as if latch'd by fays & elves—
> And from them comes a silver flash of light
> As from the Westward of a Summer's night;
> Or like a beauteous woman's large blue eyes
> Gone mad through olden songs and Poesies—
>   See what is coming from the distance dim!
> A golden galley all in silken trim!
> Three rows of oars are lightening moment-whiles
> Into the verdurous bosoms of those Isles.
> Towards the Shade under the Castle Wall
> It comes in silence—now tis hidden all.
> The clarion sounds; and from a postern grate
> An echo of sweet music doth create
> A fear in the poor herdsman who doth bring
> His beasts to trouble the enchanted spring:

In these extracts from the epistle, the stuff of high poetry rather than poetry itself, there is more of Keats the individual than in his finished work: the completeness of the poetic conception is manifest, but the detachment of pure creation is not yet attained.

In the 'Nightingale' ode the above picture is transmuted into three lines:

> The same that oft-times hath
> Charm'd magic casements, opening on the foam
> Of perilous seas, in faery lands forlorn.

But Keats was no longer a boy who could find a refuge in dreams of natural and pictured beauty. On this mortal earth we

> . . . shadow our own Soul's daytime
> In the dark void of Night. For in the world
> We jostle—

His flag is not yet 'unfurl'd on the Admiral staff' so that he dare not yet philosophize:

> Things cannot to the will
> Be settled, but they tease us out of thought.
> Or is it that imagination brought
> Beyond its proper bound, yet still confined,—
> Lost in a sort of Purgatory blind,
> Cannot refer to any standard law
> Of either earth or heaven?—It is a flaw
> In happiness to see beyond our bourn—
> It forces us in Summer skies to mourn:
> It spoils the singing of the Nightingale.

He is now at that stage of development when the cruelty and the miseries of the world sit heavy and enigmatic on the shoulders of the young. On 'a Lampit Rock of green sea weed' lapped by the waves he sat one evening:

> The rocks were silent—the wide sea did weave
> An untumultuous fringe of silver foam
> Along the flat brown sand. I was at home,
> And should have been most happy—but I saw
> Too far into the sea; where every maw
> The greater on the less feeds evermore:—
> But I saw too distinct into the core
> Of an eternal fierce destruction,
> And so from Happiness I far was gone. . . .

> The Shark at savage prey—the hawk at pounce
> The gentle Robin, like a pard or ounce,
> Ravening a worm—

But this is no food for a sick man, so

> Away ye horrid moods,
> Moods of one's mind! You know I hate them well,
> You know I'd sooner be a clapping bell
> To some Kamschatkan missionary church,
> Then with these horrid moods be left in lurch—
> Do you get health—and Tom the same—I'll dance,
> And from detested moods in new Romance
> Take refuge—

The new romance was 'Isabella, or the Pot of Basil.' Very soon we find him writing to George for his folio Shakespeare in which he had placed the first few stanzas.

In a letter to Haydon of April 8th Keats gives us a further revelation of the workings of the poetic mind in speaking of

The innumerable compositions and decompositions which take place between the intellect and its thousand materials before it arrives at that trembling delicate and snail-horn perception of Beauty.

The delight of spring is coming upon the countryside, the primroses are out and

The Hedges by this time are beginning to leaf—Cats are becoming more vociferous—young Ladies that wear Watches are always looking at them— Women about forty five. think the season very backward—Ladie's Mares have but half an allowance of food—

but it is still rainy. Both brothers were feeling the effects of the dull, wet weather. 'Tom is quite low-spirited—It is impossible to live in a country which is continually under hatches.' In three weeks they had only six fine days. The wet weather gave Keats plenty of time within doors to finish his revision of *Endymion* and to work upon 'Isabella.' He sent his preface to *Endymion* to Reynolds for criticism. It had a strong personal note and to those who did not know him might have appeared inconsistent. 'I have written to please myself, and in hopes to please others, and for a love of fame' might not come well from a man who spoke of his 'modesty and non-opinion of himself.' Reynolds condemned it as, from the point of view of the public, affected and 'Huntian.' Keats bowed to Reynolds's superior knowledge of the book-world and rewrote the preface; defending, however, the imputed arrogance which arose from a knowledge of his high calling. 'I would fain escape the bickerings that all Works not exactly in chime bring upon their begetters—but this is not fair to expect, there must be conversation of some sort and to object shows a man's consequence.' 'I have not,' he wrote, the slightest feel of humility towards the Public—or to anything in existence, —but the eternal Being, the Principle of Beauty, and the Memory of great Men—When I am writing for myself for the mere sake of the Moment's enjoyment, perhaps nature has its course with me—but a Preface is written to the Public; a thing I cannot help looking upon as an Enemy, and which I cannot address without feelings of Hostility—If I write a Preface in a supple or subdued style, it will not be in character with me as a public speaker. . . .

I never wrote one single Line of Poetry with the least Shadow of public thought.

. . . I could not live without the love of my friends—I would jump down Ætna for any great Public Good—but I hate a Mawkish Popularity.—I cannot be subdued before them—My glory would be to daunt and dazzle the thousand jabberers about Pictures and Books—I see swarms of Porcupines with their Quills erect "like lime-twigs set to catch my Winged Book" and I would fright 'em away with a torch.

Not that, he said, his preface was much of a torch, but he could not keep out of it 'an undersong of disrespect to the Public.' He must write another 'without a thought of those people.'

Keats was now looking forward to the walking-tour he had planned to take with Charles Brown during the summer, a preliminary to more extended travel. 'If my Books will help me to it,—thus I will take all Europe in turn, and see the Kingdoms of the Earth and the glory of them.'

To us it is odd to think of a poet anticipating any considerable gain from poetry. But this was a verse-reading age: of two popular poets Byron had been given £1000 for a single canto of *Don Juan* and Tom Moore £3000 for *Lalla Rookh*. It would seem however that Keats, rather than under-estimating the intelligence of the public, was over-estimating it if he thought that such rare and original work as his would bring in sums large enough to allow of much travel, even in a modest way.

Endymion was published towards the end of April. On the 27th Keats sent a list of errata to Taylor and apologized for having left to him 'all the trouble of Endymion.' Although Cowden Clarke had some hand in the correcting of the proofs, Taylor appears to have done the main part of it with minute attention, even emending certain lines with the poet's consent. Keats philosophized sadly to him,

young Men for some time have an idea that such a thing as happiness is to be had and therefore are extremely impatient under any unpleasant restraining—in time however, of such stuff is the world about them, they know better and instead of striving from Uneasiness greet it as an habitual sensation, a pannier which is to weigh upon them through life.

On the first reading in the House of a bill for the prevention of cruelty to animals it was suggested that asses should be included. The Members rocked with laughter at the idea of the familiar beast of burden being protected. With this in mind Keats's metaphor of the pannier, too often loaded beyond the pitiful little creature's strength, gains in effect.

Keats was getting his impatient, ebullient nature under control. While at Teignmouth he was insulted at the theatre, probably by one of those troublesome fellows among whom it was the fashion to come in at half price and interrupt the performance with drunken outcries. Keats did not fight him. A few years nearer boyhood this would have been an irresistible provocation. Even now he was a little ashamed of the admission of pacifism. We hear only of one fight in adult years; the thrashing of a lout in Hampstead whom he found tormenting a kitten.

There may have been money-worries to add their weight to 'the burden of the mystery' at this time. We know that once Keats had to borrow from his landlady. That, however, might happen to the improvident as well as the needy: Keats was never careful with money.

On April 27th it was still raining. 'There is a continual courtesy between the Heavens and the Earth—The heavens rain down their unwelcomeness and the Earth sends it up again to be returned to-morrow.' It is not surprising to hear that Tom was worse.

Keats was determined to enlarge the bounds of his intellect not only in travel but in severe study. He who had been 'hovering for some time between an exquisite sense of the luxurious and a love for Philosophy' must now take the harder road. He wrote to Reynolds:

I . . . shall learn Greek, and very likely Italian—and in other ways prepare myself to ask Hazlitt in about a years time the best metaphysical road I can take. For although I take Poetry to be Chief, yet there is something else wanting to one who passes his life among Books and thoughts on Books— I long to feast upon old Homer as we have upon Shakespeare, and as I have lately upon Milton. If you understood Greek, and would read me passages, now and then, explaining their meaning, 'twould be, from its mistiness, perhaps a greater luxury than reading the thing one's self.

In a letter on May 3rd he expressed his attitude more generally in magnificent metaphor:

The difference of high Sensations with and without knowledge appears to me this—in the latter case we are falling continually ten thousand fathoms deep and being blown up again without wings and with all the horror of a bare shoulderd creature—in the former case, our shoulders are fledge, and we go thro' the same air and space without fear.

An extensive knowledge takes away 'the heat and fever'; it helps to 'ease the Burden of the Mystery.'

Were I to study physic or rather Medicine again, I feel it would not make the least difference in my Poetry; when the Mind is in its infancy a Bias is in reality a Bias, but when we have acquired more strength, a Bias becomes no Bias. Every department of Knowledge we see excellent and calculated towards a great whole.

He was glad he had not given his medical books away and would look through them from time to time to keep 'alive the little I know thitherwards.' This does not exactly square with Reynolds's statement that Keats never spoke of his student days except to regret that he had endured 'a one of them.'

There was an occasion when, if the story be true,[1] he was glad to exercise his late profession. Wells (or Horne) told an old school-fellow that, some time after Keats had abandoned medicine, they were walking together when Keats hurried forward to the help of a poor man who had met with an accident. His leg was broken and Keats immediately set it 'in a masterly manner.' As they walked away Keats remarked that 'there was great pleasure in alleviating suffering; but it was a dreadful profession, on account of having to witness so much.'

But, however much he might respect knowledge, actual experience is of the highest value:

. . . axioms in philosophy are not axioms until they are proved upon our pulses: We read fine things but never feel them to the full until we have gone the same steps as the Author.— . . . now I shall relish Hamlet more than I ever have done. . . . You are sensible no Man can set down Venery as a bestial or joyless thing until he is sick of it. . . . Until we are sick, we understand not; in fine, as Byron says, "Knowledge is Sorrow," and I go on to say that, "Sorrow is Wisdom"—and further for aught we can know for certainty "Wisdom is folly"!—

The lighter touch in the last phrase led him on to some gay nonsense and from thence he returned to high seriousness in that wonderful parable, a 'simile of human life':

I compare human life to a large Mansion of Many Apartments, two of which I can only describe, the doors of the rest being as yet shut upon me. The first we step into we call the infant or thoughtless Chamber, in which we remain as long as we do not think. We remain there a long while, and notwithstanding the doors of the second Chamber remain wide open,

---

[1] From a letter to the *Literary World*, April 4th, 1871. The writer describes his informant as 'Mr. Horne, the author of the drama of Joseph and his Brethren.' The author of this drama was Charles Wells.

showing a bright appearance, we care not to hasten to it; but are at length imperceptibly impelled by the awakening of this thinking principle within us—we no sooner get into the second Chamber, which I shall call the Chamber of Maiden-Thought, than we become intoxicated with the light and the atmosphere, we see nothing but pleasant wonders, and think of delaying there for ever in delight: However among the effects this breathing is father of is that tremendous one of sharpening one's vision into the heart and nature of Man—of convincing one's nerves that the world is full of Misery and Heartbreak, Pain, Sickness and oppression—whereby this Chamber of Maiden Thought becomes gradually darken'd and at the same time on all sides of it many doors are set open—but all dark—all leading to dark passages—We see not the ballance of good and evil. We are in a Mist. *We* are now in that state—We feel the "burden of the Mystery." . . .
. . . Now if we live, and go on thinking, we . . . shall explore them. . . .

He had been comparing the ethical values of Milton and Words-worth and had come to the conclusion that Wordsworth had the finer message, more by reason of 'the general and gregarious march of intellect' than by any individual greatness of mind. Milton was bound as a man of his time to place too much emphasis on the benefits of Protestantism and to consider it 'under the immediate eye of heaven.'

Continuing his parable:

Your third Chamber of Life shall be a lucky and a gentle one—stored with the wine of love—and the Bread of Friendship.

This graceful reference to Reynolds's future marriage may have been written with a purpose. Reynolds was ill and in poor spirits. Anxious, in view of his engagement, to insure a more certain livelihood, he had decided to become a lawyer and was now an articled clerk.

Reynolds disliked the law and did not do well in it in spite of exceptional opportunities. Rice, who had paid his articles, took him into partnership as soon as he was qualified and later abandoned the practice to him. Reynolds continued to write, but under the names of 'John Hamilton' and 'Edward Herbert': it was considered beneath the dignity of a professional man, or at least unwise, to be known as a writer. This divided interest may have helped seriously to injure his prospects and to prevent him from becoming either the writer he could have been or a good lawyer. Although John Reynolds had a certain success in his day he would, but for his association with Keats and Thomas Hood, be forgotten. But this was in the future; at present he was sitting uncomfortably on an office stool and trying to adapt himself to his chosen profession.

In Keats a native strength of mind was triumphing over dark circumstance; 'Tom had spit a *leetle* blood this afternoon, and that is rather a damper.' Tom was getting tired of Devonshire and restless to return to Town. The brothers decided to leave Teignmouth before they had planned.

Perhaps Keats felt some regret at leaving Devon, now, in spite of the rain, at the height of its beauty. The fields and hedgerows were rich with flowers and the wild cherry, the golden gorse, the myrtle and hydrangea bloomed to the edge of the sea. 'I shall,' he wrote, 'breathe worsted stockings' (on the restless legs of the Bentley boys) 'sooner than I thought for.' But he was looking forward to walks upon the Heath with Reynolds and rejoicings together over that new acquisition the black-letter Chaucer printed in 1596. Treasures of this kind were, in an age hardly awake to the glories of the old poetry, within the means of moderate purses.

At the beginning of May (before the 11th[1]) Keats was on his long weariful journey back to London with poor Tom so ill that at Bridport he lost a quantity of blood. They travelled in a chaise at least as far as Honiton, avoiding the longer, hilly journey up to Exeter by taking the coast road through Dawlish to Starcross, then up to Exminster and over the Exe by the Countess Weir Bridge. From Honiton Keats sent back to the kindly Mrs. Jeffrey a note saying that Tom had, so far, stood the journey well, and at one stage Tom wrote to 'the girls' thanking them for a parting present of flowers.

Back in Hampstead they found that George, unsuccessful in obtaining employment, had determined to emigrate to the back settlements of North America and turn farmer, taking with him Georgiana Wylie as wife. The prospect to Keats of the loss of a brother he loved, and on whom he leaned in wordly affairs, brought on the numb feeling again, 'the feel of not to feel it.' He wrote to Bailey:

I am in that temper that I were under Water I would scarcely kick to come to the top. I know very well 'tis all nonsense . . . I feel no spur at my Brothers going to America, and am almost stony-hearted about his wedding.

But there was a haven, a refuge in the sympathy of his friends, and he expressed it in a lovely simile, ' 'tis like the Albatross sleeping on its wings.'

Fate had already dealt none too kindly with Keats; now she was to weave into the web of his life darker and darker strands. But she wove on the bright warp of essential poetry friendship-threads of a lovely hue. In the allegory of his life, of the lives of all poets, it is perhaps easier to grasp the significance of the suffering, but the images of happiness have their primal meaning too. There must be light to darkness and for the shadow, the sun.

[1] *See* Haydon's *Diary*, vol. II, p. 198.

CHAPTER XIII

Endymion (1818)

KEATS himself wrote with regard to *Paradise Lost*, 'There is always a great charm in the openings of great poems.' *Endymion* opens with a line that is a household word and continues in a vein of rich, quiet beauty which sets the tone of the whole poem. In this first section there is the germ of all the beauty that is *Endymion*; 'sweet dreams,' and 'quiet breathing,' 'the sun, the moon, Trees old and young,' 'daffodils with the green world they live in,' 'clear rills,' 'the mid forest brake,' 'fair musk-rose blooms,' and 'the mighty dead, All lovely tales that we have heard and read.'

The story of Endymion has a dew upon it. It has not the actuality of the later work: the beings in it are not strongly-coloured, bold and definite but shadowed forth in 'dim dreams' and only occasionally emerge clear and bright from the shifting many-hued cloud of youthful imaginings. In 'The Eve of St. Agnes' though a stanza can be admired for its own beauty, it is a stanza of the complete poem and must be related to what went before and what follows, but here the accomplished passages can be picked out from the body of the work. And yet, fluid, unequal as *Endymion* is, it is an entity, a whole informed with an individual and rich poetic imagination; 'a little Region to wander in,' a world as complete and touched with new life as any Spenser made. Perhaps to realize the full enchantment of this dream-world we must read *Endymion* in youth when we can take in our stride the immature and 'mawkish' passages and travel with the shepherd-prince on earth, in air and water, with that ease of imagination we brought earlier to *The Arabian Nights* or to our own loved fairy-tales. The maturer mind will pick and choose, finding in its wanderings 'food for a Week's stroll in Summer'; a delight in mirrored nature and in passages of wrought poetry and pregnant thought.

Keats himself intended the poem to be an allegory. Endeavours have been made to work the fable out, but never with complete success. It is generally accepted, however, that the main thread is the quest of the poet after spiritual beauty.[1] To each of us the poem will yield something different: to me it appears that there is in it too the eternal quest for the love of woman. This was a strong element in the romantics and many, like poor Shelley, did not get beyond 'the desire

[1] For an interesting analysis of this and its kinship with the theme of *Oberon*, see Mr. Beyer's *Keats and the Daemon King*.

of the moth for the star,' that nympholeptic longing which made them look in every woman for a goddess. 'Some of us,' Shelley wrote sadly, 'have in a prior existence been in love with an Antigone, and that makes us find no full content in any mortal tie.' Keats was set more firmly on the earth; he was the more normal man and as poet could perhaps divine that physical love (the Indian maid) could blend with ideal love or beauty (the Moon goddess) in a perfect union.

The psychological value of physical love has been hailed as a modern discovery but it had its roots in the new freedom of emotion and thought at the beginning of the last century. There are indications that the relations between man and woman were talked of in Hunt's circle. Barry Cornwall tells us that Hunt himself 'had a crochet or theory about social intercourse (between the sexes) to which he never made any converts.' This used to irritate Hazlitt who said: 'Damn him, it's always coming out like a rash. Why doesn't he write a book about it, and get rid of it.' Bailey, although he admired *Endymion*, published two letters (signed N. Y.) in praise of it in the *Oxford University and City Herald*, and recommended the book to Oxford booksellers, deplored 'the moral part of it' and thought the poem 'indelicate.' He criticized to Taylor, 'The approaching inclination it has to that abominable principle of *Shelley's* that *Sensual Love* is the principle of *things*. Of this I believe him (Keats) to be unconscious and can see how by a process of imagination he might arrive at so false, delusive and dangerous a conclusion.'

On January 30th Keats sent to Taylor the passage in Book I, line 777, beginning 'Wherein lies happiness' with this comment:

. . . such a preface is necessary to the subject. The whole thing must I think have appeared to you, who are a consequitive Man, as a thing almost of mere words—but I assure you that when I wrote it it was a regular stepping of the Imagination towards a Truth. My having written that Argument will perhaps be of the greatest Service to me of anything I ever did. It set before me at once the gradations of Happiness even like a kind of Pleasure Thermometer—and is my first Step towards the chief attempt in the Drama—the playing of different Natures with Joy and Sorrow.

'the playing of different Natures with Joy and Sorrow.' The 'Argument' then is of supreme importance in the poem:

> "Wherein lies happiness? In that which becks
> Our ready minds to fellowship divine,
> A fellowship with essence; till we shine,
> Full alchemiz'd, and free of space. Behold
> The clear religion of heaven! Fold
> A rose leaf round thy finger's taperness,

And soothe thy lips: hist, when the airy stress
Of music's kiss impregnates the free winds,
And with a sympathetic touch unbinds
Æolian magic from their lucid wombs:
Then old songs waken from enclouded tombs;
Old ditties sigh above their father's grave;
Ghosts of melodious prophecyings rave
Round every spot where trod Apollo's foot;
Bronze clarions awake, and faintly bruit,
Where long ago a giant battle was;
And, from the turf, a lullaby doth pass
In every place where infant Orpheus slept
Feel we these things?—that moment have we stept
Into a sort of oneness, and our state
Is like a floating spirit's. But there are
Richer entanglements, enthralments far
More self-destroying, leading, by degrees,
To the chief intensity: the crown of these
Is made of love and friendship, and sits high
Upon the forehead of humanity.
All its more ponderous and bulky worth
Is friendship, whence there ever issues forth
A steady splendour; but at the tip-top,
There hangs by unseen film an orbed drop
Of light, and that is love: its influence,
Thrown in our eyes, genders a novel sense,
At which we start and fret; till in the end,
Melting into its radiance, we blend,
Mingle, and so become a part of it,—
Nor with aught else can our souls interknit
So wingedly: when we combine therewith,
Life's self is nourish'd by its proper pith,
And we are nurtured like a pelican brood.
Aye, so delicious is the unsating food,
That men, who might have tower'd in the van
Of all the congregated world, to fan
And winnow from the coming step of time
All chaff of custom, wipe away all slime
Left by men-slugs and human serpentry,
Have been content to let occasion die,
Whilst they did sleep in love's elysium.
And, truly, I would rather be struck dumb,
Than speak against this ardent listlessness:
For I have ever thought that it might bless
The world with benefits unknowingly;
As does the nightingale, upperched high,
And cloister'd among cool and bunched leaves—
She sings but to her love, nor e'er conceives
How tiptoe Night holds back her dark-grey hood.
Just so may love, although 'tis understood
The mere commingling of passionate breath,

Produce more than our searching witnesseth:
What I know not: but who, of men, can tell
That flowers would bloom, or that green fruit would swell
To melting pulp, that fish would have bright mail,
The earth its dower of river, wood, and vale,
The meadows runnels, runnels pebble-stones,
The seed its harvest, or the lute its tones,
Tones ravishment, or ravishment its sweet
If human souls did never kiss and greet?''

Endymion, his quest not yet begun, speaks of human love, or desire.
His thoughts turning to his immortal love, he adds:

"Now, if this earthly love has power to make
Men's being mortal, immortal; to shake
Ambition from their memories, and brim
Their measure of content; what merest whim,
Seems all this poor endeavour after fame,
To one, who keeps within his steadfast aim
A love immortal, an immortal too . . .
                          . . . No, no, I'm sure,
My restless spirit never could endure
To brood so long upon one luxury,
Unless it did, though fearfully, espy
A hope beyond the shadow of a dream"

In the fourth book there is an important passage when Endymion,
having caught a lovely glimpse of the moon in heaven, turns to the
Indian maid and finds her vanishing. Still reclining on his winged steed
his spirit goes into the 'native hell' where the ghosts of buried griefs
arise only to 'linger weeping' for a brief space,

                              . . . for the pierce
Of new-born woe it feels more inly smart:

This is despair, a state of mind common to us all. But here there
follows a difficult passage:

                    . . . the man is yet to come
Who hath not journeyed in this native hell.
But few have ever felt how calm and well
Sleep may be had in that deep den of all.
There anguish does not sting; nor pleasure pall:
Woe-hurricanes beat ever at the gate,
Yet all is still within and desolate.
Beset with plainful gusts, within ye hear
No sound so loud as when on curtain'd bier
The death-watch tick is stifled. Enter none
Who strive therefore: on the sudden it is won.

> . . . Happy gloom!
> Dark Paradise! where pale becomes the bloom
> Of health by due; where silence dreariest
> Is most articulate; where hopes infest;
> Where those eyes are the brightest far that keep
> Their lids shut longest in a dreamless sleep.
> O happy spirit-home! O wondrous soul!
> Pregnant with such a den to save the whole.
> In thine own depth. Hail, gentle Carian!
> For, never since they griefs and woes began,
> Hast thou felt so content: a grievous feud
> Hath led thee to this Cave of Quietude.

The retreat into the 'Cave of Quietude' Mr. Middleton Murry (*Studies in Keats*) claims as a mystic experience, but few of us have the gift or power of mysticism to follow him into those hidden regions of the spirit. My own interpretation is that Endymion, alone and forlorn, had to gather together the shattered pieces of his life and in pain of spirit withdraw into himself and there find himself. His young dreaming spirit had gone forth questing for the Moon-goddess and in that search he had been subject to the natural influences of earth, air and water with only the outward ethereal influence of the moon to sustain and guide him. This influence had not been strong enough to protect him from the physical beauty of the Indian maid and the transient human sympathy aroused by her weeping. He had lost himself and now he must withdraw into the fastness of his own being to find himself, to gain that inner control which alone enables a human being to give himself wholly and completely in love; the love that is stronger than death.

Returning to earth and finding the Indian maid once more beside him he decides upon a comfortable second-best, the love of the Indian maid and an abiding joy in nature. He is determined to put aside his love for Cynthia until the hour shall come

> When we shall meet in pure elysium.

But to a man loved by an immortal, to Keats touched with the divine fire and intuitively wise, the second-best is not possible and he is denied his earthly comfort. The Indian maid herself forbids it. She cries:

> "I may not be thy love: I am forbidden— . . .
> .   .   .   We might commit
> Ourselves at once to vengeance; we might die;
> We might embrace and die: voluptuous thought!"

To the human being voluptuous thought, voluptuous love alone is not food for the spirit but death. Endymion makes his renunciation:

" 'Mong men, are pleasures real as real may be:
But there are higher ones I may not see,
If impiously an earthly realm I take."

In this asceticism of spirit both he and the Indian maid prepare to retire from the world but the miracle happens, as it happens in rare cases to men and women who achieve a perfect love. The Indian maid is transformed into the Moon goddess: physical love between two controlled beings, masters of themselves, is fused with the spiritual love which is Beauty and a part of that love which passeth all understanding.

Love, Beauty, Truth, all these things were to merge in Keats's mind, a spiritual entity: in *Endymion* he is groping through the mists of unformed thought and imperfect poetic imagination towards all three.

In that candid preface which delivered him whole into the hands of the reviewer-slaughterers he said 'the reader . . . must soon perceive a great inexperience, immaturity and every error denoting a feverish attempt, rather than a deed accomplished . . . there is not a fiercer hell than the failure in a great object,' and in the unpublished preface, 'Before I began I had no inward feel of being able to finish; and as I proceeded my steps were all uncertain.' *Endymion* is a growth, a progression; he was in the 'go-cart,' learning to walk as he learnt in his eighteenth-century childhood to exercise his young limbs. The Keats who wrote the last word of *Endymion* at Burford Bridge in November had in a few months emerged, growing in strength, beauty and colour, from his chrysalis. Of the earlier *Endymion* period, when he was struggling to free himself, he wrote:

The imagination of a boy is healthy, and the mature imagination of a man is healthy; but there is a space of life between, in which the soul is in a ferment, the character undecided, the way of life uncertain, the ambition thick-sighted: thence proceeds mawkishness, and all the thousand bitters which those men I speak of must necessarily taste in going over the following pages.

'Those men I speak of' are those 'who are competent to look, and who do look with a jealous eye, to the honor of English literature.'

The preface ends in these lovely, balanced lines:

I hope I have not in too late a day touched the beautiful mythology of Greece, and dulled its brightness: for I wish to try once more, before I bid it farewell.

Apart from the great passages, there are in *Endymion* scattered

phrases which start out of the page, so pregnant, so vivid are they and
so classic in their simplicity:

> ... old Deucalion mountain'd o'er the flood,
> Or blind Orion hungry for the morn;

of the god of love,

> ... awfully he stands,
> A sovereign quell is in his waving hands;
> No sight can bear the lightning of his bow;

the Dramatic ending to Book II:

> The visions of the earth were gone and fled—
> He saw the giant sea above his head.

To the moon:

> O Moon! far-spooming Ocean bows to thee,

of Glaucus' bewitched love:

> ... Cold, O cold indeed
> Were her fair limbs, and like a common weed
> The sea-swell took her hair.

Many of the literary influences at work in *Endymion* have been
traced by scholars, with the recent inclusion of Sotheby's translation of
Oberon, but there is still a wealth of contemporary literature to be
examined. As an instance, the journeying of Endymion through earth,
water and air has rightly been attributed to Ovid's

> FIRE, AIRE, EARTH, WATER, all the Opposites[1]
> That strove in *Chaos*, powerful Love unites;

but may not the travels through earth, water and air in Southey's
The Curse of Kehama have to some extent kindled Keats's imagination?
He could hardly have avoided reading this strongly coloured and
dramatic poem which had run into four editions by 1818. It might too
have suggested to him the Indian maid.

Dr. Spurgeon has in her 'descriptive study' *Keats's Shakespeare*
pointed out the close analogy between Shakespearean passages and

---

[1] *See* Mr. Blackstone's The *Consecrated Urn* for a consideration of Keats and the quaternary
elements, points of the compass, etc.)

passages in *Endymion*. I give a few striking examples from *The Tempest*
and *A Midsummer Night's Dream*:

> Sometimes a thousand twangling instruments
> Will hum about mine ears;

> . . . . the swift treble pipe, and humming string.

> And pluck the wings from painted butterflies,
> To fan the moon-beams from his sleeping eyes:

> . . . yet, his eyelids,
> Widened a little, as when Zephyr bids
> A little breeze to creep between the fans
> Of careless butterflies:

> And for night-tapers, crop their waxen thighs,
> And light them at the fiery glow-worm's eyes,

> And, while beneath the evening's sleepy frown
> Glow-worms began to trim their starry lamps,

The Shakespearean passages above are all doubly marked, both
underscored and lined at the side, in Keats's seven-volume edition.
Although clearly derivative Keats's corresponding lines are not
imitative. He has wrought his memories into new and individual
conceptions.

Of those many adjectives not always happily used ending in -y, of
which 'pipy,' 'sluicy,' 'surgy' and 'towery' appear to be his own
coinage, Dr. de Sélincourt pointed out that they may have been
employed in the cause of melody to lighten the metre. The disappear-
ance of the lightly stressed terminal vowel syllables in English has led
to a definite loss of grace and lightness in rimed couplets. Dr. Bridges
pointed out that Chaucer's

> As thick as motës in the sonnë beams

becomes in Milton

> As the gay motes that people the sunbeams

He commented on the successful use of the lightly accented -y in

> In desolate places, where dank moisture breeds
> The pipy hemlock to strange undergrowth;

The archaic unelided -ed so much used by Keats in his early poems may have had something of the same purpose. This weakness he converted to a strength in his later work in such perfect usage as in

> .   .   . her vespers done,
> Of all its wreathéd pearls her hair she frees;
> Unclasps her warméd jewels one by one;
> Loosens her fragrant boddice;

and

> As when, upon a trancéd summer-night,
> Those green-rob'd senators of mighty woods,
> Tall oaks, branch-charméd by the earnest stars,

Endymion, in spite of Keats's growing reputation in the literary world, sold little better than the 1817 volume. Taylor himself was disappointed in the poem and probably did not anticipate a large sale. He had enjoyed the first book and after reading it had suggested publication in quarto provided Haydon would, as promised, provide a frontispiece for it. Haydon, however, who made a song to Keats about doing it as a favour he had not accorded to any other man, said he would draw a head of Keats in chalk but never went beyond the suggestion. The poem was denied the dignity of quarto. Probably this was a practical advantage; it was by 1818 rather old-fashioned to publish in quarto and, as Byron once pointed out to Hunt, it was 'the worst possible size for circulation.'

Reasons for the unpopularity of *Endymion* are many; the first and strongest being, of course, the difficulty every original genius has in making his voice heard in his own generation. Then there was his avowed connection with Hunt, the new-fangled poet of the Cockney School and libeller of princes. Keats himself reminded the public of this by an attack upon the ruling powers at the beginning of Book III:

> There are who lord it o'er their fellow-men
> With most prevailing tinsel: who unpen
> Their baaing vanities, to browse away
> The comfortable green and juicy hay
> From human pastures;
>
> .   .   .   . dight
> By the blear-ey'd nations in empurpled vests,
> And crowns, and turbans.

This was talk as dangerous and as unpalatable to the rich and fashionable buyers of books as Communism is to-day. Of this passage Keats himself said 'with much simplicity, "It will easily be seen what I think of the present ministers." '

The sub-title of the book was misleading to a public who thought of a romance as a love-story in a wild and Radcliffian setting. The astute Taylor had early realized this and advised the omission of 'A Poetic Romance,' but Keats had insisted, saying that a romance 'is a fine thing notwithstanding the circulating Libraries.'

Another weakness from the selling point of view was pointed out by a reviewer who said that 'nobody cares for mythological subjects nowadays.' The public in that post-war travelling age, in an age when reading was becoming rapidly more general and books more accessible, wanted something new. They liked highly coloured stories in novel settings. The East was fashionable. Not only did Southey's *The Curse of Kehama* go through four editions in eight years but his *Thalaba the Destroyer* was published in three editions between 1801 and 1814. Byron and Moore were paid huge sums for their poems in exotic settings and Campbell's *Gertrude of Wyoming*, a sensational story of the virgin lands of romance in North America, was immensely popular. Lustrous dark-eyed maidens, Eastern gods, peris, shadowy and sinister demons, the burning Ghat, Red Indians, djinns and afrids were the strong fare palatable to a wide public that nowadays would only tolerate its works of fiction in prose form. Scotland too was almost as novel to the readers of this age as the more distant lands of romance. Chiefs and pibrochs, castles and forays and above all the fashionable mountain scenery helped to create the vogue for the Wizard of the North. Among the older generation didactic poems with such titles as 'The Pleasures of Hope,' 'The Pleasures of Memory' were still enjoyed.

Then, apart from the thinness of the 'story' of the poem, there was what Bailey called its 'moral.' *Endymion* to people incapable of grasping its imaginative content contained a very doubtful moral or no moral at all. Reading aloud was general and family reading an institution. A generation that finds the 'kisses' and 'slippery blisses' of the poem either tiring, immature or amusing can scarcely realize the horror of the father of a family reading to a bevy of sewing daughters if he came across a passage like this:

> . . . he found
> The smoothest mossy bed and deepest, where
> He threw himself, and just into the air
> Stretching his indolent arms, he took, O bliss!
> A naked waist:

or

> Enchantress! tell me by this soft embrace,
> By the most soft completion of thy face,
> Those lips, O slippery blisses, twinkling eyes,
> And by these tenderest, milky sovereignties—

And, most damning of all to the reading public, there were the adverse reviews in the great Tory organs, the *Quarterly* and *Blackwood's*. It is difficult now to realize the deadly power of these journals. When Hazlitt's *Characters of Shakespeare's Plays* came out nearly two editions were sold in about three months. Then the *Quarterly* published a review in which they made the astounding statement that Hazlitt knew nothing whatsoever about Shakespeare, and there were no more copies sold.

Then there was the dread epithet of 'Cockneyism.' The pundits of the north, ever jealous of the reputation of their 'Athens,' were only too ready to bring this charge; a charge the full force of which cannot be realized nowadays. The old antagonism between Court and City had in some measure survived right into the nineteenth century and now the Arts were under the patronage of a ruler who prided himself on being a connoisseur.

The aristocracy was still inclined to despise and suspect the rising middle-classes and powerful enough to make their influence felt. Francis Place, the social and political reformer, was also a West End tailor of fashion. He had a large library of books above his shop which he kept sedulously concealed from his patrons. One day a clumsy assistant let an influential lord see into the library and Place's profits dropped by more than a thousand a year. The noble lord resented his tailor reading and said that the fellow couldn't cut his breeches properly if his head were full of such things. A tradesman was expected to be ignorant. In *Blackwood's* review of *Endymion* Keats was dubbed apothecary's apprentice: an apothecary was nothing more than a genteelish tradesman. The claims of 'ploughboy poets,' Clare or Bloomfield, might with safety be condescendingly recognized and there was the precedent of the now established Burns; but not those of a Cockney fellow.

Keats, whether from pride or distaste, had never talked of his origins. It must have been a bombshell to him to read:

Of all the manias of this mad age, the most incurable, as well as the most common, seems to be no other than the *Metromanie*. The just celebrity of Robert Burns and Miss Baillie has had the melancholy effect of turning the heads of we know not how many farm-servants and unmarried ladies; our very footmen compose tragedies, and there is scarcely a superannuated governess in the island that does not leave a roll of lyrics behind her in her bandbox. To witness the disease of any human understanding, however feeble, is distressing; but the spectacle of an able mind reduced to a state of insanity is of course ten times more afflicting. It is with such sorrow as this that we have contemplated the case of Mr. John Keats. This young man appeared to have received from nature talents of an excellent, perhaps even of a superior order—talents which, devoted to the purpose of any useful profession, must have rendered him a respectable, if not an eminent citizen. His friends, we understand, destined him to the career of medicine, and he was bound apprentice some years ago to a worthy apothecary in town. But all has been undone by a sudden attack of the malady to which we have alluded. Whether Mr. John has been sent home with a diuretic or composing draught to some patient far gone in the poetical mania, we have not heard. This much is certain, that he has caught the infection, and that thoroughly.

Keats might have felt the more bitter if he had known it was a personal friend who put this handle into the treacherous grasp of Lockhart and Wilson, that irresponsible pair who sheltered behind the anonymity of 'Z'. An attack was unexpected: in spite of a threat in October, 1817, when Keats had been referred to as an 'amiable and infatuated bard-ling,' it had been thought that the 'Mother of Mischief' would deal comparatively gently with *Endymion*; a friend of Lockhart, J. H. Christie, having met Keats in London and reported favourably on him. Lockhart had said that if Christie would write a short review of Keats's new work 'in admonition to leave his ways etc. and in praise of his natural genius' he would publish it.

In the meantime Bailey had gone north to a Cumberland curacy. While staying with Bishop Gleig in Stirling he met Lockhart and pleaded with him on Keats's behalf, pointing out that his connection with Leigh Hunt was a purely private one, in no sense political; and unwarily giving him details of Keats's early life. With a pang perhaps of misgiving he asked that this information should be regarded as a confidence: Lockhart replied that certainly it should not be used by *him*. This is the version of the story given by Archdeacon Bailey to Lord Houghton in 1849, but to Taylor on August 29th of this year he told a different tale; the ominous name of Lockhart was not mentioned. 'I met a man in Scotland who is concerned in that publication, (*Blackwood's*) who abused poor Keats in a way that, although it was at the Bishop's table, I could hardly keep in temper. I said I supposed then he would be attacked in Blackwoods. He replied 'not by *me*', which should convey the insinuation he would by someone *else*. . . .' Thus, prefacing his account with the remark that he feared *Endymion* would be 'dreadfully cut up' in *Blackwood's*, Bailey disingenuously paved the way for the attack and dexterously shielded himself from the reproach of causing Keats to be dubbed 'apothecary's boy,' since this half-confession would be taken by his candid friend as a full one.

It would seem as if Bailey let his tongue run away with him. It is only fair to add that he did try to make amends, calling on Mr. Black-wood and telling him roundly that his conduct was 'infamous.' He asked to be allowed to print a letter in his journal in defence of Keats, but Blackwood refused. Bailey then wrote an article in defence of his friend and attacking *Blackwood's* and sent it to Constable's *Edinburgh Magazine*, but it was rejected.

Endymion was dismissed as 'calm, settled, imperturbable drivelling idiocy.' Hunt's prediction of the future greatness of Keats in *The Examiner* was referred to as 'precocious adulation' which

confirmed the wavering apprentice in his desire to quit the gallipots, and at the same time excited in his too susceptible mind a fatal admiration for the character and talents of the most worthless and affected of all the versifiers of our time.

Hunt was called the author of the 'odious and incestuous "Story of Rimini." ' Keats's youthful praise in the 1817 volume of Hunt and Haydon was ridiculed:

The nations are to listen and be dumb! and why, good Johnny Keats? because Leigh Hunt is the editor of the Examiner, and Haydon has painted the judgment of Solomon, and you and Cornelius Webb, and a few more city sparks, are pleased to look upon yourselves as so many future Shakespeares and Miltons! The world has really some reason to look to its foundations!

They 'roasted' Keats for his young unwary utterances about high poetic aims in 'Sleep and Poetry.' His attack on Pope was called the reviling of an uneducated and flimsy stripling. Then they turned their attention to the group of juvenile verses in the 1817 volume:

From some verses addressed to various individuals of the other sex, it appears . . . that Johnny's affections are not entirely confined to objects purely etherial.

Taking the lines from the verses in the 1817 volume addressed To * * * *, referring to the girl's breasts 'like two twin lilies', and

> The little loves that fly
> Round about with eager pry

they called them 'prurient and vulgar lines, evidently meant for some lady east of Temple-bar.'

In *Endymion* 'Cockney rhymes,' and the 'loose, nerveless versification' were condemned as Huntian, but

Mr. Hunt is a small poet, but he is a clever man. Mr. Keats is a still smaller poet, and he is only a boy of pretty abilities, which he has done everything in his power to spoil . . . Endymion . . . has as much to do with Greece as it has with "old Tartary the fierce."

They quoted a good deal but ignored the finest passages, making much of the 'mawkish' lines, and ended with:

It is a better and a wiser thing to be a starved apothecary than a starved poet; so back to the shop Mr. John, back to the "plasters, pills, and ointment boxes," &c. But, for Heaven's sake, young Sangrado, be a little more sparing of extenuatives and soporifics in your practice than you have been in your poetry.

Keats had said that if *Blackwood's* attacked him he should be compelled to call the writer out, but it was impossible to challenge a ghost, a shadow. These two cowards had refused to come forward to any of *The Examiner's* taunts or threats.

When in early 1824 this review came into George's hands his anger was deep. He wrote to Dilke that 'a cudgelling should have been his (Blackwood's) reward if he had been within my reach; John was the very soul of courage and manliness, and as much like the *holy Ghost*, as *Johnny Keats*.'

The attack had one pretty sequel. An admirer in Devon sent Keats a sonnet beginning

> Star of high promise!—not to this dark age
> Do thy mild light and loveliness belong;—

and predicting fame through the ages. At the end was a direction to 'turn over.' He turned over and found a banknote for twenty-five pounds. He wrote to George in America: 'This appears to me all very proper—if I had refused it—I should have behaved in a very braga-dochio dunder-headed manner—' But the present 'galls him a little' and he is not sure that, if ever he should meet with the donor, he would not return it.

The sonnet and note were sent through Taylor and Hessey and in the case of non-delivery were to be returned to a 'Mr. P. Fenbank P.O. Teignmouth.' Mr. Blunden has suggested that 'Mr. P. Fenbank' was Richard Woodhouse, who had taken this roundabout way of sending the gift that Keats should not suspect any of his friends and feel hurt in his pride. When Keats was setting out on his last voyage to Italy Woodhouse gave him a letter in which he pressed him to call on him for money if he needed it and ending,

> "one, whose hand will never scant
> From his poor store of fruits all *thou* canst want."—

These are the two last lines of the sonnet sent in 1818 by 'Mr. P. Fenbank.'

Taylor, fearing an adverse criticism in the *Quarterly*, had called upon the editor to ask him not to review *Endymion* in a political partisan spirit. The saturnine William Gifford received him with cold civility and Taylor carried away no hope of mercy. Gifford gave the book for review to John Wilson Croker, a die-hard in the Popean school. Haydon had also made an attempt to soften the editor's heart: he had begged Mrs. Hoppner, the wife of the artist and a friend of Gifford's, to go and see him. In Haydon's own words:

She told me she found him writing with his green shade before his eyes, totally insensible to all reproach or entreaty. "How can you, Gifford, dish up in this dreadful manner a youth who has never offended you?" "It has done him good," replied Gifford; "he has had £25 from Devonshire." Mrs. Hoppner was extremely intimate with Gifford, and she told me she had a great mind to snatch the manuscript from the table and throw it in the fire. She left Gifford in a great passion, but without producing the least effect.[1]

Haydon was confusing the two attacks in the Tory organs and he has not made it clear whether this call was made after or before the review came out. The circumstances, however, are not here so important as the atmosphere of implacability he evokes.

The review was in a copy of the journal dated April, but appearing in the dilatory editorial manner of that time in September. Croker professed to find *Endymion* unreadable:

we have made efforts almost as superhuman as the story appears to be, to get through it . . . we have not been able to struggle beyond the first of the four books . . . It is not that Mr. Keats, (if that be his real name, for we almost doubt that any man in his senses would put his real name to such a rhapsody), it is not, we say, that the author has not powers of language, rays of fancy, and gleams of genius—he has all these; but he is unhappily a disciple of the new school of what has been somewhere called Cockney poetry; which may be defined to consist of the most incongruous ideas in the most uncouth language . . . This author is a copyist of Mr. Hunt; but he is more unintelligible, almost as rugged, twice as diffuse, and ten times more tiresome and absurd than his prototype, who . . . generally had a meaning.

He quoted the unwise admission in the preface of 'great inexperience, immaturity and every error denoting a feverish attempt, rather than a deed accomplished,' and professed to see no meaning even in this. On a further passage 'The two first books, and indeed the two last, I feel sensible are not of such completion as to warrant their passing the

---

[1] *Autobiography*, p. 251. I have been unable to corroborate or correct this passage from the Journals.

press,' Croker quite reasonably commented that if that were Keats's own estimate of the work the first book will suffice to give him an idea of the whole. He would have spared him the 'fierce hell' of criticism if he 'had not begged to be spared that he might write more.' To a writer as young, criticism would be salutary in putting him 'in the right way.' The story 'seems to be mythological,' but he could not grasp it:

At first it appeared to us, that Mr. Keats had been amusing himself and wearying his readers with an immeasurable game at *bouts-rimés*; but, if we recollect rightly, it was an indispensable condition at this play, that the rhymes when filled up shall have a meaning . . . our author . . . has no meaning. . . . There is hardly a complete couplet inclosing a complete idea in the whole book.

He continued to criticize in his old-fashioned way, making wilful nonsense of some of the opening lines, picking out 'new words' coined 'in imitation of Leigh Hunt,' and including among them Elizabethan words. He ended with the promise that if anyone bought *Endymion* and got beyond the first book and found a meaning he would, if that person informed him of his success, 'return to the task which we now abandon in despair, and endeavour to make all due amends to Mr. Keats and to our readers.'

There may have been some party-bias in this, but it was probably, so far as it went, a genuine criticism. The ears of the old-fashioned Croker,[1] irreverently nicknamed the 'Talking Potatoe,' were accustomed to this:

> TWILIGHT'S soft dews steal o'er the village-green,
> With magic tints to harmonize the scene.
> Stilled is the hum that thro' the hamlet broke,
> With round the ruins of their antient oak
> The peasants flocked to hear the minstrel play,
> And games and carols closed the busy day.

The above is the opening to 'The Pleasures of Memory' by the last of the 'silk-stocking' poets of the eighteenth century, Samuel Rogers. It is no wonder that when Croker came upon this,

> A THING of beauty is a joy for ever:
> Its loveliness increases; it will never
> Pass into nothingness; but still will keep
> A bower quiet for us, and a sleep
> Full of sweet dreams, and health, and quiet breathing.

he felt it was all wrong.

[1] Dubbed by the indignant Woodhouse in a letter to Keats 'a cobbling, carping, decasyllabic, finger-scanning, criticaster.'

The criticism of the *Quarterly* was countered on October 11th by an article in the *Alfred, West of England Journal*, the Exeter paper, by Reynolds, attributing party rancour:

no one but a Lottery Commissioner and Government Pensioner (both of which Mr. William Gifford, the Editor of the Quarterly Review, is) could, with a false and remorseless pen, have striven to frustrate hopes and aims, so youthful and so high as this young poet nurses.

To an enthusiastic praise of Keats he added quotations from some of the loveliest passages. But the *Alfred* was a provincial organ; though the article might have helped sales locally it could have little effect against the blarings of the *Quarterly* and *Blackwood's*. There was also a well-written laudatory paragraph in *The Chester Guardian*. The writer thought *Endymion* likely to be 'caviar to the general' but containing, apart from the finer joy to be extracted from it by classical scholars, many beauties within the comprehension of the lesser informed. He attacked the *Quarterly's* 'contemptible piece of flippancy' intended to 'put down' a young Liberal aspirant.

Two letters were written to the editor of *The Morning Chronicle* in protest against the bitterness of the *Quarterly* critique. The first was signed J. S. In it the writer suggested that the 'Admiralty Scribe' (Croker was Secretary to the Admiralty Board) should 'compare the "Battle of Talavera" with "Endymion."' The poem suggested for comparison was by Croker himself. The second letter was signed R. B. and came from the Temple. The writer contented himself by giving quotations from the one book handled by Croker and leaving the reader to 'judge whether the Critic who could pass over such beauties as these . . . is very implicitly to be relied on.'

The Liberal organ, Baldwin's *London Magazine*, in a review as late as April, 1820, followed the same line, protesting against attempts to 'blight and wither the maturity of genius.' *Endymion*, though 'not a poem at all,' is 'an ecstatic dream of poetry . . . an involuntary outpouring of the spirit of poetry.' After summarizing favourably and quoting, the writer added, 'We cannot refrain from asking, is it credible that the foregoing extracts are taken, almost at random, from a work in which a writer in the most popular . . . critical journal of the day, has been unable to discover anything worthy to redeem it from mere contempt.' The critic considered Keats's works, although sometimes faulty in construction, 'richer in promise than any other that we are acquainted with, except those of Chatterton.'

Apart from the personal attack on Keats in *Blackwood's*, the vilest of the adverse reviews was that in *The British Critic* of June, 1818, the organ

of the powerful Tory Church party. It began: 'This is the most delicious
poem, of its kind, which has fallen to our notice,' leading the unwary
reader to expect a favourable critique. It continued in the old weariful
way of reference to Hunt and then embarked on an ill-written, garbled
and nonsensical account of *Endymion*, misquoting lines and making
sheer balderdash of the story. The quality of the 'humour' of the writer
can be gathered from such sentences as these: ' "there blossom'd
suddenly a magic bed of sacred ditamy" (Qu. dimity?)'; '. . . he fell
into a "stupid sleep" from which he was roused by "a gentle creep,"
(N.B.—Mr. Tiffin is the ablest bug-destroyer of our days).' The lines,

> Who lov'st to see the hamadryads dress
> Their ruffled locks where meeting hazels darken;

he mauled in 'Pan was a god "who loves to see the Hamadryads
dress." ' Of the 'mawkish' passages he said, with the typical prudery of
a dirty-minded man:

not all the flimsy veil of words in which he would involve immoral images
can atone for the impurity; and we will not disgust our readers by retailing
to them the artifices of vicious refinement, by which, under the semblance
of "slippery blisses, twinkling eyes, soft completion of faces, and smooth
excess of hands," he would palm upon the unsuspicious and the innocent,
imaginations better adapted to the stews.

The review ended:

We do most solemnly assure our readers that this poem, containing 4074
lines, is printed on very nice hot-pressed paper, and sold for 9/– by a very
respectable London bookseller. Moreover, as the Author has put his name
in the title page, and told us, that though he is something between man and
boy, he means by and by to be "plotting and fitting himself for verses fit to
live." We think it necessary to add that it is all written in rhyme, and for the
most part, (when there are syllables enough) in the heroic couplet.

This was a high-handed journal. In a May issue it had dismissed
Canto IV of *Childe Harold* with the comment, 'it would be very well for
an ordinary prize poem at the University.'

The Literary Journal for May 17th and 24th had a friendly and
understanding review with copious quotation. The reviewer took up
the volume with a feeling of distaste for 'In this *poetizing age* we are led
to look with an eye of suspicion on every work savouring of rhyme.'
He failed to respond to the first thirty lines and then he began to elevate
his 'critical eye-brows' and exclaimed: 'And this is poetry!' The

passage in which Glaucus hails Endymion as the man who is to release
him from his thousand years of decrepitude he quotes, saying that it
'will strongly remind the reader of the rapturous exclamations of Ariel,
when promised his freedom by Prospero.' There seems to be no parallel
passage in *The Tempest*, but the writer has probably run together a
recollection of the song, 'Where the bee sucks' and Ariel's words:

> That's my noble master!
> What shall I do? say what; what shall I do?

which has something of the movement of four lines of Glaucus' speech:

> O Jove, I shall be young again, be young!
> O shell-borne Neptune, I am pierc'd and stung
> With new-born life! What shall I do? Where go,
> When I have cast this serpent-skin of woe?

The writer of course could not keep Mr. Hunt out but he said:

The measure of this poem, which is so nearly allied to that of Chaucer,
frequently reminds us of Mr. Hunt's "Rimini", though many of the faults
so justly attributed to that author, have been avoided in the present work.
Indeed, with the exception of two passages, we are induced to give our most
unqualified approbation of this poem: and first,

> . . . The sleeping kine
> Couch'd in thy brightness, dream of fields divine:

This may be a very happy thought, and extremely poetical; but in our
finite judgment, the giving to the brute creation one of the greatest and most
glorious attributes of a rational being, is not only very ridiculous, but
excessively impious.

A richly period touch! The review ended in this graceful compliment:

And from the following passage we dissent most decidedly, as we feel
persuaded, that genius, like that possessed by Mr. K., may with safety
venture in the highest walks of poetry:

> O 'tis very sin
> For one so weak to venture his poor verse
> In such a place as this. O do not curse,
> High Muses! let him hurry to the ending.

There appeared in *The Champion* for June 8th an excellent review
which, the writer (probably John Scott), had delayed intentionally so

as not to injure *Endymion* with the 'great critical authorities.' He demanded fair reviews on sound principles: he himself 'cares not two straws for public opinion.' He thought *Endymion* too good to have a popular success, compared Keats with the great poets and quoted a good deal, giving the Hymn to Pan almost in full, declaring it to be 'among the finest specimens of classic poetry in our language.' Referring to

> Fair creatures! whose young children's children bred
> Thermopylæ its heroes—not yet dead,
> But in old marbles ever beautiful.

he pronounced the last line 'as fine as that in Shakespeare's sonnets, "And beauty making beautiful old rhyme" ' (Sonnet 106), adding, 'And there are not a dozen finer in Shakespeare's poems.' The review was unfinished; a conclusion was promised for a future issue, but did not appear.

It is a matter to regret that we have no criticism from Hunt. Although Hunt's feelings in regard to *Endymion* were mixed, even one of his skilled 'special pleadings' would have been of literary value; but he knew that a notice from his pen could only do harm to the book with the great Tory organs. He reprinted in full, however, the notice in *The Chester Guardian*, Reynolds' long article, and referred to the *Quarterly* review in a footnote:

We congratulate most *sincerely*, our young friend JOHN KEATS on the involuntary homage that, we understand, has been paid to his undoubted genius, in an article full of grovelling abuse.

He also commented on J. S.'s letter protesting against a certain 'half-witted, half-hearted Review' in the *Quarterly*. J. S. had remarked ironically that Mr. Keats might attain to praise from the *Quarterly* if he would give up 'his friendships, his principles, and his politics.' On this Leigh Hunt commented: 'We really believe so; but Mr. Keats is of a spirit which can afford to dispense with such approbation, and stand by his friends.' Hunt's brother, John, gave *Endymion* a more reticent support by printing the 'Hymn to Pan' in his short-lived weekly publication, *The Yellow Dwarf*.

Of private opinions we have very few except the partial admiration of close friends. We know that Shelley found *Endymion* difficult to get through, though later he could enjoy 'the treasures of poetry it contains.' The Hymn to Pan he thought on first reading 'the surest promise of ultimate excellence.' A friend of Woodhouse's in Bath said, in reference to the passages quoted in derision in the *Quarterly* review: 'If these are the worst passages what can the best be?' There is also a letter, dated March 29th, 1819, from a lady to Woodhouse which runs:

Mrs Colonel Green's Compliments to Mr Woodhouse and feels exceedingly obliged to Mr W—— for the perusal of *Endymion* and the other trifle— There are a great number of beauties in the *former* which speak highly for the authors growing Genius—A Stranger perhaps might fancy him too *wild* in some of his passages but Mrs G knowing the Author at a time when the *Fire* of his imagination appeared agitated with a *Thirst* for *fame*—can easily excuse him *for the*—*sudden bursts* of *enthusiasm* which *pervades* his *affectionate Constitution*. Should Mrs G—— ever see the Author she certainly must rally him—for a great *Mistake*—commited in the Book of trifles and which *by this time he must* be *a very great* Judge. Mrs G begs to be kindly remembered to him and should at all times be happy to see both Mr Woodhouse and the Author of Endymion—

Mr. Gittings identifies this lively and slightly incoherent lady (living in Duncan Terrace, Islington) as the wife of Colonel Thomas Green, late of the 6th Regiment of Native Infantry, Madras Presidency.

Woodhouse's sister, staying in 1820 with Mrs. Neville (Mary Frogley), at Esher, met some ladies who refused to see any beauty in *Endymion* or, indeed, in any of Keats's writings. She tried them with 'that beautiful and grand sonnet to the "Sea," ' and when that failed to interest them 'gave them up as lost *muttons*.'

Through the Nevilles Keats received a tribute from the Misses Porter, popular writers of the day. Jane Porter, the author of *Scottish Chiefs*, wrote the letter, the main part of which Keats copied out in the letter to America of December 16th. She and her sister were 'very much delighted' with *Endymion*. He did not quote the end of the letter which spoke of genius which 'always burns its brilliant way thro' every obstacle,' and expressed in rather high-falutin tones regret that Chatterton had not the manliness of mind or 'the magnanimity of patience' to live and fulfil his high destiny. On the letter he commented:

Now I feel more obliged than flattered by this—so obliged that I will not at present give you an extravaganza of a Lady Romancer.

This seems a little ungrateful, especially as the lady had taken the trouble to write when she was very unwell with a 'still adhæsive cold.' Keats's attitude to the women writers of his day was expressed in a letter to Reynolds on September 21st, 1817:

The world, and especially our England, has, within the last thirty years been vexed and teazed by a set of Devils, whom I detest so much that I almost hunger after an acherontic promotion to a Torturer, purposely for their accommodation. These Devils are a set of Women, who having taken a snack or Luncheon of Literary scraps, set themselves up for towers of Babel in Languages Sapphos in Poetry—Euclids in Geometry—and everything in nothing. . . . I had longed for some real feminine Modesty in these things, and was therefore gladdened in the extreme on opening the other day . . . a Book of Poetry written by . . . "the matchless Orinda."

He then quoted in full the poem to her friend, Mrs. Awbrey.

Keats, living in Well Walk, might have encountered Mrs. Joanna Baillie, the then-famous author and dramatist who was considered to give literary distinction to Hampstead by her residence at Bolton House: in the irony of fate *The Times*, at her death, called her 'a poet whose fame is indelibly inscribed on literature.' How astonished she and her blue-stocking friends would have been to know that an obscure young man living in lodgings in Well Walk would so totally eclipse her light! Although Keats disliked her kind and would have probably included among the 'Devils' her more didactic friend, Mrs. Barbauld, he might have found himself in agreement with the latter on one point; 'young ladies ought to have such a general tincture of knowledge as to make them agreeable companions for a man of sense, and to enable them to find rational entertainment for a solitary hour.'

An opinion of real literary value is that expressed by Sir James Mackintosh, publicist, historian, statesman and philosopher, one of the original contributors to the *Encyclopædia Britannica*, and a man who had a reputation for multifarious reading and learning. Mackintosh, at this time a man of fifty-three, was an advanced liberal who worked in the cause of the reform of the criminal code, Catholic Emancipation and the Reform Bill, and had just been appointed Professor of Law and General Politics in the East India Company's college at Haileybury. Taylor wrote to him in the December of 1818, sending a copy of *Endymion* with this comment, 'its faults are numberless,' but they are those of 'real Genius.' He mentioned Keats's age, that he was an orphan and gave particulars of his brothers and sister:

These are odd particulars to give, when I am introducing the work and not the man to you,—but if you knew him, you would also feel that strange personal interest in all that concerns him.

Commending the finest passages to Sir James, Taylor asserted that 'if he lives, Keats will be the brightest ornament of this Age.'

Sir James Mackintosh openly protested against the mode of

criticism employed against *Endymion*. He wrote in a letter to an un-known correspondent: 'such attacks will interest every liberal mind in the author's success,' and to Taylor, in July, 1819: 'I very much admire your young poet, with all his singularities. Where is he? and what high design does he meditate?' The admiration of this highly intelligent public man is all the more pleasing because he had been a doctor: it is the first instance of the strong interest taken in Keats by medical men down to our own day.

If Taylor's ulterior motive in sending *Endymion* to Sir James Mackintosh had been to elicit the active sympathy of *The Edinburgh Review* he was not successful. The great Liberal organ made no sound. Keats's comment was: 'The cowardliness of the *Edinburgh* is worse than the abuse of the *Quarterly*.'

The Edinburgh review are affraid to touch upon my Poem. They do not know what to make of it—they do not like to condemn it and they will not praise it for fear—They are as shy of it as I should be of wearing a Quaker's hat. The fact is they have no real taste—they dare not compromise their Judgements on so puzzling a Question. If on my next Publication they should praise me and so lug in Endymion—I will address them in a manner they will not at all relish.

This was exactly what did happen, but the Keats of 1820 was too ill and dispirited to make his protest.

When in 1820 Jeffrey himself reviewed *Endymion* he said there was probably no other book he would 'sooner employ as a test to ascertain whether any one had in him a native relish for poetry.' There was one man of letters who would have dissented heartily from this, Thomas de Quincey. On the subject of *Endymion* he was vigorous: 'The very mid-summer madness of affectation, of false vapoury sentiment, and of fantastic effeminacy, seemed to me combined in Keats's Endymion, when I first saw it near the end of 1821. The Italian poet Marino has been reputed the greatest master of gossamer affectation in Europe. But *his* conceits showed the palest of rosy blushes by the side of Keats's bloody crimson.'

The admirer most useful to posterity was the young lawyer, Richard Woodhouse. He had each volume of Keats's published works inter-leaved, wrote in them explanatory notes and alternative readings and kept copies of unpublished poems. He called it his 'collection of Keatsiana,' and was anxious to include complimentary sonnets to Keats, though he sometimes had to get them in a roundabout way. Probably Keats himself was both embarrassed and amused by Woodhouse's consideration for posterity.

Among Keats's presentation copies of *Endymion* was one to Hazlitt who made the blank leaf serve for an effusion to the heroine of the *Liber Amoris*. The little lodging-house flirt was no fit bedfellow for Peona or Cynthia, but imagination can transform and at least she was rare and lovely in the eyes of the infatuated Hazlitt.

A few more copies of *Endymion* were later sold on the comparative success of the 1820 volume, but the main body of the edition languished unwanted and unbound on Taylor's shelves. Eventually Edward Stibbs, a bookseller, bought the remainder at a penny-halfpenny a copy, paid twopence-halfpenny for the binding and sold it very slowly at eighteenpence. In 1933 a dealer paid two thousand, four hundred pounds for a presentation copy of *Endymion*.

But in May, 1818, these disappointments, the shock of these attacks, were still to come. Keats, relieved that the long poem he had laboured on for so many months was published and behind him, was busy in Hampstead preparing for his brother's wedding and emigration. Although in that state of mind when action is mechanical and the world profitless, he looked forward to a pleasure to come. He was going, after George's departure, on a walking-tour in the north with that congenial companion, Charles Brown.

CHAPTER XIV

George's Departure and the Walking-Tour
(May—August, 1818)

GEORGE was to be married at the end of May and to start in the middle of June on his long, hazardous journey to Louisville, Kentucky, in the backwoods of America; going equipped with more enthusiasm than experience and risking one thousand one hundred pounds, most of his available capital. He took with him, however, letters of introduction from Taylor who had a cousin in Philadelphia.

It would seem hazardous enough for an untravelled lad of twenty-one without, so far as we know, any experience of farming, to go as settler into a strange country alone, but even more so when he took with him a wife. Most of the common friends of the Keatses and Wylies regarded the scheme as, to say the least of it, highly imprudent. Mrs. Reynolds was definite in her disapproval. Dilke, who looked hopefully towards the New World as a future home of 'Godwin-perfectibility,' was the only one to applaud the enterprise of the young couple. Mrs. Wylie was very naturally blamed for allowing Georgiana, who was just under age at marriage, to go. But these were times when men took risks in the new lands and it was the duty of their women to share them. Perhaps Mrs. Wylie made her private protest.

Georgiana was a high-spirited girl and may well have taken the law in her own hands. Youth does not see difficulties and dangers in adventure; but one would like to know something of the young girl's feelings when she bore her first child within a year of marriage far away from her mother and friends. At first Georgiana was not happy among the people of her adoption and does not seem ever to have felt quite at home in America. However, she settled down and lived to bear eight children, take a second husband and to enjoy a lively old age.[1] Miss Alice Keats, her grand-daughter, has told us that she was 'rather severe with little children whom she liked to behave properly.' Somewhere about the middle of the century Georgiana wrote to Mrs. Dilke advising her not to let her son marry too soon as 'it is so unpleasant to be called Grandmamma. I have a perfect horror of it, and am as much disposed to gaiety as ever.'

Keats was willing that George, who had been 'more than a brother to him,' who was 'his greatest friend,' should go temporarily out of his

---

[1] She died at Lexington, Kentucky, April 5th, 1879.

life. 'He is,' he wrote, 'of too independant and liberal a Mind to get on in trade in this Country—in which a generous Man with a scanty recourse must be ruined. I would sooner he should till the ground than bow to a Customer—there is no choice with him—he could not bring himself to the latter.'

This attitude of George's must have been inexplicable to the good Abbey. What should a tradesman do but bow to a customer? And at that time if he were an aristocratic one you bowed very low. It would seem highly improper pride in the son of a livery-stable keeper to keep a stiff back; a pride which could only be attributed to the dangerous Jacobinical notions the boys had got into their heads.

Keats did not contemplate a long separation from his brother, but planned, if he were alive, to pay George a visit within three years. These hints of the fear of an early death might be taken as portents, as a foreknowledge of incipient tubercular trouble, but they may have been merely a reflection of the all too frequent deaths of young men. The expectation of life was considerably lower then. It was, too, a characteristic of the morbid side of the romantic movement to lay an emphasis on death.

In speaking of his sister-in-law to Bailey, Keats wrote:

To see an entirely disinterrested Girl quite happy is the most pleasant and extraordinary thing in the world—it depends upon a thousand Circumstances—on my word 'tis extraordinary. Women must want Imagination and they may thank God for it—and so may we that a delicate being can feel happy without any sense of crime. It puzzles me and I have no sort of logic to comfort me—I shall think it over.

It might well have astonished him that Georgiana could let her present happiness swamp all consideration of the future dangers his vivid imagination and his medical experience might foresee: and, weighed down as he was by 'the burden of the mystery,' that any human being could find even temporarily unalloyed happiness. He was not yet in love himself.

On June 22nd he, Brown, George and Georgiana set out on the coach for Liverpool from 'The Swan with Two Necks' in Lad Lane, now Gresham Street. At Redbourn near St. Albans, Henry Stephens, in practice there, came to see them while they took dinner at the inn. Stephens has given us an account of the meeting and this description of the young bride:

Rather short, not what might be called strictly handsome, but looked like a being whom any man of moderate Sensibility might easily love. She had an imaginative poetical cast.—Somewhat singular and girlish in her attire. . . . There was something original about her, and John seemed to regard her as a being whom he delighted to honour, and introduced her with evident satisfaction.

Girlish in her attire . . . Henry Stephens appears to criticise Georgiana's dress, which probably consisted of a fairly full muslin gown with a waist under the armpits, a short spencer and either a 'coal-scuttle' bonnet or a rustic straw hat tied under the chin with ribbons. But in regard to her character he seems, at a single meeting, to show more perspicuity than Charles Dilke who, in a comment written in his copy of Lord Houghton's *Life*, described her as 'a lively ignorant girl unaccustomed to society.' Georgiana evidently had personality enough to impress a stranger.

George and Georgiana settled down at the Crown Inn, Liverpool to await the sailing of their ship. The last good-byes were said over night. Keats and Brown took coach in the morning for Lancaster (one of the recognized starting-off points for a tour of the Lakes) before the young couple were awake.

As he bowled along on top of the coach was Keats thinking, not only of his brother George and his new sister, but of Tom in his lonely Hampstead lodging? He had not wanted to leave his brother but may, being far from fit himself, have been recommended change and exercise by the doctor, whom we know he consulted: Dr. Sawrey, having been amazed to see how well Tom looked on his return from Teignmouth, must have thought it safe for him to be left in the care of Mrs. Bentley and friends. Dr. Sawrey, and some of Tom's friends, teased the boy, telling him he wasn't really ill at all. They made him laugh so much he was temporarily quite unwell; managing however, to put into his mind that 'confinement and low spirits' had been 'his chief enemies,' and to infuse into him a hope of recovery which soon buoyed him up again.

He was not, however, equal to much exertion. In a lively letter to the Misses Jeffrey, Keats had written: 'Tom is taken for a Madman and I being somewhat stunted am taken for nothing—We lounge on the Walk opposite as you might on the Den.' With the typical irony of our English climate it became fine and warm after they left Teignmouth. Tom himself was hopefully planning to go on holiday during John's intended absence of four months, and even to live for a time in a foreign land: in May he had told Marianne Jeffrey of an intention to 'go by vessell to some port in the Adriatic or down the Rhine through Switzerland and the Alps into Italy most likely the town of Pavia—there to remain untill I have acquired a stock of Knowledge and strength which will better enable me to bustle through the world.'

Whether this was a settled possibility in the minds of the brothers or merely the dream of a sick boy we do not know. We have seen earlier how Keats himself had been planning to travel on the Continent; perhaps he had meant to join Tom before the winter. But if Tom in the meantime could not travel himself, he would be able to enjoy his brother's tour at second hand in long journal letters, and have the solace of a supply of books from Taylor's hospitable shop.

However, even though he might have felt tolerably secure in leaving Tom in the care of Mrs. Bentley and under the kindly supervision of friends, Keats must have been thinking of him with some regret as he went off away from his family with Brown. Brown, an eminently tactful man, would leave him to his thoughts. He attached Keats to him as friend by not pushing his claim; by making him feel at liberty to frequent his house without directly mentioning how much he enjoyed his company.

Brown kept a diary of the walking-tour. In 1840 he published in *The Plymouth and Devonport Weekly Journal* four instalments of an article based on this diary. Unfortunately these only carry us up to Ballantrae in Ayrshire: the diary itself has not come to light.

They found Lancaster preparing for a parliamentary election. There was great excitement in the town. Brougham, the great Whig lawyer, had dared to challenge the traditional right of the Tory family of Lowther to the monopoly of the seat. Lord Lowther, fearing for more than the usual turmoil and trouble an election meant in those days of public balloting, had induced the Government to send soldiers up. The troops were at present being kept at a discreet distance from the scene of action. It seems as if industrial troubles were adding fuel to the smouldering fire of discontent over delays in electoral reform: Parson Newton of Wath, who visited Lancaster later in the summer of 1818, tells us that Lancaster was almost a dead port; there were only three vessels in harbour, grass grew along the quay walls and the bridge was broken.

Drink flowed freely on these occasions and ruffians collected in and about the town alert for mischief. The inns were full of carousing visitors. Keats and Brown had to wait two hours for their dinner and retired for the night with some relief in a private house.

They arose at the Spartan hour of four o'clock in the morning to find it pouring with rain: they read and talked Milton until seven. Milton at four in the morning! Perhaps even Keats's enthusiasm for poetry was not equal to this, for he was restless and impatient. Brown, no doubt with his spectacles twinkling, preached patience out of *Samson Agonistes*. When the rain subsided into a Scotch mist they 'chose to consider it appropriate and complimentary,' and set out.

Just as they left the town they heard a labourer observe with some sarcasm:

"There go a couple of gentlemen! Having nothing to do, they're finding out hard work for themselves."

They walked four miles of muddy roads to Bolton-le-Sands and fortunately secured breakfast there before the rain descended once more. The local weather prophets told them it would be wet all day, but, as so often happens in hilly country, the clouds suddenly and unexpectedly cleared at midday and they set off again. They were walking towards that long arm of the mountains that stretches down to the sea in Morecambe Bay and two miles ahead of Bolton had their first fine view. The still hovering clouds lent a misty charm to the horizon. At Burton they turned into 'The Green Dragon,' asking impatiently what they could have for dinner. A voice replied in a 'gruff-and-grum' tone:

"Nothing! You can have nothing here!"

'It was the Green Dragon himself, in the shape of a tall corpulent figure, with the largest face that ever man was blessed with, a face like a target; and one that a starving traveller would be tempted to shoot at.' This 'unfeeling lump' told the hungry men that his house was full of soldiers and that he could do nothing for them. They secured a dinner at the King's Arms, where a voluble landlady lamented that she could not offer them a bed as her house too was army-ridden; she had even had to refuse two parties of carriage folk. So after dinner they had reluctantly to step out into the rain again.

Protected by their oilskin capes, they trudged along towards Kendal. Wet and discouraged, they welcomed the sight of a dirty little roadside inn, only to be repelled by a formidable landlady, smoking a pipe, who said she too was full. She told them of a wayside house at a hamlet called Endmoor, and here again, after more muddy, rain-splashed walking, they found a cold welcome. The landlady, Mrs. Black, eyeing their knapsacks, took them for poor travellers who would not have the price of a meal on them. However, after being assured that they did not carry their own food, she warmed visibly and said she would give them a lodging, although her house was all in a 'squeer' from a general whitewashing.

They spent the evening in the kitchen, the general room of the inn, with the landlady, her son, an old soldier who yarned about the late wars, and a man 'as drunk as a sponge.' The drunkard, fortunately for their comfort, took himself off early after staggering out of his corner and lunging at Brown with an enquiry as to the wares he carried. Did he sell spectacles and razors? Walking-tours being unusual at this time, our two pedestrians were constantly being taken for pedlars. Brown was

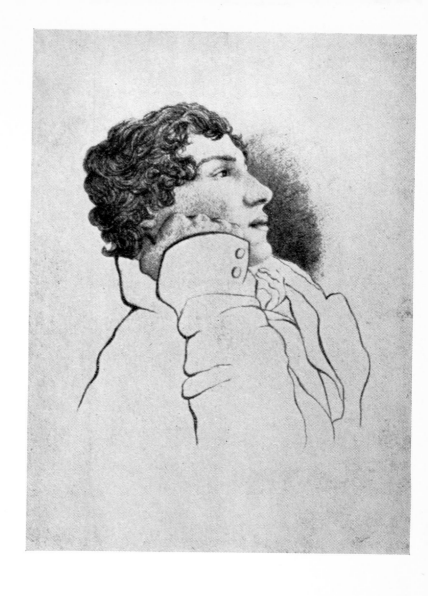

John Keats
From a drawing by Charles Brown in the National Portrait
Gallery

John Keats
From a sketch by B. R. Haydon (1831) in the possession of
Professor Willard B. Pope. Copyright strictly reserved

thought to be a spectacle-seller, the pair on his nose being taken for a badge of his trade. On finding out his mistake the old toper made sudden and profuse apologies, whispering in Brown's ear:

"I never offend any man, not I! so if you'll give me something to drink, why, I'll take it!"

Finding that this broad hint fell upon stony ground he stumbled out of the inn, mumbling and hiccupping.

As Keats and Brown took tea after their supper Mrs. Black noted that they took no sugar. This astonished and pleased her, and she pointed out to her son how economical it was. Did the two men abstain from sugar as a protest against the slave-trade? This was not unusual. However, no such motive came within the landlady's simple ken; only the economy of the habit impressed her. The next morning, on their departure, she wanted to take something off their reckoning as she had not been obliged to supply them with the then expensive item of sugar.

They awoke with relief to a day which, although dull, was fine, walked to Kendal and thence down to the shores of Windermere. The larks overhead and the fresh mountain air filled them with delight amongst the wild, unfamiliar scenery; scenery which Brown, whose narrative is in the familiar ecstatic style of the period, calls 'romantic.' Before descending to the hamlet of Bowness on the shores of the lake they both stopped short. Windermere lay spread beneath them against the rugged elevation of the peaked mountains. A little island thick with feathery trees lay immediately below, lapped by the clear water. Keats's bright eyes darted up to a mountain-peak 'beneath which was gently resting a silver cloud' and back again to the faery island.

"How can I believe in that?" he exclaimed. "Surely it cannot be!" 'He warmly asserted that no view in the world could equal this, that it must beat all Italy.' They walked on until they could see the end of the lake. Keats thought it "more and more wonderfully beautiful." The fern and the bright furze, the clustering trees, before them the mountains, and the living moving water. . . . It was a scene the beauty of which, intensified through the eyes of the young poet he had loved, lingered long in Brown's memory. The greyness of the day only added a softened grace to the landscape by a light mist before the mountains.

This was the first time Keats had seen a mountain with the exception of a distant view of the Welsh mountains on their way up to Liverpool. To the dullest of us it is an amazing experience. Brown, in his narrative, dilated on the awe-inspiring quality of the scene and burst into poetic quotation, but Keats, with his usual reticence, was content to write in his journal-letter to Tom: 'I have an amazing partiality for mountains in the clouds.'

It was now time for dinner. They walked into Bowness and found the inn there 'spacious and flourishing under the patronage of tourists; for whom the whole conduct was as much after the London fashion as possible.' A man was putting off in a boat to fetch fish for dinner and they went with him, Keats taking an oar. To their surprise he merely hauled up some fishing-pots, wooden cages in which the salmon trout were jumping alive. They enjoyed a hasty bathe while the trout were cooking.

The luxury of the inn and its modern furnishing offended the two romantics who yearned for more of sylvan simplicity. Then, as now, the presence of gaping tourists marred the enjoyment of the beauty-spot; though one is glad to think Keats was spared the orange-peel, paper-bag and cigarette-carton mess made by modern charabanc trippers. He told Tom:

There are many disfigurements to this Lake—not in the way of land or water. No; the two views we have had of it are of the most noble tenderness—they can never fade away—they make one forget the divisions of life; age, youth, poverty, and riches; and refine one's sensual vision into a sort of north star which can never cease to be open lidded and stedfast over the wonders of the great Power. The disfigurement I mean is the miasma of London. I do suppose it contaminated with bucks and soldiers, and women of fashion—and hatband ignorance. The border inhabitants are quite out of keeping with the romance about them, from a continual intercourse with London rank and fashion. But why should I grumble? They let me have a prime glass of soda water—

Later, when they were in the bleak and unfrequented Highlands, no doubt Keats would have given much for the ample food and drink, the comfort of the Bowness Inn: now he was but newly set out on his journey fresh and eager to rough it in the adventure of a tour on foot.

After dinner they walked along the lake to Ambleside at the northern extremity; slowly, because the beauty of the country so often stayed their steps. This walk is best given in Keats's own words:

We walked . . . along the border of Winandermere all beautiful with wooded shores and Islands—our road was a winding lane, wooded on each side, and green overhead, full of Foxgloves—every now and then a glimpse of the Lake, and all the while Kirkstone and other large hills nestled together in a sort of grey black mist.

The wind had arisen and the rustle of Keats's 'inland sea,' the singing of birds and the sound of the water whipped into waves and slapping against the shore added a joy of sound to the delight of the eyes.

At Ambleside they met with a tiresome person, an intruder upon country quiet from London, who began immediately to talk about himself in a consequential tone. Brown, thinking to profit by the unwelcome intrusion, asked him some practical questions about routes and lodgings, but the bore was deaf to all enquiry. He carefully explained that, although dressed roughly and suitably for walking as they were, he was a gentleman, an Oxford man, and, to give the statement verisimilitude, quoted the classics.

Keats had, soon after the encounter, unceremoniously walked on ahead, leaving Brown to grapple with the numbskull who went on to discourse about his uncle's carriage, Almack's and the opera and of the futile attempt of the Bowness Inn to ape a London hotel. Brown, with characteristic persistence, determined to make some use of him, asked what route he had taken. "Oh!" he replied, carelessly, "I can hardly tell you the names of the places." He slid into a glib account of how his father traced a long pedigree, though he himself thought nothing of a silly pride of rank and birth. Numbskull he might appear to be, but Brown was beginning from his smooth patter to suspect him as 'London sharper.' He found difficulty in disentangling himself however: it was hard to be ruthless 'because no provocation ought to ruffle the temper of Ambleside.'

The day was crowned by a reading aloud of 'Isabella, or the Pot of Basil,' which Keats had just finished. The finishing of a poem does not, of course, necessarily mean that the poet has just completed the last stanza; but one would like to think that by the shores of Winandermere, to the quiet sounds of the rustling of trees outside his window, and the lapping of the water, Keats wrote:

> And so she pin'd, and so she died forlorn,
>   Imploring for her Basil to the last.
> No heart was there in Florence but did mourn
>   No pity of her love, so overcast.
> And a sad ditty of this story born
>   From mouth to mouth through all the country pass'd:
> Still is the burthen sung—"O cruelty,
> "To steal my Basil-pot away from me!"

As Keats wished to call on Wordsworth during the day they got up the next morning at Ambleside to have a walk before breakfast. In Keats's own words:

. . . we went to see the Ambleside water fall. The morning beautiful—the walk early among the hills. We, I may say, fortunately, missed the direct path, and after wandering a little, found it out by the noise—for, mark you, it is buried in trees, in the bottom of the valley—the stream itself is interesting throughout with "mazy error over pendant shades." Milton meant a smooth river—this is buffetting all the way on a rocky bed ever various—but the waterfall itself, which I came suddenly upon, gave me a pleasant twinge. First we stood a little below the head about half way down the first fall, buried deep in trees, and saw it streaming down two more descents to the depth of near fifty feet—then we went on a jut of rock nearly level with the second fall-head where the first fall was above us, and the third below our feet still—at the same time we saw that the water was divided by a sort of cataract island on whose other side burst out a glorious stream—then the thunder and the freshness. At the same time the different falls have as different characters; the first darting down the slate-rock like an arrow; the second spreading out like a fan—the third dashed into a mist— and the one on the other side of the rock a sort of mixture of all these. We afterwards moved away a space, and saw nearly the whole more mild, streaming silverly through the trees. What astonishes me more than any- thing is the tone, the coloring, the slate, the stone, the moss, the rock-weed; or, if I may say so, the intellect, the countenance of such places. The space, the magnitude of mountains and waterfalls are well imagined before one sees them; but this countenance or intellectual tone must surpass every imagi- nation and defy any remembrance. I shall learn poetry here and shall henceforth write more than ever, for the abstract endeavor of being able to add a mite to that mass of beauty which is harvested from these grand materials, by the finest spirits, and put into etherial existence for the relish of one's fellows. I cannot think with Hazlitt that these scenes make man appear little. I never forgot my stature so completely—I live in the eye; and my imagination, surpassed, is at rest—

. . . 'the thunder and the freshness' . . . 'streaming silverly through the trees' . . . how clearly he brings before us the sight, the sound and the moist smell of a waterfall. 'I never forgot my stature so com- pletely. . . .' There are signs in the letters that Keats felt his lack of inches. I have wondered whether his frequent use of the word 'tip-toe' may not have had a physical cause. He must often have had to lift himself above his natural height to see that which other men would have well upon the level of the eye.

In descending the waterfall, however, his slightness of figure was an advantage. Towards the level of the bottom it was necessary to grasp the trees and edges of rock to prevent a headlong tumble which might mean death or a serious injury. The older and heavier Brown followed nervously and with caution. 'I never was,' he wrote, 'a sure-footed beast.'

After 'a Monstrous Breakfast' they went up to Rydal Mount only to find that all the Wordsworth family were from home. Keats was very disappointed. He wrote a note for Wordsworth and put it over Dorothy's portrait while Brown admired the view from the window. Keats's disappointment was tinged with bitterness because

Wordsworth had gone to Lowther Hall to help the Tory candidate in canvassing; but in fairness to Wordsworth he admitted that the Lowthers were old friends.

After visiting another waterfall they walked along by the side of Rydal Water which, by comparison with Windermere, looked small and bare. Brown disliked the reeds as he passed them but from a distance thought they added beauty to the lake by shadowing-in the banks. They now came in sight of Helm Crag and at once recognized

> That ancient woman seated on Helm-Crag

the fantastic heap of stones which look like some gigantic primitive old woman on the summit. Did they seek that 'tall rock' on 'Rotha's banks' where 'Joanna' stood with Wordsworth and laughed to see the rapt expression on the poet's face before the mountain view, when

> The rock, like something starting from a sleep,
> Took up the lady's voice, and laughed again:
> That ancient woman seated on Helm-Crag
> Was ready with her cavern: Hammer-Scar,
> And the tall steep of Silver-how, sent forth
> A noise of laughter; southern Loughrigg heard,
> And Fairfield answered with a mountain tone:
> Helvellyn far into the clear blue sky
> Carried the lady's voice,—old Skiddaw blew
> His speaking trumpet;—back out of the clouds
> Of Glaramara southward came the voice:
> And Kirkstone tossed it from his misty head.

Surely Keats was too young to resist trying to call up the echo himself.

They walked from thickly wooded Westmorland, through a long pass among treeless mountains, into Cumberland to the foot of Helvellyn which was veiled in heavy rolling clouds. Here Keats wrote to George and included in the letter an acrostic on his new sister's name. He reserved the letter for an addition the next day and went to bed.

After a restless night with fleas as bedfellows they awoke to find heavy clouds still enveloping the mountain and a drizzling rain below and had to forgo their plan of climbing Helvellyn. When the clouds had cleared enough to enable them to set out for Keswick they found the country had changed; the mountains were now based by sloping foothills and less craggy than in Westmorland. The entrance into Keswick Vale they thought more lovely than Windermere. A visit to the Falls of Lodore must be described in Keats's own words:

I had an easy climb among the streams, about the fragments of Rocks, and should have got I think to the summit, but unfortunately I was damped by slipping one leg into a squashy hole. There is no great body of water, but the accompaniment is delightful; for it oozes out from a cleft in perpendicular Rocks, all fledged with Ash and other beautiful trees. It is a strange thing how they got there. At the south end of the Lake, the Mountains of Borrowdale are perhaps as fine as anything we have seen.

The 'Ash and other beautiful trees' appear in his 'Ode to Psyche' as the 'dark-clustered trees' that

> Fledge the wild-ridged mountains steep by steep;

It was a pity that the previous dry weather had lessened the waters of Lodore. When Parson Newton visited them a month later the water was in full spate, swollen by the rain which marred the holiday of our travellers. He could hear the roar two miles off.

In the evening they went on to see the Druid's circle standing immeasurably old and grim on the top of a lone hill. Here in the narrative and the journal-letters we have two parallel descriptions it is interesting to compare. Brown's has a pedestrian quality. He describes the circle in detail, giving the position of the stones. This is Keats's:

We had a fag up hill, rather too near dinner-time, which was rendered void by the gratification of seeing those aged stones, on a gentle rise in the midst of Mountains, which at that time darkened all around, except at the fresh opening of the Vale of St. John.

In his 'aged stones,' shadowed by the mountains but for one long shaft of light, conveys the sinister and lonely quality of the megaliths far more subtly and faithfully than Brown's guide-book description. He makes no comment on them. Brown, writing, it is only fair to say, for general reading, ends with 'Surrounded by a majestic panorama, the spot is suited to render the human mind awestruck, and possibly with the ignorant, superstitious.' Keats's gloss to this ancient poem of the human spirit can be found in 'Hyperion':

>   . . . a dismal cirque
> Of Druid stones, upon a forlorn moor,
> When the chill rain begins at shut of eve,
> In dull November, and their chancel vault,
> The Heaven itself, is blinded throughout night.

In the town of Keswick they saw the mountain scenery in a camera obscura. We do not know the effect of this minikin view on Keats, but Brown remarks that the reduction of the vastness does away with much of its beauty and proves that mountain scenery cannot be put on canvas.

At the inn they were affronted by another whiff of the 'miasma of London' in the person of 'a yawning dandy' who came from his bedroom at midday 'and sat at his breakfast reading a bouncing novel.' Here Keats finished his letter to George and 'G minor'; but he finished it too late. When the letter reached Liverpool the young couple had sailed away.

The next day they ascended Skiddaw with two other men and a guide at four o'clock in the morning. In Keats's own words:

It promised all along to be fair, and we had fagged and tugged nearly to the top, when, at half-past six there camè a Mist upon us and shut out the view; We did not, however, lose anything by it: we were high enough without mist, to see the coast of Scotland; the Irish Sea; the hills beyond Lancaster; and nearly all the large ones of Cumberland and Westmoreland, particularly Helvellyn and Scawfell. It grew colder and colder as we ascended, and we were glad, at about three parts of the way, to taste a little rum which the Guide brought with him, mixed, mind ye with Mountain water, I took two glasses going and one returning. . . . So we have walked ten miles before Breakfast to-day. . . . All felt, on arising into the cold air, that same elevation which a cold bath gives one. I felt as if I were going to a Tournament.

Brown, a man of full habit and not a poet, found the climb fatiguing and somewhat disappointing. Half-way up he was so tired that it sounded to him like cruelty when the guide told them they had to go as far again. The panorama he considered only attractive in virtue of its strangeness. The mountains 'became comparatively insignificant.' He hated the jolting, jarring jog-trot down. 'A man's inside seems mixing together like a Scotch haggis.'

Passing along Bassenthwaite they were astonished by the total change in scenery; highly cultivated fields and dales like those in Devon, only not so luxuriant. They left Cumberland and Westmorland behind them without regret, intending to pass through them, following another route, on their way home.

When they reached the inn at Ireby, 'a dull beggarly looking place,' they heard a thumping and thudding on the ceiling and were told that the lads and lassies were having their dancing lesson above. It was the custom there, as in Scotland, for every child who could afford it to learn to dance. Keats and Brown went upstairs and found 'fine, healthy, cleanly-dressed' youngsters practising their steps with concentration. Brown wrote:

The instant the fiddle struck up, the slouch in the gait was lost, the feet moved, and gracefully, with complete conformity to the notes; and they wove the figure, sometimes extremely complicated to my inexperienced eyes, without an error, or the slightest pause. There was no sauntering half-asleep country dancer among them; all were inspired, yet by

> Nae cotillion brent-new frae France,
> But hornpipes, jigs, strathspeys and reels
> Put life and mettle in their heels.

This is the considered narrative of a practised journalist. Compare it with the sketch hastily dashed down by one who perhaps saw, felt and heard more acutely than any man of his time:

. . . we were greatly amused by a country dancing-school holden at the Inn, it was indeed "no new cotillon fresh from France". No, they kickit and jumpit with mettle extraordinary, and whiskit, and friskit, and toed it, and go'd it, and twirl'd it, and wheel'd it and stamped it, and sweated it, tattooing the floor like mad; The difference between our country dances and these Scottish figures is about the same as leisurely stirring a cup o' Tea and beating up a batter-pudding.

Keats added:

I was extremely gratified to think, that if I had pleasures they knew nothing of, they had also some into which I could not possibly enter. I hope I shall not return without having got the Highland fling. There was as fine a row of boys and girls as you ever saw; some beautiful faces and one exquisite mouth.

The hack writer generalizes and the artist knows when to particularize.

The dancing children gave to Keats in his new mood more pleasure than the wonders of the scenery. 'I never,' he said, 'felt so near the glory of Patriotism, the glory of making by any means a country happier.'

He was anxious to reach Carlisle where letters would be awaiting them. He found one from 'sister George—very delightful indeed,' which he kept for Tom to read. ' "Merry Carlisle" did not to our thinking,' wrote Brown, 'maintain its epithet; the whole art of yawning might have been learned there.' They did not care for either cathedral or castle, and the modern courthouses, Brown thought, were, with their squab round towers adjoining the square Gothic buildings, 'like a tea-caddy and a low sugar dish placed side by side.'

Neither man was now in a mood for complete enjoyment of what they saw. They had walked one hundred and fourteen miles in five days and were fatigued, though would only admit to being a little tired in the thighs and to slightly blistered feet. They decided to cover the duller country between Carlisle and Dumfries by coach. Brown thought Greta Green 'a sad ominous place for a young couple, poverty-struck and barren.'

At Dumfries they found themselves, to their amazement, in a foreign country: they had thought Scotch towns and Scottish folk would differ little from the English of the north. This was the first time that Brown, though Scottish by descent, had crossed the Border. Dumfries 'did not wear the air of comfort belonging to an English town.' They noticed the primitive cottages from which there was no outlet for smoke but by the door.

The people they thought 'more serious and solidly inanimated than necessary.' Brown found their speech 'tedious, slow and drawling,' but Keats was interested in the dialect and, with his quick ear, caught the characteristic rhythm. 'In Devonshire,' he noted, 'they say: "Well, where be ye going?" Here it is: "How is it all wi' yoursel?" ' He has also in this acute piece of observation delineated one aspect of the Scottish character. The Scot may be more curious to know where his neighbour is going but he will not ask at once in the direct manner of the simpler Southron. They were particularly struck by the caution of the Scot. Keats told his brother:

The first well-dressed Scotchman we had any conversation with, to our surprise, confessed himself a Deist. The careful manner of his delivering his opinions, not before he had received several encouraging hints from us, was very amusing.

They missed the grace of laughter. Brown said:

Except two or three girls, who returned our "speerings," (alias usual salutations) on the road, with a sort of grin, we did not perceive an approach to a laugh. If laughter, as it is said, proves our distinction from other animals, the line does not seem to be correctly drawn between them and these northerns.

Arriving at Dumfries on July 1st, the day of the annual horse fair, they saw many of these girls on the road, most of them carrying their shoes and stockings in their hands ready to put on just before they entered the town. Keats was offended by 'their large splay feet.'

There was one thing in Scotland which at once met with their whole-hearted approval, the 'whuskey.' 'Very smart stuff it is . . . very pretty drink, and much praised by Burns.' This fiery potation of the north had not yet reached the Sassenach.

Their first visit in Dumfries was to the tomb of Burns. A man on the coach had pointed it out to them on the way 'with a deal of life: "There!

de ye see it, amang the trees—white, wi' a roond tap." ' Brown's
reaction to the monument was formal and didactic; he reflected on the
need for well-kept memorials of 'great men in the intellectual world. . . .
They may excite emulation, they must inspire reverence and gratitude,
two feelings of which man is susceptible, to the improvement of his
nature.'

Keats did not find the memorial to his taste, 'though on a scale
large enough to show they wanted to honour him.' His personal
reaction was clouded by 'the feel of not to feel it.' Fatigue, the consciousness of the loss of one brother and the illness of the young one,
numbed his spirit. We shall see later that he felt, too, the weight of the
misery of Burns's life. He wrote this sonnet:

> —On visiting the Tomb of Burns—
> The Town, the churchyard, and the setting sun,
>   The Clouds, the trees, the rounded hills all seem
>   Though beautiful, cold—strange—as in a dream,
> I dreamed long ago, now new begun
> The short-liv'd paly Summer is but won
>   From Winter's ague, for one hour's gleam;
>   Though sapphire-warm, their stars do never beam,
> All is cold Beauty; pain is never done
> For who has mind to relish Minos-wise,
>   The Real of Beauty, free from that dead hue
>   Sickly imagination and sick pride
> Cast wan upon it! Burns! with honor due
>   I have oft honour'd thee. Great shadow; hide
> Thy face, I sin against thy native skies.[1]

It is clear from lines eleven and twelve that as Keats stood by the
grave of Burns his mind went out to that other dead poet whose tomb
he had seen in September and in whose thoughts he had lived so intensely for the last year. He remembered Hamlet's utterance:

> Thus conscience doth make cowards of us all
> And thus the native hue of resolution
> Is sicklied o'er with the pale cast of thought.

The reference to Minos, the impartial half-human judge of the
underworld, was probably directly due to a recent reading of the
'Inferno': Cary's three-volume pocket edition of his translation of the
Commedia was the only book Keats carried with him. But the Minos of
the 'Inferno' is a ghastly figure which in its horrid swish of the tail, to
indicate to what circle of hell the unfortunate sinner shall descend, does
not suggest a serene impartiality in effect. The reading of Canto V of
the 'Inferno' must have sent his mind back to the classical story.

[1] *See* Appendix VI.

This desire to escape from a personal view of life, to have clear before him the final issue unfalsified by 'sickly imagination and sick pride,' was to grow stronger and stronger within him. Keats was as yet scarcely out of that dark wood where his soul was 'in a ferment,' when he wrote, feeling on his pulses the cruelty of the world:

> Pleasure is oft a visitant; but pain
> Clings cruelly to us, like the gnawing sloth
> On the deer's tender haunches:

To Tom he wrote:

This Sonnet I have written in a strange mood, half-asleep. I know not how it is, the Clouds, the Sky, the Houses, all seem anti-Grecian and anti-Charlemagnish—

Of 'anti-Grecian and anti-Charlemagnish' there has been no satisfactory explanation. It has been suggested he is saying that for him the flat, unfamiliar Scottish lowlands have neither the charm of warm, smiling southern beauty nor of the dreams of chivalry. This may have truth but surely it is not a complete interpretation. We could only perhaps get at Keats's true meaning if we could evoke the shade of Tom who knew the private family language and who understood him best.

The rubbing of Keats's knapsack having split his coat he had to send it to a Dumfries tailor to be 'fortified at all points.' After visiting the ruins of Lincluden College they set out south-westward for Galloway, a country seldom visited by tourists at that time. They had intended to see Mrs. Burns while they were in Dumfries but we hear nothing of a visit to her.

Their next halt was at Dalbeattie where they had been recommended to lodge with a Mr. Murray who kept a combined public-house and general shop. On arrival they found that a fast had been appointed in the parish for that day and Mr. Murray was from home. Mrs. Murray, perhaps taking them again for profitless customers who merely wanted a bed for the night, stood in the doorway humming and ha-ing, "dinna ken what to say!" However, the hungry travellers managed to persuade her and at length she admitted them.

They liked the look of the village which was clean, neat and snug. There were children about the street, 'clean and healthy-faced,' dressed with especial care for the religious occasion. One chubby boy, unused to strangers, stared at them hard in some alarm. Rather tactlessly they called him a fat pig and he immediately set up a howl. An 'auld wife' came darting out and rated them. She was 'nae pleased to see bairns made game of.'

The unfailing balm to a small boy's wounded feelings was

administered: his fingers closed over the silver sixpence 'with a true Scotch grasp,' said Brown, 'tight as the claw of a lobster.' He went off to a group of children who were sitting in a circle with their hands before them in perfect silence. Brown and Keats took this for a normal or abnormal quietness of behaviour and thought it was no wonder that they grew up into staid men and women. It is more probable that they were either 'playing fasts' or had been threatened into unnatural soberness to suit the solemn day.

A 'sonsie lassie' put her head out of a cottage door. The men looked at her.

"There's a pretty girl!" Out came her shoulders. "A very pretty girl indeed!"

'She stretched her neck out, like a goose in a coop for more of the barley.' But, no doubt with the elders of the Kirk in mind, she 'maintained an unbecoming gravity.'

Mr. Murray proved to be a somewhat complacent gentleman who boasted that he had a better retail trade than any shopkeeper in Dumfries and took as much as sixty-three pounds in a day. "This village," he said, "did not exist thirty years ago; at that time it was a bog, full of rocky stones. The gentleman who built it died the very day I had my leg cut off."

Perhaps this was his accustomed conversational gambit; of course, the eyes of his two quests immediately travelled downwards to his feet which looked perfectly normal. But Mr. Murray boasted, besides a thriving business, a fine artificial limb on which he walked as well as any man and 'was more active than most men with their two natural legs.'

The next morning they set out for Kirkcudbright, following Mr. Murray's directions, through fine country with wooded hills and craggy mountains to the right and 'a lovely landscape, wherein a lough of the sea appeared like a lake, to the left. A small bush-covered island near the shore added to the charm.' For the most part they walked through cornfields or skirted small forests. They were now in Scott country.

Brown started talking about *Guy Mannering* which Keats had not read. Naturally Meg Merrilies figured largely in Brown's description of the book. Presently they came to 'a little spot . . . among fragments of rock, and brambles, and broom, and most tastefully ornamented with profusion of honeysuckle, wild-roses, and fox-glove, all in the very blush and fullness of blossom.'

Keats halted and cried:

"Without a shadow of doubt, on that spot, old Meg Merrilies has boiled her kettle!"

He said nothing more on the subject, but when they reached the village of Auchencairn and were sitting at breakfast, both writing,

Brown noticed that Keats's letter to his sister did not seem to be running in regular prose. Keats told him he was giving Fanny a ballad on Meg Merrilies. Brown asked if he might copy it but was told that it was only a trifle and wasn't worth the trouble. Neither Brown nor posterity has agreed with Keats's verdict. Apart from its wistful beauty the ballad is perhaps Keats's most amazing extempore: he had not (so far as we know) ever handled the ballad measure before.

After seeing the ruined Abbey at Dundrennan they walked on towards Kirkcudbright. They had by this time become more used to Scottish reserve and were liking the people better. Brown felt that the 'cold, solemn Dumfries is a befitting place wherein to write a libel on the Scotch.' They admired a neatness of clothing, particularly of the women, and thought the English labouring classes compared unfavourably in that respect. They liked the civility of the peasants and found them intelligent. Brown was distressed by the women's bare feet but Keats could now admire the beauty of a girl's foot unspoiled in shape by freedom from shoes and particularly against the green of the grass.

At Kirkcudbright Keats continued his letter to Fanny, writing the doggerel rimes of which I have quoted the third verse in Chapter I. I give now the first and last verses:

There was a naughty Boy	There was a naughty Boy
A naughty boy was he	And a naughty Boy was he
He would not stop at home	He ran away to Scotland
He could not quiet be—	The people for to see—
He took	There he found
In his Knapsack	That the ground
A Book	Was as hard
Full of vowels	That a yard
And a shirt	Was as long,
With some towels—	That a song
A slight cap	Was as merry,
For night cap—	That a cherry
A hair brush	Was as red—
Comb ditto	That lead
New Stockings	Was as weighty
For old ones	That fourscore
Would split O!	Was as eighty
This Knapsack	That a door
Tight at's back	Was as wooden
He rivetted close	As in england—
And followéd his Nose	So he stood in
To the North	His shoes
To the North	And he wonderd
And follow'd his nose	He wonderd
To the North.	He stood in his
	Shoes and he wonder'd.

The 'naughty boy' was probably an indirect reference to Mr. Abbey's disapproval. We know that he had termed Keats and Brown 'Don Quixotes.' There is no money to be made out of tilting at windmills; nothing to be gained by wearing out shoe-leather and staring at mountains.

Keats continued his letter:

My dear Fanny I am ashamed of writing you such stuff, nor would I if it were not for being tired after my day's walking, and ready to tumble into bed so fatigued that when I am asleep you might sew my nose to my great toe and trundle me round the town like a Hoop without waking me—Then I get so hungry—a Ham goes but a very little way and fowls are like Larks to me—A Batch of Bread I make no more ado with than a sheet of parliament; and I can eat a Bull's head as easily as I used to do Bull's eyes—I take a whole string of Pork Sausages down as easily as a Pen'orth of Lady's fingers—

'Parliament' was a thin flat cake made of sticky gingerbread; 'Lady's fingers' large white peppermints pink ringed.

They were now heading towards Wigtown but went out of the direct road in order to walk by the sea. At Creetown they came upon a crowd of men, women and children; so large a crowd that it looked like an emigration. On making enquiries they found that at high tide each day the whole population of the village went down to wash themselves on the shore, separating the sexes by a high jutting rock. This was a thing to be admired and wondered at in an era when cleanliness of person, although coming into fashion, was not yet a rule of life.

They rounded the top of Wigtown Bay and headed for Port Patrick in order to cross to Ireland to see the Giant's Causeway. The weather had turned very hot. Six miles beyond Glenluce they were relieved to see the Irish Mail Coach overtaking them. They stopped it and arrived at Port Patrick 'in a jiffy.' Lacking the detail of Brown's journal here— he left out the Irish portion of the tour—we do not know how long the crossing took them. In rough weather it could last as long as four hours, but as the day was fine there was probably only a fair and serviceable breeze blowing.

On the boat there were two old men singing ballads; one on the Battle of the Boyne and another about 'Robin Huid' with the refrain, 'Before the King you shall go, go, go, before the King you shall go.'

They had intended to spend a week in Ireland but found that living was three times more expensive than in Scotland and as costly as a fashionable London hotel. They had been told that it was only forty-eight miles to the Causeway but found them to be Irish miles! So they contented themselves with a walk to Belfast, staying the night there and returning to Donaghadee and Port Patrick the next day. From Port Patrick Keats wrote to Tom:

The dialect on the neighbouring shores of Scotland and Ireland is much the same—yet I can perceive a great difference in the nations from the Chambermaid at this nate Inn kept by Mr Kelly. She is fair, kind and ready to laugh, because she is out of the horrible dominion of the Scotch Kirk. A Scotch girl stands in terrible awe of the Elders—poor little Susannas—They will scarcely laugh—they are greatly to be pitied and the Kirk is greatly to be damn'd. These Kirkmen have done Scotland good (Query?) they have made Men, Women, Old Men Young Men old Women young Women, boys, girls and infants all careful—so that they are formed into regular Phalanges of savers and gainers—such a thrifty army cannot fail to enrich their Country and give it a greater appearance of comfort than that of their poor irish neighbours—These Kirkmen have done Scotland harm—they have banished puns and laughing and Kissing (except in cases where the very danger and crime must make it very fine and gustful). I shall make a full stop at Kissing for after that there should be a better paren*t* thesis: and go on to remind you of the fate of Burns.

Poor unfortunate fellow—his disposition was Southern—how sad it is when a luxurious imagination is obliged in self defence to deaden its delicacy in vulgarity, and in things attainable that it may not have leisure to go mad after things which are not. No Man in such matters will be content with the experience of others—It is true that out of suffrance there is no greatness, no dignity; that in the most abstracted Pleasure there is no lasting happiness: yet who would not like to discover over again that Cleopatra was a Gipsey, Helen a Rogue and Ruth a deep one? I have not sufficient reasoning faculty to settle the doctrine of thrift—as it is consistent with the dignity of human Society—with the happiness of Cottagers—All I can do is by plump contrasts—Were the fingers made to squeeze a guinea or a white hand?—Were the Lips made to hold a pen or a Kiss? And yet in Cities Man is shut out from his fellows if he is poor, the Cottager must be dirty and very wretched if she be not thrifty—The present state of society demands this and this convinces me that the world is very young and in a verry ignorant state—We live in a barbarous age. I would sooner be a wild deer than a Girl under the dominion of the Kirk, and I would sooner be a wild hog than be the occasion of a Poor Creatures pennance before those execrable elders.

His general impression of Ireland was not happy:

. . . we had too much opportunity to see the worse than nakedness, the rags, the dirt and misery of the poor common Irish—A Scotch cottage, though in that sometimes the Smoke has no exit but at the door, is a pallace to an irish one. . . . We had the pleasure of finding our way through a Peat-Bog—three miles long at least—dreary, black, dank, flat and spongy: here and there were poor dirty creatures and a few strong men cutting or carting peat . . . What a

tremendous difficulty is the improvement of the condition of such people.
I cannot conceive how a mind 'with child' of Philanthropy could grasp at
possibility—with me it is absolute despair.

At a miserable house of entertainment half way between Donaghadee
and Bellfast were two Men Sitting at Whiskey—one a Laborer and the other
I took to be a drunken Weaver—The Laborer took me for a Frenchman and
the other hinted at Bounty Money saying he was ready to take it. On calling
for the Letters at Port patrick the man snapp'd out 'what Regiment'?
. . . The two Irishmen I mentioned were speaking of their treatment in
England when the Weaver said—'Ah you were a civil Man but I was a
drinker.'

In this letter occurs the celebrated description of the Duchess of Dunghill:

On our return from Bellfast we met a Sadan—the Duchess of Dunghill—It
is no laughing matter tho—Imagine the worst dog kennel you ever saw
placed upon two poles from a mouldy fencing. In such a wretched thing
sat a squalid old Woman squat like an ape half starved from a scarcity of
Buiscuit in its passage from Madagascar to the cape,—with a pipe in her
mouth and looking out with a round-eyed skinny lidded inanity—with a
sort of horizontal idiotic movement of her head—squab and lean she sat and
puff'd out the smoke while two ragged tattered Girls carried her along. What
a thing would be a history of her Life and sensations.

From Port Patrick they walked northwards to Stranraer at the
bottom of Loch Ryan and thence into Ayrshire, enjoying the beauties of
rich glens, mountain and stream and the grey ocean hurling himself
against the rocky shore and filling the sounding caverns. The coast, the
wooded glens were lovely enough but now they were to enter the vale
of Glen App. 'The entrance to it was like an enchanted region.' They
were back among the mountains they loved.

With the mountains came the rain but not enough to damp their
enthusiasm or to obscure the atmosphere. They began to climb up and
up, filling their lungs with the exhilarating air. I will give this part of
the walk and its climax of joy in Keats's own words. It is a pleasure to
follow the movement of his prose and to note how the arrangement of
words and of vowel-sounds convey with the utmost economy of language
not only the changing scenery itself, but the effect of walking among it.

When we left Cairn our Road lay half way up the sides of a green mountainous shore, full of Clefts of verdure and eternally varying—sometimes up
sometimes down, and over little Bridges going across green chasms of moss
rock and trees—winding about every where. After two or three Miles of this
we turned suddenly into a magnificent glen finely wooded in Parts—seven

Miles long—with a Mountain Stream winding down the Midst—full of cottages in the most happy Situations—the sides of the Hills coverd with sheep—the effect of cattle lowing I never had so finely. At the end we had a gradual ascent and got among the tops of the Mountains whence In a little time I descried in the Sea Ailsa Rock 940 feet hight—it was 15 Miles distant and seemed close upon us—the effect of ailsa with the peculiar perspective of the Sea in connection with the ground we stood on, and the misty rain then falling gave me a complete Idea of a deluge. Ailsa struck me very suddenly —really I was a little alarmed.

The last two sentences run on breathlessly: Keats was reliving the sudden shock, the intaken breath when he saw for the first time the great bird-haunted rock, the giant's stepping-stone from Arran to the mainland.

The rain now beginning to fall in good earnest, they hurried down to Ballantrae, and there met with their first dirty inn in Scotland. 'The Post-chaise' was the best inn but they had been warned not to go there as the landlord was 'a little in trouble.' This they found to be a typically Scotch understatement; the landlord of 'The Post-chaise' had just been arrested for robbing the Paisley Bank. As they came into the town they met with a lassie who took them for travelling jewellers and shewed great eagerness to see their shining wares.

They met an old man who talked well and animatedly, so they asked him if he had ever seen Burns or what he knew of him.

"I ha ne-er seen that Burns," he answered, "but I perfectly approve o' him; for he may ha' had, and so in fac' I think, some guid sense; an' what I nae much ken o', he had a clever knack o' rhyming."

Retired for the night in their bad lodging they were kept awake by tearing, howling winds that shook and shuddered at the windows and doors and lashed the raging sea. Did Keats as he tossed and turned in his dirty uncomfortable bed meditate the sonnet to the great rock standing out there, firm in the bed of the roaring ocean, 'in the Lap of Thunder'? He wrote it at Girvan where the Craig was only ten miles from the land, but I give the sonnet here, because I feel in it the voice of the storm.

To Ailsa Rock

Hearken thou craggy ocean pyramid,
  Give answer by thy voice the Sea fowls screams!
  When were thy shoulders mantled in huge Streams?
When from the Sun was thy broad forehead hid?
How long ist since the mighty Power bid
  Thee heave to airy sleep from fathom dreams—
  Sleep in the Lap of Thunder or Sunbeams,
Or when grey clouds are thy cold Coverlid—

> Thou answerst not for thou art dead asleep
>   Thy Life is but two dead eternities
> The last in Air, the former in the deep—
>   First with the Whales, last with the eagle skies—
> Drown'd wast thou till an Earthquake made thee steep—
>   Another cannot wake thy giant Size!

Keats considered this the only sonnet of any worth he had written of late. At Ballantrae he composed at Brown's request 'a Galloway Song' in dialect to palm off upon the antiquarian Dilke as a genuine article, but decided that it was not good enough. The Song, a lover's lament over the marriage of his lady to another, was suggested by meeting a wedding-party as they entered the town.

Here Brown's published account unfortunately ends: his more pedestrian narrative adds valuable detail to Keats's own story in the letters.

Keats was agreeably surprised at the fertility of Burns's country: he had imagined Ayrshire as 'more desolate, his (Burns's) rigs of Barley seemed always to me but a few strips of Green on a cold hill—O prejudice! it was as rich as Devon' with a beauty thrown into relief by the mountains of Arran, 'black and huge over the Sea,' to which the Craig stands a lone sentinel. They were now going up towards Ayr, passing through Girvan, Kirkoswald, where Burns went to school, and Maybole.

Keats had promised his brother a comparison between the Scotch and Irish and he sent it to him from Kirkoswald. Although interesting, the comparison is, in the nature of things, but superficial. The most outstanding passage in it is perhaps this: 'The Scotchman has made up his Mind within himself in a Sort of snail shell wisdom—the Irishman is full of strong headed instinct—The Scotchman is farther in Humanity than the Irishman—there he will stick perhaps when the Irishman shall be refined beyond him—'

As they came nearer to Ayr, Burns was much in their minds and they made enquiries about him on the way. 'We came down,' Keats wrote to Reynolds, 'upon everything suddenly——'

there were in our way the "bonny Doon", with the Brig that Tam O'Shanter crossed—Kirk Alloway, Burns's Cottage and then the Brigs of Ayr—First we stood upon the Bridge across the Doon; surrounded by every Phantasy of Green in tree, Meadow and Hill,—the Stream of the Doon, as a Farmer told us, is covered with trees from head to foot—you know those beautiful heaths so fresh against the weather of a summers evening—there was one stretching along behind the trees.

They went down to Burns's Cottage, then a whiskey-shop,

and took some Whiskey—I wrote a sonnet for the mere sake of writing some lines under the Roof—they are so bad I cannot transcribe them—the Man at the Cottage was a great Bore with his Anecdotes—I hate the Rascal—his Life consists in fuz, fuzzy, fuzziest—He drinks glasses five for the Quarter and twelve for the hour,—he is a mahogany faced old Jackass who knew Burns— He ought to have been kicked for having spoken to him. He calls himself "a curious old Bitch"—but he is flat old Dog—I sho^d like to employ Caliph Vatheck to kick him—O the flummery of a birth place! Cant! Cant! Cant! It is enough to give a spirit the guts-ache—Many a true word they say is spoken in jest—this may be because his Gab hindered my sublimity—The flat dog made me write a flat sonnet.

Keats destroyed his sonnet, but not before the careful Brown had taken a copy. Dante Gabriel Rossetti wrote to H. Buxton Forman, 'for all Keats says about it himself, it is a fine thing.'

Of Burns, Keats wrote to Reynolds:

His Misery is a dead weight upon the nimbleness of one's quill—I tried to forget it—to drink Toddy without any Care—to write a merry Sonnet—it wont do—he talked with Bitches—he drank with blackguards, he was miserable—We can see horribly clear in the works of such a Man his whole Life, as if we were God's spies.

On their way to Ayr they dined with a traveller whose notions of Shakespeare were a trifle mixed. Talking of Kean,

He said he had seen him at Glasgow 'in Othello in the Jew, I mean, er, er, er, the Jew in Shylock' He got bother'd completely in vague ideas of the Jew in Othello, Shylock in the Jew, Shylock in Othello, Othello in Shylock, the Jew in Othello &c &c &c he left himself in a mess at last—Still satisfied with himself he went to the Window and gave an abortive whistle of some tune or other—it might have been Handel.

From Ayr they went to Glasgow where they admired the Cathedral and the fine stone buildings:

We enterd Glasgow last Evening under the most oppressive Stare a body could feel—When we had crossed the Bridge Brown look'd back and said its whole population had turned to wonder at us—we came on till a drunken Man came up to me—I put him off with my Arm—he returned all up in Arms saying aloud that, 'he had seen all foreigners bu-u-ut he never saw the like o' me—I was obliged to mention the word Officer and Police before he would desist—

The population of Glasgow had some cause for astonishment if Brown was then wearing the costume he described later in a letter to Dilke from Inverness, calling himself 'an odd figure.' He wore a tartan coat and trousers, a plaid thrown over his shoulders, a white hat, and carried, beside his knapsack on his back, a stout stick in his hand. His spectacles were always an object of interest. Keats called him the Red Cross Knight, and declared his own shadow was ready to split its sides as it followed him. He himself was content to confine an oddity of attire to a fur cap.

When they came to Loch Lomond they were again offended by the 'miasma' of tourists. 'Steam Boats on Loch Lomond,' said Keats, 'and Barouches on its sides take a little from the Pleasure of such romantic chaps as Brown and I.'

The lower end of the loch where it narrows into the Leven caught his imagination. He gave Tom a neat pen-and-ink sketch of it, adding colour notes. He said:

the Evening was beautiful nothing could surpass our fortune in the weather —yet was I worldly enough to wish for a fleet of chivalry Barges with Trumpets and Banners just to die away before me into that blue place among the mountains—

Perhaps Keats had at the back of his mind the 'four mann'd and masted barges' of canto 1, section 16 of 'The Lady of the Lake' although he has reversed the barges and substituted trumpets for bagpipes. It was the fashion in Keats's circle to speak of Scott as a popular versifier but no one who had been a boy at the beginning of the century could escape his influence, especially on his native soil. We find above in the same letter a fragment of a rough story made up by Brown on the names of the places with which they had come in contact, beginning 'The Lady of the Lake went to Rock herself to sleep on Arthur's seat and the Lord of the Isles etc.'

They now walked through 'tremendous glens' towards Loch Fyne and had gone fifteen miles before breakfast, making for a place called Rest and be Thankful, only to find it was not an inn but a stone seat. They had to carry their empty stomachs on weary feet for another five miles. As they passed in the early morning through Glencro, they were 'pleased with the noise of Shepherds Sheep and dogs in the misty heights' above. For some time they could only hear them but at length 'two came in sight creeping among the Craggs like Emmets.'

Keats was glad, when they came to the banks of Loch Fyne, a lough of the sea, to bathe the dust off himself in the salt water. He came out 'quite pat and fresh except for the cursed Gad flies—damn 'em they have been at me ever since I left the Swan and two necks.' He made up for Tom a set of doggerel rimes, joyous and Georgian in tone, on the possible usages of gadflies and their stings,[1] of which this is a fair sample:

> Is there a Man in Parliament
> Dum founder'd in his speech
> O let his neighbour make a rent
> And put one in his breech.

They rounded the top of Loch Fyne to Inverary, that fine old town on the edge of the water. The county families of Argyll spent their winters in Inverary and there were many large houses, dominated by the Duke's castle. Keats found the castle 'very modern but magnificent.' Its setting was beautiful among woods 'old enough to remember two or three changes in the Crags above them.' He enjoyed a band, almost certainly the Duke's own band of brass and drums, playing by the castle. But soon a piper struck up and it was too much for his Sassenach ears. 'I thought the beast would never have done.'

Brown's feet were painful through walking in new shoes and he was glad to rest that evening. Keats went alone to a performance by barn-stormers of that once popular drama from the German, *The Stranger*. He found both play and performance intolerable and at times a positive torture. Bagpipes were employed to heighten dramatic tension: 'at the heartrending shoemending reconciliation the Piper blew amain.' The adjective 'shoemending' is a just one for the last scene of this play. Indeed, the whole of *The Stranger* is wretched cobbler's work.

The next morning it rained and thundered but they did not mind. The state of Brown's feet demanded a rest in any case. When he was again able to set off they went across to Loch Awe, walked twenty miles down its banks and on to Kilmelfort on the coast, opposite Luing Island.

. . . the near Hills were not very lofty but many of their steeps beautifully wooded—the distant Mountains in the Hebrides very grand the Saltwater Lakes coming up between Crags and Islands fulltided and scarcely ruffled—sometimes appearing as one large Lake, sometimes as three distinct ones in different directions—At one point we saw afar off a rocky opening into the main Sea—We have also seen an Eagle or two. They move about without the least motion of Wings when in an indolent fit—

They were now in Gaelic-speaking country though many of the people could speak English. Their enjoyment was a little marred by the state

---

[1] It seems worth while recalling here that in late Latin and in Italian literature the gadfly is not infrequently used as a symbol of the poetic frenzy.

of Brown's feet and by the food which in these unfrequented regions
was lamentably poor. It had been difficult at times to get good pro-
vender in Wigtown and Galloway but here a poor diet was the rule.
Eggs and oat cake revolted them; there was no white bread to be had.
One day they rejoiced in a small chicken and a bottle of port, but that
was a happy exception. Fortunately they could take a gill of whiskey
with their meals; this must have helped to digest the sickening quantity
of eggs and 'the cursed oatcake.' When Keats did encounter a bit of
white bread he fell upon it 'like a sparrow.'

They saw to their surprise very few kilts but, said Keats: 'At Fort
William they say a Man is not admitted into Society without one—the
Ladies there have a horror at the indecency of Breeches.' The inn at
Kilmelfort they found well furnished and comfortable though they
were kept awake at night by 'some Whiskey Men' who 'sat up clattering
Gaelic' into the morning. The old grandmother of the house, 'intelligent though not over clean,' made them some snuff as there was none
to be had in the village. They were again affronted here by the poverty
of 'the wretched black Cottages scented of peat smoke which finds its
way out by a door or by a hole in the roof.'

Walking in the Highland country Keats had not forgotten Burns:
he was composing those lines in polter's measure, 'There is a joy in
footing slow across a silent plain' and probably wrote them down about
this time. In them are thoughts of Burns and of his beloved brothers
and sister. There is a sober sadness in the poem.

They walked fifteen miles north in heavy rain to Oban, the port for
the Hebrides, wanting to cross to Staffa. Staffa was an expensive place
to visit. They were asked seven guineas 'and those rather extorted . . .
like paying sixpence for an apple at the playhouse.' However, they
managed to make a bargain for crossing to Mull, a walk across the
island and a visit to Iona, the isle of ancient sanctity on its opposite
shore. In those wild, Gaelic-speaking regions it was necessary to take a
guide. They took ferry to Kerrara and again to Mull. On Kerrara
they saw, looming high on a gaunt rock, the ruins of Gylen Castle
whose casements opened in days gone by on 'foam of perilous
seas.'

On Mull they had a disagreeable walk of thirty-seven miles over
'bog and rock and river' with, said Keats, 'our Breeches tucked up and
our Stockings in hand,' spending the night in their clothes in a
small smoky shepherd's hut with an earthen floor 'full of Hills and
Dales.'

Their attitude to the scenery on Mull is interesting. The traveller of
the earlier part of the eighteenth century was apt to dismiss the mountains of Scotland as barbarous: in steep and dangerous passes, with the

fear of robbers ever before him, he had little temptation or opportunity to admire the view. Travelling more securely Keats and Brown could enjoy to the full the glories of the hills; although Brown, accepting the 'gothic' beauties of a Salvator Rosa landscape as 'romantic,' demanded a clothing of trees. In this noisy, man-ridden age the lover of lone beauty faced with a notorious 'beauty-spot' contaminated by the fumes of petrol and litter-strewing cockneys on holiday yearns for wide bird-haunted open spaces, for the bare beauty of moor, bog and fen under changing skies. But our two romantics found the bareness of the Hebrides ugly. The element of discomfort again had its effect; there might be no danger to life and limb, but there were then no pleasant dry roads across the island. And unfortunately Keats caught a bad cold in Mull.

Brown, who had been enquiring about his ancestors in the Highlands, now came closer to his own kin. On Luing Island where he thought his grandfather had been born, he 'chatted with ane who had been a Miss Brown and who I think,' said Keats, 'from a likeness must have been a Relation':

—he jawed with the old Woman—flatterd a young one—kissed a child who was affraid of his Spectacles and finally drank a pint of Milk—They handle his Spectacles as we do a sensitive leaf—

The people were kind. Once when they lost their way and inquired at a cottage, a young woman 'without a word threw on her cloak and walked a Mile in a missling rain and splashy way to put us right again.' They liked their guide who was friendly and helpful and sang them Gaelic songs.

They crossed the mile of sea to Iona, saw the burial-places of ancient kings and chieftains, collected or bought some Scotch pebbles for Fanny and then hired a boat 'at a bargain' for Staffa. Keats's impressions of Staffa must be given in his own words:

—One may compare the surface of the Island to a roof—this roof is supported by grand pillars of basalt standing together as thick as honeycombs. The finest thing is Fingal's Cave—it is entirely a hollowing out of Basalt Pillars. Suppose now the Giants who rebelled against Jove had taken a whole Mass of black Columns and bound them together like bunches of matches—and then with immense Axes had made a cavern in the body of these columns —of course the roof and floor must be composed of the broken ends of the Columns—such is fingal's Cave except that the Sea has done the work of excavations and is continually dashing there—so that we walk along the sides of the cave on the pillars which are left as if for convenient Stairs—the roof is arched somewhat gothic wise and the length of some of the entire side pillars is 50 feet—About the island you might seat an army of Men each on a pillar. The length of the Cave is 120 feet and from its extremity the view into the sea through the large Arch at the entrance is very grand—the colour of the columns is a sort of black with a lurking gloom of purple therein—For solemnity and grandeur it far surpasses the finest Cathedral—At the extremity of the Cave there is a small perforation into another cave, at which the waters meeting and buffetting each other there is sometimes produced a report as of a cannon heard as far as Iona which must be 12 Miles—As we approached in the boat there was such a fine swell of the sea that the pillars appeared rising immediately out of the crystal—But it is impossible to describe it.

He composed here the poem which is almost an apocalypse, beginning:

> Not Aladin magian
> Ever such a work began.

in which he conjured up the spirit of Lycidas whose body, Milton had supposed, might have been hurled 'beyond the stormy Hebrides.' The memory of Fingal's Cave went in its epic grandeur into 'Hyperion.'

On their way back to Oban they had a vivid sight of 'nature red in tooth and claw,' of that cruel aspect of life which had been puzzling and hurting Keats for months past. A swarm of seagulls attacking a shoal of herrings, 'with now and then a porpoise heaving about among them for a supper.' So great was the destruction of the fish that the water was 'literally spangled with herring scales.'

A sore throat, the fatal harbinger of disease and suffering, already troubling Keats, they rested at Oban for a day or two. The bad weather did not improve his condition. When the throat felt easier they set off north, and at Letterfinlay, about twelve miles from Ben Nevis, Keats wrote his brother a fine letter headed,

> Ah mio Ben.

They had made the ascent of Ben Nevis, and as it is the highest mountain in Great Britain, Keats made up his mind never to climb another 'in the empire.'

I am heartily glad it is done—it is almost like a fly crawling up a wainscoat—Imagine the task of mounting 10 Saint Pauls without the convenience of Stair cases.

They started at five in the morning with a guide 'in the Tartan and

Cap' and 'after much fag and tug and a rest and a glass of whiskey' they attained to the first rise. After some level walking in a 'heath valley in which there was a Loch' they mounted to the last three miles 'of a stony ascent' where they went among the loose stones,

large and smal sometimes on two sometimes on three, sometimes four legs— sometimes two ₁nd stick, sometimes three and stick, then four again, then two, then a jump, so that we kept ringing changes on foot, hand, stick, jump, boggle, stumble, foot, hand, foot, (very gingerly) stick again, and then again a game at all fours.

They must have envied the four legs of the dog which accompanied them, keeping all the time a sharp look-out for the red deer on Nevis; but neither he nor his human friends saw one.

Half-way up they passed large patches of snow and nearer the summit came into a thick mist. The chasms in the mountain, many of them snow-filled, Keats thought 'the finest wonder of the whole':

These Chasms are 1500 feet in depth and are the most tremendous places I have ever seen—they turn one giddy if you choose to give way to it—We tumbled in large stones and set the echoes at work in fine style. Sometimes these chasms are tolerably clear, sometimes there is a misty cloud which seems to steam up and sometimes they are entirely smothered with clouds.

After a while the mist cleared away only to reveal, not clear distances, but

large Clouds about attracted by old Ben to a certain distance so as to form as it appear'd large dome curtains which kept sailing about, opening and shutting at intervals here and there and everywhere; so that although we did not see one vast wide extent of prospect all round we saw something perhaps finer—these cloud-veils opening with a dissolving motion and showing us the mountainous region beneath us through a loop hole—these cloudy loop holes ever varying and discovering fresh prospect east, west north and South. Then it was misty again and again it was fair—then puff came a cold breeze of wind and bared a craggy chap we had not yet seen though in close neighbourhood—Every now and then we had over head blue Sky clear and the sun pretty warm. . . . There is not a more fickle thing than the top of a Mountain—what would a Lady give to change her headdress as often and with as little trouble!

On the summit Keats stood triumphantly on a pile of stones 'and so got a little higher than old Ben himself.' He was tired, but not too weary to commemorate the ascent by a fine sonnet:

Read me a Lesson, muse, and speak it loud
　　Upon the top of Nevis blind in Mist!
I look into the Chasms and a Shroud
　　Vaprous doth hide them; just so much I wist
Mankind do know of Hell: I look o'erhead
　　And there is sullen mist; even so much
Mankind can tell of Heaven: Mist is spread
　　Before the Earth beneath me—even such
Even so vague is Man's sight of himself.
　　Here are the craggy Stones beneath my feet;
Thus much I know, that a poor witless elf
　　I tread on them; that all my eye doth meet
　　Is mist and Crag—not only on this height,
　　But in the world of thought and mental might—

The descent was 'vile.' Keats 'felt it horribly.'

They had been entertained by the story of a certain Mrs. Cameron, a woman of fifty and 'the fattest woman in all Inverness shire' who had got up the mountain with the aid of her servants. Keats said: 'She ought to have hired Sysiphus.' He wrote some delightful verses on her (unfortunately too long to quote) for his brother's entertainment. They are in the form of a spirited dialogue between the fat lady and the mountain.

About this time he received a letter from a friend enclosing an invitation from Blackwood, who must have been informed of the original intention of the walkers to return through Edinburgh. The friend (probably Bailey, whom Keats had intended to visit at Carlisle as he went south) urged Keats to accept and to try to conciliate the owner of the powerful Tory organ.

It is possible that if Keats had complied the virulent attack on him in *Blackwood's Magazine* might have been avoided. The pundits of the north were not unwilling to be placated. Haydon thought it worth while, in the winter of 1820 when his picture was to be exhibited in Scotland, to visit 'the very camp of the enemy, where Blackwood reigned' and to make himself agreeable to Lockhart and Wilson, the twin personalities of 'Z.' Keats, however, as one would expect, rejected his friend's proposal with indignation and scorn.

At Inverness, Keats wrote a letter to Georgiana's mother:

It was a great regret to me that I should leave all my friends, just at the moment when I might have helped to soften away the time for them. I wanted not to leave my brother Tom, but more especially, believe m , I should like to have remained near you, were it but for an atom of consolation after parting with so dear a daughter; My brother George has ever been more than a brother to me, he has been my greatest friend, and I can never forget the sacrifice you have made for his happiness. As I walk along the Mountains here I am full of these things, and lay in wait, as it were, for the pleasure of seeing you, immediately on my return to town. I wish above all things, to say a word of Comfort to you, but I know not how. It is impossible to prove that black is white. It is impossible to make out, that sorrow is joy, or joy is sorrow—

He then referred to a tale Tom had written him of Mrs. Wylie calling in some alarm on Haslam; having read in a newspaper of a man in a fur cap falling over a precipice in Kirkcudbrightshire:

If it was me, I did it in a dream, or in some magic interval between the first and second cup of tea; which is nothing extraordinary when we hear that Mahomet, in getting out of Bed, upset a jug of water, and whilst it was falling, took a fortnight's trip as it seemed, to Heaven; yet was back in time to save one drop of water being spilt.

He said he had only seen one other fur cap and that was at Carlisle which

I dare say was the unfortunate one. I dare say that the Fates seeing but two Fur caps in the North, thought it too extraordinary, and so threw the Dies which of them should be drowned. The lot fell upon Jonas. I dare say his name was Jonas. . . . Stop! let me see!—being half-drowned by falling from a precipice is a very romantic affair—why should I not take it to myself? Keep my secret & I will. How glorious to be introduced in a drawing-room to a Lady who reads Novels, with "Mr So-and-so—Miss So-and-so; Miss So-and-so, this is Mr So-and-so who fell off a precipice and was half-drowned.'

Such a reputation would make his fortune!

His throat being now much worse Keats consulted a doctor. 'Thin and fevered,' far too unwell to continue the journey, he decided to go home by sea from Cromarty. While they awaited a ship Brown and he visited Beauly Abbey, making afterwards together a set of verses on a heap of skulls lying there which they took to be those of the old monks.

When Keats had left him Brown continued the tour alone. He must have been an exceptionally strong man. Six weeks of average walking of twenty miles a day through difficult country in bad weather, latterly on a poor diet, does not seem to have lowered his physique. He and Keats had been, in his own words, 'always moving—moving from one place to another, like Dante's inhabitants of the Sulphur Kingdom in search of cold ground.' Every night when they arrived at an inn Brown was still fresh enough to write 'volumes of adventure to Dilke.' Keats commented on this nightly industry to Bailey:

When we get in of an evening and I have perhaps taken my rest on a couple of Chairs he affronts my indolence and Luxury by pulling out of his Knapsack 1st his paper—2ndly his pens and last his ink . . . I say now why not Bailey take out his pens first sometimes—But I might as well tell a hen to hold up her head before she drinks instead of afterwards.

Keats was, fortunately, not sea-sick on the voyage beyond 'a little Qualm now and then.' He, the only Englishman on board, was forced to live on beef all the way 'not being able to eat the thick Porridge which the Ladies managed to manage with large awkward horn spoons into the bargain.' The journey, not made more pleasant by a dawning toothache, took nine days. Keats landed at London Bridge on August 18th.

His tour would have been cut short in any case: Tom was much worse and the doctor had said his brother must be advised. As Dilke's letter had not reached Keats before he left Cromarty he was spared anxiety on the voyage.

Mrs. Dilke tells us that he came back as brown as a berry and 'with scarcely any shoes left, his jacket all torn at the back, a fur cap, a great plaid and his knapsack.' A sore throat, the toothache and the shock of Tom's condition might well have made him gloomy, but Keats was never a man to worry friends with his troubles. He was outwardly cheerful. He sat down in a comfortable stuffed chair and wriggled himself in with enjoyment, saying with a grin:

" 'Bless thee, Bottom! bless thee! thou art translated.' "

CHAPTER XV

The Death of Tom (August—December, 1818)

KEATS's first thought after he had recovered from the first shock of his brother's relapse was to write to his little sister. He made the best of Tom's condition but added: 'I shall ask Mr. Abbey to let me bring you to Hampstead.' In his letter there is a charming glimpse of one of Fanny's youthful ambitions, 'I would not advise you to play on the Flageolet however I will get you one if you please.'

Fanny was now fifteen. She had asked her brother to speak to her guardian about her school and he had promised to do so. Mr. Abbey wanted to take her away, considering perhaps that she had now as much education as was good for a girl. But Fanny was happier at Miss Caley's. There she must have been fairly free to indulge her own fancies since she talked of playing on the flageolet: apparently the letters she received were not censored by her headmistress, for those from her brother were often decidedly outspoken with regard to her guardian and his wife. She asked her brother to try to persuade Abbey to allow her to remain at school.

Fanny was brought up to see poor Tom who was so pleased that he found it hard to let her go. But he became so agitated on her departure that Keats was doubtful whether a further visit would be wise.

Mr. Abbey, too, had a decided doubt, but not from any consideration for Tom: he had found out from Fanny that she had been taken to see some friends of her brothers. When Keats called on him to arrange a day for Fanny to come up to Hampstead again he would not give his consent. Keats had to write Fanny a difficult letter explaining why she could not come and hinting that it would have been more prudent not to mention those visits. Telling a child not to be open with her guardian is not a wise proceeding: her brother felt the embarrassment. This is how he put it:

I do not mean to say you did wrongly in speaking of it, for there should rightly be no objection to such things: but you know with what People we are obliged in the course of Childhood to associate; whose conduct forces us into duplicity and falsehood to them. To the worst of People we should be openhearted: but it is as well as things are to be prudent in making any communication to any one, that may throw an impediment in the way of any of the little pleasures you may have. I do not recommend duplicity but prudence with such people. Perhaps I am talking too deeply for you: if you do not now, you will understand what I mean in the course of a few years.

Determined not to submit to such tyranny Keats again called on Mr. Abbey, obtaining the concession of one more visit to Tom 'between this (November 5th) and the Holy-days.' Mr. Abbey could not at that period have been actuated by any fear of the child contracting the disease: we can only, therefore, set his conduct down to callousness. He must have known how desperately ill his other ward was. However, Keats, by dint of persistence, extracted permission for a few more visits. We hear nothing of any active interest taken in Tom by Abbey although he was still legally under his guardianship. Keats was unlikely, in the circumstances, to be able to persuade Abbey to allow Fanny to remain at school.

Keats had by now read the cruel Tory reviews of *Endymion*. He was naturally enough hurt and discouraged, but soon recovered his poetic balance. After his return he dined at Taylor's in company with Woodhouse and in the first bitterness engendered by *Blackwood's* attacks declared he would write no more; anyhow, it was not worth while for there was now nothing original that could be said in poetry.

Woodhouse, not realizing that the artist lives more completely in his mood than most men, had taken this as a final decision, and, when the *Quarterly* review came out, wrote a long, kindly, thoughtful letter encouraging Keats by argument and praise to know his own worth and 'reverence the lyre.' Keats, already at work on 'Hyperion,' must have grinned somewhat shamefacedly over this letter. In thanking Woodhouse for his friendly solicitude he tried to explain himself thus:

1st. As to the poetical Character itself (I mean that sort of which, if I am anything, I am a Member; that sort distinguished from the wordsworthian or egotistical sublime; which is a thing per se and stands alone) it is not itself —it has no self—it is every thing and nothing—It has no character—it enjoys light and shade; it lives in gusto, be it foul or fair, high or low, rich or poor, mean or elevated—It has as much delight in conceiving an Iago as an Imogen. What shocks the virtuous philosopher, delights the camelion Poet. It does no harm from its relish of the dark side of things any more than from its taste for the bright one; because they both end in speculation. A Poet is the most unpoetical of any thing in existence; because he has no Identity— . . . filling some other Body—The Sun, the Moon, the Sea and Men and Women who are creatures of impulse are poetical and have about them an unchangeable attribute—the poet has none; no identity—he is certainly the most unpoetical of all God's Creatures. If then he has no self, and if I am a Poet, where is the Wonder that I should say I would write no more? Might I not at that very instant have been cogitating on the Characters of Saturn and Ops? It is a wretched thing to confess; but is a very fact that not one word I ever utter can be taken for granted as an opinion growing out of my identical nature—how can it, when I have no nature? When I am in a room with People if I ever am free from speculating on creations of my own brain, then not myself goes home to myself: but the identity of every one in the room begins so to press upon me that I am in a very little time annihilated—not only among Men; it would be the same in a Nursery of children: I know not whether I make myself wholly understood: I hope enough so to let you see that no dependance is to be placed on what I said that day.

This possession of Keats by the personalities of others appears to me to be more strongly the attribute of Keats as born dramatist than as pure poet. He went on to speak of his purpose in life:

I am ambitious of doing the world some good: if I should be spared that may be the work of maturer years—in the interval I will assay to reach to as high a summit in Poetry as the nerve bestowed upon me will suffer. The faint conceptions I have of Poems to come brings the blood frequently into my forehead. All I hope is that I may not lose all interest in human affairs—that the solitary indifference I feel for applause even from the finest Spirits, will not blunt any acuteness of vision I may have. I do not think it will—I feel assured I should write from the mere yearning and fondness I have for the Beautiful even if my night's labours should be burnt every morning, and no eye ever shine upon them.

Keats ended by saying that perhaps even now he was not speaking from himself, but in an assumed character; but the next sentence he could assure Woodhouse was from himself:

I feel your anxiety, good opinion and friendliness in the highest degree, and am

>   Your's most sincerely
>   John Keats.

Keats, as a man of common-sense, would see that a good deal of the abuse of the Tory journals had been brought upon himself by his open partisanship of Leigh Hunt and of the liberal cause. As Haydon very sensibly remarked, war is war, and if you enter into it you must abide the consequences. After all, *The Examiner* had been, and continued to be, highly provocative.

Hazlitt was at this time similarly attacked in *Blackwood's*, and, although he himself had made many personal attacks on others, was furiously angry and issued proceedings.[1] Hazlitt was a man whose touchiness amounted to mania. If a friend inadvertently passed him in

[1] The suit was settled out of court, Blackwood's paying a lump sum with costs.

the street he would construe it into an insult. It was not, therefore, likely that he would take a gross attack from *Blackwood's* with calm. In Keats, on the other hand, pride and the dignity of his high vocation precluded retaliation. The old belligerent spirit was conquered: his friends speak of him as gentle and ever ready to make excuses for others. The praise of friends and the protests in the public press against the virulence of the Tory attacks gave him pleasure, but did not alter his own opinion of 'the slipshod Endymion':

Praise or blame has but a momentary effect on the man whose love of beauty in the abstract makes him a severe critic on his own Works. My own domestic criticism has given me pain without comparison beyond what Blackwood or the Quarterly could possibly inflict, and also when I feel I am right, no external praise can give me such a glow as my own solitary reperception & ratification of what is fine.

. . . I have written independently without *Judgment.*—I may write independently, & *with Judgment* hereafter. The Genius of Poetry must work out its own salvation in a man: It cannot be matured by law and precept, but by sensation & watchfulness in itself. That which is creative must create itself—In Endymion, I leaped headlong into the Sea, and thereby have become better acquainted with the Soundings, the quicksands, & the rocks, than if I had stayed upon the green shore, and piped a silly pipe, and took tea & comfortable advice.—I was never afraid of failure; for I would sooner fail than not be among the greatest.

Keats was now nursing his brother: so heavy was the penalty imposed on his finely attuned nature of suffering with those he loved that he was sometimes obliged to go out, although he had meant to spend the necessarily long hours beside the sick-bed in study. Even in that other world of reality, his Shakespeare, he could not escape a consciousness of the dying boy, dying 'with an exquisite love of life.' On October 4th, a Sunday evening, Keats was reading *King Lear*. In Act III he underlined the words 'poore Tom,' putting the date in the margin.

Dilke had been ill and was away now recuperating in Hampshire. Keats tried to write him a cheerful letter and succeeded in the main, but could not restrain himself from breaking into:

I wish I could say Tom was any better. His identity presses upon me so all day that I am obliged to go out—and although I intended to have given some time to study alone I am obliged to write, and plunge into abstract images to ease myself of his countenance his voice and feebleness—so that I live now in a continual fever—it must be poisonous to life although I feel well. Imagine 'the hateful siege of contraries'—if I think of fame of poetry it seems a crime to me, and yet I must do so or suffer—I am sorry to give you pain—

I am almost resolv'd to burn this—but I really have not self possession and magninimity enough to manage the thing otherwise—after all it may be a nervousness proceeding from the Mercury—

We know now in the light of medical knowledge that the continued doses of mercury would be, apart from the hours of watching in an airless sick-room, 'poisonous to life,' a life already shadowed, if not yet threatened by disease.

At first in composition Keats took the midway course of translation. He made a free rendering of Ronsard's sonnet on Cassandra, fitly turning the beautiful line, 'Amour coula ses beautez en mes veines' into :

> Love pour'd her beauty into my warm veins.

Unfortunately the translation lacks the last two lines: Keats had no longer the original before him and could not remember the content of them. It was probably this copy of Ronsard borrowed from Woodhouse which led him to a more complete poetic conception. The ode, 'A Michel de l'Hôpital,' is one of the recognized sources of 'Hyperion.' Very soon the huge phantasms of the Titans were taking shape in his brain.

There was another element in the conflict within Keats's young mind and that was the thought of Woman. Keats had felt the normal desire for love and marriage. In July he had written to Reynolds, now engaged to Eliza Drewe:

I have spoken to you against Marriage, but it was general, the Prospect in those matters has been to me so blank, that I have not been unwilling to die —I would not now, for I have inducements to Life—I must see my little Nephews in America, and I must see you marry your lovely Wife—My sensations are sometimes deadened for weeks together—but believe me I have more than once yearne'd for the time of your happiness to come, as much as I could for myself after the lips of Juliet.—From the tenor of my occasional rhodomontade in chit-chat, you might have been deceived concerning me in these points—upon my soul, I have been getting more and more close to you every day, ever since I knew you, and now one of the first pleasures I look to is your happy Marriage—the more, since I have felt the pleasure of loving a sister in Law.

The expression of despair at his own lack of prospect in marriage seems over-strong for a handsome young man of only twenty-two. It is evident from his letters that for this there was more than one cause.

On September 22nd he wrote to Reynolds about a woman who was momentarily disturbing his mind:

I never was in love—yet the voice and the shape of a Woman has haunted me these two days—at such a time when the relief, the feverous relief of Poetry seems a much less crime—This morning Poetry has conquered—I have relapsed into those abstractions which are my only life—I feel escaped from a new strange and threatening sorrow.—and I am thankful for it.— There is an awful warmth about my heart like a load of Immortality.

The girl was a cousin of Reynolds, a Miss Jane Cox, from the East Indies. Keats wrote more fully of her in his journal-letter of October to George and Georgiana:

At the time I called M^rs. R. was in conference with her up stairs and the young Ladies were warm in her praises down stairs, calling her genteel, interesting and a thousand other pretty things to which I gave no heed, not being partial to 9 days wonders—Now all is completely changed—they hate her; and from what I hear she is not without faults—of a real kind: but she has others which are more apt to make women of inferior charms hate her. She is not a Cleopatra, but she is at least a Charmian. She has a rich eastern look; she has fine eyes and fine manners. When she comes into a room she makes an impression the same as the Beauty of a Leopardess. She is too fine and too conscious of her Self to repulse any Man who may address her—from habit she thinks that nothing *particular*.

From Jane Austen's letters we know that 'being particular' was, in plain English, flirting.

I always find myself more at ease with such a woman; the picture before me always gives me a life and animation which I cannot possibly feel with anything inferior—I am at such times too much occupied in admiring to be awkward or on a tremble. I forget myself entirely because I live in her. You will by this time think I am in love with her; so before I go any further I will tell you I am not—she kept me awake one Night as a tune of Mozart's might do—I speak of the thing as a passtime and an amuzement than which I can feel none deeper than a conversation with an imperial woman the very 'yes' and 'no' of whose Lips is to me a Banquet. I dont cry to take the moon home with me in my Pocket nor do I fret to leave her behind me. I like her and her like because one has no *sensations*—what we both are is taken for granted—

From Keats's letter to Reynolds it would seem that if he were not a little in love with this young woman his admiration of her came very near to it.

He had little conversation with his Charmian because of 'the Miss Reynoldses on the look out':

—They think I don't admire her because I did not stare at her—They call her a flirt to me—What a want of Knowledge? She walks across a room in such a manner that a Man is drawn towards her with a magnetic Power. This they call flirting! they do not know things. They do not know what a Woman is.

Miss Jane Cox, a beauty, heiress and the darling of her grandfather (though at this time she had temporarily quarrelled with him) was probably far less self-conscious with men than the average middle-class girl of her day. Apart from the stultifying of their intellects from lack of education and experience of the world, the restraint on women in society, a constant deference to an artificial decorum, put up between them and men a barrier in intercourse.

An easy companionship, an intellectual intercourse with a member of the opposite sex is, I think, essential to an artist; this Keats had lacked. Losing the women of his family so early, his companionship had been almost entirely masculine. He had come nearest to intimacy with Georgiana, but she had been snatched from him. His letters to the Reynolds girls and to the Misses Jeffrey suggest a relationship of easy fun rather than frank intimacy. He had been seeing less of the Misses Reynolds of late and he had given to Bailey as a reason:

I am certain that our fair friends are glad I should come for the mere sake of my coming; but I am certain I bring with me a Vexation they are better without— . . . I am certain I have not a right feeling towards Women— at this moment I am striving to be just to them but I cannot—Is it because they fall so far beneath my Boyish imagination? When I was a Schoolboy I thought a fair Woman a pure Goddess, my mind was a soft nest in which some one of them slept, though she knew it not—I have no right to expect more than their reality. I thought them etherial above Men—I find them perhaps equal—great by comparison is very small. . . .
. . . When I am among Women I have evil thoughts, malice spleen—I cannot speak or be silent—I am full of Suspicions and therefore listen to nothing—I am in a hurry to be gone—You must be charitable and put all this perversity to my being disappointed since Boyhood.

The lack of family contact with women added to his feeling of inadequacy towards them sharpened his awareness of femininity. Later, when he was absorbed in Fanny Brawne, he told her that there had been a time 'when even a bit of ribband was a matter of interest to me.'

The only way to cure this feeling of antagonism towards women was, he thought, to try 'to find the root of the evil,' but 'an obstinate Prejudice can seldom be produced but from a gordian complication of feelings, which must take time to unravell and care to keep unravelled.' Perhaps one cause of his uneasiness, probably the root cause, is unconsciously revealed when he adds: 'I do think better of Woman-kind than to suppose they care whether Mister John Keats five feet high likes them or not.' Keats was very short, and this would, in the absence of the excessive vanity some small men possess, put him at a disadvantage with women. A woman finds it hard to take seriously a man who only reaches up to her shoulder. In this she is logically wrong, but perhaps biologically right.

In another way Keats's experience of women was not normal. He had spent five impressionable years in medicine; he had seen women sick, in childbirth and enduring the agonies of the operation table. In his greatness of heart he suffered with them. Bailey once asked him in a letter: 'Why should Woman suffer?' Keats replied:

Aye. Why should she? "By heavens I'd coin my very Soul and drop my Blood for Drachmas"! These things are, and he who feels how incompete the most skyey Knight errantry is to heal this bruised fairness is like a sensitive leaf on the hot hand of thought.

Later he wrote, 'were it in my choice I would reject a petrarchal coronation—on account of my dying day, and because women have Cancers.'

John Keats, therefore, knew about women both too much and too little. It has been suggested that he was over-sexed, but I find no evidence of this beyond, perhaps, one sentence in a letter to Tom. He says: 'With respect to Women I think I shall be able to conquer my passions hereafter better than I have yet done.' But this, written less than a fortnight after the letter to Bailey about his ill-ease with women and in his following letter to Tom, may well refer to his feeling of antagonism in their presence.

It was probably Marianne who made him feel uncomfortable at the Reynolds's. Dilke describes her as a girl of somewhat saturnine beauty, not popular with many. She had the defects of her qualities. Later, although she loved her husband, Marianne had many hardships and trials in married life over which her spirit triumphed. The hard girl developed into a magnificent woman. Jane Reynolds must surely have been delightful: she married dear Tom Hood who adored her. The literal quality of her mind tempted him to play on her many little domestic practical jokes which she received with what appears to have been a quite exceptional sweetness of temper.

It is possible that Keats had not until now felt strongly that inward loneliness of the unmated. The family tie was a strong one; his love for his brothers and his little sister (so far as he was allowed to indulge an affection for her) had been in some measure a vicarious satisfaction.

There was too, the close friendship with Reynolds. But now one brother was gone, the other almost lost to him, the friend engaged to be married and his desire for the companionship of his young sister thwarted by her guardian. The idea of marriage had been brought forcibly to his mind by the mating of a brother with a girl who seemed an ideal companion and by the happy engagement of his friend. What had seemed a vague project for the future was now brought home to him. He was thinking a good deal about the relation between man and woman.

Keats now met with another woman who interested him. He does not tell us her name.[1] We only know that he had met her before at Hastings and that she lived at 34 Gloucester Street, Queen Square (now Old Gloucester Street). He encountered her near Lamb's Conduit Street; at first passing her by, but turning back, to be greeted with evident pleasure. I continue the story in Keats's own words to George:

We walked on towards Islington where we called on a friend of hers who keeps a Boarding School. She has always been an enigma to me—she has been in a Room with you and with Reyholds and wishes we should be acquainted without any of our common acquaintance knowing it. As we went along, some times through shabby, sometimes through decent Streets, I had my guessing at work, not knowing what it would be and prepared to meet any surprise—First it ended at this House at Islington: on parting from which I pressed to attend her home. She consented, and then again my thoughts were at work what it might lead to, tho' now they had received a sort of genteel hint from the Boarding School.

Back at Gloucester Street they went up to her sitting-room:

a very tasty sort of place with Books, Pictures a bronze statue of Buonaparte. Music, aeolian Harp; a Parrot, a Linnet—a Case of choice Liqueurs &c, &c. &c. She behaved in the kindest manner—made me take home a Grouse for Tom's dinner—Asked for my address for the purpose of sending more game—As I had warmed with her before and kissed her—I thought it would be living backwards not to do so again—she had a better taste: she perceived how much a thing of course it was and shrunk from it—not in a prudish way but in as I say a good taste. She contrived to disappoint me in a way which made me feel more pleasure than a simple Kiss could do— She said I should please her much more if I would only press her hand and go away. Whether she was in a different disposition when I saw her before —or whether I have in fancy wrong'd her I cannot tell. I expect to pass some pleasant hours with her now and then: in which I feel I shall be of service to her in matters of knowledge and taste: if I can I will.

I have no libidinous thought about her—she and your George are the

[1] *See* Appendix VII.

only women à peu près de mon age whom I would be content to know for
their mind and friendship alone.

Keats visited this lady several times, taking home with him more
presents of game. Very soon a stronger interest absorbed his attention
and probably he completely forgot her. But she is of value in indicating
his growing need for an intimacy with a woman.

The high conception of love set out in the idealized love-story in
Endymion was to him no longer a condition unattainable by man. To
George and Georgiana he wrote this significant passage:

Your content in each other is a delight to me which I cannot express—
The Moon is now shining full and brilliant—she is the same to me in Matter,
what you are to me in Spirit—If you were here my dear Sister I could not
pronounce the words which I can write to you from a distance; I have a
tenderness for you, and an admiration which I feel to be as great and more
chaste than I can have for any woman in the world.

He also wrote:

As a Man in the world I love the rich talk of a Charmian; as an eternal
Being I love the thought of you. I should like her to ruin me, and I should
like you to save me.

To the thought of Georgiana and that other friendly woman he added
the conception of woman as mistress; an integral part of a perfect
union, a true marriage.

No doubt Keats was, like many sensitive beings and perhaps most
artists, shy and a little afraid of marriage; the surrender is so complete
a thing and the risk of unhappiness, of the miserable savour of the half-
loaf, so great that the disturbance to an essential integrity of being is
feared in prospect. He said he hoped he would never marry:

Though the most beautiful Creature were waiting for me at the end of a
Journey or a Walk; though the carpet were of Silk, the Curtains of the
morning Clouds; the chairs and Sofa stuffed with Cygnet's down; the
food Manna, the Wine beyond Claret, the Window opening on Winander
mere, I should not feel—or rather my Happiness would not be so fine, my
Solitude is sublime. Then instead of what I have described, there is a
Sublimity to welcome me home. The roaring of the wind is my wife and
the Stars through the window pane are my Children. The mighty abstract
Idea I have of Beauty in all things stifles the more divided and minute
domestic happiness—an amiable wife and sweet Children I contemplate as
part of that Beauty—but I must have a thousand of those beautiful particles
to fill up my heart. I feel more and more every day, as my imagination

strengthens, that I do not live in this world alone but in a thousand worlds. No sooner am I alone than shapes of epic greatness are stationed around me, and serve my Spirit the office which is equivalent to a King's body guard—then "tragedy with scepter'd pall, comes sweeping by." According to my state of mind I am with Achilles shouting in the Trenches, or with Theocritus in the Vales of Sicily. Or I throw my whole being into Troilus, and repeating those lines, "I wander, like a lost Soul upon the stygian Banks staying for waftage", I melt into the air with a voluptuousness so delicate that I am content to be alone.

These things combined with the opinion I have of the generallity of women—who appear to me as children to whom I would rather give a Sugar Plum than my time, form a barrier against Matrimony which I rejoice in . . . I am as happy as a Man can be—that is in myself I should be happy if Tom was well, and I knew you were passing pleasant days—Then I should be most enviable—with the yearning Passion I have for the beautiful, connected and made one with the ambition of my intellect.

He told his brother and sister that Tom was much worse and prepared them for the end:

. . . you must my dear Brother and Sister take example from me and bear up against any Calamity for my sake as I do for your's. Our's are ties which independent of their own Sentiment are sent us by providence to prevent deleterious effects of one great, solitary grief. I have Fanny and I have you —three people whose Happiness to me is sacred—and it does annul that selfish sorrow which I should otherwise fall into, living as I do with poor Tom who looks upon me as his only comfort—the tears will come into your Eyes—let them—and embrace each other—thank heaven for what happiness you have and after thinking a moment or two that you suffer in common with all Mankind hold it not a Sin to regain your cheerfulness—

As the days darkened into November Tom grew steadily weaker. Friends were kind. Haslam did all he could to help. It is to be regretted that we know so little of William Haslam. The survival of certain letters and the destruction or the mislaying of others have given us an unbalanced estimate of the relative warmth of Keats's friendships. Haslam, whom Keats held dearly,[1] said after Keats's death that he had put his letters away so carefully that he could not find them. One, however, has come to light, giving hope that others may be still in existence.

The same applies to Cowden Clarke who would appear from the letters to drop almost entirely out of Keats's life after March, 1817. It is true that Keats saw far less of him because his parents, who had given up the school, had retired to Ramsgate and Cowden Clarke lived with

[1] Brown, letter to Lord Houghton, March 19th, 1841.

them there for several years. But the letters which might have served to remind us of a continued friendship were cut up by the Clarkes for autographs.

Severn volunteered to relieve his friend on night duty from time to time, but Keats would allow no one to take his place beside Tom. His face was haggard, his eyes strained: he told Severn that he felt his own vitality ebbing away with his brother's life. Both Severn and Haslam feared that his health might be damaged, and that he might in the end succumb to the same malady. Severn went so far as to press him not to live in the same rooms, but to take an apartment near by: but as Tom's 'only comfort' Keats would not leave his brother for a single hour.

On December 1st Tom died. Early the next morning Brown was awakened by a pressure on his hand. Keats had come to tell him his brother was dead. Brown said nothing. The two remained silent with hands clasped, thinking of Tom. Then Brown, his thoughts returning from the dead to the living, said:

"Have nothing more to do with those lodgings—and alone, too! Had you not better live with me?"

Keats pressed his hand warmly and replied: "I think it would be better."

Tom was buried on December 7th in the family grave at the City Church of St. Stephen's, Coleman Street. He was only nineteen.

CHAPTER XVI

Fanny Brawne and the Spring of 1819
(December, 1818—May, 1819)

THE good Haslam informed George of his brother's death. Keats did not write; perhaps was not in a fit state to write, until December 16th, and then his letter, a journal one, was not sent off till after January 4th. In it he said:

The last days of poor Tom were of the most distressing nature; but his last moments were not so painful, and his very last was without a pang. I will not enter into any parsonic comments on death—yet the common observations of the commonest people on death are as true as their proverbs. I have scarce a doubt of immortality of some nature or other—neither had Tom.

The rest of the letter is cheerful, giving news of Georgiana's family and friends. Since Tom's death his studies, Keats told them, had been greatly interrupted, he had 'not the Shadow of an idea of a book' in his head: his pen seemed 'to have grown too goutty for verse.' By January, however, he was able to give them those two buoyant poems, 'Ever let the Fancy roam' and 'Bards of Passion and of Mirth,' and the tender little song, 'I had a dove and the sweet dove died.'

This inability to write during most of December had two causes apart from his grief for Tom. The first was that he was in a low state of health, worn out with nursing and highly nervous, probably for a while mentally unbalanced. Severn had wanted to take him away into the West Country, but the weather had been too bad for this.

As Wentworth Place, Keats's new home, was then surrounded by open heath, small animals would penetrate into the garden. One day Dilke shot a white rabbit on his ground and Keats declared it to be the spirit of his dead brother returning to him. Perhaps the soft creature's pitiful eyes were too like the dying boy's. In those days of hard treatment of mental cases this was an absurd delusion to be either derided or ignored: the unimaginative Dilke had the rabbit cooked and brought to table, but Keats's earnest conviction had so played upon the feelings of the household that no one could touch it.

Keats's journal-letter to George and Georgiana reveals nothing of another possible cause of an inability to write, his love for Fanny Brawne. We do not now think that they were betrothed on Christmas Day, 1818,

233

but there must have been some reason for Fanny
later declaring in a letter to Keats's sister that this
had been the happiest day of her life. One thing,
however, is quite evident from a scrutiny of the
letter: Keats was doing his best not to write
about Fanny.

About December 16th there is a reference
to Fanny's mother: 'Mrs. Brawne who took
Brown's house for the Summer, still resides in
Hampstead—she is . . .' Here Keats paused,
thinking of her daughter, wrote 'her' and
crossed it through, then continuing, 'a very
nice woman.' But the daughter could not
be kept out; indeed, she might come in quite
naturally here and not arouse suspicion in the
minds of George and little George to whom he
had written in his last letter that he would
never marry. He took the plunge:

and her daughter senior is I think beautiful and
elegant, graceful, silly, fashionable and strange we
have a little tiff now and then—and she behaves
a little better, or I must have sheered off—

Silhouette of
Fanny Brawne

Some days later when he sat down to write he felt the same urge and
made an artful gambit; artful yet amusingly clumsy from a man of such
delicate perceptions, tact and power over the pen. He started off by
saying, referring particularly to his 'dear sister,' that 'as you were fond
of giving me sketches of character you may like a little pic nic of
scandal even across the Atlantic.' He then hit off a certain 'Uncle
Redhall,' referring to a party of his which he had already described
in detail to his brothers and which took place a year before; adding
carelessly:

Shall I give you Miss Brawn? She is about my height—with a fine style of
countenance of the lengthen'd sort—she wants sentiment in every feature
—she manages to make her hair look well—her nostrills are fine—though
a little painful—her mouth is bad and good—her Profil is better than her
full face which indeed is not full but pale and thin without showing any
bone—Her shape is very graceful and so are her movements—her Arms
are good her hands badish—her feet tolerable—she is not seventeen—but
she is ignorant—monstrous in her behaviour flying out in all directions,
calling people such names—that I was forced lately to make use of the term
Minx—this is I think not from any innate vice but from a penchant she has

for acting stylishly. I am however tired of such style and shall decline any
more of it.

It will be noted that the first stroke of his description is 'She is about
my height,' a pleasing fact. This would seem a strangely unflattering
portrait for a lover to draw. It was written in December: so far as we
know they had met in October or November. He had early fallen in
love. Later, he told her: 'the very first week I knew you I wrote myself
your vassal; but burnt the letter as the very next time I saw you I
thought you manifested some dislike to me.' Perhaps after the first
flash of emotion had died away he had struggled to break through the
intangible trammels which are the bitter-sweet prelude to an irrevoc-
able love and had felt resentment against her for robbing him of his
freedom. It would appear from the passage which follows in the
journal-letter that he made little effort to ingratiate himself with the
beloved:

She had a friend to visit her lately—you have known plenty such—Her face
is raw as if she was standing out in a frost—her lips raw and seem always
ready for a Pullet—she plays the Music without one sensation but the feel
of the ivory at her fingers—she is a downright Miss without one set off—
We hated her and smoked her and baited her, and I think drove her away
—Miss B—thinks her a Paragon of fashion, and says she is the only woman
she would change persons with—What a Stupe—She is superior as a Rose
to a Dandelion—

This incidentally is a commentary on Georgian manners. It was a
brutal age. At bed-time Brown said as he put out the taper what an
ugly old woman this Miss Robinson would make, and Keats groaned
aloud for at least ten minutes.

On January 2nd Keats mentioned in his journal-letter having dined
at Mrs. Brawne's, but still gave no hint of an understanding between
Fanny and himself. He merely commented: 'I never intend hereafter
to spend any time with Ladies unless they are handsome—you lose
time to no purpose.' Poor Miss Robinson! For a woman to be plain is
still a great drawback in life; then it was a tragedy.

It is on the face of it strange that even when Keats was an accepted
lover, no word was written of this to George, the brother and confidant:
but although an apparent openness of behaviour and a freedom of
communication to his friends in his letters rather obscures the fact,
Keats was an intensely reserved man where his deepest feelings were
involved. In the letters there are only two further references to Tom;
one to his grandmother in the doggerel verses 'There was a naughty
boy' he sent to his sister; and one indirect reference to his father and

mother in speaking of a letter-seal to Fanny Brawne. As it was, in view of his circumstances, bound to be a long one, the withholding of news of his engagement from his friends might be explained as a measure of prudence. Mrs. Brawne may have wished it: but it seems strange that his brother should have been kept so entirely in the dark. It is probable that disease was already taking its toll of Keats; from now on we hear frequently of the sore throat. Those with only a slight practical knowledge of tuberculosis know how it warps the mind and accentuates tendencies in the disposition of the patient. Keats had been a reserved man and was now rapidly becoming a secretive one.

With his friends he must have involved himself in many a social difficulty. He had been invited to dine with Mrs. Reynolds on Christmas Day and apparently in the absorption of his love had forgotten all about it. Finding himself with the more pleasing invitation to dine with Mrs. Brawne, he had, when at length the memory of Mrs. Reynolds's prior claim reproached him, to write an explanation and an apology a few days before Christmas. He made the singular excuse that he had accepted an invitation elsewhere, thinking he should be in Hampshire at the time. The engagement to join Brown at Chichester, and proceed for Christmas to Dilke's brother-in-law at Bedhampton, had been broken with the convenient excuse of the throat. So does love corrupt our manners and our good intentions.

Fanny Brawne was a girl of good family, the daughter of a widow who had inhabited Brown's half of Wentworth Place while he was on the walking-tour: it was Brown's habit to let his house in summer. When they removed to Downshire Hill on Brown's return the Brawnes remained on friendly terms with the Dilkes.

Dilke says that Keats met Fanny at his house in October or November. She was eighteen when they first met and as he thought her only seventeen, probably looked young for her age. His description of her was considered by her family to be a very fair one. Her eyes were a bright blue and she would often accentuate their colour by threading a blue ribbon in her hair, which was mid-brown. She seems to have been a girl who, although not an actual beauty, gave the effect of beauty by a subdued but lovely complexion and by personality. After Keats's death her hair faded and she lost her colouring. Writing in 1825, when she was deathly pale and painfully thin, Gerald Griffin, the writer, found her 'as beautiful, elegant and accomplished a girl as ever—or more so than any I have seen here.' Griffin was an Irishman. This would suggest that she had an extraordinary vivacity. In colder contemplation he admitted that her younger sister was prettier, but not so clever.

With a girl as attractive as Fanny, Keats had probably more than one rival. She was a keen dancer and probably frequented the Assembly Rooms: Keats could not dance. In February we find him wishing that his sister could teach him a few common dancing steps. Miss Brawne spoke fluent French (not a common accomplishment in those days) and a number of Frenchmen visited the house; members of that colony in Hampstead started, at the Revolution, in Oriel House and kept up in numbers by victims of Napoleonic persecution. Keats had a good book-knowledge of the language, but was unable to hold his own in rapid conversation. Miss Brawne's popularity, viewed with the jealous eyes of a passionate man violently in love, gave him many miserable hours. Probably as early in his love-story as January, 1819, he wrote those painful verses to her, beginning: 'Physician Nature, let my spirit blood!' One of the Dilkes, writing to a friend, said: 'He doesn't like anyone to look at or speak to her.'

For many years we had nothing in Fanny Brawne's own handwriting but one draft letter which those who dubbed her hastily vulgar suburban flirt could twist to their advantage, but since the publication of thirty-one letters, written from September, 1820 to June, 1824,[1] those who held steadily to a very different view could justify themselves.

The writer of these letters was a lively, practical young woman, not intellectual, perhaps, but of a keen intelligence. In Keats's lifetime she may have enjoyed to the full parties, dancing and admiration, but after her lover's death she led a quiet, retired life, shunning and disliking society. Fanny was a great reader; not of poetry but of novels, though she could laugh at herself for wasting time on 'such trash.' Her bias was towards the brighter side of life, with a devotion to the theatre, and a decided preference for comedy.

Later she wrote. Her son stated that her work was published in *Blackwood's Magazine*, but no trace of her name as contributor can be found: in *Blackwood's*, however, there appeared in February, 1942 a story previously held by Mr. M. Buxton Forman in manuscript, 'Nickel List and His Merry Men, or Germany in the 17th Century,' a horrible tale of robbery, torture and lingering death. Nickel List was the robber refined and immortalized by Schiller as 'Karl Moor.' The narrative is presented plainly and straightforwardly in good English, and with a detachment curious in one of Fanny Brawne's generation.[2] The impersonality of presentment seems more characteristic of the last decade of the nineteenth century, thirty years after her death. The choice of subject certainly supports her own claim to strong nerves.

Fanny Brawne would surely have made an excellent wife for Keats;

---

[1] *Letters of Fanny Brawne to Fanny Keats*, 1820–1824. Edited by Fred Edgcumbe. The Oxford University Press 1937.

[2] Mr. Forman, however, suspected the work may be a translation from a German original.

intelligent enough to appreciate, encourage and respect his work and not too keenly interested to break in upon his solitary thinkings and creations. Her own pen might indeed have contributed to the limited exchequer of a poet. She was practical in worldly affairs and he certainly was not. She had a sense of humour and loved fun: this would have been common, delightful ground. She was a woman lovely and clever enough to supply the 'Charmian' element and one with solid enough qualities to 'wear well,' and although lively, of equable temperament.

Much is demanded of an artist's wife, but one feels that the fine, sensible girl we now know Fanny to have been would not have failed Keats. One thing is abundantly clear; she loved him with her whole heart. No one anxious to get a clear picture of the last years of Keats's life can afford to neglect the reading of these letters. Here and, so far as we know, here only, did Keats's love break through her reserve and cry her feelings aloud. On May 23rd, 1821, exactly three months after his death, she wrote:

All his friends have forgotten him, they have got over the first shock, and that with them is all. They think I have done the same, which I do not wonder at, for I have taken care never to trouble them with any feelings of mine, but I can tell you who next to me (I must say *next* to me) loved him best, that I have not got over it and never shall—It's better for me that I should not forget him but not for you, you have other things to look forward to—and I would not have said anything about him for I am afraid of distressing you but I did not like to write to you without telling you how I ielt about him and leaving it to you whether the subject should be mentioned fn our letters—

Later Fanny supplied to Thomas Medwin for his *The Life of Percy Bysshe Shelley*[1] a passage on Keats largely repudiating the popular notion that he was 'snuffed out by an article,' killed by the reviewers. Of their first acquaintance in the late summer or autumn of 1818 she wrote:

We met frequently at the house of a mutual friend, but neither then nor afterwards did I see anything in his manner to give the idea that he was brooding over any secret grief or disappointment. His conversation was in the highest degree interesting, and his spirits good, excepting at moments when anxiety regarding his brother's health dejected them. . . . An hereditary tendency to consumption was aggravated by the excessive susceptibility of his temperament, for I never see those often quoted lines of Dryden, without thinking how exactly they applied to Keats:

[1] See H. Buxton Forman's edition, Oxford University Press, 1913, p. 296. Medwin did not reveal the writer's name. The mutual friend was Mrs. Dilke.

> The fiery soul, that working out its way,
> Fretted the pigmy body to decay.

Neither Reynolds nor Severn liked Fanny. Reynolds called her 'that poor idle thing of womanhood to whom he has unaccountably attached himself,' and Severn thought her a cold and conventional mistress. He considered the figure of Sacred Love in Titian's picture, 'Sacred and Profane Love,' to be an accidentally authentic delineation of Fanny Brawne. The picture shows a woman of serene glance, plump softly aquiline features and hair of a light brown verging on chestnut. The only portrait we have of her is a miniature painted in later life, showing a thinner face and darker hair, but the same clear, steady look. The shape of the mouth, with a full lower lip, is strikingly similar. A photogravure of the miniature can be seen in *The Letters of John Keats* and also in the volume of Fanny Brawne's letters.

It is probable that in the dislike of these two friends there was more than a little jealousy. A man is seldom satisfied with his friend's choice of a love, and Keats's friends were strongly attached to him. He made little or no exertion to acquire friends, but the glowing genius and the rich humanity within him drew like a magnet.

One may guess that Fanny Brawne, as girls are apt to do, in stepping into Keats's life overthrew all his plans. In a letter to Haydon towards the end of December he spoke of 'a little money which may enable me to study and to travel three or four years.' He was anxious to 'exist without troubling the printer's devil.' But he evidently had not the heart to carry out this intention.

This admission of money in hand was an unwise one. Haydon, who had been asking for a loan, now in the grip of money-lenders and at his wits' end to know where to turn pressed him again. Keats, temporarily short of money, applied to Taylor with the naïve admission that twenty of the thirty pounds for which he asked were for a friend. Apparently Taylor jibbed and Keats had to approach his trustee, but 'from the alertness and suspicion of Abbey: and especially from the affairs being still in a Lawyer's hand—who has been draining our Property for the last 6 years,' he was unsuccessful. He was clearly not aware of the extent of his current resources; he left his accounts entirely in Abbey's hands. Keats had persisted until April, and when this explanation of his inability to lend was sent to Haydon he replied in a characteristically unreasonable and selfish way.

Keats was hurt. He said that he had recently been engaged 'on a Book' but that Haydon had maimed him again. He would, if Haydon still could not obtain the money elsewhere, take him into the City and see what he could do with Abbey in the way of personal persuasion. Did the cautious Abbey meet Haydon and capitulate to his bounding, buoyant personality? The thought of the possible interview is amusing. Keats certainly did succeed in raising the money from somewhere.

The humble, unselfish tone of Keats's letters to this man whose struggling 'genius' he and many of his contemporaries placed far too high is both pathetic and ironic to us who, but for the journals, his letters and connection with the great men of his time, would have almost wholly forgotten that clumsy Phæton, the painter Haydon.

Apart from the memory of Tom, money worries and the menace of a constantly recurring sore throat, this period must have been for Keats a singularly happy one. Not only could he delight in his love, but he had the tranquillity of a congenial house-mate in Brown, and the homes of both the Dilkes and the Brawnes were thrown open to him. For Mrs. Brawne he had a deep affection. The torch of his life flamed up in a blaze of poetry and most of his finest work was done now; in January 'The Eve of St. Agnes,' in February the fragment of 'The Eve of St. Mark,' in April 'La Belle Dame sans Merci,' the 'Ode to Psyche', the 'Ode on a Grecian Urn,' and in May the 'Ode to a Nightingale.'

The letters to Fanny Keats during these months are more frequent. He seemed in his new happiness to yearn after his little sister and probably longed to show her to his love. But Abbey was definite in his refusal to allow her to visit at Hampstead again: the two Fannys did not meet until months after Keats's death. Abbey even went so far as to try to prevent Fanny receiving letters from her brother.

There is one delightful elder-brotherly touch in a letter at the beginning of February. Fanny was restless and discontented at having to leave school, but the time will come, he told her, when she would be more pleased with life:

look forward to that time and, though it may appear a trifle, be careful not to let the idle and retired Life you lead fix any awkward habit or behaviour on you—whether you sit or walk—endeavour to let it be in a seemly and if possible a graceful manner.

In March Fanny was presumably being prepared for Confirmation and faced by a set of questions on dogma which frightened her, she sent them to John. Had he not written to her: 'In all your little troubles think of me with the thought that there is at least one person in England who if he could would help you out of them'? Keats went up to town and selected a little book for her; a book which Mrs. Marie Adami has suggested may have been *The Catechism set forth in the Book of Common Prayer*, 1817. He also set down the answers to her questions clearly and concisely, ending his letter 'Your affectionate Parson John.' This letter and the last letter from her brother, written and signed for him by

Fanny Brawne, were, with H. Buxton Forman's knowledge, withheld from the packet she sent over to him from Spain in 1881 for publication in his four-volume edition, *The Poetical Works and other Writings of John Keats*. They remained in her family as heirlooms.

In January Keats and Brown had gone down into Hampshire,[1] heralded by a letter from Mrs. Dilke to her father-in-law in which she wrote of Keats: 'You will find him a very odd young man, but good-tempered and very clever indeed.' The stay at Bedhampton and Chichester was comparatively uneventful. Keats's throat being troublesome, he did not go outside the garden more than two or three times, but employed his enforced retirement in writing 'The Eve of St. Agnes,' mentioned modestly to his brother as 'a little Poem.'

One expedition he did make of dubious entertainment; an excursion in the rain to see a Chapel consecrated. He told George and little George about it in his own lively manner:

Brown I and John Snook the boy, went in a chaise behind a leaden horse Brown drove, but the horse did not mind him—This Chapel is built by a Mr Way a great Jew converter—who in that line has spent one hundred thousand Pounds. He maintains a great number of poor Jews—Of course his communion plate was stolen—he spoke to the Clerk about it—The Clerk said he was very sorry—adding 'I dare shay your honour its among ush' . . . they sanctified the Chapel—and it being a wet day consecrated the burial ground through the vestry window.

The aspersion on the converts must not be taken too seriously. It is probably only an early example of a popular music-hall jest.

There is an amusing joint letter from Brown and Keats, full of shocking puns, addressed to Dilke at the Navy Pay Office. In Keats's portion this occurs: 'Viz. Remember me to Wentworth Place and Elm Cottage —not forgetting Millamant—' Elm Cottage was surely Mrs. Brawne's residence, for to whom else but Fanny could Keats give the name of the 'fashionable' and 'strange' Millamant, perhaps the most fascinating heroine of the English theatre? This message, unless it were either a joke or an attempt to throw dust in Dilke's eyes, would suggest that he was not corresponding with Fanny during this absence; there are no letters extant. This fact seems to invalidate the idea that they came to some sort of understanding in December; though it is difficult to know how else to explain the statement in Fanny's letter to the other Fanny in 1821 that the Christmas Day of three years ago was 'the happiest day I had ever spent.' She might have first realized his love

[1] *See* Appendix VIII.
[2] Probably on Downshire Hill, Hampstead, at the top of Pilgrim's Lane.

for her on that day; but the burst of fine poetry from him in the spring does not suggest the unsettled mind of an unaccepted lover.

Keats had not been for some months now in the mood for society. The trouble in his throat kept him in from the winter night air and he had his work and his other sweet absorption. His friends saw little of him unless they came up to Hampstead. The Wylies he visited with regularity for Georgiana's sake. Severn was with him a good deal. They walked together and Keats took him to visit the Brawnes. Mrs. Brawne took a strong liking for Severn: it is probable that with a jealous eye upon him he was not given much opportunity to improve acquaintance with her daughter. Severn was a handsome, lively young man.

With the immediate Leigh Hunt circle Keats was now entirely out of sympathy. He had visited at Novello's in December and commented: 'there was a complete set to of Mozart and punning—I was so completely tired of it that if I were to follow my own inclinations I should never meet any one of that set again, not even Hunt.' It is noticeable that Keats was finding mankind in the mass more and more tiring. Once he had been a sociable man. Apart from the lack of savour to a lover in company when the beloved is absent, the disease was probably already slightly warping his mind, making him self-conscious and suspicious. Keats had always spoken of himself as suspicious by nature, but his friends saw no signs of it. If this were so, and he were not merely more clear-sighted than most men, he succeeded in completely disguising it in the earlier days.

There was one friend in whom, together with Reynolds and Rice, his judgment had been at fault. Keats had taken Bailey to be much simpler and more straightforward than he was. At Oxford Keats had pitied his friend sighing gustily after 'a little Jilt in the country' who would have none of him,

little supposing as I have since heard, that he was at that very time making impatient Love to Marian Reynolds—and guess my astonishment at hearing after this that he had been trying at Miss Martin.

The 'little Jilt' was probably Tamsine Leigh, to whom, her granddaughter said, according to family gossip, Bailey had proposed.

Mr. M. Buxton Forman remarks in defence of Bailey that Keats might have been misinformed about Miss Martin who married another Bailey whose Christian name was Edward. Bailey, after proposing to Marianne and being rejected, had begged her to take time to think it over. He then went north and the next thing the family heard was that he was engaged to Miss Gleig, a daughter of the Bishop of Brechin.

He showed his correspondence with Marian to Gleig—returnd all her Letters and asked for his own—he also wrote very abrupt Letters to Mrs Reynolds. . . . The great thing to be considered is—whether it is want of delicacy and principle or want of Knowledge and polite experience—and again Weakness—yes that is it—and the want of a Wife—yes that is it. . . . Marians obstinacy is some excuse—but his so quickly taking to miss Gleig can have no excuse—except that of a Ploughmans who wants a wife.

To do Bailey justice his friends do not seem to have suspected a mercenary motive, although a Bishop can be quite a useful father-in-law to a curate.

Marianne's 'conduct has been very upright throughout the whole affair—She liked Bailey as a Brother.' Bailey does not sound an ingratiating lover; he 'used to woo her,' said Keats, 'with the Bible and Jeremy Taylor under his arm.'[1] Keats felt secure in a condemnation of Bailey's conduct because Rice, Bailey's great friend, who 'would not make an immature resolve,' had abandoned him entirely. With himself in mind perhaps, Keats added, speaking of the Reynolds women:

If you mentioned the word Tea pot some one of them came out with an a propos about Bailey—noble fellow—fine fellow! was always in their mouths —this may teach them that the man who redicules romance is the most romantic of Men—that he who abuses women and slights them—loves them the most—that he who talks of roasting a Man alive would not do it when it came to the push—and above all that they are very shallow people who take everything literally.

He added to that a fine, thoughtful utterance:

A Man's life of any worth is a continual allegory—and very few eyes can see the Mystery of his life—a life like the scriptures, figurative—which such people can no more make out than they can the hebrew Bible. Lord Byron cuts a figure—but he is not figurative—Shakespeare led a life of Allegory: his works are the comments on it—

In this journal-letter to George, perhaps with a hope of marriage in mind, Keats mentions a plan to obtain a physician's degree up in Edinburgh.

I am afraid I should not take kindly to it; I am sure I could not take fees— and yet I should like to do so: it's not worse than writing poems, and hanging them up to be fly-blown on the Review shambles.

He had also been to see Mr. Abbey who had suggested he should

---

[1] Perhaps Bailey was less of a prig than appears: he was at this time contemplating the editing of Jeremy Taylor's Works. See *Keats Circle*, I, pp. 11 & 125.

become a hat-maker. It will be remembered that Mr. Abbey had himself an interest in hat-making.

Another passage in this letter is a prelude to the 'Ode on Indolence.' In playing cricket he had got a black eye from a blow with the ball; the second only he had had in his life and that, curiously enough, outside the fighting schooldays. Was that other black eye an honourable badge of his fight with the butcher-boy[1] in the previous month? Keats had found him tormenting a kitten and had fought with him in a blind-alley in Hampstead for nearly an hour until the brute had to be led home.

We are indebted for this information to Cowden Clarke who came to take his leave of him before going to live permanently with his family at Ramsgate: so was this friend of his vigorous youth spared the pain of seeing him gradually succumb to the dread disease. Keats was apparently at this time 'in fine health and spirits.'

This second black eye had shaken him up and after the application of a leech Keats had gone to bed.

This morning I am in a sort of temper indolent and supremely careless: I long after a stanza or two of Thomson's Castle of indolence. My passions are all asleep from my having slumbered till nearly eleven and weakened the animal fibre all over me to a delightful sensation about three degrees on this side of faintness—if I had teeth of pearl and the breath of lillies I should call it langour—but as I am I must call it Laziness. In this state of effeminacy the fibres of the brain are relaxed in common with the rest of the body, and to such a happy degree that pleasure has no show of enticement and pain no unbearable frown. Neither Poetry, nor Ambition, nor Love have any alertness of countenance as they pass by me: they seem rather like three figures on a greek vase—a Man and two women who no one but myself could distinguish in their disguisement. This is the only happiness; and is a rare instance of advantage in the body overpowering the Mind.

When he wrote, or finished, the 'Ode on Indolence' in May the man and two women (on a type of Greek vase a Bacchus or priest in god's guise followed by two priestesses) became three female figures, Love, Ambition and his 'demon poesy.' This ode, though imperfect and unpolished, is full of cloudy beauty. There is no distinct colour in it; the highest note is that suggested when the spell of the shadowy enchantment is lifting in the 'newly budded vine' about the open window. There are few high vowels and the consonants are blurred. The movement of it seems to shift and change softly like a dove-coloured cloud. One line, purely romantic, is haunting:

My sleep hath been embroider'd with dim dreams.

[1] In a letter to Dilke, May 7th, 1830, George called his opponent 'a scoundrel in livery.'

But in March, writing to his brother, Keats could not detach himself from reality so completely. He has heard that Haslam's father is dying and must go to town the next day to see his friend. 'This is the world; thus we cannot expect to give way many hours to pleasure.' He went on to reflect that few of us can get near to that state of disinterestedness which was so often before him as man's goal. 'Even so we have leisure to reason on the misfortunes of our friends; our own touch us too nearly for words.' In a piece of beautiful balanced prose he set down in part his new attitude to life:

From the manner in which I feel Haslam's misfortune I perceive how far I am from any humble standard of disinterestedness—Yet this feeling ought to be carried to its highest pitch as there is no fear of its ever injuring Society—which it would do I fear pushed to an extremity—For in wild nature the Hawk would lose his Breakfast of Robins and the Robin his of Worms—the Lion must starve as well as the swallow. The greater part of Men must make their way with the same instinctiveness, the same unwandering eye from their purposes, the same animal eagerness as the Hawk. The Hawk wants a Mate, so does the Man—look at them both they set about it and procure one in the same manner. They want both a nest and they both set about one in the same manner—they get their food in the same manner—The noble animal Man for his amusement smokes his pipe—the Hawk balances about the Clouds—that is the only difference of their leisures. This it is that makes the Amusement of Life—to a speculative Mind. I go among the Fields and catch a glimpse of a Stoat or a fieldmouse peeping out of the withered grass—the creature hath a purpose and its eyes are bright with it. I go amongst the buildings of a city and I see a Man hurrying along—to what? the Creature has a purpose and his eyes are bright with it. But then, as Wordsworth says, "we have all one human heart"—there is an ellectric fire in human nature tending to purify—so that among these human creatures there is continually some birth of new heroism. The pity is that we must wonder at it: as we should at finding a pearl in rubbish.

I have no doubt that thousands of people never heard of have had hearts completely disinterested: I can remember but two—Socrates and Jesus—their Histories evince it. What I heard a little time ago, Taylor observe with respect to Socrates may be said of Jesus—That he was so great a man that though he transmitted no writing of his own to posterity, we have his Mind and his sayings and his greatness handed to us by others. It is to be lamented that the history of the latter was written and revised by Men interested in the pious frauds of Religion. Yet through all this I see his splendour.

Keats had grown since he sat upon a rock by the sea and 'saw too distinct into the core of an eternal fierce distruction.'

He then fell again into that speculation of a superior being looking down and seeing with amusement man's activities, the small strife of a human quarrel, as he himself is entertained, 'with the alertness of a Stoat or the anxiety of a Deer.'

Though a quarrel in the Streets is a thing to be hated, the energies displayed in it are fine; the commonest Man shows a grace in his quarrel—By a superior being our reasonings may take the same tone—though erroneous they may be fine—This is the very thing in which consists poetry; and if so it is not so fine a thing as philosophy—For the same reason that an eagle is not so fine a thing as a truth—Give me this credit—Do you not think I strive —to know myself? Give me this credit—and you will not think that on my own account I repeat Milton's lines

> "How charming is divine Philosophy
> Not harsh and crabbed as dull fools suppose
> But musical as is Apollo's lute"—

No—not for myself—feeling grateful as I do to have got into a state of mind to relish them properly—Nothing ever becomes real till it is experienced— Even a Proverb is no proverb to you till your Life has illustrated it.

This idea of some being looking down on the world goes like a silver thread through his life from the moon as 'Maker of sweet poets,' from the moon-goddess in *Endymion* to the conception of a fixed star 'which can never cease to be open lidded and stedfast over the wonders of a great Power' linked in this rich period of poetic growth with love, that basic force which alone gives a man full power and contentment, in the sonnet, 'Bright Star, would I were stedfast as thou art.'

The 'Bright Star' sonnet was copied by Fanny Brawne into the first volume of Cary's 'Dante' which had been given to her by Keats, and in which he himself had written down the sonnet, 'A Dream, after reading Dante's episode of Paolo and Francesca.'

On the 'Dream' sonnet Keats wrote to his brother:

The fifth canto of Dante pleases me more and more—it is that one in which he meets with Paolo and Francesca—I had passed many days in rather a low state of mind, and in the midst of them I dreamt of being in that region of Hell.

The dream was one of the most delightful enjoyments I ever had in my life—I floated about the whirling atmosphere as it is described with a beautiful figure to whose lips mine were joined as it seem'd for an age—and in the midst of all this cold and darkness I was warm—even flowery tree tops sprung up and we rested on them sometimes with the lightness of a cloud till the wind blew us away again—I tried a Sonnet upon it—there are four-teen lines but nothing of what I felt in it—O that I could dream it every night—

As Hermes once took to his feathers light
When lulled Argus, baffled, swoon'd and slept
So on a delphic reed my idle spright
So play'd, so charm'd so conquer'd, so bereft
The dragon world of all its hundred eyes
And seeing it asleep so fled away:—
Not to pure Ida with its snow cold skies,
Nor unto Tempe where Jove grieved that day,
But to that second circle of sad hell,
Where in the gust, the whirlwind and the flaw
Of Rain and hailstones lovers need not tell
Their sorrows—Pale were the sweet lips I saw
Pale were the lips I kiss'd and fair the form
I floated with about that melancholy storm—

This journal letter, so rich in poetry, contains beside, 'La Belle Dame sans Merci,' 'The Ode to Psyche,' the two sonnets on Fame, 'To Sleep,' 'If by dull rhymes our English must be chain'd' (an experiment in form), and that poem of sorrow :

Why did I laugh tonight? No voice will tell:
    No God no Deamon of severe response
Deigns to reply from heaven or from Hell—
    Then to my human heart I turn at once—
Heart! thou and I are here sad and alone:
    Say, wherefore did I laugh? O mortal pain!
O Darkness! Darkness! ever must I moan
    To question Heaven and Hell and Heart in vain!
Why did I laugh? I know this being's lease
    My fancy to its utmost blisses spreads:
Yet could I on this very midnight cease
    And the world's gaudy ensigns see in shreds.
Verse, fame and Beauty are intense indeed
But Death intenser—Death is Life's high mead.

Keats is careful to explain that the sonnet was the outcome of a passing mood and 'written with no Agony but that of ignorance,' but it is hard to believe that this was the case. George knew nothing nor was he to be given any hint of that great consuming love, at once a joy and a pain.

Keats had also of late been hurt by a painful reminder of his dead brother's sufferings and of a wanton cause for their increase. In turning over old papers he had found the 'Amena' correspondence. We can guess from the careful way Tom docketed in his clerkly hand letters received that he was by nature methodical. He seems to have made copies of the letters sent in reply to 'Amena.' It would appear that he had to a certain extent kept John in the dark about the correspondence.

We do not know when the deception was revealed, but it was said that his misery at the discovery threw Tom into a far worse state of health. Keats, on discovering who was responsible for the hoax, dropped Wells's acquaintance. The last mention of Wells in the letters is in January, 1818, but this does not, of course, fix the date of the termination of their friendship.

Keats in his anger at Wells's deception vowed revenge in a passage of this journal-letter:

I do not think death too bad for the villain—The world would look upon it in a different light should I expose it—they would call it a frolic—so I must be wary—but I consider it my duty to be prudently revengeful. I will hang over his head like a sword by a hair. I will be opium to his vanity—if I cannot injure his interests—He is a rat and he shall have ratsbane to his vanity—I will harm him all I possibly can—I have no doubt I shall be able to do so—

Probably his threats came to nothing; though he did take one step, perhaps with the purpose of getting advice from a man he trusted, in sending two of the letters to his friend Thomas Richards.

But in the greatness of his mind Keats could rise up from the fire of thwarted passion and of anger. The following passage not only amplifies the speculation on life given above but links on to the 'Chambers of Life' allegory of the year before (see page 161):

The common cognomen of this world among the misguided and superstitious is 'a vale of tears' from which we are to be redeemed by a certain arbitrary interposition of God and taken to Heaven—What a little circumscribed straightened notion! Call the world if you Please "The vale of Soul-making". Then you will find out the use of the world. . . . I say 'Soul making' Soul as distinguished from an Intelligence—There may be intelligences or sparks of the divinity in millions—but they are not Souls till they acquire identities, till each one is personally itself . . .'

I will call the *world* a School instituted for the purpose of teaching little children to read—I will call the *human heart* the *horn Book* used in that School —and I will call the *Child able to read, the Soul* made from that *School* and its *hornbook*. Do you not see how necessary a World of Pains and troubles is to school an Intelligence and make it a Soul? A Place where the heart must feel and suffer in a thousand diverse ways! Not merely is the Heart a Hornbook, It is the Minds Bible, it is the Minds experience, it is the teat from which the Mind or intelligence sucks its identity. As various as the Lives of Men are— so various become their Souls, and thus does God make individual beings, Souls, Identical Souls of the Sparks of his own essence—This appears to me a faint sketch of a system of Salvation which does not affront our reason and humanity—I am convinced that many difficulties which christians labour under would vanish before it—there is one which even now Strikes me—the Salvation of Children—In them the Spark or intelligence returns to God without any identity—it having had no time to learn of and be altered by the heart—or seat of the human Passions— . . .

Seriously I think it probable that this System of Soul-making—may have been the Parent of all the more palpable and personal Schemes of Redemption, among the Zoroastrians the Christians and the Hindoos.

This surely is a remarkable utterance for a man of twenty-four. It is possible that his mind had been stimulated by the meeting a few days before with that inspired talker, Coleridge.

Years after Coleridge gave two separate accounts of this meeting, and neither of them tallies with Keats's version. Coleridge suggests only a momentary encounter and gives details which, from a knowledge of Keats at this period, cannot be accepted. He speaks of Keats's figure as 'loose,' 'slack,' and says that Keats, after leaving him, turned back with: "Let me carry away the memory, Coleridge, of having pressed your hand!" Coleridge, feeling a heat and dampness in the poet's hand, remarked to his companion, Mr. Green, that there was death in it. This comment, as remembered, might have been no more than an excusable touch of drama in an old man who long survived the young one or—which seems more likely—might have been actually made after some later meeting with Keats on their communal ground, the Heath; though, as a genius of acute perception and some medical knowledge, it is possible that on this occasion Coleridge might have perceived in an apparently robust young man signs of disease beyond the already troublesome sore throat.

Keats himself says he met Coleridge in Millfield Lane, Hampstead, with Mr. Green, his demonstrator at Guy's, and joined them 'after enquiring by a look whether it would be agreeable.' They walked at an 'alderman-after-dinner pace' for nearly two miles. The tide of Coleridge's mellifluous conversation flowed over him; that marvellous talk 'far above singing,' 'the music of thought.' He touched in his tangential way on many subjects: Keats gave a rough list of them to his brother. Among them were, 'Nightingales, Poetry—on Poetical Sensation—Metaphysics—Different genera and species of Dreams . . . a dream accompanied by a sense of touch—single and double touch— A dream related.' Keats told his brother that he heard Coleridge's voice as he came towards him and heard it as he moved away. 'I had heard it all the interval—if it may be called so. He was civil enough to ask me to call on him at Highgate.' So far as we know Keats did not call. Perhaps the first impact with such a determined talker had stunned him; but the memory of that meeting was soon to crystallize in the sonnet, 'On a Dream,' the above philosophical passage and, a month later, in the 'Ode to a Nightingale.'

On the lighter side Keats's letter to George contains the extempore 'When they were come unto the Faery's Court,' the 'Chorus of Faeries,' the verses on Brown in the Spenserian manner which, taken conversely, give us a vivid picture of the full-fleshed, worldly man, a reference to the velocipede 'the nothing of the day,' his critique on Reynolds's *Peter Bell* and a piece of rich hyperbole on a thin lady for whom Henry Wylie had an inclination. It is seldom that these joyous passages can be extracted from the main body of a letter, but this one is fortunately self-contained :

Says I, Will Henry have that Miss ——, a lath with a boddice, she who has been fine drawn—fit for nothing but to be cut up into Cribbage pins, to the tune of 15–2 ; one who is all muslin ; all feathers and bone ; once in travelling she was made use of as a lynch pin ; I hope he will not have her, though it is no uncommon thing to be *smitten with a staff* ; though she might be very useful as his walking-stick, his fishing-rod, his tooth-pick, his hat-stick (she runs so much in his head)—let him turn farmer, she would cut into hurdles ; let him write poetry, she would be his turn-style. Her gown is like a flag on a pole ; she would do for him if he turn freemason ; I hope she will prove a flag of truce ; when she sits languishing with her one foot on a stool, and one elbow on the table, and her head inclined, she looks like the sign of the crooked billet—or the frontispiece to Cinderella or a tea-paper wood-cut of Mother Shipton at her studies ; she is a make-believe—She is bone *s*ide a thin young 'oman—But this is mere talk of a fellow creature ; yet pardie I would not that Henry have her—Non volo ut eam possideat, nam, for, it would be a bam, for it would be a sham—

Reynolds's *Peter Bell* was an anonymous skit in anticipation of Wordsworth's poem and written in a few hours after seeing the advertisement of *Peter Bell*. Taylor and Hessey published quickly : it was soon 'in every bookseller's window in London,' and within two months had run through three editions. The joke was made more pungent by the fact that Reynolds had intuitively hit upon the stanza form selected by Wordsworth for his *Peter Bell*. Reynolds made fun of the homelier side of Wordsworth's muse in such lines as :

> 'Tis Peter Bell—'tis Peter Bell,
> Who never stirreth in the day ;
> His hand is wither'd—he is old !
> On Sunday he is us'd to pray,
> In winter he is very cold.

As the parody progressed the verses became more absurd :

His stick is made of wilding wood,
His hat was formerly of felt,
His duffel cloak of wool is made,
His stockings are from stock in trade,
His belly's belted with a belt.

It ends magnificently. 'Peter Bell,' surveying the tombstones in the churchyard by the light of a lantern, comes to Wordsworth's grave. At this discovery he mutters the inscription:

He mutters ever—'W.W.
Never more will trouble you, trouble you.'

Keats's review of this 'false Florimel' in *The Examiner* was, in his own words, 'a little politic—I say something for and against both parties.' The more the author 'may love the sad embroidery of the *Excursion*, the more will he hate the coarse samples of Betty Foy and Alice Fell.' Here Keats was true to the majority of the younger readers of Wordsworth. He added that in the present work there was 'such a pernicious likeness in the scenery, such a pestilent humour in the rhymes, and such an inveterate cadence in some of the stanzas' that 'this Simon Pure is in points the very man.' Reynolds had taken as motto to his parody, 'I do affirm that I am the REAL SIMON PURE.' To his brother wrote Keats: 'I and my conscience are in luck to-day': he could speak his mind and still be politic to the other party. 'If we are,' he continued in his notice, 'one part amused with this, we are three parts sorry that any one who has any appearance of appreciating WORDSWORTH, should show so much temper at this really provoking name of *Peter Bell*.'

Viewed impartially, Reynolds's joke was not perhaps in the best of taste though the richness of it mitigated its impudence. It was followed by several other anonymous parodies. This unwelcome publicity stimulated the sale of the real *Peter Bell* so that a second edition was soon called for. People bought it to compare with the parodies. In his second edition Wordsworth, however, inadvertently capped the joke: he cut out many of the more humourless lines. Reynolds's *Peter Bell*, reaching Italy, stimulated Shelley into contributing yet another *Peter Bell* in the same year, *Peter Bell the Third*, by Miching Mallecho, Esq.

The preface Reynolds put into the mouth of the pseudo-Wordsworth is so amusing an exaggeration of Wordsworth's egotism that perhaps a portion of it might be quoted here:

It has been my aim and my achievement to deduce moral thunder from buttercups, daisies, celandines, and (as a poet, scarcely inferior to myself, hath it) "such small deer." Out of sparrows' eggs I have hatched great truths, and with sextons' barrows have I wheeled into human hearts, piles of the weightiest philosophy.

At the pleasant house in Hampstead there were changes imminent. The Dilkes' boy, Charles Wentworth, now nine years of age, had entered Westminster School. Charley was his father's idol. 'One would think,' said Keats, 'Dilke ought to be quiet and happy—but no—this one Boy makes his face pale, his society silent and his vigilance jealous.' Dilke left the comfortable house and garden he had made for himself, went to live in Town lodgings near the school, and Mrs. Brawne moved into Wentworth Place.

Mrs. Brawne's decision to occupy the Dilke house seems to suggest that, however improvident the match with an impecunious poet, she did not intend to discourage it. Perhaps the young people were too determined for her. Keats and Fanny were not yet, so far as we know, formally engaged, but they certainly were by early summer.

Keats at first thought of lodging elsewhere: the letter of the strict etiquette of the day might have demanded this. But the thought of having his beloved so near him must have overcome the prudent resolution. In May the two lovers were living in joined houses under one roof and in a common garden.

CHAPTER XVII

The Isle of Wight and Winchester (May—October, 1819)

WENTWORTH PLACE is not large. Dilke, in the fashionable phrase-
ology of the day, described the two houses as cottages, but to us they are
not that. The rooms are high and well proportioned. Excluding the
basement, Brown's house had four and Dilke's five rooms. Dilke's two
living-rooms were divided by folding-doors and could be thrown into
one large enough in which to give a party. The house would just hold
in comfort Mrs. Brawne and her three children; beside Fanny there
were Sam, a boy of fourteen, and a little sister, Margaret. In 1838 the
two houses were bought by Miss Chester, an actress who had formerly
held the Court appointment of reader to George IV: she converted
them into one house with the addition of a large drawing-room.

Wentworth Place, now the Keats Memorial House, is full of the
peace and dignity of age, though tragedy has owned it. Keats was ill
and unhappy within its walls; in 1828 Sam Brawne[1] died there of the
same disease; and in November, 1829, Mrs. Brawne came to a terrible
end. Holding aloft a candle to light a friend out of the house, her dress
caught fire and she died as the result of burns.

In the garden, the design of which is little altered since Keats's
day, there are some fine old trees. The glory of them is a two hundred-
years-old mulberry now supporting his great age with a crutch but still
producing abundant fruit. The plum tree under which the 'Nightingale' Ode is said to have been written was still there until recently, an
ivy-clad stump. Before the house grew a hedge of laurustinus, now
replaced by a wooden fence. Water was obtained from a conduit
which was not long ago uncovered in the course of drain repairs.

To a man in love the period of engagement is necessarily a trying
one: to Keats, an ardently passionate man, the nearness of his beloved
must have been almost unbearable. There are indications in his letters
that she herself was not yet fully awakened to love. The response is
often far slower in a woman and Fanny was young. Before his death
she had learned to love him wholly.

Although his love for her inspired most of his finest work, Keats
could not write when he was near her: work in some form or other was,
apart from the creative urge within him, a necessity, as money was
short. He would soon have temporarily to leave Wentworth Place

[1] His grave is in St. Martin's Burial Ground, Camden Town.

because of Brown's habit of letting his house for the summer. At the end of May Keats wrote to Miss Jeffrey asking her to find a cheap lodging for him but not in, or too near Teignmouth: there the memory of Tom would be too painful. He spoke of an alternative to this retirement:

I have the choice as it were of two Poisons (yet I ought not to call this a Poison) the one is voyaging to and from India for a few years; the other is leading a fevrous life alone with Poetry—This latter will suit me best; for I cannot resolve to give up my Studies.

The idea of becoming a surgeon on board ship may have originated in Dr. Darling, Haydon's doctor, who had himself served in an East Indiaman. A voyage might materially have benefited Keats's health: although the conditions on board were at that time so rough, he was a good sailor. The fresh salt air might have proved a drastic remedy. A distraction of interests would not have hurt his mind and might have prevented morbidities that hastened the progress of the disease. This he realized in part: did he not 'strive to know' himself? In a second letter to Miss Jeffrey he wrote:

Your advice about the Indiaman is a very wise advice, because it just suits me, though you are a little in the wrong concerning its destroying the energies of Mind: on the contrary it would be the finest thing in the world to strengthen them—To be thrown among people who care not for you, with whom you have no sympathies forces the Mind upon its own resources, and leaves it free to make its speculations of the differences of human character and to class them with the calmness of a Botanist. An Indiaman is a little world. One of the great reasons that the English have produced the finest writers in the world is, that the English world has ill-treated them during their lives and foster'd them after their deaths. They have in general been trampled aside into the bye paths of life and seen the festerings of Society.

After developing this idea by examples he added:

I have been very idle lately, very averse to writing; both from the overpowering idea of our dead poets and from abatement of my love of fame. I hope I am a little more of a Philosopher than I was, consequently a little less of a versifying Pet-lamb.

Miss Jeffrey had suggested to him the lovely village of Bradley. Keats, however, decided not to go there for the moment as Rice, ill and obliged to leave London for a time, had asked him to accompany him to the Isle of Wight. Living, he assured Keats, could be very cheap on the seaward side of the Island. Cheapness was a prime necessity; by

early June Keats was too poor to afford the coach-fare to Walthamstow to see his sister. A return of the sore throat prevented him from
walking.

In June Abbey showed Keats a letter from George containing news
of an event Keats had been eagerly anticipating in writing to America.
George had a daughter. Keats had assumed the 'little child o' the
western wild' would be a boy and predicted he would become the first
American poet. There are clear indications in the letters that if he had
not felt responsibility for the young sister inevitably in the clutch of
Abbey Keats might, after Tom's death, have followed George: it is
curious to reflect that if he had done so he himself would have been the
first American poet, at least by adoption.

In writing to Fanny of the birth of a niece Keats added less agreeable news; that, according to Abbey, Mrs. Midgley Jennings was
threatening to file a further petition against the estate. If she won her
case Abbey 'would be decidedly in the wrong box.' 'If it goes against
him,' Keats told Haydon in a letter, 'I must in conscience make over to
him what little he may have remaining.' Abbey also told Keats, quite
falsely, that Tom's money from the grandmother,[1] on which Keats had
been counting for his relief, might be held until Fanny came of age.

Whether Abbey had any basis for this last assertion we shall never
know as Mrs. Jennings' deed of settlement was later lost, but we can
say there was no ground for a further petition to Chancery by Mrs.
Midgley. Here Abbey, either a foolish man or a sly one, seems to have
worked upon Keats's ignorance both of money matters and the will,
going so far as to state that even if Mrs. Midgley failed in her action
there would be heavy costs for the estate to pay.

With our fresh knowledge of the Keats's affairs the question forcibly
arises, was Abbey an honest man? Although he could not touch the
money lying in Chancery (the capital of the mother's annuity and the
grandfather's direct legacy Keats's share of which should have been
claimed in 1816 when he came of age) it was, to say the least, gross
negligence on Abbey's part to keep the knowledge of it to himself or, if
unaware of the money's existence, not to have properly informed himself as guardian of the terms of John Jennings' will. Abbey could not
touch the money in Chancery but he could handle that left by Mrs.
Jennings for her grandchildren's benefit; legally in the case of Fanny
and by consent in that of Keats who was so careless in his affairs. It
will be remembered that when Fanny came of age, Abbey being in her
opinion on the verge of bankruptcy, Dilke managed to wrest her money
out of her guardian's hands, but with great difficulty.

---

[1] According to George's letter to Dilke, April 10th, 1824, £1,100, of which £100 went to
Fanny over and above her share of one third.

Keats, now obliged to depend on Brown for daily sustenance, asked Haydon to return the money lent him, writing 'your Pocket must needs be very low having been at the ebb tide so long: but what can I do? mine is lower.' As he put it to George in his own vivid way: 'Now in this see-saw game of Life I got nearest to the ground and this chancery business rivetted me there so that I was sitting in that uneasy position where the seat slants so abominably.'

An application to Haslam, to whom George had lent money, resulted in the prompt repayment of a part, but Haydon could not or would not return one penny; nor does he, in his monstrous egotism, have appeared to bother about the matter although Keats had made it clear his income might cease entirely. Keats, thinking Haydon might at least have tried to sell some drawings, could no longer feel a warmth towards Haydon: the acquaintance continued but not in the same intimacy.

It was this cooling and an uncomfortable sense of obligation which probably led Haydon, always influenced in his attitude towards others by his own self-centred emotions, his own conveniences, to defame Keats after death; representing him, not only in his Journal but to Miss Mitford and others, as a spineless boy who, after the attacks in the Tory press, 'was scarcely ever sober for weeks together.' One of Haydon's instances of 'irregularities' to Miss Mitford was that he 'covered his tongue & throat as far as he could reach with cayenne pepper in order to have the delicious coolness of claret in all its glory.' This sounds like a mere boyish prank, a student's trick: Albert Smith tells us that the wags in his medical school (Middlesex) used cayenne pepper in their broad joking. When a man came into the dissecting-room dazed with heavy drinking the night before they would give him a pot of beer laced with cayenne and, when this had taken its effect, prop him up in a corner to have his sleep out.

By July 1st Keats was at Shanklin, staying in a cottage a little back from the sea. 'Our window,' he told his sister, 'looks over house tops and Cliffs onto the Sea, so that when the Ships sail past the Cottage chimneys you may take them for Weathercocks.' Eglantine Cottage, which local tradition pointed out as his lodging, was at the south end of the High Street. Now only part of the back premises remain, the original front door being a back door.[1]

On the way down Keats had been caught on top of the coach in a heavy shower of rain. He was far from well; not made the better for living with Rice, whose illness and suffering weighed upon him, and feeling the wrench of the parting from his beloved whom he would not see for a long time and might never see again. He had told her tha,, if

[1] Eglantine Cottage now bears a plaque.

Wentworth Place
From a water-colour by E. J. Lambert of Hampstead, in the
possession of Mrs. Fred Edgcumbe

Charles Armitage Brown
From the original bust by Andrew
Wilson, Rome, 1828, in the Keats
Memorial House

his Fate did not turn up a winning or at least a court card, he would never return to London. He wrote to her:

I have never known any unalloy'd Happiness for many days together: the death or sickness of some one has always spoilt my hours—and now when none such troubles oppress me, it is you must confess very hard that another sort of pain should haunt me. Ask yourself my love whether you are not very cruel to have so entrammelled me, so destroyed my freedom. Will you confess this in the Letter you must write immediately and do all you can to console me in it—make it rich as a draught of poppies to intoxicate me—write the softest words and kiss them that I may at least touch my lips where yours have been. For myself I know not how to express my devotion to so fair a form: I want a brighter word than bright, a fairer word than fair. I almost wish we were butterflies and liv'd but three summer days—three such days with you I could fill with more delight than fifty common years could ever contain. But however selfish I may feel, I am sure I could never act selfishly. . . . Though I could centre my Happiness in you, I cannot expect to engross your heart so entirely—indeed if I thought you felt as much for me as I do for you at this moment I do not think I could restrain myself from seeing you again tomorrow for the delight of one embrace. But no—I must live upon hope and Chance. In case of the worst that can happen, I shall still love you —but what hatred shall I have for another!

Fanny in her reply evidently made some protest against his decision to keep away from her, asking whether their next meeting depended on 'horrid people.' Perhaps some prudent elderly friends had broken in upon their young delight with talk of money, an establishment and the risks of matrimony on love and poetry, and she thought that Keats had been unduly influenced by them. Mrs. Brawne was wise enough not to interfere, though she privately hoped that her daughter's fancy for this charming but poor young man would 'go off.' Keats replied to his love's protest:

Do understand me, my love, in this. I have so much of you in my heart that I must turn Mentor when I see a chance of harm beffaling you. I would never see any thing but Pleasure in your eyes, love on your lips, and Happiness in your steps. I would wish to see you among those amusements suitable to your inclinations and spirits; so that our loves might be a delight in the midst of Pleasures agreeable enough, rather than a resource from vexations and cares. But I doubt much, in case of the worst, whether I shall be philosopher enough to follow my own Lessons: if I saw my resolution give you a pain I could not.

She had also protested that he thought too much of her beauty and that he had implied that she did not love him. He continued:

Why may I not speak of your Beauty, since without that I could never have lov'd you. I cannot conceive any beginning of such love as I have for you but Beauty. There may be a sort of love for which, without the least sneer at it, I have the highest respect and can admire it in others: but it has not the richness, the bloom, the full form, the enchantment of love after my own heart. So let me speak of your Beauty, though to my own endangering; if you could be so cruel to me as to try elsewhere its Power. You say you are affraid I shall think you do not love me—in saying this you make me ache the more to be near you.

We find him indulging like any common man in all the sweet lunacies of love, kissing her handwriting in the hope that she has done the same and sleeping with her letters under his pillow. Love had made Keats humble as he had never been before. He had been humble in his attitude to ultimate achievement in poetry, to Shakespeare, to Milton, but to the world at large had shown, and still continued to show, the legitimate pride of conscious genius. Love must bring a humbling of the spirit in a feeling of unworthiness. So does it help the growth of the soul. He could now contemplate with equanimity himself struggling in the scrum of life, in the ignoble scramble for a livelihood; writing to Reynolds:

I have of late been moulting: not for fresh feathers and wings: they are gone, and in their stead I hope to have a pair of patient sublunary legs. I have altered, not from a Chrysalis into a butterfly, but the Contrary, having two little loopholes, whence I may look out into the stage of the world: and that world on our coming here I almost forgot. The first time I sat down to write, I co^d scarcely believe in the necessity of so doing. It struck me as a great oddity. Yet the very corn which is now so beautiful, as if it had only took to ripening yesterday, is for the market: so why sh^d I be delicate—

Towards the end of July Brown came to Shanklin and Rice took his departure, much to Keats's relief. He liked Rice, he felt he knew and liked him better for having lived with him, but his illness was a heavy burden; made the more trying by his valiant attempts to mask pain by a forced jollity. Brown's robust health was ever a satisfaction and restful to Keats. With Rice he had not been able to work much. The two were 'like Sauntering Jack and idle Joe.' But now the dire shadow of sickness no longer fell between him and the man he lived with, Keats began to write and study with intensity. The one blot on his pleasure at Brown's arrival was the account he brought of an indisposition of Miss Brawne's. He wrote to her:

You cannot conceive how I ache to be with you: how I would die for one hour——for what is in the world? I say you cannot conceive; it is impossible

you should look with such eyes upon me as I have upon you: it cannot be.
. . . If you should ever feel for Man at the first sight what I did for you, I am
lost. Yet I should not quarrel with you, but hate myself if such a thing were
to happen—only I should burst if the thing were not as fine as a Man as you
are as a Woman.

Apparently Keats did not share his friends' opinion of him as a
good-looking, an exceptionally striking man:

I hold that place among Men which snubnos'd brunettes with meeting
eyebrows do among women—they are trash to me—unless I should find one
among them with a fire in her heart like the one that burns in mine. You
absorb me in spite of myself—you alone: for I look not forward with any
pleasure to what is call'd being settled in the world; I tremble at domestic
cares—yet for you I would meet them, though if it would leave you the
happier I would rather die than do so.

The letter ended with:

I will imagine you Venus to-night and pray, pray, pray to your star like a
Heathen.
                                        Yours ever, fair Star.[1]

This would suggest that the sonnet, 'Bright Star, would I were stedfast
as thou art,' was written in the 'little coffin' of a bedroom at Shanklin
which, when he left his cheerful friend and the abstractions of his work,
was filled with his love's warm presence. He could now at least lose the
keen consciousness of her being during the day. At work with Brown
upon the tragedy *Otho the Great*, he saw her only dimly 'through the
mist of Plots speeches, counterplots and counterspeeches—'

The Lover is madder than I am—I am nothing to him—he has a figure like
the Statue of Maleager and double distilled fire in his heart. Thank God for
my diligence! were it not for that I should be miserable. I encourage it, and
strive not to think of you—but when I have succeeded in doing so all day
and as far as midnight, you return as soon as this artificial excitement goes off
more severely from the fever I am left in—

'Diligence' would seem a mild word for his feverish activity; at
work upon 'Lamia' and possibly 'Hyperion,' writing the dialogue of
Otho and yet, to Brown's amazement, entirely absorbed for a part of
the day in the study of Greek and Italian. Keats's mental capacity was
so great that surely it would, apart from disease, griefs and his devouring love, have worn out the strongest body. From time to time he

[1] *See* Appendix IX.

speaks of himself as an idle man, but this term could only have been a comparative one.

Keats and Brown wrote their tragedy, to a great extent a pot-boiler, with Kean in their eye. Keats had no illusions about it; calling it a 'tolerable tragedy.' Compared with the turgid dramas of the time, *Otho* was more than tolerable. The speeches are short, clear, easy to 'get over' and carry on the story. The plot is, together with the characters, frankly melodramatic. In 1838 Severn made some effort to get it performed by gifted English amateurs in Rome but without success. The actors were enthusiastic, but it looks as if Brown put difficulties in the way. It was not until 1950 that *Otho* was put upon the stage in London, by the Preview Theatre Club.[1]

The method of collaboration was not a happy one. In four acts Keats 'only acted as Midwife' to the plot as Brown gave it, supplying the dialogue without enquiry as to the course of the action. When they arrived at the fifth act he demanded to know the plot and rejected some of Brown's suggestions as too melodramatic and possibly evocative of giggles from the audience. He wrote this act 'in accordance with his own views.' The two had a good deal of fun over writing the play, both making absurd suggestions. Brown wanted an elephant introduced, but Keats objected that they had 'not historical reference within reach to determine as to Otho's Menagerie.' To his brother Keats gave a few lines which he apparently considered to be fine ones:

> Not as a Swordsman would I pardon crave,
> But as a Son: the bronz'd Centurion
> Long-toil'd in foreign wars, *and whose high deeds*
> *Are shaded in a forest of tall spears,*
> *Known only to his troop,* hath greater plea
> Of favour with my Sire than I can have—

The italics are Keats's own. I think he could have quoted finer lines. When the villain Albert dies, groaning, Ludolph exclaims:

> There goes a spotted soul
> Howling in vain along the hollow night—

and speaks of

> His most uneasy moments, when cold death
> Stands with the door ajar to let him in.

His hope for the success of this play was, not only that it would bring him in some money, but that it would add to his worldly reputation and help him to market his poems to better advantage.

[1] *See* K.-S.M.*Bulletin* IV, 1952, also No. XX, 1969, 'The Romantic Poets in the Theatre' by J. C. Trewin.

My name with the literary fashionables is vulgar—I am a weaver boy to them—a Tragedy would lift me out of this mess. And mess it is as far as it regards our Pockets.

Keats was not, however, too sanguine. To this statement of his every playwright will sigh out a doleful acquiescence: 'There cannot be greater uncertainties east, west, north, and south than concerning dramatic composition.' His hopes of an early performance were already dashed by the news that Kean was going to America.

It is typical of his extreme conscientiousness in art that Keats had not turned his attention to the drama long before. The theatre was starved for good plays, and with all the men he knew connected with the theatre, Reynolds, Dilke, Brown himself and others, it would have been easy to get consideration. One of his ambitions was 'to make as great a revolution in modern dramatic writing as Kean has done in acting.' The fine work of 1819 was regarded as a mere preliminary to dramatic composition: referring to 'The Eve of St. Agnes,' he wrote to Taylor:

Two or three such Poems if God should spare me, written in the course of the next 6 years, wo^d be a famous Gradus ad Parnassum altissimum. I mean they would nerve me up to the writing of a few fine plays—my greatest ambition when I do feel ambitious.

It is interesting, although futile, to speculate how the survival of this great restless brain might have affected the literature and the thought of the century and especially how it might have stimulated growth in the theatre. Keats and Kean would have made a formidable combination. The art of play-writing might not have dwindled away into crude melodrama, or the miserable and artificial translations from the French, to wait so long for the first reviving touch of Tom Robertson. Kean's acting tended to the naturalistic, and we may take it from Keats's remark above that his revolution in dramatic writing would have been in the same direction; the direction the drama has actually taken up to modern times. It is probable that there were men of the theatre with an eye on young Keats and that even the imperfect and conventional *Otho* made some stir, for a notice of his death was put in the *Theatrical Pocket Magazine* for 1821.

When they had finished *Otho* in late August, Brown pointed out a subject for a tragedy in the reign of Stephen, beginning with his defeat by the Empress Maud and ending with the death of his son Eustace.

"The play must open," he said, "with the field of battle when Stephen's forces are retreating. . . ."

"Stop!" cried Keats. "I have been too long in leading-strings. I will do all this myself."

He then immediately wrote the bare two hundred lines that are the fragment *King Stephen*.

This fragment, although reminiscently Elizabethan, is genuine stuff. The construction of it is close, a rare quality in a first play. There is not a word wasted or a simile employed which does not add to the total effect. He plunges too directly into the action for the comfort of the audience, but that is a common and venial fault in young play-wrights. To the vanquished army, retiring in confusion, we get the conquering enemy contrasted in a vivid phrase:

> . . . 'Tis a gallant enemy;
> How like a comet he goes streaming on.

This came out of observation. There had been a comet visible while Keats was at Shanklin.

After the turmoil of the first scene amid the conquered we are taken among the victors, breathing freely again, and the scene opens with a serene and beautiful passage:

> Now we may lift our bruised vizors up,
> And take the flattering freshness of the air,
> While the wide din of battle dies away
> Into times past, yet to be echoed sure
> In the silent pages of our chroniclers.

Keats, a true dramatist, at once makes use of this idea to develop the story as the First Knight inquires:

> Will Stephen's death be mark'd there, my good Lord,
> Or that we gave him lodging in yon towers?

But Stephen is not yet captured. Stephen at bay is given incisively:

> His gleaming battle-axe being slaughter-sick,
> Smote on the morion of a Flemish knight,
> Broke short in his hand;

The narrative leads directly on to the third scene, where we find Stephen unarmed, but still superb in defiance; only quailing before the insult of a blow from a common soldier. He claims death as a right if he cannot surrender to the Duke of Gloucester. The scene ends fittingly in the sound of trumpets proclaiming the triumph of might against his single valour and we are left in suspense as to his fate.

Scene 4 is the Presence Chamber of the victorious Empress Maud, and here occurs an amusing human touch. Maud makes a rather pompous speech about bending an attentive ear to sage advisers and demanding from them plain speaking. When she sees that Gloucester intends to take her at her word and plead for the fallen King she stops him before a dozen words are out of his mouth. Gloucester goes and the Earl of Chester tries to turn Maud against him by hints of over-courtesy to the fallen King. He works upon the weak Empress and she cries:

> A frost upon his summer!

To which Chester quickly rejoins:

> A queen's nod
> Can make his June December. Here he comes.

But, alas, he does not come nor ever will come. The fragment ends here.

This plunging deep into 'imaginary interests' was the only relief from a 'throng of Jealousies that used to haunt' him. Keats's mind was now 'heap'd to the full; stuff'd like a cricket ball.' The tormenting thought of Fanny Brawne was now comparatively remote. He told her so frankly, secure that she would understand. 'I know the generallity of women would hate me for this.' He was in a mood detached: the vexed question of ways and means, of means to attain her, no longer worried him:

> It may be a proud sentence; but, by heaven, I am as entirely above all matters of interest as the Sun is above the Earth—and though of my own money I should be careless; of my Friends I must be spare.

There is little love in this letter. Keats was not happy enough for 'silken Phrases, and silver sentences.' He could no more use soothing words to her than if he were at that moment 'engaged in a charge of Cavalry.' He had hurt Fanny's pride in his last letter by saying:

> So you intend to hold me to my promise of seeing you in a short time. I shall keep it with as much sorrow as gladness: for I am not one of the Paladins of old who livd upon water grass and smiles for years together—

And now protested that this was written 'in simple innocent childish playfulness'; he had not really intended to imply compulsion on her part. Anyhow, finances would prevent him seeing her. He was living on his friend's money.

Keats was tired of Shanklin and wanted to get away from it. He had begun to dislike the view of the sea from their window and 'the voice of the old Lady over the way[1] was getting a great Plague.' One may guess that a soft climate did not suit him; that, much as he might admire the luxuriancies of the Island, when he was among the lush, leafy lanes and the rounded hills he viewed them with a bilious eye. He had stoutly maintained the beauty of Devonshire among the grander scenes of the north, but while under 'the Acrasian spell' of its climate had railed against it. He was, too, by nature a roamer and never cared to be long in one place; hoping after marriage never to 'settle—turn into a pond, a stagnant Lethe—a vile crescent, row or buildings. Better be imprudent moveables than prudent fixtures.' Brown and he had decided to go across to Winchester where there might be the additional advantage of a library.

He had been working far too hard and had taken little exercise, never getting farther than Bonchurch. Perhaps Brown, too, was feeling the effect of confinement; a week before they left the Island he set out, knapsack on back, to tramp about. Keats became so absorbed in his work that when Brown returned, although he liked 'his society as well as any Man's,' he had broken in upon him 'like a Thunderbolt.'

It was while they were still at Shanklin that Brown made the drawing of Keats now in the National Portrait Gallery. He had been out sketching and Keats, who had accompanied him, had playfully challenged him to a trial of skill. On the return to their lodging Keats was tired. As he lounged back with his fist against his cheek, Brown opened his portfolio, took out paper and pencil and quietly set to work.

Keats enjoyed his crossing to the mainland. He wrote to Fanny Brawne:

One of the pleasantest things I have seen lately was at Cowes. The Regent in his Yatch . . . was anchored opposite—a beautiful vessel—and all the Yatchs and boats on the coast, were passing and repassing it; and curcuiting and taking about it in every direction—I never beheld any thing so, silent, light, and graceful—

A small naval boat heavily manned came too near their vessel: their bowlines caught her mast and snapped it. Keats admired the discipline of the sailors: 'Neither officer nor man in the whole Boat moved a Muscle—'

With Winchester he was charmed though he found no library there. His room was large and its outlook on to a blank wall a positive relief after a surfeit of the picturesque. He liked the wooded situation;

[1] Almost certainly a Mrs. Warder, grandmother of Mr. R. W. Warder, member of an old Shanklin family.

the 'old Buildings mixed up with Trees' and set in downs the air from which was 'worth sixpence a pint.' He enjoyed the Cathedral and above all the mellow calm of the place. The weather had been fine for a month or more now. Keats loved hot weather, 'a fair atmosphere to think in.' The only disturbance to the grateful warmth and quiet was the sound of 'a fiddle that now and then goes like a gimlet through my Ears. Our Landlady's Son not being quite a Proficient.'

In a letter to Reynolds on September 21st, he gave a delightful impression of the old, sleepy town:

Yesterday . . . was a grand day for Winchester. They elected a Mayor. It was indeed high time the place should receive some sort of excitement. There was nothing going on: all asleep: not an old maid's sedan returning from a card party: and if any old woman got tipsy at Christenings they did not expose it in the streets. The first night tho' of our arrival here there was a slight uproar took place at about 10 o' the Clock. We heard distinctly a noise patting down the high Street as of a walking cane of the good old Dowager breed; and a little minute after we heard a less voice observe "What a noise the ferril made—it must be loose"—Brown wanted to call the Constables, but I observed 'twas only a little breeze, and would soon pass over.—The side streets here are excessively maiden-lady like: the door steps always fresh from the flannel. The knockers have a staid serious, nay almost awful quietness about them.—I never saw so quiet a collection of Lions' & Rams' heads. The doors most part black, with a little brass handle just above the keyhole, so that in Winchester a man may very quietly shut himself out of his own house.

It was suggested by W. Courthope Forman that Keats's lodging in Winchester was in the west portion of Colebrook Street, a quiet backwater at the north-east of the Cathedral. On the regular walk he took for an hour before dinner he went out by the garden gate at the rear of the house, crossed Paternoster Row and

into the Cathedral yard, which is always interesting; then I pass under the trees along a paved path, pass the beautiful front of the Cathedral, turn to the left under a stone door way,—then I am on the other side of the building— which leaving behind me I pass on through two college-like squares seemingly built for the dwelling place of Deans and Prebendaries—garnished with grass and shaded with trees.

He then passed through King's Gate and into College Street (where he would go by the house in which Jane Austen died two years before), over meadows and a country alley of gardens to the foundation of St. Cross, the ancient and beautiful hospital for old men about which Trollope wrote thirty-six years later in *The Warden*. From St. Cross he walked through open country beside 'a beautifully clear river.' To Reynolds he wrote:

How beautiful the season is now—How fine the air. A temperate sharpness about it. Really, without joking, chaste weather—Dian skies—I never lik'd stubble fields so much as now—Aye better than the chilly green of the Spring. Somehow a stubble-plain looks warm—in the same way that some pictures look warm—This struck me so much in my Sunday's walk that I composed upon it.

The poem was a masterpiece in which he caught all the rich serenity of our English September when the weather is kind to us, the 'Ode to Autumn.'

> Season of mists and mellow fruitfulness,
> Close bosom-friend of the maturing sun;

His only regret was that in this halcyon weather he had not been well enough to bathe, either in the sea at Shanklin or in the clear, cool river.

The old quiet of Winchester set his mind swinging back to that ancient town of Canterbury which has remained more mediæval in character than the Hampshire cathedral town; to Canterbury and Chaucer and to the fragment of a poem he had written in the spring and promised to send to George. He now copied it in his journal-letter saying: 'I know not whether I shall ever finish it.' The fresh beauty of 'The Eve of St. Mark,' the serene poem with its loved detail, makes us marvel, I think, more than in any other poem at Keats's ability to use words as if they were new, as new as when 'old Chaucer used to sing.' There is the clean bright effect of an illumination, a pre-Pre-Raphaelite presentation without the mannered stiffness of that movement:

> Her shadow, in uneasy guise,
> Hover'd about, a giant size,
> On ceiling-beam and old oak chair,
> The parrot's cage, and panel square;
> And the warm angled winter screen,
> On which were many monsters seen,
> Call'd doves of Siam, Lima mice,
> And legless birds of Paradise,
> Macaw and tender Avadavat,
> And silken-furr'd Angora cat.
> Untir'd she read, her shadow still
> Glower'd about, as it would fill
> The room with wildest forms and shades,
> As though some ghostly queen of spades
> Had come to mock behind her back,
> And dance, and ruffle her garments black.

The influence of 'Christabel' on the metre comes out clearly in the last
two lines. Compare them with

> The one red leaf, the last of its clan,
> That dances as often as dance it can.

If all the letters to Fanny Brawne have come down to us, there are
none between August 16th and September 14th. In the 'flint-worded'
letter of August 16th he had said that he must not give way to the
thought of her, 'but turn to my writing again—if I fail I shall die hard.'
Persuaded as he was that Fanny did not love him greatly, Keats may
have thought it kinder in view of his harsh circumstances to neglect her
and so give her an excuse to break off the connection.

She must have been badly hurt and all the more as she did not
apparently understand his work or place a high value on it, considered
impersonally. He himself did not resent this but rejoiced that Fanny
liked him for himself alone and was not one of those women who 'would
like to be married to a Poem and to be given away by a Novel.' She
might not feel anxiety for his welfare as she could hear of his movements through letters from Brown to the Dilkes, but she would be
wounded both in her pride and her love. Probably she danced more,
visited more, laughed a little louder and became outwardly more
'silly, fashionable and strange.' But she still loved him.

Keats had been forced to continue borrowing from Brown although
Brown was 'not at all flush.' Brown's generosity to Keats was all the
greater in a man who, according to his friends, was by nature rather
'near'. His means were small and he had always eked them out by
sharing his home with another man, so that the five pounds a month
Keats paid him when they were housekeeping together must have
been a welcome addition to his income.[1] It is true that after Keats's
death he presented to George a bill *with interest*, but this addition,
savouring more of the money-lender than the friend, can be explained
by a knowledge of Brown's character. He had a rigid sense of justice
and the courage of his opinions, and was violently prejudiced against
George who he considered had not only neglected to supply his brother,
but had taken money from him at a time when he needed it sorely.
Dilke, who later knew more about the Keats's money affairs than anyone, made a complete defence of George, but Brown would hear none
of it. The dispute led unhappily to the breaking of an old friendship.

In August Keats and Brown were reduced almost to shillings and
something had to be done. Keats wrote reluctantly to Taylor asking
for a loan secured by a bill with Brown's name to it. Brown affixed a

---

[1] From unpublished letters of Dilke's and Brown's in the Keats Museum.

note to the letter corroborating this and promising ample security. Keats mentioned the tragedy from which they hoped 'to share moderate Profits,' adding:

I feel every confidence that if I choose I may be a popular writer; that I will never be; but for all that I will get a livelihood—I equally dislike the favour of the public with the love of a woman—they are both a cloying treacle to the wings of independence. I shall ever consider them (People) as debtors to me for verses, not myself to them for admiration—which I can do without. . . .

You will observe at the end of this if you put down the Letter 'How a solitary life engenders pride and egotism!' True: I know it does—but this Pride and egotism will enable me to write finer things than any thing else could—so I will indulge it. Just so much as I am humbled by the genius above my grasp, am I exalted and look with hate and contempt upon the literary world—

This was, to say the least, high-handed to a publisher who has lost on a previous publication and from whom he wanted to borrow money. The phrase about the love of woman does not strike pleasantly on the ear with the thought of the patient, waiting girl at Hampstead.

Taylor was naturally rather taken aback by this letter and forwarded it to Woodhouse for his opinion. That constant admirer's comment was 'I wonder how he came to stumble upon that deep truth that "people are debtors to him for his verses and not he to them for admiration".—Methinks such a conviction on anyone's mind is enough to make half a Milton of him.' Although at the moment short of money, Woodhouse would be glad to help with a loan. He could spare fifty pounds. 'Whatever,' he wrote, 'People regret that they could not do for Shakespeare or Chatterton, because they did not live in their time, that I would embody into a Rational principle and (with due regard for certain expediencies) do for Keats.'

Two of the contingencies Woodhouse wished to avoid, however, was that Brown should share in the loan and that Keats might lend some of it to one or other of his needy friends. 'I wish he could be cured of the vice of lending—for in a poor man, it is a vice.' He also thought that an obligation on the part of Keats might eventually prove beneficial to 'the business.'

Keats's letter, before being sent to on Woodhouse, had been forwarded from Fleet Street to Taylor at Retford; this, with the necessary return of the letter, entailed a good many days' delay of which Keats could know nothing. He wrote again, this time asking merely for 'a Month's cash.' He and Brown had written to several friends but all their correspondence seemed to be dropping into a void.

Four days later Hessey sent him a bank post bill for thirty pounds,

money which had been privately supplied by Woodhouse. In acknow-
ledging it Keats told him that Brown had been able to borrow from a
friend in Hampshire and he himself had heard that there was a sum of
money waiting for him at the post office at Chichester, sent there by
mistake. Apart from this money they now had sixty pounds between
them. He said cheerfully: 'To be a complete Midas I suppose some one
will send me a pair of asses ears by the waggon—'

In the middle of September he was hurried to Town by a letter
from George which must be placed before Abbey. George was in
desperate need of money. The young couple were living at Henderson,
Kentucky, in the same house with Audubon, the naturalist. Audubon
had persuaded George to take shares in a boat carrying cargoes up and
down the Ohio river, the boat had sunk and George's money was lost.
They were living at the moment on a loan from a kindly neighbour.
When Mr. Abbey read the letter 'he appeared really anxious about it'
and promised he would forward some money due to George as quickly
as possible. He 'behaved extremely well' to Keats and invited him to
drink tea on the following Monday evening.

Keats had arrived in Town on the morning of Saturday, September
11th. The appointment with Abbey obliged him to stay over the week-
end. He called in at Fleet Street, found that Taylor was still at Retford
and then spent melancholy hours 'walking about the streets as in a
strange land.' Reynolds was in Devonshire and the Dilkes away. The
Reynolds women, once his dear friends, he seems by this time to have
completely turned against. They disapproved, we know, of his engagement to Fanny Brawne: perhaps, directly or indirectly, he knew of this.
Hampstead he would not visit. The miserable day was ended up by
going half-price to Covent Garden Theatre.

When he entered Taylor and Hessey's shop that morning Keats
had found Hessey and Woodhouse talking together. He told them about
the threatened Chancery suit, implying that he had come up to
London to dissuade his aunt from proceeding with it; with characteristic
family pride saying nothing of George's difficulties.

He had brought up with him the manuscripts of 'Lamia' and 'The
Eve of St. Agnes.' No doubt with the urgent necessity of making money
in mind, he asked Hessey if they could be published immediately.
Hessey was not responsive to the idea.

Woodhouse invited Keats to breakfast next morning in the Temple.
Keats stayed with his friend until three in the afternoon when Woodhouse departed on holiday to Weymouth. They talked of his poetry
and Keats read 'Lamia' to him. Woodhouse found it difficult entirely
to catch the meaning of the poem: Keats read it badly and he was, he
said, always slow to catch the purport of poetry, needing to read it over

several times. But Woodhouse realized the drama of the story. He wanted to know why Keats had not mentioned 'Isabella' to Hessey. Keats said he could not bear it now; he thought it 'mawkish.' Wood-house defended 'its great tenderness and simplicity' and assured Keats that 'Isabella' would please the public more than 'The Eve of St. Agnes.' Woodhouse was right in thinking that 'Isabella' would appeal strongly to his own generation.[1] A simple story, easy to follow and full of what modern editors call 'heart interest,' it was of their own world and its pathos within their comprehension.

Keats showed his revised 'Eve of St. Agnes' to Woodhouse and on one important point Woodhouse 'abused it for a full hour by the Temple clock.' In the thirty-sixth stanza Keats had indicated quite clearly that a physical union took place between the two lovers. Wood-house objected that this rendered the poem 'unfit for ladies, and indeed scarcely to be mentioned to them.' Keats retorted that he did not write for ladies but for men; 'he should despise a man who would be such a eunuch in sentiment as to leave a maid, with that Character about her, in such a situation: and should despise himself to write about it etc., etc., etc., and this sort of Keats-like rhodomontade.'

Thus Woodhouse reported the matter to Taylor. Taylor's reply was definite:

I cannot but confess to you that it excites in me the Strongest Sentiments of Disapprobation—Therefore, my dear Rich^d, if he will not so far concede to my Wishes as to leave the Passage as it originally stood, I must be content to admire his Poems with some other Imprint.

The two versions we possess, though clear enough in intent to the initiate, might be limited to a dream-marriage in the minds of the innocent: it must therefore be presumed that Keats took this threat to heart.

He walked with his friend to the coach and they took leave in the noisy yard. Woodhouse had taken his place inside the coach when Keats, looking up at him, promised to write, saying:

"And if it *should be in verse*, I daresay you will forgive me."

All this Woodhouse told Taylor, adding 'I make no apology for stuffing my letters with these Keatsiana. I am sure nothing else I could say would half the Interest. And I deem myself in luck to have such a subject to write about.'

Keats dined that day with Georgiana's mother and brothers. He did not show them George's letter, 'for better times will certainly come and why should they be unhappy in the meantime.'

---

[1] It was a favourite with Charles Lamb.

The next morning he wrote a letter to Hampstead:

Am I mad or not? I came by the Friday night coach and have not yet been to Hampstead. Upon my soul it is not my fault. I cannot resolve to mix any pleasure with my days: they go one like another undistinguishable. If I were to see you to day it would destroy the half comfortable sullenness I enjoy at present into downright perplexities. I love you too much to venture to Hampstead, I feel it is not paying a visit, but venturing into a fire. . . . Knowing well that my life must be passed in fatigue and trouble, I have been endeavouring to wean myself from you: for to myself alone what can be much of a misery? As far as they regard myself I can despise all events: but I cannot cease to love you. This morning I scarcely know what I am doing. . . . I shall return to Winchester to-morrow; whence you shall hear from me in a few days. I am a Coward, I cannot bear the pain of being happy: 'tis out of the question: I must admit no thought of it.

Yours ever affectionately
John Keats.

This letter appears a selfish one unless, convinced that Fanny did not love him much, he was being cruel to be kind. George's difficulties, which he felt bound to relieve in future so far as it lay in his power, had raised a further barrier between him and his love. Fanny Brawne was, after all, only nineteen and at that age to an ordinary girl life is full, emotion facile and the memory short.

But Fanny was not an ordinary girl. In the fascination of his love, the preoccupation with his own feelings, he could not have studied her nature and seen behind the lively manner, the easy social grace, an intense reserve of feeling. One feels she was an inarticulate woman; certainly after his death she could speak of her love to no one except Fanny Keats.

During the day Keats went over to Walthamstow to see his sister and in the evening kept his appointment with Abbey. His guardian was friendly over the tea-cups. He had evidently, however much he might deplore the eccentricity of John's conduct, accepted him as an established poet. After all, there might be money in it. Look at Lord Byron—not that he approved of the fellow. And, of course, Byron was Lord Byron. This boy was only John Keats. In Keats's own words, he then

began blowing up Lord Byron while I was sitting with him, however says he the fellow says true things now & then; at which he took up a Magasine and read me some extracts from Don Juan, (Lord Byron's last flash poem) and particularly one against literary ambition.

When Keats left Abbey he went up Cheapside, but returned to put some letters in the late post at the General Post Office in Lombard Street and met Mr. Abbey in Bucklersbury. They walked together through the Poultry as far as the hatter's shop in which Abbey had an interest. Abbey spoke of the shop in such a way as to imply that he wanted Keats 'to make an offer to assist him in it.'

It is a curious fact that at 74 Cheapside, where Cheapside and Bucklersbury join Poultry, there was a hat manufacturer (also of 23, New Bond Street) named Joseph Keats. This Joseph Keats died somewhere in 1816, or early 1817, and his widow announced in 'The Times' for January 29, 1817 that she would carry on the business. The shop was not far from Abbey's warehouse and only two doors from 76 Cheapside where the Keats brothers had lived in 1816 and early 1817. Perhaps there was a family connection here, and an interest, friendly or financial, taken in the widow by Keats's guardian. There was also at 1 Pancras Lane an 'R. and J. Keats, warehousemen.' Added to this, in Poultry itself there was, at No. 14, a second firm of hatters, Keats & Co.

Keats did not return to Winchester the next day but remained in Town until Wednesday the 15th. We do not know his movements beyond that, some time over the long week-end, he went to see Rice, and met Haslam there. Haslam was in a like case with himself, in love. Keats, in his letter to George, professes to find Haslam's love 'very amusing.'

Nothing strikes me so forcibly with a sense of the rediculous as love. A Man in love I do think cuts the sorryest figure in the world. Even when I know a poor fool to be really in pain about it, I could burst out laughing in his face. His pathetic visage becomes irrisistable. . . . Somewhere in the Spectator is related an account of a Man inviting a party of stutterers and squinters to his table. 't would please me more to scrape together a party of Lovers, not to dinner—no to tea. There would be no fighting as among Knights of old.

He then gave George 'a few nonsense verses' on the subject, beginning:

> Pensive they sit, and roll their languid eyes.
> Nibble their toasts, and cool their tea with sighs,

The verses are amusing and yet painful reading. Keats was, to use a colloquialism, laughing on the wrong side of his face.

Keats, after a return to Winchester, did not (so far as we know) write to Fanny. It would seem as if he had temporarily succeeded in stifling his love and had attained to some serenity of mind. On September 21st he wrote to Reynolds; 'I am surprized at the pleasure I live alone in' (Brown had 'gone a-visiting'), and 'I have lately shirk'd some friends of ours, and I advise you to do the same, I mean the blue-devils—I am never at home to them.' He told his brother:

Whenever I find myself growing vapourish, I rouse myself, wash and put on a clean shirt brush my hair and clothes, tie my shoe-strings neatly and in fact adonize as I were going out—then all clean and comfortable I sit down to write.

To Reynolds he said:

I have given up Hyperion—there were too many Miltonic inversions in it—Miltonic verse can not be written but in an artful or rather artist's humour. I wish to give myself up to other sensations. English ought to be kept up. It may be interesting to you to pick out some lines from Hyperion and put a mark × to the false beauty proceeding from art, and one ‖ to the true voice of feeling. Upon my soul 'twas imagination I cannot make the distinction—Every now & then there is a Miltonic intonation—But I cannot make the division properly.

He wrote on the same day to George:

The Paradise lost though so fine in itself is a corruption of our Language—it should be kept as it is unique—a curiosity—a beautiful and grand Curiosity. The most remarkable Production of the world. A northern dialect accommodating itself to greek and latin inversions and intonations. The purest english I think—or what ought to be the purest—is Chatterton's . . . Chatterton's language is entirely northern. I prefer the native music of it to Milton's cut by feet. I have but lately stood on my guard against Milton. Life to him would be death to me.

Keats was at work on the revised 'Hyperion,' 'The Fall of Hyperion,' and in the promised letter to Woodhouse gave him two extracts from it. This fragment was his final serious work before illness gripped him, and in one sense it is his greatest. He had experienced the amazing adventure of the *Divina Commedia* in the great original. Characteristically, since it touched him so nearly, Keats refers to it baldly and briefly in his letters, saying 'the reading of Dante is well worth the while.'

There is a debt in 'The Fall of Hyperion' to the Divine Comedy both in form and in individual passages. Dante's poem is a voyaging of the soul and so is the second 'Hyperion.' It is an emanation of the innermost spirit of Keats, the *Purgatorio* of the suffering man; a reading in the horn-book of the heart. Keats had up till now walked proudly wrapped in the poetic mantle; he had not questioned his great destiny. Love had brought him a new humbleness of spirit, her greatest gift to the soul.

The exact purport of 'The Fall of Hyperion' is hard to grasp but a deep humility pervades it. Keats must have been reading with attention Canto XII of the *Purgatorio* where, on the side of the mount, Dante is purged from pride. There are the same difficult steps in the climb upward as in the approach to the altar in 'Hyperion' and the same easy ascent when once the first painful effort has been made. In Dante's progress the last climb is made easy by an angel beating his forehead with his wings. The subconscious memory of this angel has merged into a simile:

> I mounted up
> As once fair angels on a ladder flew
> From the green turf to Heaven.

Both Moneta and Dante's angel are clad in white.

Some measure of the doubt as to his purpose, his meaning in life, may have come from increasing debility and a natural despondency engendered by disappointed hopes and frustrated love, but in the main it struck deeper. All humanity, believer and unbeliever, must come back at length to the Sermon on the Mount: 'Blessed are the meek, for they shall inherit the earth.' Shakespeare, Socrates, Christ; they had all to experience this healing despair. It is a part of the allegory of life, a process in the making of the soul.

He made a final determination to write for the Press. He had played with the idea for many months but now his mind was made up. If his health had permitted, the humdrum pursuit of journalism would surely not have harmed Keats any more than Shakespeare was injured by his life as an actor. Keats's critical powers and the rich, racy quality of his prose would soon have lifted him out of the rut. He wrote to Brown, Reynolds and Dilke announcing his determination and asked Dilke to find him a cheap lodging in Westminster.

The letter to Brown was a difficult one. This project had been talked over between them and Brown had dissuaded him. Keats wrote shyly, protesting his affection and gratitude to his friend and regretting that the money he had been forced to take from Brown had deprived him in the very prime of life, of pleasures which it was 'his duty to procure.' He could not live at Hampstead next winter. 'I like xxxxxxxxx[1] and I cannot help it.' He will 'fag on as others do,' applying to Hazlitt for information about markets. He had 'got into a habit of mind of looking towards' Brown 'as a help in all difficulties,' but must now stand on his own feet. 'If,' he told Brown, 'you have anything to

[1] The crosses, in a misleading number, were substituted for Fanny's name by Brown, whose copy is our only source.

gainsay, I shall be even as the deaf adder which stoppeth her ears.'
To Dilke he had written:

Even if I am swept away like a Spider from a drawing room I am determined
to spin—home spun any thing for sale. Yea I will traffic. Any thing but
Mortgage my Brain to Blackwood. . . . You may say I want tact—that is
easily acquired. You may be up to the slang of a cock pit in three battles. It is
fortunate I have not before this been tempted to venture on the common.
I should a year or two ago have spoken my mind on every subject with the
utmost simplicity.

The underlying bitterness comes to the surface in the phrase 'on the
common.' For a woman to go 'on the common' meant that she became
the lowest type of prostitute, a street-walker. But there was a compen-
satory thought. He might be able to do something in a small way on
behalf of 'The Liberal side of the Question' before his death.

Fearing that his good friend Brown might be made unhappy on
his behalf Keats wrote him on the same day a second letter in which he
said:

Imaginary grievances have always been more my torment than real ones.
You know this well. Real ones will never have any other effect upon me than
to stimulate me to get out of or avoid them. This is easily accounted for. Our
imaginary woes are conjured up by our passions, and are fostered by
passionate feeling: our real ones come of themselves, and are opposed by an
abstract exertion of mind. Real grievances are displacers of passion. The
imaginary nail a man down for a sufferer, as on a cross; the real spur him up
into an agent.

By 'imaginary woes' he did not mean troubles conceived in the mind
and having no grounds in reality, but the travail of the spirit. We can
link up his use of the word 'imaginary' with the passage in the letter of
March 13th from Teignmouth, in which he divided 'Ethereal things'
under three heads: 'Things real—things semi-real—and no things.'
Under things real he put the existences of sun, moon and stars and
under things semi-real 'Love, the Clouds &c which require a greeting
of the Spirit to make them wholly exist.'

Though Keats was made in his short life to suffer much, and was
bound by the fineness of his nature to suffer more acutely than the
common man, he had the saving gift of humour. In his darkest hours
humour would bubble up. Not only at this time did he play a practical
joke on Brown, concocting a false note of complaint from his summer
tenant at Wentworth Place, but he enjoyed a joke against himself.

There was an old Major and a youngish wife living in the same house at Winchester. One day when Keats was 'reading as demurely as a Parish Clerk' in his room there was a rap on the door. On answering it he found no one there. This happened several times. 'This must be the Major's wife,' he said to himself, 'at all events I will see the truth.' So he went out, rapped at the Major's door and walked in, 'to the utter surprise and confusion of the Lady who was in reality there.' After a difficult and confused explanation he made his escape. Later he found that 'a little girl in the house was the Rappee. 'If,' he commented, 'the Lady tells tits I shall put a very grave and moral face on the matter with the old Gentleman, and make his little Boy a present of a humming top.'

Keats's letters to Brown concerning his new plans had been directed to him at Mrs. Snook's at Bedhampton. In all he wrote four letters but received no reply. These letters were redirected to old Mr. Dilke's at Chichester but Brown did not arrive there until the fourth letter had been written, sent and redirected. According to Brown's son, Brown had in the meantime gone over to Ireland to marry Abigail Donaghue.

Based somewhat rashly on insufficient evidence (her very name has been given incorrectly) opinion has not been kind to Brown in regard to his treatment of Abigail Donaghue: now, however, from information received from Brown's granddaughter, Mrs. Mina Osborne, we can modify that opinion. All we formerly knew was that by this peasant woman, at one time in his employ at Wentworth Place, Brown had in 1820 a son, Charles ('Carlo,' or 'Carlino') who in old age stated that his parents had been married by Roman Catholic rites in Ireland.

At the end of 1820 Abigail was back at Wentworth Place. On 21st December Brown wrote to Keats in Rome: 'Abby is living with me again, but not in the same capacity,—she keeps to her own bed, & I keep myself continent. Any more nonsense of the former kind would put me in an awkward predicament with her. One child is very well . . . In the mean time the child thrives gloriously . . .' Carlino was born on July 16th, 1820, 'within the sound of Bow Bells' while Brown was on his second visit to Scotland.

When the boy was two years old Brown took him abroad, refusing to allow Abigail to follow and giving as his reason for leaving England that he feared the child, whom he dearly loved, might be taken from him on the same grounds that Shelley lost his children by Harriet; because he was a free-thinker. Actually the child was illegitimate and would be the property of his mother.

It had previously been suggested that Brown, without regard to the feelings of Abigail, deliberately begot a child of healthy stock or took advantage of a casual connection to secure one, placating the mother's scruples by a marriage he knew to be at that time illegal but which would be accepted by an ignorant woman of Roman Catholic faith as binding. We now gather, from family tradition and papers once in the possession of Mrs. Osborne, that Abigail was far from being a dull, crassly ignorant creature; that she came of a Killarney family 'much mixed up' in rebel activities who, she being 'something of a firebrand,' sent her to London to keep her out of it; that she was 'extremely bigoted and consequently would be married nowhere but in her own church.'

Abigail Donaghue, or O'Donaghue, was, according to her grand-daughter, a very pretty lively woman with a gift of repartee which delighted Brown: he made her his wife against the opposition of friends and to the end of his days, though separated from Abigail, regarded himself as a married man, making her an allowance which continued after his death. Carlo as a boy stayed with the grandmother in Killarney and, when he returned to England about 1848, would have visited his uncles if Brown's lawyer, Mr. Skynner, had not strongly advised against it, considering 'they merely wanted to see if they could get money out of him to assist them in their political activities.'

Abigail was alive in 1870 when she wrote her son a letter 'occupied chiefly with a tirade against the English for dispossessing the O'Donaghues in Tudor times.'

If Brown did return from Ireland in the autumn of 1819 a married man, or prospective one, he was no less devoted to the affairs of his friend. When the delayed letters reached him he hurried to Winchester in an endeavour to dissuade Keats from writing for the Press; but had, however, after discussion, to agree that Keats was taking the only course open to him, though, Brown insisted, he should not live alone. On this point Keats was adamant: by early October he was established at 25 College Street, Westminster.

CHAPTER XVIII

His Illness (October 1819—August 1820)

DILKE had known how to choose a lodging for a writer determined on a steady course of work. The ancient houses of College Street, overlooking the Abbey gardens, quiet, secluded, could give Keats a memory of mellow cloistered Winchester.

But Keats found it impossible to work. The thought of Fanny Brawne, now so much nearer to him, fevered his blood. The detachment he had won for himself in Winchester fast melted away.

Severn, who visited him soon after his arrival in Town, had expected to see Keats much improved in appearance after his long sojourn in the country, but found him looking ill. He seemed, however, to be in high spirits and was full of his poetry. To Severn it was an evening of delight. He heard, or read, all the poems written since last June. 'Hyperion' came richly to him with such inevitability that lines from it haunted his memory to the end of his long life. He begged Keats to finish the poem, exclaiming that it might have been written by John Milton. This was the wrong thing to say. His friend immediately retorted, that was just the point; he did not want to put his name to a poem that might have been written by John Milton but to one that was unmistakably written by John Keats.

Severn did not much care for 'Lamia' and regretted that his friend's mind 'seemed much more taken up by a rhymed story about a serpent-girl.' He promised, however, to reserve his judgment and to return another night to hear it read aloud. His arduous labours as miniaturist and aspiring painter in oils prevented him for a week or two, and when he did come Keats was gone.

After a few days of futile attempts to work in Westminster Keats had been irresistibly drawn to Hampstead. After a day of rich delight he wrote to Fanny:

I am living to day in yesterday: I was in a complete fascination all day. I feel myself at your mercy. Write me ever so few lines and tell me you will never for ever be less kind to me than yesterday—. You dazzled me. There is nothing in the world so bright and delicate.

Brown had been with them during the evening and had concocted, to tease his friend, some story against him. 'I felt,' wrote Keats, 'it would be death to me if you had ever believed it—though against any one else I could muster up my obstinacy.' He protested that he lived only in her kindness and put in a postscript such a wealth of love that over the long years and in cold print one can feel the yearning and the heart-break of it: 'Ah hertè mine!'

Two days later he wrote again. He had been trying to copy out some verses but his mind was full of her and he could 'not proceed with any degree of content.'

Upon my Soul I can think of nothing else. The time is passed when I had power to advise and warn you against the unpromising morning of my Life. My love has made me selfish. I cannot exist without you. I am forgetful of every thing but seeing you again—my Life seems to stop there—I see no further. You have absorb'd me. I have a sensation at the present moment as though I was dissolving . . . I have no limit now to my love . . . 'Tis richer than an Argosy of Pearles. Do not threat me even in jest. I have been astonished that Men could die Martyrs for religion—I have shudder'd at it. I shudder no more—I could be martyr'd for my Religion—Love is my religion—I could die for that. I could die for you. My Creed is Love and you are its only tenet. You have ravish'd me away by a Power I cannot resist; and yet I could resist till I saw you; and even since I have seen you I have endeavoured often 'to reason against the reasons of my Love'. I can do that no more—the pain would be too great. My love is selfish. I cannot breathe without you.

After three days of futile endeavour Keats was up again at Hamp-stead for a long week-end and determined to live there once more. His prudence, his unselfish thought for her were also thrown to the winds. He gave himself up to love. He wrote to Fanny, saying:

I must impose chains upon myself. I shall be able to do nothing. I should like to cast the die for Love or death. I have no Patience with any thing else—if you ever intend to be cruel to me as you say in jest now but perhaps may sometimes be in earnest be so now—and I will—my mind is in a tremble, I cannot tell what I am writing.

By October 20th he was back living with Brown. He succeeded in chaining himself down to fairly steady work, but the journalism determined on was not, so far as we know, pursued, or even begun, unless 'The Cap and Bells' was written with a market in view. He told Taylor he had abandoned his hope of immediate gain from his poems and would publish nothing already written though he hoped 'to publish a Poem before long and that I hope to make a fine one':

As the marvellous is the most enticing, and the surest guarantee of harmon-ious numbers I have been endeavouring to persuade myself to untether

Fancy and let her manage for herself. I and myself cannot agree about this at all. Wonders are no wonders to me. I am more at home amongst Men and Women. I would rather read Chaucer than Ariosto.

He had been reading Ariosto in the autumn and found himself a little impatient. The poet's diffuseness worried him and the more so since he read with difficulty in Italian and could not manage more than six or eight stanzas at a time. Though earlier, as we may see in the 1817 volume, he had been influenced, entranced by the poets of chivalry, for him now Ariosto's marvels were too remote from the world of men and women.

Keats was ripe for the great dramatic adventure; probably still at work on the *Stephen* fragment and reading in Holinshed with an eye on the Earl of Leicester's history. The poem he mentioned to Taylor may have been the revised 'Hyperion', on which he was still at work, though it might have been an entirely new conception. At the end of his letter to Taylor he called it 'this Poem that is to be.'

If 'The Cap and Bells,' or, as he himself preferred to call it, 'The Jealousies,' were a piece of journalism it was a well-timed one. As a satire the main subject of it seems to be the unedifying matrimonial and love affairs of the Prince Regent.

The Prince's relations with Princess Caroline were already occupying the public mind and, although feeling did not yet run high, London was taking sides.[1] The 'first gentleman in Europe' with his reckless extravagance and an eccentricity of conduct hovering on the borders of insanity, was unpopular. Economic conditions had improved slightly in 1817 and 1818, but they were now almost back to the miserable level of 1816. Gangs of roughs mobbed the Regent's coach and howled round Carlton House: the 'Adonis of fifty' felt it wiser to stay as much as possible within its walls or to retire to his world of exotic unreality at the Brighton Pavilion.

Brown was a shrewd man, and it was he who suggested the writing of a comic and satirical fairy-tale: it is highly probable that the first intention of 'The Cap and Bells' was to produce an ephemeral work with a ready sale. The success of *Don Juan* referred to by Keats as 'Lord Byron's last flash poem' had probably led the thoughts of both men to a satirical work.

Without an exhaustive examination of contemporary journals, records and letters it is difficult to disentangle all the threads of 'The Cap and Bells,' the very intention of which is not fully revealed in the unfinished state of the poem. But from the point of view of an easy

---

[1] Even Mr. Abbey threw himself into the fray, signing a *Times* letter, together with other City men. *See also* Appendix X.

popularity it would appear as if Keats had weakened his appeal by an apparent confusion of theme: there are distinct hits at Lord Byron's matrimonial disaster as well as the Prince Regent's. Also the form of the poem does not look promising for a popular success. The machinery of fairies and magic is delightful enough but clouds the main purpose, if we have guessed that purpose aright. The wit is over-delicately barbed; its arrows would seem too light, too feathery for satire.

There are also signs of weariness in the writing. Keats is for the first time using up old material in an uncreative manner. Bertha Pearl at Canterbury and the 'legend-leaved book' are too reminiscent of 'The Eve of St. Mark' and an affront to many in this flimsier setting. We know that Keats wrote at random with no design for either development or plot. This would in itself suggest a loss of power, a relaxing of the discipline he had imposed on himself since he put *Endymion* behind.

Brown probably realized the weaknesses of the poem but was only too glad to encourage Keats in work that could, without too great a strain, occupy him happily during a part of the day. He wrote rapidly and easily, sitting with Brown who copied out the stanzas as they were finished: in the evening, alone in his room, he was at work on 'The Fall of Hyperion.'

Brown was worried about his friend. Under an outward serenity, an unnatural quietness of manner, Keats was profoundly miserable. It was not long before he fell into a state of wretched apathy, unable to write, unable to exercise his intellect in study. He felt himself to be a failure. His friends remonstrated and reasoned with him. He answered them patiently but the old affectionate vivacity of response was gone. He became for the first time careless of his health, trying to support his failing spirits by a recourse to laudanum. When Brown by a fortunate accident discovered this he reproached him, saying that he of all people should realize the danger of even the few drops he was taking; securing from Keats a promise that he would never again touch the drug without his knowledge. 'Nothing,' said Brown, 'could induce him to break his word when given.'

If Keats could have brought himself to finish 'The Cap and Bells' and the satire of the finished poem had been made plain he might, when the old King died early in January, have caught the tide of popular interest. The question immediately arose in the public mind, was the Princess Caroline to become Queen? Feeling ran high. During the following months a host of pamphleteers and satirists arose on either side to reap a rich harvest.

But worldly success was not for Keats: even in the matter of the play he had been unlucky. It had been accepted at Drury Lane Theatre and Brown was under the impression that it would be performed that season with Kean as Ludolph. This was all that the friends could desire. The play had been sent in under an assumed name. Presumably if the tragedy were successful the identity of Keats as part author would be triumphantly revealed to confound the Tory critics. Brown's plan had been to make his friend popular in spite of his detractors and with as short a delay as possible; but later he was informed that *Otho the Great* could not be performed until the spring or following autumn. He withdrew it for submission to Covent Garden. Keats had, in the first flush of hopeful enthusiasm, rejected with scorn the idea of a performance at that theatre, saying that there was a wretched set of actors there. Swallowing his disappointment, he now said bravely: ' 'Twould do one's heart good to see Macready in Ludolph.' The tragedy was rejected. Brown had a suspicion that it had not even been read.

But if Keats had himself failed in a new venture, he could rejoice in the success of a friend. Severn had taken an important step forward in his project of abandoning miniature for historical painting; he had won the coveted Academy Gold Medal and with the additional honour of receiving the award after an interval of twelve years during which the Council had considered no entry to have reached the required standard. Keats went up to Town to see the picture, demanding from Severn a promise to return the compliment by going with him 'to see a Poem I have hung up for the Prize in the Lecture Room at the surry Institution.' The subject set by the Academy had been Spenser's 'Cave of Despair.' Keats ended his letter to Severn by 'You had best put me into your Cave of despair.'

The inroads of disease on his mind are visible in his letters now. The old vivid interest in men and in things of the mind is gone. There is a new current of bitterness. The world is dull. He hates his fellow-men.

This increasing bitterness of mood led to a certain brutality of utterance. The tone of his letters to George had sometimes been in part coarse after the manner of the age, but in his next letter, a short one written with visible effort, he put in a bawdy rime of Rice's although he must have known that 'little George' would see or want to see the letter. It was, to say the least, an error of taste.

The rime in itself is ugly, but honest bawdry does not unduly disturb the modern mind. In a letter to Rice, however, there is a passage which I find peculiarly revolting and one which would not have been possible from Keats in health. He tells a story of a man whose wife, being pregnant, demands a bit of her husband's foot to eat and continued to demand more. He gives her a second piece thinking she may be carrying twins. When she asks for a third he 'stabb'd her with the knife, cut her open and found three Children in her Belly two of them very comfortable with their mouths shut, the third with its eyes and mouth stark staring open.' The story may have originated with Brown who found enjoyment in a type of earthly fable he called a fairy-tale; but it is evident from his gusto in the telling, it had caught Keats's imagination. From a man who had seen the travail of childbirth and had written so tenderly of women's sufferings, it cannot, even allowing for the brutal sexual attitude of the times, be accepted as normal.

Some critics attribute this increasing bitterness of mood to a growing jealousy and suspicion of Fanny Brawne, basing their assumption on some lines written down on the manuscript of 'The Cap and Bells'.

> This living hand, now warm and capable
> Of earnest grasping, would, if it were cold
> And in the icy silence of the tomb,
> So haunt thy days and chill by dreaming nights
> That thou would wish thine own heart dry of blood
> So in my veins red life might stream again,
> And thou be conscience calm'd—see here it is—
> I hold it towards you.

Others believe this to be merely a scrap of dialogue for a projected play, and I agree with them. The fragment is dramatic in form and feeling, and if addressed to Fanny would not have been written on a manuscript of which Brown was making the fair copy. From two love-poems attributed to this autumn Keats's main grief against Fanny would seem to have been his failing powers which he blamed entirely on to his absorbing love for her; as in the 'Lines to Fanny' placed by Lord Houghton in October:

> How shall I do
> To get anew
> Those moulted feathers, and so mount once more
> Above, above
> The reach of fluttering Love,
> And make him cower lowly while I soar?

In the sonnet 'To Fanny', written later when love could no longer be resisted, he cries out to her to give him all, herself, her soul, or he will die, or living on, perhaps, her 'wretched thrall'

> Forget, in the mist of idle misery,
> Life's purposes,—the palate of my mind
> Losing its gust, and my ambition blind!

There is one poem written at this time which is finer and happier reading than the 'Lines' or the above sonnet 'To Fanny.' It is wrought poetry; has less of immediate feeling poured painfully into verse and is more truly 'emotion recollected in tranquillity'. It is the more to be prized, I feel, because we are apt to forget that Fanny brought him, besides anxious misery, brief hours of intense happiness:

> The day is gone, and all its sweets are gone!
>   Sweet voice, sweet lips, soft hand, and softer breast,
> Warm breath, light whisper, tender semi-tone,
>   Bright eyes, accomplish'd shape, and lang'rous waist!
> Faded the flower and all its budded charms,
>   Faded the sight of beauty from my eyes,
> Faded the shape of beauty from my arms,
>   Faded the voice, warmth, whiteness, paradise—
> Vanish'd unseasonably at shut of eve,
>   When the dusk holiday—or holinight
> Of fragrant-curtain'd love begins to weave
>   The woof of darkness thick, for hid delight;
> But, as I've read love's missal through to-day,
> He'll let me sleep, seeing I fast and pray.

To the agonizing consciousness of failing power and the pains of thwarted love was now added the ever-present worry of ways and means. George too was badly in need of money and receiving little from Abbey.

In early January, rendered desperate by poor circumstances, George came over to England to raise capital and took back with him seven hundred pounds. After Keats's death Brown declared this money to have been all John's by right. George, he said, had only left behind him less than one hundred pounds, not sufficient even to cover John's debts. Dilke was staunch in George's defence. It is impossible to disentangle the Keats's financial affairs, but it would seem as if George, though not business-like, was a strictly honourable man: though he was under no legal obligation to do so and was at the time, in Abbey's words, 'working like a Turk over in America,' after Keats's death he paid within a few years every shilling of his brother's debts.

There is no doubt that when George returned to America with the seven hundred pounds he left in Keats's mind resentment and some bitterness; but it was a mind warped by sorrow and disease. Keats complained to Fanny Brawne that George had acted selfishly, but he supposed that married life made a man selfish. His sense of honour would prevent a word of discontent to George himself, to whom he had in his letters promised help to the fullest extent in his power. George on his side was unhappy. His brother had changed. The old intimacy, the mutual confidence, was gone.

George told Dilke after Keats's death that not one penny of the sum he took with him was John's, but that he had led John to believe that some of it was his in order that he might the more easily help him with money when he could: the brothers had been used to consider their money as one common fund. John had been in such a depth of melancholy that George feared to tell him the true state of affairs; that his own exchequer was depleted. Knowing Keats's lack of money-sense he might easily deceive him. That he did deceive him was unfortunate for it added one more grief and resentment to his load of misery. It would seem a stupid and clumsy thing to have done; though probably the money was safer with George because of Keats's incurable habit of lending. We know from Brown that even after they had been in such a tight corner at Winchester, Keats could not forbear lending some of the money returned to him or loaned by Taylor.

If George had been able, as he hoped in early June, to send John two hundred pounds, Brown's view of his conduct might not have been so jaundiced. At the time Brown himself had to allow that some of George's trouble in sending money was due to the difficulties of exchange in an undeveloped country. As it was, after Keats's death Brown could admit nothing good of George: he was dishonest, heartless and extravagant. Much of this prejudice he communicated to Fanny Brawne.

We do not know whether Keats told his brother of his engagement. There is no message to Fanny in George's letter to him on June 18th, but this is no evidence. They were a reticent family. Although he liked and valued her so highly, Keats himself had sent no messages to his future sister-in-law in his earlier letters to George. Also it is probable that George felt some resentment against Fanny Brawne. Even if John did not tell him directly of his engagement he must have been aware that his brother was deeply in love. Fanny told his sister in after years that George disliked her: he may have put down to her account much of his brother's unhappiness. She on the other hand may have been cold to him, feeling that he had not treated John well.

Actually George seems to have obtained some money from an outside source. It was not, he said, 'all ours by right.' Perhaps Mr. Abbey advanced a sum.

Keats did not see a great deal of his brother, being unfit to accompany him on the visits he felt bound to pay. With George often absent and Brown, a jealous suspicious Brown, with them when he was at Wentworth Place, there could not have been many hours alone together for intimacy and mutual confidences. George himself was quiet and preoccupied. Keats had the impression that he was not well. His brother could not in the circumstances have been in full spirits.

He had left many hundreds of miles away a girl-wife and the baby of whom he thought and talked often after the manner of young fathers. There was constant anxiety about what he should be able to take back to them and how 'little George' was faring on the scanty allowance left behind. For the journey over, which cost him one hundred and fifty pounds, he had been obliged to borrow.

Keats wrote a letter to little George; a letter as cheerful as he was able to make it, giving her the gossip and the nonsense she liked. He told her that he and her husband had dined with Taylor and then George had gone alone to see Haslam and his 'innamorata' at Deptford. Keats himself ought, though it was against his inclination, to visit her, for Haslam had been so kind to them. But, he said:

A Man is like a Magnet, he must have a repelling end—so how am I to see Haslams lady and family if I even went, for by the time I got to greenwich I should have repell'd them to Blackheath and by the time I got to Deptford, they would be on Shooters hill, when I came to shooters Hill, they would alight at Chatham and so on till I drove them into the Sea, which I think might be inditeable.

In this letter occurs the well-known passage about Rice, Reynolds and Richards, 'three witty people all distinct in their excellence' and the delightful 'Twang dillo dee' nonsense. His gloom shadows over other parts of the letter. He said to her:

If you should have a Boy do not christen him John, and persuade George not to let his partiality for me come across. 'Tis a bad name, and goes against a Man. If my name had been Edmund I should have been more fortunate.

George and Georgiana disregarded this and named their fifth child, born in 1827, John. I do not know whether he throve in circumstances, but he probably did in health. He lived to be ninety, dying in 1917.

George left London for Liverpool on January 28th, never to see his brother again. He had not even the consolation of receiving the smallest token of his brother: not a single book or manuscript or personal belonging was sent him after Keats's death. The only thing remaining to him, except John's letters which he treasured, was a book of transcripts of poems largely copied by himself and taken back on this voyage.

By the middle of January Keats had made up his mind to go out of London. He must attempt to work and hoped it might again be possible away from Fanny. He stayed on, however, in Hampstead until the end of the month, and on February 3rd was taken seriously ill. There had been a spell of cold, snowy weather while George was in

England, but now the thaw set in. Keats went to Town and, in that new carelessness of health, returned at night on top of the coach without a greatcoat. He was at first chilled to the bone, but when he came into Wentworth Place at eleven o'clock he was in a high fever, flushed and nervous. If Brown had not known such a state in him was impossible, he would have thought Keats was drunk. Brown insisted he should go at once to bed.

As Keats was getting into bed, a cold bed, for neither seem to have thought of the warming-pan, he coughed slightly. He said to Brown who had just entered the room: "That is blood from my mouth." Brown went nearer and saw in the gloom that he was looking down closely at the sheet.

"Bring me the candle, Brown, and let me see this blood."

All his excitement, his feverish intoxication were gone now. In the circle of light from the candle Brown saw upon the bed a single drop of blood. Keats looked steadily at it. When at length he turned his face towards Brown and spoke, his voice was quiet and calm.

"I know the colour of that blood. It's arterial blood. I cannot be deceived in that colour. That drop of blood is my death-warrant. I must die."

Brown ran for a surgeon and, after the astonishing fashion of the time, he was bled. Brown remained by his bedside until, at five in the morning, he fell into a quiet sleep.

When the blood came up into his mouth, half-suffocating him, he thought of his love. As he lay for those five hours awake and still, in the shadows, he thought of her. During the first days of illness the thought of Fanny obsessed him in every waking hour.

The next day he wrote:

Dearest Fanny, I shall send this the moment you return. They say I must remain confined to this room for some time. The consciousness that you love me will make a pleasant prison of the house next to yours. You must come and see me frequently: this evening, without fail—when you must not mind about my speaking in a low tone for I am ordered to do so though I *can* speak out.

It is probable that the absence of Fanny from home was a fiction on Brown's part to keep him quiet; a fiction kindly meant but ineffective. Brown was not, he said himself, a good liar. In a postscript Keats said he had 'been looking for the stage the whole afternoon.' This might mean that he was from time to time raising himself on his elbow to look out of the window, over the fields, in the hope of seeing the London coach rolling up towards the Bird in Hand in the High Street and, a few minutes later, a small familiar figure coming across to

Wentworth Place. This movement would have damaged the ruptured lung. It is essential that a hæmorrhage patient should lie perfectly still on his back for some days.

Evidently he began to suspect that he was being fobbed off with a tale. Why did she not come to see him? Then Brown said to him that perhaps her mother was out and she must wait until she returned. At length he extorted a confession that she had been there all the time. He ended his postscript with: 'Had I known this I could not have remain'd so silent all day.'

There were regular visits from Fanny and an interchange of notes. She sent him always a written good-night. His notes were cheerful and, on the whole, optimistic about himself. She was not to know of his inward conviction that he must die. His native humour soon bubbled up again. Telling how the thought of her had obsessed him, he added: 'Tis true that since the first two or three days other subjects have entered my head.'

His sister was not forgotten. In a letter to her on the 7th he minimized his illness, but added, in case worse news must be sent: 'If I should be long confined I shall write to Mr Abbey to ask permission for you to visit me.' By the 9th he had been brought down from his back bedroom and a bed made up for him in the front parlour. He wrote to Fanny Keats:

How much more comfortable than a dull room up stairs, where one gets tired of the pattern of the bed curtains. Besides I see all that passes—for instance now, this morning, if I had been in my own room I should not have seen the coals brought in. On sunday between the hours of twelve and one I descried a Pot boy. I conjectured it might be the one o'Clock beer—

There was open Heath before Wentworth Place then with the exception of two half-built houses which 'seemed dying of old age before they were brought up.' One of these was the present Eton Lodge. The Heath was then a village common used for grazing and drying clothes, for gathering sticks for humble fires. Keats gave his sister a vivid description of what he saw there to amuse a half-hour in her dull life with the Abbeys:

Old women with bobbins and red cloaks and unpresuming bonnets I see creeping about the heath. Gipseys after hare skins and silver spoons. Then goes by a fellow with a wooden clock under his arm that strikes a hundred and more. Then comes the old french emigrant, (who has been very well to do in france) with his hands joined behind on his hips, and his face full of political schemes. . . . As for those fellows the Brickmakers they are always passing to and fro. I mus'n't forget the two old maiden Ladies in well walk who have a Lap dog between them that they are very anxious about. It is a corpulent Little Beast whom it is necessary to coax along with an ivory-tipp'd cane. Carlo our Neighbour Mrs Brawne's dog and it meet sometimes. Lappy thinks Carlo a devil of a fellow and so do his Mistresses. Well they may—he would sweep 'em all down at a run; all for the Joke of it.

He was vexed to hear from Fanny Keats a few days later that she was not allowed enough pocket-money by Abbey. Fanny was in her seventeenth year now. He told her that Abbey had also treated himself and George badly by withholding money from them and compelling George to take a long and costly journey to England in order to exact it. He may have had fresh information about the conduct of their affairs by Abbey, but otherwise this does not square with his earlier statement that Abbey was doing his best; that it was lawyers and litigation past and to come that was ruining them.

The irritable suspiciousness natural to the mind of the consumptive may have been increased by Abbey's neglect of himself. Brown wrote twice during Keats's illness but Abbey did not reply. He had not inquired how Keats had been living all these months nor seemed to take the slightest interest beyond mentioning in December the possibility of a tea-brokerage for him. Keats thought this over: if he did not want to keep it himself he could hand it over to George. Anyhow it would mean easy profit without much work. He had again approached Abbey on the subject and the changeable old man put him off, representing and enlarging on the onerous duties the brokerage would entail. 'His mind,' Keats commented, 'takes odd turns.'

In spite of being given, according to the treatment of the day, so small a quantity of food that 'a mouse would starve on it,' by the 11th, eight days after the attack, Keats was able to walk for a quarter of an hour in the garden. He had good care and attention from his friends; 'so many presents of jam and jellies,' he told his sister, 'that they would reach side by side the length of the sideboard.' But his nervousness increased. The doctor felt obliged to limit Fanny Brawne's visits as they excited him beyond his strength.

The marvel is that his powerful and restless mind was not more affected. Forbidden to write or to read poetry, he was shut in a hot room and half-starved on a vegetable diet. Knowing the inordinate appetites of consumptives and the large allowance of food, and especially flesh foods, now given them this would seem wanton cruelty; but it was the orthodox treatment. There is a pathetic letter in the Keats Museum, written by Tom to Dilke in the summer of 1818, complaining that invalids 'are supposed to have delicate stomachs; for my part I should like a slice of underdone surloin.'

Keats had now, except for occasional visits and the precious notes, to try to find satisfaction in glimpses of his love through the window. Fanny kept to the house and garden until he wrote to her: 'Let me not longer detain you from going to Town—there may be no end to this imprisoning of you.' He felt himself obliged to suggest again that he should free her from their engagement. It is no wonder that he wrote: 'I wish I had even a little hope.'

But she would not be freed. She had been very tender towards him since his attack. Perhaps, girl-like, Fanny had previously taken his love for granted but now, with the thought of the recent death of Tom from the same disease, she must have realized that she might lose him. Soon after his attack she wrote, being too shy to say it to him, that she hoped he would not think her cold. Rendered, perhaps, by anxiety and confinement a little nervous herself, she suggested that he might wish to forget her. He replied:

My dearest Girl, how could it ever have been my wish to forget you? how could I have said such a thing? The utmost stretch my mind has been capable of was to endeavour to forget you for your own sake seeing what a chance there was of my remaining in a precarious state of health. I would have borne it as I would bear death if fate was in that humour: but I should as soon think of choosing to die as to part from you.

After he had received her refusal to give him up he had written:

My greatest torment since I have known you has been a fear of you being a little inclined to the Cressid; but that suspicion I dismiss utterly and remain happy in the surety of your Love, which I assure you is as much a wonder to me as a delight.

The weather was not kind. With the wind sighing round the house and rain streaming against the windows he lay brooding on his love. The doctor took advantage of the weather to try to give him hope; he would be better when the sun began to shine again. He thought with longing of the spring, the tender 'greening' when

> early budders are just new,
> And run in mazes of the youngest hue
> About old forests; while the willow trails
> Its delicate amber; and the dairy pails
> Bring home increase of milk.

He wrote to Rice:

I shall follow your example in looking to the future good rather than brooding upon present ill. I have not been so worn with lengthen'd illnesses as you have therefore cannot answer you on your own ground with respect to those haunting and deformed thoughts and feelings you speak of. When I have been or supposed myself in health I have had my share of them, especially within this last year. I may say that for 6 Months before I was taken ill I had not passed a tranquil day. Either that gloom overspred me or I was suffering under some passionate feeling, or if I turn'd to versify that acerbated the poison of either sensation.

The Beauties of Nature had lost their power over me. How astonishingly (here I must premise that illness as far as I can judge in so short a time has relieved my Mind of a load of deceptive thoughts and images and makes me perceive things in a truer light)—How astonishingly does the chance of leaving the world impress a sense of its natural beauties on us. Like poor Falstaff, though I do not babble, I think of green fields. I muse with the greatest affection on every flower I have known from my infancy—their shapes and colours are as new to me as if I had just created them with a superhuman fancy. It is because they are connected with the most thought-less and happiest moments of our Lives. I have seen foreign flowers in hot-houses of the most beautiful nature, but I do not care a straw for them. The simple flowers of our spring are what I want to see again.

It would seem as if Rice in his wisdom had guessed at 'the deformed thoughts and feelings' behind the revolting story of the man and his wife in Keats's last letter to him; and that he had explained to himself such an uncharacteristic utterance by a mention in his letter of the effect of long and frequent illnesses in his own case. Perhaps Keats was in a sense reassuring his friend by his revelation of a more normal outlook since the attack.

To Fanny he wrote of how he had pondered during long wakeful nights on himself and on fame:

"If I should die," said I to myself, "I have left no immortal work behind me —nothing to make my friends proud of my memory—but I have lov'd the principle of beauty in all things, and if I had had time I would have made myself remember'd." Thoughts like these came very feebly whilst I was in health and every pulse beat for you—now you divide with this (may *I* say it?) "last infirmity of noble minds" all my reflection.

After three weeks of confinement Keats felt himself to be progressing very little. He said so frankly to his love. But the spring was near now:

Do you hear the Thrush singing over the field? I think it is a sign of mild weather—so much the better for me . . . That Thrush is a fine fellow. I hope he was fortunate in his choice this year.

He asked her not to return any more of his books. 'I have great pleasure in the thought of you looking on them.' It was one of his joys in love to help her to share his tastes in reading. Under his guidance her young mind was developing. She who had once been lured by the fashionable siren voice of the sophist Byron could now admit him to be not among the finer spirits.

In his dull confinement and enforced seclusion from the world of letters a pretty compliment came Keats's way and gave him pleasure. B. W. Procter (Barry Cornwall) had called, and had afterwards sent him a copy of his *Marcian Colonna* with a note in a humble strain as from a lesser to a great man. He asked Keats to send him an early copy of his next work with an inscription.

The formality of the note suggests a recent, or only a slight, acquaintance. In his reminiscences Procter wrote that he only saw Keats a few times before he went to Italy: it seems, however, almost impossible that these two young men, moving in the same literary circle, had not met earlier. The description of Keats given by Procter certainly does not suggest an ill man. Procter was charmed with 'his bright and open countenance, his ability in discussion and simplicity of bearing.' There are also two suggestions of an early acquaintance with Procter in a holograph of the sonnet 'On the Grasshopper and Cricket' with a note 'This is Keats's handwriting *B.W.P.*' and a copy of the *Poems*, 1817, presented by Keats to Procter on December 30th, 1818.

On sending his letter with the presentation copy after the visit Procter wrote in a postscript 'I wish you would set me the example of leaving off the word 'Sir.' ' A few days later he sent Keats his *Dramatic Scenes* and *A Sicilian Story*, a version of the Boccaccian tale out of which Keats himself had made 'Isabella or the Pot of Basil.' Rather disappointingly, in writing to Reynolds of the incident, Keats did not criticize *A Sicilian Story* but he did say with reference to the *Dramatic Scenes*:

I confess they tease me—they are composed of Amiability—the Seasons, the Leaves, the Moon &c. upon which he rings (according to Hunt's expression) triple bob majors. However that is nothing—I think he likes poetry for its own sake, not his.

Surely a sound criticism of 'Barry Cornwall's' pretty pipings; pipings that emulate, perhaps from a noble consciousness of the worth of poetry, the strains of an heroic trumpet. Hunt's 'triple bob majors' must have been derived from some lines of Barry Cornwall's in 'Gyges' and refer to his deliberate use of the *ottava rima* in lighter verse after the manner of Byron:

The old 'ottava rima,' (quite a pleasure,
  To poets who can make their triplets chime
Smoothly . . .

Keats was now slightly better and sleeping tolerably well. For a while his notes to Fanny were more cheerful and there are touches of the old humour. He had been amusing himself with 'two volumes of Letters written between Rousseau and two Ladies in the perplexed strain of mingled finesse and sentiment in which the Ladies and gentlemen of those days were so clever.' It was prevalent still, he said, 'among Ladies of this Country who live in a state of reasoning romance.' (A lady of this melting type was, a decade later, observed with amusement by the young Charles Dickens and satirized in his Julia Mills.) Keats wondered

What would Rousseau have said at seeing our little correspondence! What would his Ladies have said! I don't care much—I would sooner have Shakspeare's opinion about the matter. The common gossiping of washerwomen must be less disgusting than the continual and eternal fence and attack of Rousseau and these sublime Petticoats.

His innate sense of style never deserted him even in his darkest hours. About this time Keats coined a word worthy of adoption into our language. While enjoying some black currant jelly he

made a little mark on one of the Pages of Brown's Ben Jonson, the very best book he has. I have lick'd it but it remains very purple—I did not know whether to say purple or blue . . . purple . . . may be an excellent name for a colour made up of those two, and would suit well to start next spring.

Fanny gave him a ring on which their joint names were engraved. He wrote:

The power of your benediction is of not so weak a nature as to pass from the ring in four and twenty hours—it is like a sacred Chalice once consecrated and ever consecrate. I shall kiss your name and mine where your Lips have been—Lips! why should a poor prisoner as I am talk about such things. Thank God, though I hold them the dearest pleasures in the universe, I have a consolation independent of them in the certainty of your affection. I could write a song in the style of Tom Moore's Pathetic about Memory if that would be any relief to me. No 'twould not. I will be as obdurate as a Robin. I will not sing in a cage.

In a letter expressing once more his utter devotion to her he wrote what is sweet for a woman to hear, though dearer still after years of marriage: 'You are always new.'

By March 4th he was decidedly better but still weak from being kept on a small amount of 'pseudo-victuals.' This process of semi-starvation affected his heart. On March 6th he was attacked by violent palpitations. On March 8th Dr. Robert Bree attended him.

Dr. Bree was a specialist on respiratory disorders and under the patronage of the Duke of Sussex, son of George III, whom he attended for asthma. He gave a good hope of recovery, saying that 'there was no pulmonary affection and no organic defect whatever.' It is unlikely that in examining Keats Dr. Bree had the advantage of the stethoscope which had only been invented in Paris in the previous year: but he was not the first or the last doctor to diagnose wrongly in Keats's case.

In two days' time Keats was up again and able to walk in the garden; although so nervous that he could not bear the smallest excitement.

Brown had all this time been nursing him devotedly. In the first dark hours of illness he sat by his bed far into the night. Brown was on the whole, with his robust health, good spirits and general tact, a good attendant for Keats, but the coarse element in his nature at times betrayed him. Characteristically he admired Hogarth and cherished his prints. He was peculiarly deft with his hands, so deft he could write the Pater Noster on a scrap of paper the size of a little finger nail. During the long hours of watching he passed the time by making accurate and careful sepia drawings of heads from the prints, many being from that ghastly scene in a madhouse, No. 8 in the series 'The Rake's Progress.' These drawings, on small cards, are now exhibited in the Keats Memorial House.

One day he brought home in triumph Hogarth's 'Credulity, Superstition and Fanaticism,' a picture the subject of which must have had an unusually strong appeal to his free-thinking mind, and showed it with pride to Keats. Hogarth is strong and even rank meat to many stomachs, and to a sick man, even though he were a Georgian, he must have been peculiarly nauseous. The new picture gave Keats a sleepless night.

Brown knew well how intensely Keats loved Fanny, but in his relations with the lovers he was unable to tread delicately enough near a man whose nerves were in a painfully morbid condition. Embarrassed perhaps by emanations of young love, Brown joked too heavily and a little stupidly with Fanny. Confinement to the house and anxiety had affected the girl's health and perhaps made her at times a little hysterical so that she laughed rather too loudly and unwisely, made the more nervous by the dark, pained eyes of her lover. A man deeply in love is naturally jealous of every man under fifty: the poor diseased mind enlarged upon very word they uttered and brooded over it. This was probably the starting-off point for the new access of jealousy.

Keats had professed himself secure in her affection, had told Fanny she must go out again and take up in some measure her old life, but now he asked himself, what did she do, and whom did she meet? When she went to Town was it only to see Mrs. Dilke? Fanny Brawne must have needed at this time infinite patience and all the support her love for him could give her.

Brown too must have been sorely tried. It is not likely that Keats's generosity of temper or his gratitude to Brown could always restrain him from indulgence in covertly hostile moods or in that irritability which is one of the most distressing symptoms of phthisis. Brown must have noticed that Fanny never now visited her lover when he was at home. Keats had asked her not to.

On March 12th Keats was at work on a revision of 'Lamia' and by March 25th felt well enough to go up to Town to be present at a private view of Haydon's 'Christ Entering Jerusalem,' finished at last. The grandiose painter had, on borrowed money, hired the great Egyptian Hall in which to exhibit it, sending out invitations to the rank and fashion of the day. Some distinguished and exalted people had already viewed the picture in the studio and been sufficiently impressed to speak well of it to others. The hall was soon crowded with (to quote the *Autobiography*) 'the ministers and their ladies, all the foreign ambassadors, all the bishops, all the beauties in high life . . . all the geniuses in town, and everybody of any note.' This catalogue was characteristically all-embracing, but certainly many distinguished people did come to quiz the picture and went away profoundly impressed.

Keats and Hazlitt sat together in a corner happy in their friend's triumph. It is to be hoped that Keats remained to enjoy one incident. When the room was thronged Mrs. Siddons came majestically in and stood before the picture where a group of people were murmuring against the Christ's head, considered unorthodox in presentment; but when Mrs. Siddons (I quote Haydon's own words) in her solemn and sublime tone, said 'It is decidedly successful! and its paleness gives it an awful and supernatural look,' opinion was decided.

The approval of the great woman, which Haydon took care to publicize in the Press,[1] was enough. Fashion might safely admire the picture and the middle classes could follow their lead. The public were admitted at a charge and money rolled in. Haydon had to pay his debts, many of which were pressed by lawyers' letters. He took, in the exhibition of this picture in London, Edinburgh and Glasgow, three

[1] *See* letter of March 25th to Jerdan, of *The Literary Gazette,* in Keats House.

thousand pounds. Let us hope that he paid back what was owing to John Keats.

Approval was not universal. Many who understood painting saw the weaknesses of the picture and especially in the Christ's head, with which Haydon himself was secretly dissatisfied. He had fumbled over it, repainting it at least seven times. Perhaps there was for the failure of the Christ face a psychological cause arising out of Haydon's inordinate egotism: it bears a remarkable resemblance to himself. Indeed, in one version he did take himself as model.

John Northcote, the Academician, an acid relict of the past century, came and spoke his mind: "Mr. Haydon, the ass is the Saviour of your picture." This remark may have had a double edge to it. Charles and Thomas Landseer were pupils of Haydon. Their more famous brother Edwin had himself received in 1816 some instruction from him: there was a rumour that he had been 'permitted to paint in this animal.'

At the beginning of April the tenor of Keats's invalid life at Hampstead was broken by a small but pleasurable interest, a link with the little sister he had not been able to see for so many weeks. As Fanny Keats, no longer able to keep herself, wanted to find a home for a spaniel (evidently a fine animal), her brother told her to send it up to Hampstead for 'I think I know where to find a Master or Mistress for him.' Eleven days after, he wrote 'The Dog is being attended to like a Prince.' Later we hear of the spaniel going to Mrs. Dilke's brother, possibly Mr. Snook at Bedhampton.

Brown was now thinking of his long summer vacation. He decided again to walk in the Highlands. Brown has been blamed for leaving Keats at this time, for not breaking through his habit of letting his house; but after all he had already done much for Keats. After weeks of devoted nursing he deserved a change and could not afford it without letting his house. He could leave his friend with a clear conscience: the doctor had said there was now nothing the matter with Keats beyond 'nervous irritability and a general weakness of the whole system,' the result of the worries and anxiety of the past years and 'too great excitement of poetry.' Apparently he had prescribed a study of Geometry to his patient! Keats wrote to his sister: 'They tell me I must study lines and tangents and squares and circles to put a little Ballast into my mind.'

So sure was the doctor of recovery that he advised Keats to go north with Brown. Fortunately both Brown and Keats were wiser than he: it was agreed, however, that Keats should accompany his friend up to Scotland on the smack, returning alone, for the benefit of the sea air.

Brown's generosity to Keats did not end with the care and money he had already so freely given. He left him fifty pounds (borrowed at interest) on which to live in his absence.

Although Keats was by now leading a fairly normal life, the journey over to Walthamstow was not to be ventured upon. He longed to see his sister before he sailed. In regard to the illness of the two brothers it is difficult not to call Mr. and Mrs. Abbey a heartless pair.

Keats, setting out with Brown on the 7th of May, did not, however, go farther than Gravesend. Possibly he had overestimated his strength. The idea of a voyage beneficial to health persisted: he thought again of the old plan of going on board an Indiaman or, altenatively, of a voyage to South America. An anonymous newspaper correspondent, writing to *The Morning Chronicle* a few months after his death, stated that Keats 'once said, that if he should live a few years, he would go over to South America, and write a Poem on Liberty.' The desire of the freedom of man, a care for the Liberal question, never left him although he seldom wrote of it.

It was imperative to seek, as well as health, a livelihood. He could not continue to live on Brown. In the meantime he retired to Kentish Town and made efforts to proceed with 'The Cap and Bells;' living near Hunt and spending much of his time with him. Perhaps the growing dislike and suspicion of Hunt had been swept away, together with other morbid thoughts and feelings, in the attack. Keats was even thinking of publishing 'Hyperion' with a work of Hunt's, but apparently Reynolds dissuaded him.[1]

He lodged in Wesleyan Terrace, then a trim row in one of the prettiest villages around London, writing from there to Fanny Brawne:

I endeavoured to make myself as patient as possible. Hunt amuses me very kindly—besides I have your ring on my finger and your flowers on the table. I shall not expect to see you yet because it would be so much pain to part with you again. When the Books you want come you shall have them. I am very well this afternoon. My dearest . . .

He spent a quiet week marking the most beautiful passages in Spenser for her, 'comforting myself in being somehow occupied to give you however small a pleasure,' and on May 15th wrote cheerfully to Brown that he was 'well enough to extract much more pleasure than pain out of the summer' even though he 'should get no better.' It is not probable that Keats himself was ever deceived about his condition. Hunt and Brown both mention that during his illness he would look at his hands, which were faded and swollen in the veins, and remark that they were the hands of an old man.

[1] See *The Keats Circle*, II, 234.

From Kentish Town he wrote the first of the terrible letters to Fanny. With the progress of the disease, his growing irritable suspicions playing around her bright, delicate figure in absence, Keats wrought himself up into a raging jealousy. He was haunted by a vision of her in a shepherdess dress, perhaps a fancy costume worn at one of the hated Balls in the Long Room in Well Walk. In health he had said that he would not wish to deny her a single pleasure; now he demanded a complete sacrifice. 'You must be mine to die upon the rack if I want you.' The element of cruelty in all great love grew fungus-like and overspread the generosity of his nature.

I shall not quote much from these letters: they were not written by John Keats but by the pitiful diseased and tormented creature into which a relentless fate transformed him. Every one of us who has had experience of this dreadful disease knows how the sweetest nature can be warped and destroyed. That Fanny herself exonerated him from blame is clear from the short memoir given by her to Medwin: 'I do not hesitate to say, that he never could have addressed an unkind expression, much less a violent one, to any human being.'

It was probably at this time that he scored anew, under-scored and side-marked *Troilus and Cressida* in his folio Shakespeare. His identification of Fanny with Cressida was an insult that only a loving and understanding girl could brook. This fact alone should long ago have confounded the doubters in Fanny's love.

As far back as October, 1818, when he had probably not met Fanny, Keats wrote in sad prophecy to his brother: 'I throw my whole being into Troilus,' and repeating those lines "I wander, like a lost Soul upon the stygian Banks staying for waftage." In the early day of hope, alone on his journey to the Isle of Wight, he had unboxed a Shakespeare and cried 'Here's my comfort!' Could he in his loneliness now, a bitter loneliness of heart, find relief in the abiding beauty of his master's lines:

> I stalke about her doore
> Like a strange soule upon the Stigian bankes
> Staying for waftage . . .

In sorrow and near to death, perhaps the agony of the lines outweighed their beauty.

The weather was unkind. In his walks abroad he was driven by sudden showers from shelter to shelter. His one worldly interest was the new book to be published in July. It would, he told Brown, come out 'with very low hopes, though not low spirits, on my part.'

Keats, not now confined between four monotonous walls and kept on a low diet, was able to control his nervousness and appear tolerably

cheerful in company: one outbreak of irritability, however, he acknowledged with regret in a letter to Brown. The name of the mutual friend
to whom he was uncivil was suppressed by Brown but it would appear
to have been Dilke. In a growing discontent with the circle in which he
moved Keats had long been impatient in Dilke's society. Both the man's
dogmatic political opinions and his absurd devotion to his boy had
annoyed him. There was a fresh cause of irritation against the Dilkes:
Fanny's disliked and suspected visits to Town were to see Mrs. Dilke. He
said to Brown that he could go and 'accommodate matters' but what
was the use? He was too weary of the world. They were more happy
and comfortable than he, therefore why should he trouble himself?

He had recently spent an evening at Monkhouse's with Lamb,
Talfourd and Wordsworth, who was in Town. Keats was invited now
by another friend to sup with Wordsworth, Southey, Lamb and Haydon, but feeling his health to be improving slowly, would not risk being
out at night. He visited the Surrey Institution to see a collection of
English portraits. His old humour bubbled up in describing this to
Brown:

There is James the First, whose appearance would disgrace a "Society for
the Suppression of Women"; so very squalid and subdued to nothing he
looks.

Despite his apparent improvement in health Keats had not been
well enough to start again on 'The Cap and Bells.' The savage letters to
Fanny continued. In red-hot imagination he´saw her lightheartedly
dancing and flirting. 'I appeal to you,' he cried, 'by the blood of the
Christ you believe in: Do not write to me if you have done anything
this month which it would have pained me to have seen.'

The desperate state of his mind could not have been improved by a
letter from George telling of misfortune and sorrow. His little niece
had been 'so ill as to approach the Grave dragging our dear George
after her.' George is here, of course, 'little George' or Georgiana.
George had not prospered in his affairs and was unable yet to send the
promised two hundred pounds.

To add to Keats's worries he received an urgent summons from
Fanny Keats to come to Walthamstow. We do not know the cause:
perhaps she had broken into open rebellion against the petty tyranny
of the Abbeys.

The agitation Keats must have felt on her behalf could not have
made him the fitter for the long coach journey. He started out at once
but was soon brought to a halt by a spitting of blood and returned to
the house.

In the evening he went round to Leigh Hunt. Mrs. Gisborne, the friend of Shelley, was taking tea there. She wondered if the quiet, pale young man were the author of *Endymion* 'but on observing his countenance and his eyes I persuaded myself he was the very person.' Haydon tells us that Keats was the only man he had ever met 'who seemed and looked conscious of a high calling, except Wordsworth.'

Over the tea-cups the talk turned, as it had a way of doing at Hunt's, on music and especially on Italian and English singing. Mrs. Gisborne said that 'Farinelli had the art of taking breath imperceptibly, while he continued to hold one single note, alternately swelling out and diminishing the power of his voice like waves.' Keats who had spoken very little and in such a low voice that it was difficult to catch what he said, now observed that this must be as painful to the hearer as watching a diver descend into the hidden depths of the sea and thinking that he might never rise again. Mrs. Gisborne recorded this in her journal. She knew nothing of the hæmorrhage that day, merely writing down that Keats 'had lately been ill.' It seems probable that the Hunts did not know of it either. When Keats returned home he had another attack.

It seems likely that the medical man called on on this occasion was Dr. William Lambe who lived in Kentish Town near to the Hunts. He had attended Hunt and Shelley and was later a friend of the Leigh Hunts. Very soon we find Keats under the care of Dr. Darling; but in the meantime he seems to have been attended, or at least examined, by Dr. Lambe.

Dr. William Lambe was a well-known consultant on constitutional diseases, a generous man who would excuse or minimize fees in cases of poverty. He was regarded as something of an eccentric from his strong advocacy of vegetarianism. This view of him was probably heightened by the physical accident of his being that freak of nature, an albino. It was his belief in vegetarianism which probably brought Shelley to him as patient.

When Dr. Lambe retired into Herefordshire he took with him his case-papers. At some time these were stowed away in a leaking attic and forgotten. When they were later searched for by his great-grandson, the late Mr. H. Saxe Wyndham, they were so injured by damp as to be either illegible or entirely destroyed. From them we might have gathered valuable information about the last days in England of Keats and Shelley.

Dr. Lambe was not a general practitioner. One must suppose that he handed the case over, or back to Darling. Dr. Darling lived in Town, in Russell Square, so he could hardly have been called in at the outset.

The treatment followed the old disastrous way of 'copious bleedings and active medicines.' Keats must have been a vigorous man to survive it so long. As he could not in this condition remain in lodgings Hunt decided he must be moved to Mortimer Terrace. Hunt was himself unwell with 'a bilious fever' and Mrs. Hunt lived a harassed life coping incompetently on inadequate means with a growing family; but this large-hearted couple could always find room for the sick and suffering.

On the 24th of June an exceptionally hot spell of weather set in.[1] To Keats, in no fit state now to enjoy the heat, it was harmful. He spat blood for several days. Dr. Darling, now in attendance, agreed in consultation with Dr. Lambe that his only chance of life was to winter in Italy.

The hot weather was the cause of one pleasant minor incident. Hunt set about writing an article for *The Indicator* to be called 'A Now, Descriptive of a Hot Day.' Keats helped him and supplied 'one or two passages.' It has become almost a parlour-game for Keatsians to try to pick out the passages contributed by Keats. One, a reference to an apothecary's apprentice who thinks yearningly of the pond he used to bathe in at school, seems fairly obvious, but the other or others can be selected according to taste or inner conviction. This article is reprinted in H. Buxton Forman's *Complete Works*.

In the same number of *The Indicator* Hunt published the Dream sonnet, 'As Hermes once took to his feathers light.' He had already printed 'La Belle Dame sans Merci,' though unfortunately in the altered and weakened version. Both poems were undersigned 'Caviar.' Since the attacks on *Endymion* Keats had not used his own name in periodicals. Elsewhere he had employed the sign of a dagger thrusting downwards.

Keats did not remain long in bed. Downstairs in the midst of the untidy, crowded household there must have been many nerve-racking moments; even in comparative health, company, and especially noisy child-life, had of late worried him. But this was better than solitude. He was among friends, and there was the refuge of Hunt's writing-room, the cheer of his buoyant bright society.

In the midst of this home life, familiar of old in the happy early days of the Vale of Health, the image of Fanny haunted him in every known detail of her life at Wentworth Place. 'I see,' he wrote, 'every thing over again eternally that I ever have seen.' Miserably enough, jealous suspicion was now extended to his friends:

My friends have behaved well to me in every instance but one, and there they have become tattlers, and inquisitors into my conduct: spying upon a secret I would rather die than share it with any body's confidence. For this

[1] Mrs. Gisborne's diary. "I have never suffered so much since I left Rome."

I cannot wish them well, I care not to see any of them again. If I am the Theme, I will not be the Friend of idle Gossips. Good gods what a shame it is our Loves should be so put into the microscope of a Coterie.

In his despair he could no longer believe in a life to come.

I long to believe in immortality. I shall never be able to bid you an entire farewell. If I am destined to be happy with you here—how short is the longest Life. I wish to believe in immortality—I wish to live with you for ever.

He added a tender apology for his unkindness to her:

If I have been cruel and unjust I swear my love has ever been greater than my cruelty which lasts but a minute whereas my Love come what will shall last for ever.

In the whole letter he urged her to keep secret the bond between them. Fanny, by nature reserved, obeyed this command of love long after he was lost to her. The letter ended with: 'I will be as patient in illness and as believing in Love as I am able.'

Under this delusion of prying eyes the writing and the sending of letters to her must have been difficult to him. Once in a letter against the opening 'My dearest Girl' he put a note: 'I do not write this till the last that no eye may catch it.'

Mrs. Gisborne, seeing him again on July 12th, was 'much pained by the sight of poor Keats, under sentence of death from Dr. Lambe. He never spoke and looks emaciated.' The 'sentence of death' may have been dramatic exaggeration; certainly Dr. Lambe concurred in 'bleak' Dr. Darling's hope for recovery if he would winter in a warm climate. Keats also came again under the observant eyes of little Mary Victoria Novello who was brought up to see her beloved Mr. Hunt. He was half-reclining, she tells us, on 'some chairs that formed a couch for him.' Mrs. Hunt cut a silhouette of Keats in this position. Mary Novello to the end of her long life never forgot the last time she saw Keats.

One day Hunt took him for a drive towards Hampstead. They alighted at Well Walk and sat on a bench there. The shadow of Tom fell upon him. For the first time his proud spirit failed and he broke down before Hunt. 'He suddenly,' Hunt said, 'turned upon me, his eyes swimming with tears, and told me he was dying of a broken heart.'

On August 10th a messenger called at Mortimer Terrace with a letter for Keats. Mrs. Hunt, busy with one of her children, told the maid to take it to him. The woman, leaving her the next day, was in a spiteful mood: perhaps she had resented the extra work put upon her by the presence of a young invalid. She gave the letter to Thornton Hunt, a boy of ten, with an injunction not to hand it to his mother until the day after she had left. On the 12th the boy gave it to Mrs. Hunt with the seal broken. Mrs. Gisborne, recording the incident, says that the letter 'contained not a word of the least consequence.' But it was from Fanny Brawne.

Keats broke down completely, weeping for several hours. Disregarding entreaties and apologies, he left the house and went up to Hampstead.

He intended, as soon as he had explained the mishap to Fanny and received some measure of consolation from her, to go back to live with Mrs. Bentley. During Tom's illness Mrs. Bentley had become to the boys more than a landlady; she was their friend. Keats had felt his brother's death too poignantly to venture much into Well Walk and had more than once reproached himself with a neglect of her. Now he would take up his old quarters there. But Mrs. Brawne insisted that he should stay with her and be cared for by Fanny and herself as long as he remained in England.

In his last letter to Fanny he had written:

Every hour I am more and more concentrated in you; everything else tastes like chaff in my Mouth. I feel it almost impossible to go to Italy—the fact is I cannot leave you, and shall never taste one minute's content until it pleases chance to let me live with you for good. . . . I shall never be able any more to endure the society of any of those who used to meet at Elm Cottage and Wentworth Place. The last two years taste like brass on my Palate. If I cannot live with you I will live alone. I do not think my health will improve much while I am separated from you.

Now he was living with her on the closest terms of intimacy possible without marriage. The curious expression 'the last two years taste like brass on my Palate' can be paralleled in 'Hyperion':

Instead of sweets, his ample palate took
Savour of poisonous brass and metal sick:

The first mention of the taking of mercury for his health was two years and ten months before this, in October, 1817. We do not know how long he continued to take it: mercury, however, was a recognized medicine for consumption. A physical effect of continued doses of mercury is a brassy taste in the mouth. A mind, however great and powerful, is imprisoned in the body. Much of the unhealthy suspicion and jealousy which marred his love might in the early stages of the disease have been due to the faulty medical treatment of the time.

Keats was in a highly nervous condition. He wrote to Fanny Keats on August 14th, 'a person I am not quite used to entering the room half choaks me.' He was not, he believed, yet in consumption, 'but would be were I to remain in this climate all the Winter.' In his own heart he knew this to be otherwise. He was handing on to Fanny for her consolation the official view of his health.

On August 12th he had received a generously worded letter from Shelley at Pisa. Percy and Mary Shelley both urged that he should take up residence with them.

Shelley had kept up his first vivid interest in Keats in spite of a lack of response. Copies of his works were always sent to him. In regard to *Endymion*, Shelley wrote:

I have lately read your Endymion again & ever with a new sense of the treasures of poetry it contains, though treasures poured forth with indistinct profusion. This, people in general will not endure, & that is the cause of the comparatively few copies which have been sold.—I feel persuaded that you are capable of the greatest things, so you but will.

The Cenci had already been presented to Keats and *Prometheus Unbound* would follow. Of his own work Shelley wrote:

The Cenci . . . was studiously composed in a different style "Below the *good* how far! but far above the *great*" In poetry *I* have sought to avoid system & mannerism; I wish those who excel me in genius, would pursue the same plan—

Keats's reply to the invitation was grateful but ambiguous. He wrote: 'If I do not take advantage of your invitation it will be prevented by a circumstance I have very much at heart to prophesy.' He ended his letter: 'In the hope of soon seeing you.' The first sentence may refer either to a possibility of Brown as companion, or to the dearer hope of his love accompanying him.

About the poetry of them both, he wrote to Shelley:

I am glad you take any pleasure in my poor Poem;—which I would willingly take the trouble to unwrite, if possible, did I care so much as I have done about Reputation.

I received a copy of the Cenci. . . . There is only one part of it I am judge of; the Poetry, and dramatic effect, which by many spirits nowadays is considered the mammon. A modern work it is said must have a purpose, which may be the God—*an artist* must serve Mammon—he must have "self concentration" selfishness perhaps. You I am sure will forgive me for sincerely remarking that you might curb your magnanimity and be more of an artist, and 'load every rift' of your subject with ore. The thought of such discipline must fall like cold chains upon you, who perhaps never sat with your wings furl'd for six Months together. And is not this extraordinary talk for the writer of Endymion! whose mind was like a pack of scattered cards— I am pick'd up and sorted to a pip. My Imagination is a Monastery and I am its Monk. . . .

I am in expectation of Prometheus every day. Could I have my own wish for its interest effected you would have it still in manuscript—or be but now putting an end to the second act. I remember you advising me not to publish my first-blights, on Hampstead heath—I am returning advice upon your hands. Most of the Poems in the volume I send you have been written above two years, and would never have been publish'd but from a hope of gain; so you see I am inclined enough to take your advice now.

It will be remembered that there was in Shelley's pocket at death a copy of *Lamia* doubled back.

'. . . who perhaps never sat with your wings furl'd for six Months together.' How just and how beautiful a picture of the ethereal Shelley.

Keats had been censured for these frank remarks. Ardent Shelleyans regard them as impertinence. I do not see how they can be considered so. Keats and Shelley were, except to a small circle, little-known minor poets in their day: of the two, regarded not as men, but as poets, Keats probably had the wider reputation. And after all, Shelley had thrown down the challenge for Keats to take up. It was done good-naturedly and with a high respect on both sides. And in regard to Keats's advice to 'load every rift' with ore Mr. John Buxton has recently pointed out that Keats was not the first or the last critic who has failed to recognise Shelley's unique quality; his employment of a style largely unadorned with epithet moving, in the Greek manner, through a skilful use of verbs. Shelley, though linked in men's minds with those Romantic poets who looked back to Shakespeare and the Elizabethans, was moving out of time, a star that dwelt apart.

There was no more poetry for Keats. He asked Hunt to send him up 'The Cap and Bells,' which had been left behind him at Mortimer Terrace, but it is not likely that he added a word to it. His final achievement lay before him in the 1820 volume. He knew that the book was praised and admired by many and that his friends were proud; but it was only the palest shadow of his dreams and ambitions. The thought of the dread journey to an alien land haunted him day and night. But he was with Fanny. When he was dying, far away from her, he told Severn that the last summer days at Wentworth Place were the only peaceful ones he had ever spent.

CHAPTER XIX

The 1820 Volume

'LAMIA, Isabella, The Eve of St. Agnes, and other Poems' was published in the first week of July at seven and sixpence. Taylor seems at first to have thought of publishing the book in five separate pamphlets at three shillings each, 'the whole in 1 Vol. 8vo., price 12 & 6.' There is a pencil note to this effect on the back of the 'Lamia' manuscript.

Taylor was enthusiastic about the book. He wrote: 'If it does not sell well, I think nothing will ever sell well again. I am sure of this, that for Poetic Genius there is not his equal living, and I would compare him against anyone with either Milton or Shakespeare for Beauties.' Hessey was equally pleased and said that he thought no single volume of poems had ever, taken as a whole, given him more real delight. One hundred and sixty copies were subscribed for and Hessey reported with gratification to Taylor who was at Bath, on the day of publication a copy of *Endymion* was sold.

The book went fairly well: it had excellent reviews and probably would have sold much better if it had not appeared at an unfortunate time. Keats's ill luck held. The Town was gone mad over the attempt of George IV to pass 'The Bill of Pains and Penalties' through Parliament in order to rid himself of his wife, Princess Caroline, who was now in London claiming her rights as Queen. The attempt to prove adultery, supported by discreditable witnesses, was so unpopular that the Bill was thrown out, but not until November 10th. The sea of pamphlets, lampoons and caricatures rose higher. Every detail of the unsavoury process was eagerly scanned by the public, who had little thought for buying or reading printed matter on any other subject.

The bookselling trade suffered badly. Publicity gained by the good reviews was lost to Keats. Sales fell off and as late as March, 1822, not five hundred copies of *Lamia* had been sold.

Feeling ran almost as high in Scotland. In Edinburgh the mob raged about the city breaking the windows of the citizens who would not illuminate with candles for 'the Queen.' This was a pretty habit of Georgian crowds. But one private individual in East Lothian read *Lamia* and admired it so much that he wrote begging Keats to come and make a long stay with him, promising him quiet in which to work, 'soothing affection' and 'a select and extensive' library of books.

This generous soul was John Aitken, afterwards editor of *Constable's*

Miscellany, but now merely a teller (cashier) in a bank. Aitken's good offices did not end here: he wrote to James Hogg praising Keats as 'a sweet-tempered inoffensive young creature' with 'a real genius for poetry.'[1]

Taylor and Woodhouse made the final choice of the poems to be published. Keats was too ill to be troubled in the matter. Perhaps all the available poems were not before them: it seems strange that they omitted the best of the sonnets, 'Meg Merrilies' and, above all, 'La Belle Dame sans Merci.' 'La Belle Dame sans Merci' is so familiar to us, so closely knit to the name of Keats, that it is easy to forget it was not included in the 1820 volume.

This ballad had a stronger effect on mid-Victorian verse than perhaps any other of Keats's poems. As the Kelmscott Press edition of Keats was printed the work was brought sheet by sheet to William Morris for inspection. When the page containing 'La Belle Dame sans Merci' came before him Morris began to read it quietly but soon looked up in hot indignation. The editor had used the revised version with 'wretched wight' for 'knight at arms,' the fourth and fifth verses transposed and the changes in the seventh Keats had made to avoid the 'kisses four' which he feared were too particular a catalogue. Rapidly changing the poem back to its original form Morris exclaimed: "Why, this was the germ from which all the poetry of my group has sprung!"

Why had this one short poem such an influence? Surely because it contained in concentrated form and with a human appeal the strong magic, the primal quality brought back into English poetry by Coleridge, coming deviously to us through the German,[2] to be grafted on such rooted British stock as:

> There were twa sisters sat in a bour,
>   *Binnorie, O Binnorie!*
> There cam a knight to be their wooer
>   *By the bonnie milldams o' Binnorie,*

'La Belle Dame sans Merci' is now a part of our heritage from childhood and its slow, magic rhythm has almost the force of a rune:

> O what can ail thee, Knight at arms
>   Alone and palely loitering?
> The sedge has wither'd from the Lake
>   And no birds sing!

[1] *See* 'Letter to his Reviewer,' *Blackwood's*, October, 1820.
[2] For Keats's knowledge of other German works beside *Oberon*, *see* letter to Woodhouse, September 21st, 1819.

Keats's own generation might have called the poem affected and would certainly have held it to be irregular. Taylor, who knew his business, perhaps deliberately rejected it. The comparatively dull 'Robin Hood,' in a strain made familiar by Scott, was quoted in full by more than one reviewer.

'Lamia,' the first poem in the volume, Keats himself thought would be popular. He wrote: 'I am certain there is that sort of fire in it which must take hold of people in some way—give them either pleasant or unpleasant sensation. What they want is a sensation of some sort.' Although Keats had declared earlier that he 'never wrote one single Line of Poetry with the least Shadow of public thought,' it is possible that 'Lamia' was to some extent composed with the poetry-reading public in mind. Keats was needing money badly and he wanted Fanny for his wife.

Keats took trouble over the period setting of the story. He read *Archæologia Græca*, by John Potter, a heavy treatise on the antiquities of Greece, and adhered closely to the detail given.

The handling of the couplets in 'Lamia' is markedly skilful. In *Endymion* one can read line after line and forget that the poem is in couplets. This, though in itself an achievement and a direct challenge to the closed and marshalled couplets of Pope, brings the couplet too close to blank verse. The accented rimes at the end of the lines are the backbone of the couplet and make its virility. In 'Lamia' the accent is sure and the danger of monotony avoided by an occasional dropping or lightening of the accent and by the introduction of the alexandrine.

The extent of the poetic influence which had brought about this strengthening of Keats's handling of the couplet can be shown by a simple experiment:

> UPON a time, before the faery broods
> Drove Nymph and Satyr from the prosperous woods,
> Before king Oberon's bright diadem,
> Sceptre, and mantle, clasp'd with dewy gem,
> Frighted away the Dryads and the Fauns
> From rushes green, and brakes, and cowslip'd lawns,
> *A milk-white Hind, immortal and unchang'd,*
> *Fed on the lawns, and in the forest rang'd.*

The last couplet is the opening one of Dryden's 'The Hind and the Panther.'

It does not, I hope, detract from the value of the poem to suggest that the writing of the verse of 'Lamia' was to Keats something in the nature of an exercise. Shakespeare, Spenser and Chaucer were his natural ancestors; Milton and Dryden were godparents who taught him valuable lessons. In 'Lamia' the influence of Dryden is apparent and gives strength to both form and narrative, but Keats's own natural verse is more fluid and in a sense richer. There are lines in 'Lamia' which lift themselves up on the page; lines which have a fluency and a warmer beauty, such as

> Upon her crest she wore a wannish fire . . .
>
> . . . Warm, tremulous, devout, psalterian . . .
>
> . . . About a young bird's flutter from a wood.

These are not always the finest lines, but they sound in the authentic voice of Keats.

The poem is a mixture, as one of his critics pointed out, of classic and romantic; a skilful mixture, but not quite blended. The two styles are used in passages of outstanding beauty. One of the lovely romantic passages beginning 'A haunting music, sole perhaps and lone' was singled out by the reviewers as magical. Of simpler, objective beauty is

> They were enthroned, in the even tide,
> Upon a couch, near to a curtaining
> Whose airy texture, from a golden string,
> Floated into the room, and let appear
> Unveil'd the summer heaven, blue and clear,
> Betwixt two marble shafts:—there they reposed,
> Where use had made it sweet, with eyelids closed,
> Saving a tythe which love still open kept,
> That they might see each other while they almost slept;

The 'moral' of the story has been criticized and various unsatisfactory allegorical interpretations put forward. I think that in the light of his analysis of the influence of *Oberon* upon Keats's thought we may accept Mr. Beyer's suggestion; that 'in the course of its genesis 'Lamia' acquired symbolical values born of the poet's own anguish: in the *inner clash of the sensuous man*—and his need for beauty, pleasure, woman —with his *spiritual nature*—his hunger for knowledge and achievement, fame and immortality.' This we may link up with those harsh words written to Taylor from Winchester while Keats was almost certainly at work upon 'Lamia': 'I equally dislike the favour of the public with the love of a woman—they are both a cloying treacle to the wings of independence.'

Mr. Beyer also points out that, with the key given to us by allusions to *Oberon*, the opening to Part II must be regarded no longer as a

Byronic interpolation but as an essential passage in the development of the theme.[1]

'Isabella,' the earliest written of the narrative poems, a bridge between *Endymion* and 'The Eve of St. Agnes,' was, as Woodhouse predicted, the most popular in Keats's own generation. Its simple pathos was easily felt and understood, the incident of Lorenzo's ghost in the familiar tradition of the Radcliffian and German tales and plays of horror. There was too a growing fashion for Italian literature heralded two years before by the enthusiasm of the Leigh Hunt circle. Hunt had pointed out what fine subjects there were for poems in Boccaccio's tales and mentioned 'The Pot of Basil' and 'The Falcon.'

Hazlitt, in his 1818 lectures, had stated this more publicly, saying that the story of 'Isabella . . . if executed with taste and spirit, could not fail to succeed in the present day.' On this encouragement Keats and Reynolds had decided to combine in a volume of metrical translations of the *Decameron*. Reynolds's engagement and legal career prevented him from carrying out his side of the bargain and 'Isabella' was the only fruit of Keats's determination. Reynolds, in 1821, published two versions, 'The Garden of Florence' and 'The Ladye of Provence,' and B. W. Procter, taking 'The Pot of Basil' and 'The Falcon' made one into a poem and the other into a play. Hunt's *Story of Rimini* and his translations of Italian poetry had, combined with the wider knowledge of Italy brought home by the many travellers in that post-war age, widened this enthusiasm of a literary circle into something of a vogue, so that we find in 1820 even the sober *Edinburgh Magazine* writing about Italian poetry and publishing translations.

In his version of Boccaccio's tale Keats did not work direct from Boccaccio's story but from an early anonymous translation, modified in detail and treatment, published in 1684 by one 'Awnsham Churchill, at the *Black Swan* at *Amen Corner*.' His mode of presentment in the Chaucerian manner of digression and invocation probably arose from a twisted subconscious memory of a linking by Hazlitt in the lecture heard in 1818 of the *Decameron* with the tales of Chaucer which, Hazlitt had said, writers might, after the fashion of Dryden, be well advised to render into modern English.

The outburst against Isabella's brothers (stanzas XV-VII) interrupts the story, but in the Chaucerian manner. In employing the *ottava rima* he was, however, challenging public opinion: this measure with its triple rime, popularized by Byron, had come to be associated with satire or light-hearted gallantry. Though Keats's handling is here and there uncertain, it is a tribute to his general success in the

---

[1] *See* Chapter V of *Keats and the Daemon King*.

metre that no criticism was offered on this score by fine critics like Hunt and Lamb.

Keats's own opinion of the poem was, as we know, adverse. He called it 'a weak-sided Poem.' 'There is,' he wrote, 'too much inexperience of life, and simplicity of knowledge in it—which might do very well after one's death—but not while one is alive.' He thought the critics would find 'an amusing sober-sadness about it.' Reynolds, a shrewd judge of the public taste, assuring him that it had 'that simplicity and quiet pathos, which are of sure Sovereignty over all hearts,' urged Keats to publish it as quickly as possible as an answer to the *Quarterly's* ridicule of *Endymion*. In a generous letter he assessed his own value to posterity, writing: 'Do *you* get Fame,—and I shall have it in being your affectionate and steady friend.'

It is ungrateful to point out the occasional immaturities in 'Isabella' and unnecessary to praise its beauty and power; the light rich beauty of

> Parting they seem'd to tread upon the air,
>   Twin roses by the zephyr blown apart
> Only to meet again more close, and share
>   The inward fragrance of each other's heart.
> She, to her chamber gone, a ditty fair
>   Sang, of delicious love and honey'd dart;
> He with light steps went up a western hill,
> And bade the sun farewell, and joy'd his fill.

the restrained power of:

> There was Lorenzo slain and buried in,
>   There in that forest did his great love cease;
> Ah! when a soul doth thus its freedom win,
>   It aches in loneliness—is ill at peace
> As the break-covert blood-hounds of such sin:
>   They dipp'd their swords in the water, and did tease
> Their horses homeward, with convulsed spur,
> Each richer by his being a murderer.

and the pathos:

> Piteous she look'd on dead and senseless things,
>   Asking for her lost Basil amorously;
> And with melodious chuckle in the strings
>   Of her lorn voice, she oftentimes would cry
> After the Pilgrim in his wanderings,
>   To ask him where her Basil was; and why
> 'Twas hid from her: "For cruel 'tis" said she,
> "To steal my Basil-pot away from me."

'The Eve of St. Agnes,' next in the volume,[1] is enchantment. Little can or need be said about its heady and perfumed loveliness. Keats had written in 1817: 'I have the same Idea of all our Passions as of Love they are all in their sublime, creative of essential Beauty.' If this poem is not essential beauty created by love, his great love for a woman, it is a rainbow symbol of it, an arc in heaven. It seems impossible that it was written before 'Lamia.'

It has amused lovers of Keats that the subject of this lovely poem was suggested to him 'by a Mrs. Jones.' The only other fact we knew about her was that Keats had lent or given her one of his books: now, since the publication of Mr. Blunden's *Keats's Publisher*, we can mitigate the baldness of this name. She was 'the beautiful Mrs. Jones, a friend of Taylor's and her name was Isabella.'[2] In 1818 we find her giving a house-warming party at 57 Lamb's Conduit Street. After Keats's death she read and discussed with Taylor the biographical material he had collected for his intended memoir of Keats. Mr. Ridley has pointed out that Mrs. Jones probably brought the legend of St. Agnes' Eve to Keats's attention in a homely chap-book entitled *Mother Bunches Closet newly broke open.*

The management of colour in Keats's poems is always interesting and particularly so in 'The Eve of St. Agnes.' The main body of the poem is in effect rich and glowing, but on examination it will be found that colour-words are not used as frequently as one would expect. Of the colours of the spectrum only the softer *blue* and *violet* are used. Yellow is heightened and enriched into *gold*. *Red* appeared twice in an early draft, but was cut out in the final version. The violence of this colour he softened into *rose*, the colour of love, and linked it with Porphyro. *Blue* ('Blue! 'Tis the life of heaven'), the tender colour of purity, of the Virgin's cloak he reserved for Madeline. Curiously enough green, the colour of youth and hope, is not employed at all. *Silver, gold* and *black* are employed with dramatic effect; *silver* to hold to attention the constant background of cold and moonlight, *gold* to give a splendour of touch and *black* as contrast. They run as pointing threads through the web of the story.

The poem opens with the Beadsman in the ancient chapel in a chill grey world. The key-word of the first two lines is 'a-cold':

> St. Agnes' Eve—Ah, bitter chill it was!
> The owl, for all his feathers, was *a-cold*.

---

[1] Apparently Keats had wanted it to come first in the volume. *See* Brown's letter to Taylor, March 13th, 1820, *The Keats Circle*, p. 105.
[2] *See* Appendix VII.

It ends in chilling age with the same word:

> The Beadsman, after thousand aves told,
> For aye unsought for slept among his ashes cold.

The 'sculptur'd dead' are prisoned 'in *black*, purgatorial rails.' As the Beadsman leaves the icy chapel he hears in the castle 'Music's *golden* tongue,' but this bright image is immediately followed by the dulling thought of the age of the Beadsman 'flatter'd to tears.' 'Already had his death bell rung.' Then, returning to music in stanza IV,

> the *silver* snarling trumpets 'gan to chide

In three stanzas we have already *black*, *gold* and *silver*. In stanza V '*argent* revelry' warms up very slightly the silver-cold background, ushering in the 'rich array' and splendour of the ball. Madeline is introduced and the legend in which she is wrapped. Maidens, if they wish to see their lovers on this enchanted night, must 'couch supine their beauties, *lilly white*.' There is music and dancing in VII and VIII, but still no colour. The first hint of colour comes in stanza IX with Porphyro whose heart is '*on fire*' for Madeline. With the lover comes the first direct mention of moonlight, and from now on the poem is drenched in the magic of the moon, a chill wan moon, a moon of faint faery, a fitting background for the colour of love. Old Angela takes Porphyro to 'a little *moonlight* room' and

> Feebly she laugheth in the languid moon,
> While Porphyro upon her face doth look,
> Like puzzled urchin on an aged crone
> Who keepeth clos'd a wond'rous riddle-book,
> As spectacled she sits in chimney nook.
> But soon his eyes grew brilliant, when she told
> His lady's purpose; and he scarce could brook
> Tears, at the thought of those enchantments cold
> And Madeline asleep in lap of legends old.

Then comes the first note of strong colour:

> Sudden a thought came like a *full-blown rose*,
> Flushing his brow, and in his pained heart
> Made *purple* riot:

In the next stanza but one he is '*burning* Porphyro.' The colour then fades back into the pale enchantment of the legend. The lover follows the old woman 'through many a *dusky* gallery' to 'The maiden's chamber, silken, hush'd and chaste.' With the re-entrance of Madeline into the narrative the accentuating thread of *silver* comes uppermost with '*silver* taper's light,' vanishing into the soft radiance of the moon with

> Out went the taper as she hurried in;
> Its little smoke, in pallid moonshine, died:

In XXIV, with its detailed description of the room beginning 'A casement high and triple-arch'd there was,' there is no more definite colour than in

> A shielded scutcheon *blush'd* with *blood* of queens and kings.

Here the poem breaks into rich colour, but colour drenched in moonlight:

> Full on this casement shone the wintry moon,
> And threw *warm gules* on Madeline's fair breast,
> As down she knelt for heaven's grace and boon;
> *Rose-bloom* fell on her hands, together prest,
> And on her *silver* cross soft *amethyst*,
> And on her hair *a glory, like a saint:*
> She seem'd a splendid angel, newly drest,
> Save wings, for heaven:—Porphyro grew faint:
> She knelt, so pure a thing, so free from mortal taint.

Here again is the accentuating silver thread and the gold. In Madeline's unrobing there is no colour. When she is in bed the red of love may be suggested in '*poppied* warmth,' though here Keats probably intended to convey white as in the drowsing opium poppies. Heralding the full colour of love at the end of this beautiful stanza is the indirect black of '*swart* Paynims.' The colour comes fully but more delicately with the girl than in Porphyro's 'full-blown rose':

> Blinded alike from sunshine and from rain,
> *As though a rose should shut, and be a bud again.*

There is a gleam of the golden thread in *sunshine*.

There is now no colour until the story nears the height of the drama. It is heralded again by the silver, gold and black here linked with the colour of love:

> Then by the bed-side, where the faded moon
> Made a dim, *silver* twilight, soft he set
> A table, and, half anguish'd, threw thereon
> A cloth of woven *crimson, gold* and *jet*;—

In the delicate food he piles upon the table there is, surprisingly, no colour. We taste rather than see the food in smooth slipping syllables like 'lucent syrops tinct with cinnamon.' This was one of Keats's own favourite lines. In this stanza the only colour is in the first line:

> And still she slept an *azure*-lidded sleep,

Then

> These delicates he heap'd with glowing hand
> On *golden* dishes and in baskets bright
> Of wreathed *silver:* sumptuous they stand
> In the retired quiet of the night,
> Filling the chilly room with perfume light.—

There is a hint of black when the lovers embrace within the *dusk* curtains and gold is repeated in 'Broad *golden* fringe upon the carpet lies.' Madeline opens 'Her *blue* affrayed eyes.' For two stanzas there is no colour, and then:

> Beyond a mortal man impassion'd far
> At these voluptuous accents, he arose,
> Ethereal, *flush'd*, and like a throbbing star
> Seen mid the *sapphire* heaven's deep repose;
> Into her dream he melted, as the *rose*
> Blendeth its odour with the *violet*,—
> Solution sweet: meantime the frost-wind blows
> Like Love's alarum pattering the sharp sleet
> Against the window-panes; St. Agnes' moon hath set.

Blue and rose blend in their union. Here both the colour and the moonlight fade from the story in:

> Thy beauty's shield, heart-shap'd and *vermeil* dyed?
> Ah, *silver* shrine, here will I take my rest

The lovers steal away through crowded, hurrying stanzas in the dark, with only one more wavering touch of light:

> A chain-droop'd lamp was flickering by each door;
> The arras, rich with horseman, hawk, and hound,
> Flutter'd in the besieging wind's uproar;
> And the long carpets rose along the gusty floor.

Love and beauty have left the ancient castle. The poem ends as it had begun in chill and age.

The subdued and sparing use of colour, conveying rather than displaying an effect of splendour, was a lesson hardly learnt by Keats's disciples later in the century. They in giving colour to their pictures, both actual and verbal, scarcely avoided the picturesque. Browning in sardonic mood wrote in his 'Popularity':

> Hobbs hints blue,—straight he turtle eats:
>   Nobbs prints blue,—claret crowns his cup:
> Nokes outdares Stokes in azure feats,—
>   Both gorge. Who fished the murex up?
> What porridge had John Keats?

This is putting it dramatically. Browning would have admitted that Keats did not only recover in poetry the almost forgotten murex-dye, the splendour of colour; he used it as a master craftsman.

When in 1848 Lord Houghton published the *Life, Letters and Literary Remains of John Keats*, his work was 'priced and saleable at last.' Edward Moxon brought out edition after edition. Others drank the fine claret he had savoured at pleasant intervals.

The Odes in the 1820 volume are too loved and familiar to need much comment. It is a tribute to their greatness that most people qualified to judge of the merit of poetry put them in varying order. Rossetti's order was: 'Urn,' 'Psyche,' 'Autumn,' 'Melancholy,' 'Nightingale.' To take only one of the later critics, Dr. Bridges; his order was, 'Nightingale,' 'Autumn,' 'Melancholy,' 'Psyche,' 'Urn.' He placed on a line with them the 'Ode on Indolence' and the 'Ode to Sorrow' in *Endymion*, which he regarded as one of the greatest of Keats's achievements. Swinburne thought the 'Nightingale' 'one of the final masterpieces of human work in all time' and found the Odes 'unequalled and unrivalled,' saying of them:

Of these perhaps the two nearest to absolute perfection, to the triumphant achievement and accomplishment of the very utmost beauty possible to human words, may be that to Autumn and that on the Grecian Urn; the most radiant, fervent, and musical is that to a Nightingale; the most pictorial and perhaps the tenderest in its ardour of passionate fancy is that to Psyche; the subtlest in sweetness of thought and feeling is that on Melancholy. Greater lyrical poetry the world may have seen than any that is in these; lovelier it surely has never seen, nor ever can it possibly see.

The fragment 'To Maia' he called 'divine.' Colvin presumably placed the 'Grecian Urn' highest, for he called it 'a true masterpiece.' Tennyson used to recite lines from the 'Nightingale' as expressive of 'the innermost soul of poetry.' Contemporary critics thought the 'Nightingale,' 'To Autumn' and the 'Grecian Urn' the finest, although the 'Urn' was rarely quoted. The 'Nightingale' and 'To Autumn' were in a vein more familiar to contemporary romantics; of delight in nature and the contemplation of death and human sorrow. The nightingale was a natural subject to those read in old literature: it had been handled in modern poetry by Wordsworth and Coleridge.

It is typical of Keats's reserve that the three strongly personal odes, the 'Nightingale,' the 'Urn' and 'To Melancholy' are not mentioned in his letters beyond a passing light reference to the 'Nightingale.' George, on his visit to England, was copying it on a snowy day 'which is,' Keats wrote, 'like reading an account of the black hole at Calcutta on an ice bergh.'

The legend of the composition of the 'Nightingale' is fittingly romantic. One spring evening in 1819 Keats and Severn were spending the evening with some friends at the Spaniard's Inn on the Heath. Keats quietly disappeared from the company and Severn, going out in search of him, found him lying up on the little hill under the group of pines known to us as 'Constable's Firs,' and listening to a nightingale. Severn made a picture of the scene in that series of loving memories of his friend he was painting right up to his death.

Brown tells us that Keats found solace and delight in the song of a bird whose mate had nested in the Wentworth Place garden. One May morning, after sitting out under the plum-tree to the left of the house for two or three hours, he came indoors with two closely written sheets of paper in his hand. When Brown suddenly entered the room he thrust the papers behind some books, crumpling them in his haste.

It is understandable that he did not want to talk so near to its creation of such a personal poem. The close attention of Brown and of Woodhouse to his work must have been at times irksome to Keats, though without it much might have been lost to us. Brown tells us that he would write his short poems on any slips of paper that came to hand and trouble no further about them. Brown was constantly on the watch for these precious fragments of manuscript.

The conception of the happy nightingale, a conception unknown to the old poetry, came perhaps from 'The Nightingale' in *Sibylline Leaves*, a poem shadowed over by the wider fame of Keats's Ode, and its haunting line made with Coleridge's individual magic out of plain words:

> In Nature there is nothing melancholy.

Before and after Keats heard Coleridge talking of nightingales in Millfield Lane he must have read with loving concentration this 'Conversation Poem' and let it sink into his being as unconscious preparation for his own work. How lovely is the picture of the nightingales:

On moon-lit bushes,
Whose dewy leafits are but half disclosed,
You may perchance behold them on the twigs,
Their bright, bright eyes, their eyes both bright and full,
Glistening, while many a glow-worm in the shade
Lights up her love-torch.

'Leafits' was used by Keats in 'Isabella' in

So that the jewel, safely casketed,
Came forth, and in perfumed leafits spread.

The word was damned by one critic as 'affectation.' Coleridge himself altered it in later versions of his 'Nightingale' to the more commonplace 'leaflets'; perhaps as the result of a similar criticism.

The sensuous beauty of the 'Ode to a Nightingale' has an early and enduring appeal, but the restrained loveliness of the 'Ode on a Grecian Urn' is for maturer minds. The shape of the poem, the slow rise and fall of the lines are inevitable. If 'The Eve of St. Agnes' can be called the creation of 'essential Beauty' out of love, the 'Ode on a Grecian Urn' is a creation of beauty, eternal beauty out of spiritual power and contemplation. The last triumphant lines can be paralleled in the letters by utterances on Truth and Beauty, but their meaning cannot be logically explained; it can only be felt:

Beauty is Truth, Truth Beauty,—That is all
Ye know on Earth, and all ye need to know.

I have quoted not as in the 1820 volume, but as at the first publication of the ode in the *Annals of the Fine Arts* early in the same year. Of the poem there is no known holograph.[1] The version in *Lamia* was, together with other of the poems, almost certainly subjected to 'editing' by Taylor.

Matthew Arnold pointed out that in these two great odes Keats has exercised both 'the power of natural magic' and 'the power of Greek radiance'; the first in that stanza full of the beauty, the sight, the smell, the soft murmurings of an English wood in spring:

I cannot see what flowers are at my feet,
Nor what soft incense hangs upon the boughs,
But, in embalmed darkness, guess each sweet
Wherewith the seasonable month endows
The grass, the thicket, and the fruit-tree wild;
White hawthorn, and the pastoral eglantine;

[1] For transcripts *see* 'The Message of the Grecian Urn', Alvin Whitley, Keats-Shelley Memorial *Bulletin* V, 1953.

Fast fading violets cover'd up in leaves;
And mid-May's eldest child,
The coming musk-rose, full of dewy wine,
The murmurous haunt of flies on summer eves.

and in

. . . magic casements, opening on the foam
Of perilous seas, in faery lands forlorn.

and the second, 'the power of Greek radiance' in lines 5, 6 and 7 of

Who are these coming to the sacrifice?
To what green altar, O mysterious priest,
Lead'st thou that heifer lowing at the skies,
And all her silken flanks with garlands drest?
What little town by river or sea shore,
Or mountain-built with peaceful citadel,
Is emptied of this folk, this pious morn?
And, little town, thy streets for evermore
Will silent be; and not a soul to tell
Why thou art desolate, can e'er return.

These lines, Arnold said, are 'as Greek as a thing from Homer or Theocritus . . . compared with the eye on the object, a radiance and light clearness being added.'

The sources of the Ode, the living creatures 'in old marbles ever beautiful' on frieze, on vase, have been traced by Sir Sidney Colvin and abundantly illustrated in his *John Keats*. There one may see depicted the gracious movement, 'Attic shape, Fair attitude,' the pipes and timbrels and the ecstasy.

The 'Ode to Psyche' is a more conscious creation. Keats told his brother that he had composed it with great care. Its shape is accomplished. There is in it the delicacy and tenderness of young love. Psyche is a human goddess, the soul dwelling with earthly love. In 'some untrodden region' of the poet's mind her 'rosy sanctuary' is set rich in natural beauty where there shall be for her

all soft delight
That shadowy thought can win,
A bright torch, and a casement ope at night,
To let the warm Love in!

Professor Garrod has pointed out in these lines a rich content that had, I believe, escaped most people. Psyche, the soul, was represented by the Greeks as a butterfly or moth. Psyche and love are fused in a fluttering image drawn into the mind by a bright awareness, the torch of a watchful intelligence. The ode was written in the April of 1819. In July Keats wrote in his first love-letter:

For myself I know not how to express my devotion to so fair a form: I want a brighter word than bright, a fairer word than fair. I almost wish we were butterflies and liv'd but three summer days—three such days with you I could fill with more delight than fifty common years could ever contain.

The next poem in the volume is fittingly a happy one, 'Fancy.' So far as we know it was the first poem he wrote after his brother's death. There is a substratum of melancholy; the sad circumstance of his life had made happiness suspect to him but the tone of the poem is happy. The movement of the verse is joyful although it reminds us that 'Pleasure never is at home':

> Ever let the Fancy roam,
> Pleasure never is at home:
> At a touch sweet Pleasure melteth,
> Like to bubbles when rain pelteth;

The ode beginning 'Bards of Passion and of Mirth' is one which, except that it links on to the following 'Lines on the Mermaid Tavern,' might well have been omitted from the volume to make way for 'The Eve of St. Mark' or 'La Belle Dame sans Merci.' The vision of the Bards

> Seated on Elysian lawns
> Brows'd by none but Dian's fawns;
> Underneath large blue-bells tented,
> Where the daisies are rose-scented,
> And the rose herself has got
> Perfume which on earth is not;

seems rather more childish than Elysian and ungrateful to the living beauties of earth. Who wants bluebells as large as tents and perfumed daisies? The buoyant 'Lines on the Mermaid Tavern' no one could spare. The vision of the Poets

> Sipping beverage divine,
> And pledging with contented smack
> The Mermaid in the Zodiac.

has a feeling of authenticity and is much pleasanter.

'Robin Hood,' a thread of homespun rather out of place, is cheerful, however, and shows another aspect of Keats. 'To Autumn' is

John Keats in his room at Wentworth Place
From a posthumous portrait in oils by Joseph Severn in the
National Portrait Gallery

The Piazza di Spagna, Rome
From an old print

a ripe perfection and all the more grateful since we get in this uncertain climate so few of the golden days when Autumn is kind and warm, a

> Close bosom-friend of the maturing sun.

The poem is at once a living joy and a lovely memory.

The 'Ode to Melancholy' is to many the most difficult of the odes to read with understanding. Although in essence universal, it is 'period' in feeling. A fine and cultivated melancholy was an aspect of the romantic muse and one encouraged by Byron, having its roots in the eighteenth century 'graveyard school.' Keats has lifted this melancholy from a mood to a truth. There can be no pleasure without pain, no light without shadow. The law of life is contrast.

> Ay, in the very temple of Delight
>   Veil'd Melancholy has her sovran shrine,
>   Though seen of none save him whose strenuous tongue
>   Can burst Joy's grape against his palate fine;
> His soul shall taste the sadness of her might,
>   And be among her cloudy trophies hung.

In the first stanza there is again a presentment of Psyche as moth but here in reference to the soul departing from the body:

> Nor let the beetle, nor the death-moth be
>   Your mournful Psyche, nor the downy owl
> A partner in your sorrow's mysteries;

If Keats had been in health, 'Hyperion' would probably not have been given in the *Lamia* volume. Apart from its incomplete condition he regarded it with disfavour as too Miltonic and had embodied passages from it in 'The Fall of Hyperion.' On the flyleaf of the volume Taylor and Hessey apologized for its unfinished state, saying 'Hyperion' was included 'at their particular request.' This looks as if at first Keats had refused to allow it to be printed: he certainly provided no manuscript for the poem, which was set up from Woodhouse's transcript.

In a copy presented to Burridge Davenport of Hampstead, Keats struck out this advertisement, writing above: 'This is none of my doing—I was ill at the time.' The final sentence which ran: 'The poem was intended to have been of equal length with ENDYMION, but the reception given to that work discouraged the author from proceeding' he commented on angrily with 'This is a lie.'

The reviews proved how right Taylor had been to publish 'Hyperion.' The poem gained far more unqualified praise than any

other, being singled out by private as well as public critics as the finest
in the volume. Shelley found *Lamia* 'in other respects insignificant
enough, but containing the fragment of a poem called "Hyperion" . . .
it is certainly an astonishing piece of writing, and gives me a conception
of Keats which I confess I had not before.' Four months later he wrote
to the same correspondent, Peacock, 'if the "Hyperion" be not grand
poetry, none has been produced by our contemporaries.' To Hunt he
wrote that 'Hyperion' placed Keats among those destined to become
the 'first writers of the age.' Lord Byron, when he did bring himself to
read the book, said of 'Hyperion,' 'it seems actually inspired by the
Titans' and, echoing the *New Monthly*, 'as sublime as Æschylus.'

The arrangement of the poems is admirable and the putting of
'Hyperion' last an inspiration. It makes a magnificent finish and links
with the poem before, the 'Ode to Melancholy,' in the description of
Thea:

> But oh! how unlike marble was that face:
> How beautiful, if sorrow had not made
> Sorrow more beautiful than Beauty's self.

The large, sad, inevitable opening leads on from the more emotional
and bitter-sweet Ode:

> Deep in the shady sadness of a vale
> Far sunken from the healthy breath of morn,
> Far from the fiery noon, and eve's one star,
> Sat gray-hair'd Saturn, quiet as a stone.
> Still as the silence round about his lair;
> Forest on forest hung about his head
> Like cloud on cloud. No stir of air was there,
> Not so much life as on a summer's day
> Robs not one light seed from the feather'd grass,
> But where the dead leaf fell, there did it rest.

Although Keats had written in full the two last lines of the poem it
ends, the last in the volume, as his life was soon to be, broken,
incomplete.

The first public mention of *Lamia* beyond a formal advertisement
was in *The Literary Gazette* for Saturday, July 1st. A copy of Mr. Keats's
new volume of poetry 'on the eve of publication' had been received too
late for review and the journal presented 'by way of novelty the following specimens from the minor productions,' printing the 'Ode to a
Nightingale,' 'Lines on the Mermaid Tavern' and 'To Autumn.' These
quotations were probably of more value than a set review in *The
Literary Gazette*, at least if it were written by the editor, William Jerdan,

who was said by his fellow-journalists to acquire knowledge of books
sent in by cutting the leaves and smelling the paper-knife.

The most important review in July was the one almost certainly
written by Charles Lamb in *The New Times* of July, 1820. Lamb was
an ardent admirer of Keats's work and placed him, admittedly as a
poet of a different type, 'next to Wordsworth.' This was, indeed, high
praise from Wordsworth's admiring friend. Tom Hood tells us that in
later years at Colebrooke Cottage once when Wordsworth was present
there was 'a discussion on the value of the promissory notes issued by
our younger poets, wherein Wordsworth named Shelley, and Lamb
took John Keats for choice.'

Lamb headed the review with those warm, rich-hued stanzas in
'The Eve of St. Agnes' describing Madeline's unrobing and falling to
sleep in her 'soft and chilly nest,' stanzas XXIV–VII:

> Blinded alike from sunshine and from rain,
> As though a rose should shut, and be a bud again.

He wrote of them:

Such is the description which Mr. Keats has given us with a delicacy worthy
of Christabel, of a high-born damsel, in one of the apartments of a baronial
castle, laying herself down devoutly to dream on the charmed Eve of St.
Agnes; and like the radiance, which comes from those old windows upon
the limbs and garments of the damsel, is the almost Chaucer-like painting
with which this poet illumines every subject he touches. We have scarcely
anything like it in modern description. It brings us back to ancient days, and

> *Beauty making-beautiful old rhymes*

It will be remembered that *The Literary Journal* reviewer employed
this Shakespearean quotation in his praise of a line of *Endymion*.

Lamb considered 'Isabella' to be the finest poem in the volume,
especially commending 'the anticipation of the assassination . . .' in one
epithet in the narration of the ride:

> So the two brothers and their *murder'd* man
> Rode past fair Florence to where Arno's stream
> Gurgles through straiten'd banks. . . .

Of the description of Isabella and her nurse finding the body of Lorenzo
he said, quoting the stanzas XLVI–VIII, that 'there is nothing more
awfully simple in diction, more nakedly grand and moving in sentiment,
in Dante, in Chaucer, or in Spenser.' Referring to 'the divine germ' of

the story in Boccaccio he wrote, 'it is a long while since we read the original; and in this affecting revival of it we do but

Weep away a long-forgotten woe.'

In 'Lamia' Lamb pointed to the epithet 'Star of Lethe' for Hermes as 'one of those prodigal phrases which Mr. Keats abounds in, which are each a poem in a word, and which in this instance lays open to us at once, like a picture, all the dim regions and their inhabitants and the sudden coming of a celestial among them.' He found 'Lamia' 'more exuberantly rich in imagery and painting' and of 'as gorgeous stuff as ever romance was composed of.' The marvels and the splendours of the story 'are all that fairy land can do for us' but

They are for younger impressibilities. To *us* an ounce of feeling is worth a pound of fancy; and therefore we recur again, with a warmer gratitude, to the story of Isabella and the pot of basil, and those never-cloying stanzas which we have cited, and which we think should disarm criticism if it be not in its nature cruel; if it would not deny to honey its sweetness, nor to roses redness nor light to the stars in Heaven; if it would not bay the moon out of the skies, rather than acknowledge she is fair.

He made no mention of the odes or of 'Hyperion' which was the poem singled out for highest praise by the majority of the reviewers. Lamb's tastes in literature were formed when Wordsworth and his circle were in full revolt against a frozen classicism; romantic themes were dearer to him. Hunt reprinted Lamb's review in *The Examiner* with the comment, 'The poet and the critic are worthy of each other—a rare coincidence when the first is good.'

The Monthly Review for July found that the volume displayed 'the ore of true poetic genius, though mingled with a large proportion of dross.' Unread in the storehouse of Elizabethan literature, the reviewer found in Keats's boldly coined and highly individual language a frequent 'affectation of quaint phrases' but was broad-minded enough to admit that experiments must be made and that 'Innovations of every kind, more especially in matters of taste, are at first beheld with dislike and jealousy, and it is only by time and usage that we can appreciate their claims to adoption.' He continued:

Very few persons, probably, will admire Mr. Keats on a short acquaintance; and the light and frivolous never will. If we would enjoy his poetry, we must think over it; and on this very account, which is perhaps the surest proof of its merit, we are afraid that it will be slighted. Unfortunately, Mr. Keats may blame himself for much of this neglect; since he might have conceded something to established taste, or, (if he will) established prejudice, without derogating from his own originality of thought and spirit.

He found Mr. Keats 'often laboriously obscure' and sometimes indulging 'in such strange intricacies of thought, and peculiarities of expression, that we find considerable difficulty in discovering his meaning.' Unable to keep Mr. Hunt out he attributed this to Keats being 'a disciple in a school in which these peculiarities are virtues' and regretted that the young poet was 'sowing the seeds of disappointment where the fruit should be honour and distinction.'

Turning with relief to 'Hyperion,' a poem understandable because it was in the familiar Miltonic tradition, he quoted largely, putting the outstanding lines in italics. 'Isabella' was 'the worst part of the volume,' Barry Cornwall's version of the tale being 'in some respects superior.' In the outburst against commercial profiteers in stanza XVI he found evidence of 'simplicity and affectation.'

Though to consider the comparative poetic merits of 'A Sicilian Story' and 'Isabella,' would be both unprofitable and unjust to Procter (Barry Cornwall) it is useful to compare them in assessing the taste of the day. The volume to which Procter's poem gave a name went into two editions in 1820. The story, told smoothly and in a much more 'gentlemanly' manner, was far easier and a safer version for a man to read aloud to his women-folk. The horror of the tale is hidden away. The ghost is 'a dim and waving shadow.' Isabella finds her lover's body above ground and cuts away, not the head, but the heart. The process is discreetly side-tracked in

> . . . but wherefore ask
> How, tremblingly, she did her bloody task?

She buries the heart, not in a pot, but under a tree, under which she sits and weeps. When her brothers dig up the heart it is not like Lorenzo's head, 'vile with green and livid spot' but still perfect, for Isabella had embalmed it. The tree, which before had grown magically, now withers away, and Isabella retires, half-crazed, to live in a cave in the Gothick hermit tradition and is at length 'translated to a finer sphere.'

The reviewer found fault with Keats's selection of images as 'according to the tenets of that school of poetry' which held that 'any thing or object in nature is a fit material on which the poet may work; forgetting that poetry has a nature of its own, and that it is the destruction of its essence to level its high being with the triteness of every-day life.' Amazingly enough to the modern reader he gave as an example and as a mere *concetto*:

> Heard melodies are sweet, but those *unheard*
> Are sweeter; therefore, ye soft pipes, play on;
> Not to the sensual ear, but, more endear'd,
> Pipe to the spirit *ditties of no tone* :

'On Autumn' (quoted in full) brought the 'reality of Nature more before our eyes than almost any description that we can remember.' The critic ended by exhorting 'Mr. K.' to become 'somewhat less strikingly original. . . . We could then venture to promise him a double portion of readers, and a reputation which, if he persist in his errors, he will never obtain.' But 'his writings present us with so many fine and striking ideas, or passages, that we shall always read his poems with great pleasure.'

The Sun reviewed the book on July 10th, beginning: 'There are few things more delightful than the perusal of a new Volume of beautiful Poetry. . . . This delight we have just experienced in a very eminent degree.' It quoted largely from 'Hyperion,' regarding it, even in its unfinished state, as 'the greatest effort of MR. KEATS' genius, and gives us reason to hope for something great from his pen.' No space was left for criticism of the other poems in the volume which 'are very various in style, but all of great merit.' ' "Isabella" . . . is a specimen of beautiful simplicity and affecting tenderness' and of the shorter poems the 'Ode to a Nightingale' and 'On a Grecian Urn' were singled out.

The Literary Chronicle for July 29th gave an admonitory notice. The critic was disappointed in Mr. Keats for whom he 'had augured better things.' Mr. Keats must really abandon 'all acquaintance with our metropolitan poets.' He was lukewarm about the longer poems, though admitting that 'Lamia,' 'Isabella,' and 'The Eve of St. Agnes' had some fine passages in them. He ignored 'Hyperion.' 'Among the minor poems, many of which possess considerable merit' he thought the best to be the 'Ode on a Grecian Urn' and quoted it in full. In 'Bards of Passion and of Mirth,' also quoted, he found 'a pretty idea, happily expressed.' Let Mr. Keats, however, 'avoid all sickly affectation on the one hand, and unintelligible quaintness on the other. Let him avoid coining new words, and give us the English language as it is taught and written in the nineteenth century, and he will make considerable progress towards improvement.'

Gold's *London Magazine* (August, 1820) gave a long article where praise was mixed with ridicule; ridicule apparently provoked by the friendliness towards Keats of their rival, 'the pseudo London Magazine,' Baldwin's.

We frankly confess our dislike of his rhythm, and his intolerable affectation, and mistaken stringing-together of compound epithets. But still we feel he often *thinks* like a poet . . . His Endymion led us, with all its blemishes, to expect from him higher things . . . we are still sanguine of his success.

After recommending country air to strengthen the poet's nerves and a change of diet to preserve his health, there followed eleven pages of jocular summary of 'Lamia' and 'Isabella' with quotations implied as absurd.

The Guardian, a Tory paper, after remarking that journals of opposite principles had united in lauding this 'Muses' Son of Promise,' was more subtly derisive than the *London*:

> The first great merit of Mr. Keats' poetry consists in the exercise it affords to the thinking faculties. . . . It is deep and mystical—it has all the stimulating properties of a Christmas riddle—it is a nosegay of enigmas. . . .
>
> Our readers will by this time conclude that Mr. Keats is a very original poet. We perfectly accord with them. But yet he has his faults;—he sometimes descends to write naturally, and to use the common language of humanity in the expression of pleasure or grief. We hope he may correct this fault ere the Cockney chair shall become vacant.

In August there appeared in *The Edinburgh Review* a critique, not only of the new volume but of the hitherto ignored *Endymion*, written by Jeffery himself. Finding this poet, whom he had not ventured to defend against his powerful Tory rivals, now in a fair way to becoming famous he rather neatly took credit to himself by saying:

> That imitation of our older writers, and especially of our older dramatists, to which we cannot help flattering ourselves that we have somewhat contributed, has brought on, as it were, a second spring in our poetry;—and few of its blossoms are either more profuse of sweetness or richer in promise, than this which is now before us.

He 'had never happened to see either of these volumes till very lately.' This in the case of *Endymion* seems highly improbable in view of Keats's statement in a letter of September, 1819, that 'The Edinburgh review are affraid to touch upon my Poem . . . they do not like to condemn it and they will not praise it for fear—They are as shy of it as I should be of wearing a Quaker's hat.' He found 'The Cowardliness of the Edinburgh . . . worse than the abuse of the Quarterly.' From an entry in Parson Newton's diary for 1818 it would appear as if, at least in the north-west of England, the sale of the *Review* was dwindling, for some 'Ladies whiggishly inclined' complained that it had fallen off and said that many of their neighbours had exchanged it for the *Quarterly*. *The Edinburgh* for a time, perhaps, felt it had to step warily.

In his article Jeffrey concentrated on *Endymion*, giving the outline of the story and quoting copiously from the finer passages. He made a very fair criticism, though admitting its beauties generously, adding that there was probably no other book 'we would sooner employ as a test to ascertain whether any one had in him a native relish for poetry.' This was probably a side-hit at the *Quarterly* oracle, Croker. Jeffrey had allowed himself too little space for much comment on the *Lamia* volume, but quoted with approbation from 'Isabella,' 'The Nightingale,' and 'Fancy.' He found in 'Hyperion' 'passages of force and grandeur,' but the subject of it 'too far removed from all the sources of human interest, to be successfully treated by any modern author.' Keats must not 'waste the good gifts of nature on intractible themes.'

On the publication of his articles in book form later Jeffrey expressed regret that he 'did not go more largely into the exposition' of Keats's merits 'in the slight notice of them.' Perhaps we must not too much blame a harassed and busy editor for not giving the young poet support when he most needed it.

Constable's *Edinburgh Magazine*, which had given what was on the whole a fair criticism of the 1817 volume, had ignored *Endymion*: it also now changed its mind. It had predicted in 1817 that if Keats would cast off the uncleanness of 'the Cockney School,' 'taking him by himself it appears he might succeed.' In spite of the many traces of that taint in *Endymion* the reviewer began his notice of it with 'Mr. Keats is a poet of high and undoubted powers.' He thought that *Endymion*, though it contained more positive faults than *Lamia*, 'is more completely in Mr. Keats's own style; and we think that it contains, at least, as many beauties.' He criticized little but quoted freely so that readers might taste for themselves for 'after all, poetry is a matter of feeling rather than of argument,' including lines 'quoted against the author, in a London Review' (the *Quarterly*):

> "Endymion! the cave is secreter
> "Than the isle of Delos.   Echo hence shall stir
> "No sighs but sigh-warm kisses, or *light noise*
> "*Of thy combing hand, the while it travelling cloys*
> "*And trembles thro' my labyrinthine hair.*"

and finished the article with 'If this be not poetry, we do not know what is; but we must perforce leave Endymion, begging our readers to refer to it without more ado, both for their own sakes and our own.' The review on *Lamia* he promised for a later issue.

The British Critic which two years before made wilful nonsense of *Endymion* in a vulgar style, having, in view of the recognized achievement of *Lamia*, to climb down, did it with what dignity it could muster, laying all the blame for its *Endymion* critique on that dreadful Mr. Leigh Hunt.

The reviewer opened with 'If there be one person in the present day, for whom we feel an especial contempt, it is Mr. Examiner Hunt.' It was, of course, merely as a disciple of Hunt that 'Mr. Keats fell under our lash, so severely, upon the occasion of his poem of Endymion.' Upon recurring to that poem he was not unwilling to admit it some merit; at the first perusal he had not been 'in a frame of mind to appreciate.' *Endymion* must have been 'corrected by our modern Malvolio, and projected by his advice and under his superintendence. . . . The effect of this upon Mr. Keats's poetry, was like an infusion of ipecacuanha powder in a dish of marmalade.' As there is in this new volume some measure of 'the same obstacle to dispassionate judgment' the reviewer congratulated himself on his impartiality.

He again, however, pursed a moral lip. The subject of one of the poems was drawn from the works of that notoriously immoral writer Boccaccio, and the other narrative poems had stories of similar doubtful character. But in the handling of them there were fortunately no details that might 'appear calculated to wound delicacy.'

'Mr. Keats is really a person of no ordinary genius' and if he will only take *The Critic's* advice and model himself on Spenser or Milton instead of Mr. Leigh Hunt 'he need not despair of attaining to a very high and enviable place in the public esteem.' One who failed to see the influence of Spenser and of Milton on Keats's work does not demand lengthy consideration: I shall pass over the rest of the review and merely give the spirited lunge at the end of the article. Giving examples of 'affectations' in the Huntian manner, several of which, to do him justice, might be so styled, he boomed:

such innovations in language are despicable in themselves, and disgusting to the imagination of every man of virtue and taste, from having been originally *conceited*, as Mr. Keats would say, in the brain of one of the most profligate and wretched scribblers that we can remember to have even either heard or read of.

The 'profligate and wretched scribbler' published his own review of *Lamia* in *The Indicator* for August 2nd and 9th. The article is neither so rich nor so gracefully written as the 1817 review of the *Poems*; perhaps the fine point of Hunt's pen was blunted by heavy anxiety for his friend. He adopted the method of telling the story of each of the long poems 'cutting some of the richest passages out of (Keats's) verse, and fitting them in to our plainer narrative. They are such as would leaven a much greater lump. Their drops are rich and vital, the essence of a heap of fertile thoughts.' Of

> A haunting music, sole perhaps and lone
> Supportress of the faery-roof, made moan
> Throughout, as fearful the whole charm might fade.

he said: 'This is the very quintessence of the romantic.' He found fault in 'Lamia' with

the common-place of supposing that Apollonius's sophistry must always prevail, and that modern experiment has done a deadly thing to poetry by discovering the nature of the rainbow, the air, etc.: that is to say, that the knowledge of natural history and physics, by shewing us the nature of things, does away the imaginations that once adorned them. This is a condescension to a learned vulgarism, which so excellent a poet as Mr. Keats ought not to have made. The world will always have fine poetry, as long as it has events, passions, affections, and a philosophy that sees deeper than this philosophy.

With regard to 'Isabella' Hunt wrote, no doubt with his friend Lamb in mind: 'The following masterly anticipation of his (Lorenzo's) end, conveyed in a single word, has been justly admired:

> So the two brothers and their *murder'd* man, etc.

He criticized Keats's temporary failure of dramatic sense in putting in the mouth of one of the sordid brothers the exquisite metaphor:

>   ... ere the hot sun count
> His dewy rosary on the eglantine.

He quoted, remarking on their 'fervid misery,' the stanzas praised by Lamb, XLVI–VIII, and, also with strong approbation, the last heart-rending nineteen lines of the poem.

'The Eve of St. Agnes,' wrote Hunt, 'is rather a picture than a story' and quoting the stanzas singled out by Lamb, XXIV–VII, 'The description . . . falls at once gorgeously and delicately upon us, like the colours of a painted glass.'

'When Mr. Keats errs in his poetry, it is from the ill management of a good thing—exuberance of ideas.' As an example of this he gave from the 'Ode to Psyche' the line:

> At tender eye-dawn of aurorean love

adding, 'it is once or twice only, in his present volume.'

He quoted the 'Ode to a Nightingale' in full, commenting:

The poem will be the more striking to the reader, when he understands what we take a friend's liberty in telling him, that the author's powerful mind has for some time past been inhabiting a sickened and shaken body, and that in the mean while it has had to contend with feelings that make a fine nature ache for its species, even when it would disdain to do so for itself; we mean, critical malignity, that unhappy envy, which would wreak its own tortures upon others, especially upon those that really feel for it already.

This personal touch would not be pleasing to Keats; nor, I should imagine, could he feel anything but disgust for the extraordinary statement from Hunt that almost all the poems in the present volume were written four years ago, when the author was but twenty. One cannot, however one might wish to defend Hunt, regard this as anything but a journalistic disingenuousness to advertise the poems. Hunt could not, for all his natural disregard for mundane facts, have been unaware of the rough dating of most of the poems. He could not have thought they were contemporary with the 1817 volume.

'The Hyperion,' he wrote, 'is a fragment—a gigantic one, like a ruin in a desart, or the bones of a mastodon.' He quoted from it largely, including that great utterance we can link with the idea perceived in Keats's letters of a strong, serene power looking down:

> Now comes the pain of truth, to whom 'tis pain;
> O folly! for to bear all naked truths,
> And to envisage circumstance, all calm,
> That is the top of sovereignty.

He gave as 'the core and inner diamond of the poem' Book I, lines 176–304, creating the fiery beauty of the Sun-god's palace 'whose portals open like a rose, the awful phænomena that announce a change in heaven, and his inability to bid the day break as he was accustomed.' He made the valuable suggestion that Keats had left 'Hyperion' unfinished because 'our feeble tongue' cannot convey 'that large utterance of the early Gods.' Milton had failed in a like attempt and, according to Pope, had made

> God the father turn a school divine.

The moment the Gods speak, we forget that they do not speak like ourselves. The fact is, they feel like ourselves; and the poet would have to make them feel otherwise, even if he could make them speak otherwise, which he cannot, unless he venture upon an obscurity which would destroy our sympathy: and what is sympathy with a God, but turning him into a man? We allow, that superiority and inferiority are, after all, human terms, and imply something not so truly fine and noble as the levelling of a great sympathy and love; but poems of the present nature, like Paradise Lost, assume a different principle; and fortunately perhaps, it is one which it is impossible to reconcile with the other.

This is interesting, not only as general criticism, but as perhaps an indication of why Keats, whether deliberately or intuitively, had refrained from completing 'Hyperion.' The Titans are huge figures and speak greatly but they speak in grief which is in itself great. The words of the commonest man in sorrow can be natural poetry. About Hyperion himself there is a splendid pall of tragedy. The handling of Apollo, the coming sun-god, is weaker and his speech almost common-place in such lines as:

> ". . . Point me out the way
> "To any one particular beauteous star,
> "And I will flit into it with my lyre,
> "And make its silvery splendour pant with bliss."

Faltering human nature cannot depict a potent god. Dante saw God as supreme light, not personified, and the Trinity in three circles; in so far as he could put his beatitude in human terms.

The critique ended:

The author's versification is now perfected, the exuberances of his imagination restrained, and a calm power, the surest and loftiest of all power, takes place of the impatient workings of the younger god within him. The character of his genius is that of energy and voluptuousness, each able at will to take leave of the other, and possessing, in their union, a high feeling of humanity not common to the best authors who can less combine them. Mr. Keats undoubtedly takes his seat with the oldest and best of our living poets.

Keats was now an established poet. He wrote on August 20th to Brown: 'My book has had good success among the literary people.' The critiques mentioned above he must have read; those which came out in September may have missed him; the magazines were then dilatory in their appearance and he left London on September 17th. It would be a pity if he did not see *The New Monthly*. Its praise of the volume showed clearly which way the wind was blowing. *The New Monthly* was a Tory Review, owned by Colburn, the publisher (an ancestor of Hurst and Blackett) and edited officially by the poet Thomas Campbell. The reviewer said of the poems:

There is a fine freeness of touch about them, like that which is manifest in the old marbles, as though the poet played at will his fancies virginal and produced his most perfect works without toil . . . his latest works (are) as free from all offensive peculiarities—as pure, as genuine, and as lofty, as the severest critic could desire.

Of 'Lamia' he wrote:

There is in this poem a mingling of Greek majesty with fairy luxuriance, which we have not elsewhere seen. The fair shapes stand clear in their antique beauty, encircled with the profuse magnificence of romance, and in the thick atmosphere of its golden lustre!

and of 'Hyperion,' 'we do not think anything exceeds in silent grandeur the opening of the poem' and quoting Book II, lines 5–81, 'The picture of the vast abode of Cybele and the Titans—and of its gigantic inhabitants, is in the sublimest style of Æschylus.' He noted 'the gigantic stride he (Keats) has taken' and predicted 'an exalted and lasting station among the English poets.'

The Monthly Magazine or British Register gave a short notice. Keats, the reviewer felt, was now entitled 'to stand equally high in the estimation of public opinion' as Hunt or B. W. Procter. He possessed 'the faults characteristic of his school' but there was in him 'more reach of poetic capacity, more depth and intenseness of thought and feeling, with more classical power and expression' than in Procter and more originality than in either poet.

The reviewer in the September issue of Baldwin's London Magazine, now edited by John Scott, former editor of The Champion, opened with a long castigation of the Quarterly, though admitting that Keats had in some measure courted its attack by his imprudence in obtruding his political views in his work and by youthful 'affectations.' He criticized on this score the stanzas attacking the brothers of Isabella, adding: 'That most beautiful Paper . . . in our last number, on the "ledger-men" of the South Sea House, is an elegant reproof of such short-sighted views of character; such idle hostilities against the realities of life. . . . The author of Endymion and Hyperion must delight in that Paper.' The paper referred to was Charles Lamb's 'The South Sea House.' If Mr. Keats must protest against the materialism of the age let him do it in the 'bold and indignant style of Wordsworth's glorious sonnet.' The reviewer then quoted in full 'The world is too much with us.' In this peroration there are hints of John Scott's hostility to Hunt: Scott was but a mild Liberal and regarded the editor of The Examiner as a mischievous fellow.

Quoting the last two stanzas of the 'Nightingale' he said: 'it is distinct, noble, pathetic and true; the thoughts have all chords of direct communication with naturally-constituted hearts: the echoes of the strain linger about the depths of human bosoms.' Giving stanzas XXIII–IX of 'The Eve of St. Agnes' he wrote:

Let us take a passage of another sort altogether—the description of a young beauty preparing for her nightly rest, overlooked by a concealed lover, in which we know not whether most to admire the magical delicacy of the hazardous picture, or its consummate, irresistible attraction. "How sweet the moonlight sleeps upon this bank," says Shakespeare; and sweetly indeed does it fall on the half-dressed form of Madeline: it has an exquisite moral influence, corresponding with its picturesque effect.

'Hyperion' he found 'one of the most extraordinary creations of any modern imagination' and he got in another slap at the *Quarterly* with

The sorrows of this piece are "huge", its utterances "large"; its tears "big". —Alas, centuries have brought littleness since then,—otherwise a crawling, reptile of office, with just strength enough to leave its slimy traces on the pages of a fashionable Review, could never have done a real mischief to the poet of the Titans! . . . "*the reception given to that work* (Endymion) *discouraged the author from proceeding.*"

Let Mr. Croker read the following sublime and gorgeous personification of Asia, and be proud of the information thus given him—and of that superior encouragement to which it is owing that we have his Talevera in a complete state!

He then quoted Book II, lines 52-63 of 'Hyperion'. This, if written by John Scott himself, has a pathos for modern readers: in the following year, a week before Keats's death, Scott was killed in a duel with Christie, the friend of Lockhart of *Blackwood's*, as a result of his constant reprisals on the Tory organs for their unjust treatment of Liberal writers.

Towards the end of the review there was a concentrated dose of criticism, pointing out 'the principal faults' that impeded Keats's popularity. One fault was 'obscurity and confusion of language,' and as an example of 'confusion' he cited 'the epithet of "leaden-eyed" to despair, considered as a quality or sentiment.' That the old habit of personification in poetry still shackled the minds of many is clear in 'Were it a personification of despair the compound would be as finely applied, as, under the actual circumstances, it is erroneously so.'

The second fault was Keats's fondness for 'running out glimmerings of thought and indicating distant shadowy fancies . . . plain earnest minds turn away from such tricks with disgust.' The third was 'a quaint strangeness of phrase; as some folk affect an odd manner of arranging their neckcloths, etc.' He objected to Mr. Keats talking of *cutting mercy with a sharp knife to the bone*; 'we cannot contemplate the *skeleton* of mercy.' He put on a level with this razor-sharp metaphor the periphrasis, too coy perhaps for its context, 'the dainties made to still an infant's cries.'

But the reviewer is tired of criticism. 'Let us,' he said, 'then turn together all to the book itself . . . we shall there find what it will be our delight to enjoy.'

In December, giving a paragraph to Keats in his 'Essay on Poetry, with Observations on the Living Poets,' Scott repeated his criticisms but added, 'he has a happy faculty of expressing apt images by individual expression, and of hitching the faculty of imagination on a single word; such as that exquisitely imaginative line:

> She stood in tears amid the *alien* corn.

The ascetic *Eclectic Review* had in 1817 warned Mr. Keats against the frivolity of poetry in relation to the serious business of life: 'When a man has established his character in any useful sphere of exertion, the fame of a poet may be safely sought.' Now (September, 1820) as then, it acknowledged Mr. Keats to be 'a young man . . . possessed of an elegant fancy, a warm and lively imagination, and something above the average talent of persons who take to writing poetry,' but warned him against the snare of imagination and the delusion of poetry for its own sake, 'poetry, after all, if pursued as an end, is but child's play.'

The Edinburgh Magazine continued its review[1] of Keats's poems in October. The critic contented himself with presenting Keats's poetry in lavish quotation but with little comment. 'Isabella' he found 'eminently beautiful'; in 'The Eve of St. Agnes' he quoted the set of stanzas chosen for special notice by other reviewers. He was inclined to prefer the 'Nightingale' to any other poem in the book. 'We have read this ode over and over again, and every time with increased delight.' He quoted all but the first and last verse. 'Hyperion' he did not like as much as the other poems, 'yet there is an air of grandeur about it, and it opens in a striking manner.' Of the line

> Sat grey-haired Saturn, quiet as a stone

he said that it reminded him of a line in the *Mirror for Magistrates*:

> By him lay heavie sleep, cosen of death,
> Flat on the ground, and *still as any stone*;

[1] Professor Willard B. Pope suggests this review was written by John Hamilton Reynolds.

and also of a line in Chaucer. Perhaps the line he meant was from 'The Compleynte unto Pite':

> Adoun I fel, when that I saugh the herse,
> *Dead as a stoon,* whyl that the swogh me laste.

The only criticism he had to make was of the tirade against Isabella's brothers as in bad taste, but palliated it with: 'Mr. K., indeed, himself seems to have some doubts of this, and in the following beautiful stanzas intreats the forgiveness of his master. They are enough, to say the least, to wipe away the sin committed.' He quoted the invocation to Boccaccio, stanzas XIX and XX.

Following directly on this review is a set of couplets entitled 'Dian and Endymion' and signed I. R. or J. R. (the letter is worn). Though of little value in themselves, they are full of remote but unmistakable Keatsian echoes. It would be of interest to know the name of the author. One may guess he was a Scot as in the first couplet he rimes 'Endymion' with 'mŭn' (moon).

There was no reference in *Blackwood's* August number either to *Lamia* or Keats himself. On the 31st Mr. Blackwood called on Taylor in Fleet Street. Taylor, after a general chat upon books, told him they had published another volume of Keats's for his editors to make merry with. Blackwood said they were disposed to speak favourably of Mr. Keats this time. He had expected an article on *Lamia* to appear in the August issue. Taylor exclaimed against their inconsistency; how could they praise Keats after they had denied talent to him? Blackwood asserted that formerly they had felt bound to find fault but that now they could praise.

"But why," asked Taylor, "did you attack him personally?" This Mr. Blackwood had the impudence to deny. When Taylor pressed the question home with examples of *Blackwood's* abuse of Keats, Mr. Blackwood said airily, O that! that was only a joke. The writer certainly found affectation in Keats's poetry and said so. 'It was done in the fair spirit of criticism.' Taylor lost his temper.

"It was done in the spirit of the Devil, Mr. Blackwood. So if a young man is guilty of affectation while he is walking the streets it is fair in another person because he dislikes it to come and knock him down."

"No," answered Blackwood, "but a poet challenges public opinion by printing his book, but I suppose you would have them not criticized at all?"

Taylor, who privately loathed professional criticism, could not answer directly to this but replied that he thought an unsuccessful poet was punished enough in the neglect of his work, and it "seems very cruel to abuse a man merely because he cannot give us as much pleasure as he wishes. But you go beyond this—you strike a man when he is down. He gets a violent blow from the Quarterly—and then you begin."

"I beg your pardon," said Blackwood coolly, "we were the first."

It must have been difficult for Taylor to keep control of himself. But he remained cool enough to get in a subtle thrust by a reference to the manners of gentlemen and an enquiry whether these should not regulate a man's conduct in writing as well as in personal intercourse. No man would insult Mr. Keats as 'Z' had done in his company and 'Z's' attack was the baser for being anonymous; he ran no personal risk such as a man who insulted another in person did in those days when duelling still lingered on. Taylor continued:

"I feel regard for Mr. Keats as a man of real genius, a gentleman, nay more, one of the gentlest of human beings. He does not resent these things himself, he merely says of his opponents, 'They don't know me.' "

But Mr. Blackwood was not a man to be moved by this. Taylor went on in a firmer tone:

"I am happy to say that public interest is awakened to the sense of the injustice which has been done him and the attempts to ruin him will have in the end a contrary effect."

They talked about Scott's new book, *Ivanhoe*, for another ten minutes and then Mr. Blackwood took his leave with a formal bow and a good morning. On arrival he had shaken hands.

All this Taylor wrote down and sent in a letter to Hessey. He feared there might be allusion to it in 'The Mother of Mischief' and wanted to keep the conversation clear before him.

Perhaps Taylor's protest did make some impression: a short notice of *Lamia* (known to be by Lockhart) in *Blackwood's* September issue is comparatively mild:

Aug. 16.—It is a pity that this young man, John Keats, author of Endymion, and some other poems, should have belonged to the Cockney school—for he is evidently possessed of talents that, under better direction, might have done very considerable things. As it is, he bids fair to sink himself entirely beneath such a mass of affectation, conceit, and Cockney pedantry, as I never expected to see heaped together by any body, except the Great Founder of the School. What in the name of wonder tempts all these fellows to write on *Greek* fables. A man might as well attempt to write a second Anastasius without going into the east. There is much merit in some of the stanzas of Mr. Keats' last volume, which I have just seen; no doubt he is a fine feeling lad—and I hope he will live to despise Leigh Hunt, and be a poet—

—"After the fashion of the elder men of England—"

If he wants to see the story of the *Lamia*, which he has spoiled in one sense, and adorned in another—told with real truth and beauty, and explained at once with good sense and imagination, let him look to Weiland's (sic) life of Peregrinus Proteus, vol. first, I think.

The journal made a further half-apologetic reference to Keats in a review of Shelley's *Prometheus Unbound*. They were sorry to hear he was ill and wished him a speedy recovery. Mr. Keats's friends attributed his illness in great part to their castigation of *Endymion*. If this were so they expressed regret; if they had suspected the author 'of being so delicately nerved, we should have administered our reproof in a much more lenient shape and style.' Of course, they recognized all along Mr. Keats's promise of being 'a real poet in England' if he would forswear the 'Cockney School' and 'the thin potations of Mr. Leigh Hunt. We, therefore, rated him as roundly as we decently could do. . . .'

Allowing for the coarser tone of Georgian journalism what, one wonders, would 'Z' regard as indecent criticism? The editors evidently regarded their medical jokes as 'decent' for, after in this article saying, although they saw more beauties in Keats's present volume there were still the old 'Cockney' faults, they put in the same number of the magazine a rimed sneer at the 'School' including:

> We, from the hands of a cockney apothecary
> Brought off this pestle, with which he was capering,
> Swearing and swaggering, rhyming and vapouring;
> Seized with a fit of poetical fury,
> (I thought he was drunk, my good sir, I assure ye), . . .
> Loud he exclaimed, 'Behold here's my truncheon;
> I'm the Marshal of poets—I'll flatten your nuncheon.
> Pitch physic to hell, you rascals, for damn ye, a—
> I'll physic you all with a clyster of Lamia.'

In justice to Blackwood it must be said that he himself would not have handled this dirt: he does not seem to have been forceful enough to restrain Lockhart and Wilson. John Murray, at first connected with *Blackwood's Magazine*, had soon withdrawn himself in strong protest.

It is a tribute to Murray's common sense and fairness that he did not launch an attack on Keats's new volume in the *Quarterly*: Lord Byron, on receiving a copy of *Lamia*, had written: 'Pray send me *no more* poetry but what is rare and decidedly good.' Referring to the volume as 'trash' he exhorted Murray to 'flay him alive; if some of you don't I must skin him myself; there is no bearing the drivelling idiotism of the Mankin.' When he read Jeffrey's praise of Keats's poetry in *The Edinburgh Review* Byron wrote to Murray shriekingly and in such gross terms that even modern editors feel compelled to use asterisks. Byron, who had originally fallen foul of Keats for his youthful attack on Pope in the 1817 volume, was at this time the most popular poet in Europe; both as man and poet a dominant figure, a rage, a fashion, almost a tradition, and highly profitable to his publisher. In remaining silent about Keats, therefore, in the periodical he owned, Murray showed not only admirable discretion but considerable courage.

It is unlikely that Keats himself was informed of *Blackwood's* further attack or of Lord Byron's filthy abuse; all he knew of important reactions to his new volume was that, in spite of minor criticisms, he was almost unanimously hailed as a true poet. In early days, when a love of fame animated him, recognition would have been dear. Now a greater love and its loss in the shadow of the valley of death possessed him. Ambition could not touch him. His greatest work was but the forerunner of what was to come; only a slight preparation for his ancient lofty dreams. What man had said and what man could say was no comfort in the coldness of his despair.

CHAPTER XX

The Voyage to Italy (September—November 1820)

THE favourable reception of his book in literary circles, Tory and Liberal, aroused outside his immediate circle a new interest in Keats. It is likely that he received many invitations which, both from ill-health and disinclination, he refused. One, however, was accepted, and, so far as we know, it was the last engagement he fulfilled; to spend the day with Horace Smith at his house in Elysium Row, Fulham, then in the midst of open country, nursery gardens and orchards. During the afternoon Smith took his little daughter into the garden and drew her attention to 'a rather thin, pale and ill-dressed gentleman' sitting in the shade of a wide-spreading ilex tree.

"Do you see that man?" he said, "that's a poet."

The familiars of his circle came to dine at an earlier hour than usual so that they might enjoy a long evening out of doors in exceptionally beautiful weather. James and Leonard Smith were there and also the 'literary dry-salter,' Thomas Hill of Sydenham. Hill had been allowed as an especial favour by his host to send over in Keats's honour a dozen of his favourite beverage, 'some quite undeniable *Chateau Margeaux*', and this was enjoyed in the garden.

As the weeks drew on towards the shorter days the thought of the voyage to Italy weighed more and more on Keats's mind. 'This Journey,' he wrote to Taylor on August 14th, 'wakes me at daylight every morning and haunts me horribly. I shall endeavour to go through it with the sensation of marching up against a Battery.'

The financial aspect was worrying him. Mr. Abbey had promised that if no money came from George he would make a loan, but when Keats wrote for it he answered formally: 'You know that it was very much against my will that you lent your money to George. . . . Bad debts for the last two years have cut down the profits of our business to nothing, so that I can scarcely take out enough for my private expence —It is therefore not in my power to lend you any thing—I am Dear Sir Yrs—Richd Abbey. When you are able to call I shall be glad to see you, as I should not like to see you want "maintenance for the day." '[1]

In a further letter to Taylor about the voyage Keats enclosed without comment a note of how he wished to dispose of his property

---

[1] At the time (*see* Appendix I) there was lying to Keats's account unclaimed in the Court of Chancery at least £700.

after death; the property which beyond his books lay 'in the hopes of the sale of books publish'd or unpublish'd.' Brown and Taylor were to be 'first paid Creditors—the rest in nubibus—but in case it should shower pay my Taylor [tailor] the few pounds I owe him. My Chest of Books divide among my friends.'

This paper was, according to the note in Hone's *Table Book* (1828), in which it was first brought to light, submitted to Doctors' Commons but refused acceptance as a will.

On the 20th he wrote to Brown in Scotland telling him that a winter in Italy was his only chance of living. 'Not that I have any great hopes of that for, I think, there is a core of disease in me not easy to pull out.' The letter as we have it is incomplete but we may guess that he asked Brown to accompany him. He wrote again to Brown:

. . . I ought to be off at the end of this week, as the cold winds begin to blow towards evening;—but I will wait till I have your answer to this. I am to be introduced, before I set out, to a Dr Clark, a physician settled at Rome, who promises to befriend me in every way there. The sale of my book is very slow, though it has been very highly rated. One of the causes, I understand from different quarters, of the unpopularity of this new book, and the others also, is the offence the ladies take at me. On thinking that matter over, I am certain I have said nothing in a spirit to displease any woman I would care to please; but still there is a tendency to class women in my books with roses and sweetmeats,—they never see themselves dominant . . . I will say no more, but, waiting in anxiety for your answer, doff my hat, and make a purse as long as I can.

Neither letter reached Brown in time: Keats set out on his last journey without a word from him.

The thought of going alone to Italy must have added a fresh load to the burden of his misery. When Haydon saw him for the last time in Wentworth Place he was 'lying in a white bed with a book, hectic and on his back, irritable at his weakness and wounded at the way he had been used. He seemed to be going out of life with a contempt for this world and no hopes of the other. I told him to be calm, but he muttered that if he did not soon get better he would destroy himself. I used to reason against such violence, but it was no use; he grew angry, and I went away deeply affected.'

In all Haydon's accounts of Keats a large allowance must be made for exaggeration and even misrepresentation. This passage follows on a reference to Keats's 'irregularities' which from the testimony of more reliable witnesses we know to be slander. But there seems to be a fairly general agreement that his diseased mind now brooded on the former attacks on him in *Blackwood's* and the *Quarterly*. He would pore over them when alone, and although he would, as soon as anyone entered the room, thrust them aside and begin to talk of some other matter, his misery was apparent. Woodhouse reports him as saying: "If I die you must ruin Lockhart." That this vindictiveness of spirit was not native to him Fanny Brawne makes clear in her memoir already quoted: '. . . his anger seemed rather to turn on himself than on others, and in moments of greatest irritation, it was only by a sort of savage despondency that he sometimes grieved and wounded his friends.'

His friends, however, mistook a symptom for a cause. None but Brown could guess at the depth of his love for Fanny and probably nobody at this time understood the effect of his terrible disease upon the mind; so that after Keats's death far too great a stress was put upon the disastrous effect of the attacks upon him. It was also a convenient stick to lay about the shoulders of the Tories.

Haydon's account also exaggerates his weakness of body. A man who could face and survive a voyage to Italy under the hard conditions of that day must still have been tolerably active. There must have been in these last summer days many walks on the Heath with his love, the boisterous Carlo running and leaping before them; walks in which he snatched desperately at vanishing joy. But the thought of that terrible journey could never have been far from his mind.

At the beginning of September the cold winds of evening made it clear that the time had come for Keats to go. There was still no sign from Brown and any thought of his accompanying Keats must be abandoned. Fanny wanted to go with him as his wife and Mrs. Brawne agreed, saying she herself would go too. Keats must have been sorely tempted but in honour felt bound to refuse. It would seem that some outside persons offered officious advice on the subject which Fanny thought had swayed his decision. From her enmity to them in after years it would appear as if the Reynolds women were the offenders.

But Keats would scarcely need prompting. He could not subject his love to the agony of a deathbed which his medical experience enabled him to realize in its painful detail. His common sense would tell him that from the mother, too, he would be exacting much; she would leave her young boy and girl behind her and strain financial resources which were, so far as we can gather, not large. She herself was willing for love of Keats and her daughter to set aside these difficulties, but he would not permit her. In face of his definite refusal the two women put as cheerful a face on it as possible; talking of his return next summer, of an immediate marriage and life together at Wentworth Place. 'Had he returned,' Fanny wrote to his sister in the March of 1821, 'I should have been his wife and he would have lived with us.'

The money difficulty was smoothed away by Taylor who bought the copyright of *Lamia* for a hundred pounds which, when moneys owing on advances made were deducted, left Keats thirty pounds with which to make preparation. One hundred pounds had been owing against advances on *Endymion*, but this Taylor cancelled in exchange for the copyright. He also arranged a credit over in Italy for one hundred and fifty pounds. All this was done when capital was very short with Taylor and trade exceptionally bad. The credit was to be set against money expected from George; probably the two hundred pounds mentioned in a letter of June 18th to his brother and which he had hoped to send off almost immediately. Taylor, however, must have known he was running a risk of having to meet the credit in full himself. Keats had no faith in George's ability to send him money; nor, indeed, much confidence in his brother as a man of business.

Arrangements were made for Keats to sail in the *Maria Crowther*, a brig of one hundred and thirty tons, due to leave London on or about the 17th. It seemed as if he would have to go alone.

The kindly Haslam was now a married man with a child either born or expected, but this had not lessened his affection and solicitude for Keats. 'If I know what it is to love,' he wrote to Severn in Italy, 'I truly love John Keats.' He could not bear the contemplation of the solitary journey and of his friend possibly dying unknown and uncared for in a foreign land. Casting about in his mind for a companion, Haslam thought of Severn. Severn, inexperienced of life, lacking in self-confidence, to a great extent dominated by Keats, was not perhaps the best man; Haslam would have preferred the older, stronger-willed and worldly Brown, but he had vanished in the North.

Severn's leisure was always woefully meagre and summer daylight meant even longer painting hours. He had seen very little of his friend since June and did not apparently know that the Italian journey was now a settled thing; but even thought his friend to be improving in health under the care of Mrs. Brawne. One evening in early September as he sat at work in his town lodgings Haslam called. After telling Severn the situation in regard to Keats he said, "Will you go?" Unhesitantly, though the prospect must have been alarming to the modest, home-keeping youth, Severn answered, "I'll go."

Consideration and discussion soon led him to see that a winter in Rome might materially benefit him. As winner of the Academy's gold medal he could apply for their travelling scholarship. It was at this time the dream of every painter to go to Rome: a picture from there might obtain for Severn the coveted income of one hundred and thirty pounds for three years, with consequent leisure to paint what he liked and to see life outside his own country. But no one can doubt that if, on the other hand, there had been nothing in prospect for Severn he would have gone. His friend needed him and that was enough.

As things were he was throwing up a secure livelihood attained after years of struggle. He had no capital and but for a timely payment of twenty-five pounds for a miniature 'of a lady in a white satin bonnet and feathers' could not have gone at all, or only on borrowed money. He had also to face the fury of a father who was already angry with him for wishing to throw up a hard-won connection as miniaturist for the uncertain career of an historical painter.

Severn's memory, never good, became increasingly unreliable as he grew older. In varying accounts of this time he gave twenty-four hours and three days as the period of preparation for the journey. Five days are now accepted as the likely period.[1] They were days of continual rush that gave him little time for thought.

He had to go out to Hoxton to see his family, to make purchases, apply for his passport and visit Sir Thomas Lawrence in order to get introductions in Rome. She whom he called his 'angel-mother' fully sympathized and undertook, with his sisters, to get his trunk ready. His father would do nothing but make him miserable by reproaches. He was a tyrant and a man of uncertain temper, but Severn loved him, as he loved all his family. The parting from the adored mother, brothers and sisters was hard enough without the anger of his father; justifiable anger perhaps in the circumstances. Mr. Severn had a great love for his eldest son and could not be expected to see in a friend a prior claim over that son's own family and his prospects for the future. He resorted in his despair to reasoning, but Severn, as he said of himself, had 'the virtue of the donkey—obstinacy—in the highest degree.'

In the meantime Keats was with Taylor in Fleet Street awaiting the day when the *Maria Crowther* might be ready and able to depart. The last painful good-byes had been said at Wentworth Place on the 13th.[2] Keats left with Fanny a message for his sister exhorting her to avoid colds and coughs and never to go out of the greenhouse into the cold air. He asked Fanny to correspond with her and to give her a lock of his hair. Apparently Abbey was no more willing to allow his ward to visit her brother than he had been in the case of the dying Tom. His hatred of the Hampstead circle seems to have amounted to a mania: a year passed before Fanny was able by persistence and diplomacy to meet Fanny Keats and in the meantime their correspondence had to be conducted in secret.

While they were together in Fleet Street, Taylor set down on

---

[1] *See* Haslam's letter to Taylor, September 13th, 1820, *The Keats Circle*, p. 140.
[2] *See* Appendix XI.

paper the business relations between Keats and his firm; though they were so materially to Keats's benefit that they might be more truly termed a friendly agreement. Taylor and Hessey proposed in the case of any future work, and also with regard to the *Poems, Endymion* and *Lamia*, the copyrights of which they had bought, to hand over to him all clear profit and to bear the burden of losses that could not be made good. Both men had strong faith in Keats and felt that to publish for him would bring honour to their house, but even this advantage was, in the state of his health, at best problematical. The only material gain was the copyrights of two books which might be of high value in future. There was a certain sale for Keats's work and two new editions[1] but in 1846, two years before the publication of Lord Houghton's *Life*, the copyrights were sold to Edward Moxon for a small sum (probably £200). It was Moxon, not Taylor, who reaped the harvest.

At midnight on the 16th Severn reached home to take a final farewell of his family. He found his father 'sunk down in extreme grief in his armchair.' His trunk, a heavy one, stood in the room. Joseph and Tom Severn had difficulty in lifting it for conveyance to the carriage outside and Joseph was forced to ask his father to help. 'He rose up in an apparent passion of madness, and swore that if without his touching it the trunk was never to be lifted at all, it should not be touched by him.'

Severn said nothing but turned to go upstairs to take leave of his youngest brother. His father rose and stood in the doorway and, when his son attempted to pass, knocked him down. So violent was the rage of the unhappy, tormented father that Tom Severn, although nineteen and a powerful young man, had to be assisted in restraining him. There was no time for remonstrance or reconciliation. Severn had to go leaving anger and sorrow behind.

Tom was to accompany him as far as Gravesend. On the slow horse-journey through the dark and chill of night the two brothers were wrapped in gloom. Severn was, in addition to a natural distress of mind over the painful scene with his father, suffering from a liver complaint. But as they came near the south bank of the Thames with the wharves and masts looming against the pale dawn his spirits rose. A new life lay before him, and with the friend he loved most.

Keats was waiting on the wharf with Taylor, Haslam, Woodhouse and others. Taylor had with him his apprentice, William Smith Williams, who was later to become reader to Smith Elder and a friend of the Brontës. Perhaps it was he who as 'Gaston' contributed to Hone's *Table Book* in 1827 some verses on Keats (with a preliminary demand for some written memorial and an engraved portrait) in which are the following lines:

See Appendix XII.

Still do I see thee on the river's strand
Take thy last step upon thy native land—
Still feel the last kind pressure of thy hand.
A calm dejection in thy youthful face,
To which e'en sickness lent a tender grace—
A hectic bloom—the sacrificial flower,
Which marks th' approach of Death's all-withering power.

The *Maria Crowther* sailed out of the London Docks at 7 o'clock. Taylor, Woodhouse, Haslam and Tom Severn remained on board. On the way down river, Severn, always careless of detail and possibly remembering it for the first time, said that his passport had not arrived before he left. Haslam undertook to procure it and let him have it before the ship left Gravesend.

The little company of friends, although of a generation used to discomfort in travel, must have felt misgiving when they inspected the travellers' quarters. The *Maria Crowther* was a small brig with but one cabin which it seems as if the captain shared with the passengers. A woman had come on board with them, a Mrs. Pidgeon, a cheerful middle-aged woman to whom fortunately Keats and Severn took an immediate fancy. She too had to share the cabin 'with only a side-scene to retire to.'

The ship reached Gravesend about noon and waited for another passenger. The friends remained with Keats and Severn until four o'clock. I now quote from a letter Taylor wrote at her brother's request to Fanny Keats:

He did not go ashore but entered at once on the kind of life which he will have to lead for about a Month to come, dining in the Cabin with the Captain, and another Passenger (a Lady) besides Severn, the Friend who is gone with him—The Vessel waited at Gravesend for another Lady who was coming on board there.—Mr. Taylor, Mr. Haslam and Mr. Woodhouse accompanied Mr. Keats to Gravesend, and left him at four o'clock on Sunday afternoon.—He was then comfortably settled in his new Habitation with every prospect of having a pleasant Voyage.—His Health was already much improved by the Air of the River, by the Exercise and the amusement which the Sailing afforded.—He was provided with everything that would contribute to make the Time pass agreably, and with all that his Health required;

This was a rosy picture for Fanny's benefit. The ship was not only ill-equipped, but badly provisioned.

When Haslam took farewell of Severn he made an earnest request that he would write journal-letters of their life on the voyage and abroad for the benefit of Keats's friends; letters from which together with others written at the time, we obtain the most reliable details of Severn's life with Keats. It was perhaps now that Woodhouse handed to Keats a generously-worded letter saying that, though at present short of money, it would give him great satisfaction later to answer a draft of his for 'there is no one who would be more welcome than yourself to share my little Superfluities.' He asked for a lock of his friend's hair. It was arranged that Haslam should call on Fanny Keats to give her a personal account of her brother's departure. Two of the men wrote immediately to Fanny Brawne reporting that Keats's health and spirits were better than they had expected. And this was no kindly fiction on their part: all of them were agreeably surprised by his animation and his apparently improved state of health.

That evening at tea in the cabin he 'cracked his jokes' and was quite the 'special fellow of olden times.' Fortunately sleep soon overcame to quench these unnaturally high spirits. He and Severn 'serenaded' Mrs. Pidgeon 'with a snoring duett.' Severn woke up several times 'with the oddest notions—the first time in a Shoemaker's shop—the next down in a wine cellar pretty well half seas over.'

While they slept that night a small coasting vessel glided into the harbour and anchored nearly alongside the gently rocking ship. She had come from Dundee with a passenger aboard her. That passenger was Charles Brown. At daybreak, long before Keats and Severn came on deck, the ship had weighed anchor and sailed up-river on the incoming tide. Fate had been unkind enough to Keats; this last rough jest, not yet complete, would seem an unnecessary cruelty.

Charles Brown, on his pedestrian tour of the Highlands, collected on September 9th from the Dunkeld post office two of Keats's letters which had been following him round; letters written in the second week of August full of a despair which sent him hurrying home. In Brown's own words: 'On my arrival at Dundee, a smack was ready to sail, and with a fair wind. Yet I was one day too late. Unknown to each other at the time, our vessels lay, side by side, at Gravesend.'

The captain of the *Maria Crowther*, Thomas Walsh, the travellers found to be 'a good fellow' and anxious to make them as comfortable and happy as possible. After breakfast he and Severn went ashore to do some shopping. They bought, among other provisions, apples and biscuits. The captain tried to get a goat to provide milk for Keats, but was unsuccessful. On Keats's particular instructions Severn obtained 'some things from the Chymist.' made up partly from his own prescription and including a bottle of laudanum.

At dinner that afternoon Keats was 'full of his waggery—looked well—ate well—and was well.'

At six o'clock Severn's passport arrived and soon after the fourth passenger came on board. She was a Miss Cotterell, a pretty gentle girl, 'very lady-like—but a sad martyr'; also a consumptive going in search of winter warmth and sunshine. She was naturally very depressed at the prospect of the lonely voyage. The two young men did their best to cheer her. Severn tried hard to keep up with Keats in a light play of puns and joking, but, he said, 'my wit would have dropped in a minute but for Keats plying me—but I was done up for all that—leaving him sole Master—but I struck up again in my own language or Keats would have borne the Lady off in triumph.' Severn was tired out and a bad colour from incipient sea-sickness and the liver trouble. A woman friend, come to see Miss Cotterell off, enquired which was the dying man.

Severn was 'destined to pass some weeks in sad penance.' His 'dinner was a matter that always came to light.' But throughout the voyage he remained resolutely cheerful, 'made puddings and sketches' and tended the invalids. With Keats's usual ill-luck they were detained in the Channel by adverse winds for a fortnight, beating up and down distressfully and obliged to put in at various points.

Miss Cotterell was terribly ill and continually fainted away. Craving for air she wanted the port-holes kept open: if the windows remained open for long Keats would start to cough violently and sometimes bring up blood. When they were closed Miss Cotterell fainted again and would often remain insensible for five or six hours together. Mrs. Pidgeon, a woman of only surface good nature, was disobliging and worse than useless in regard to Miss Cotterell. Severn had to apply restoratives while Keats from his bunk 'dictated surgically—like Esculapius of old in basso-relievo.'

On the 19th they were off Dover Castle. The sea was rough and Keats, good sailor though he was, was sick, but 'in a most gentlemanly manner.' At night they all slept in their clothes, feeling too ill even to undress.

On the 20th they were off Brighton on a beautiful morning, able to breakfast on deck, but Keats prophesied a storm: at two o'clock it was raging furiously. By early evening water was pouring through the sky-light. They had to remain in their bunks tossed from side to side as the *Maria Crowther* pitched and rolled. Their trunks bumped incessantly about the floor. Keats was the calmest of them all. The women were terrified.

Severn managed later to get up on deck. 'The watry horizon was like a Mountainous Country—but the ship's motion was beautifully to the sea—falling from one wave to the other in a very lovely manner—the sea each time crossing the deck and one side of the ship being level with the water.' For a time he was reassured, but as it was getting dark the sea began to rush into the cabin through an opening in the planks.

He climbed down from his bunk and staggered across to Keats, saying: "Here's pretty music for you." With the greatest calmness Keats replied: "Water parted from the sea!" His mind went back perhaps to early carefree evenings at Novello's where Lamb, that wilful heretic in music, would claim for this ballad of Dr. Arne's, made popular at Vauxhall, superiority over Mozart arias.

With the pumps working incessantly, the sails squalling and the shouts of the sailors, it was a long and terrible night for the passengers 'pinn'd up in our beds like ghosts by daylight.' Severn had to tumble out from time to time to attend to the women, but the painful qualms in his stomach made him get back as soon as he possibly could. The next morning Keats bragged of his friend's 'sailorship,' saying that if he could keep on his legs in that waterlogged cabin he must have been a standing miracle. By daylight the storm had abated, but they were many miles back on their course and very soon stayed for want of wind.

They went ashore at Dungeness and scrambled over the gravel, glad to stretch their legs. Severn was astonished and delighted by the enormous waves at least ten feet high which swept curling up the shore. So long did he loiter in one spot staring at the high foaming sea that a coastguardsman came up to ask what he was doing. The stammered explanation that he was watching the waves only confirmed the suspicion of this man of earth that Severn was looking out for contraband 'which let down all the high romance which the waves had inspired.'

Detained in the Solent by a contrary wind, the ship put in at Portsmouth. They had been in the Channel ten days now. Assured that no progress could be made that day, Keats and Severn went across to Bedhampton, seven miles away, to visit the Snooks.

Here the cruel jest of fate was rounded off. Brown, bitterly disappointed at missing Keats so narrowly at Gravesend, and not caring to remain in London, had set off for Chichester where he was staying with old Mr. Dilke. If Keats had known that Brown was only ten miles distant from him he would have been doubly disappointed: from one of the letters to Fanny Keats it would appear as if the Brawnes had been expecting Brown to follow Keats to Italy. This seems to have been little more than a vivid hope. Probably necessary arrangements for Abigail and the child born in July forced Brown to remain in England. A few months later he would have gone more than willingly, but a shortage of money prevented him.

Keats maintained a resolutely cheerful manner. The Snooks thought that he looked and seemed far better than they would have expected.

In his old picturesque way he abused the captain roundly for their delay and expressed a lively dislike of Mrs. Pidgeon. Brown, writing about Keats's visit to Bedhampton, said: 'neither the boisterous weather, nor his antipathies, nor his anger, will do him harm . . . they are good physic to his mind, & will help to purge away his apprehensions.' Brown knew better than anyone, except George, the danger of brooding to Keats and his craving in mental disturbance to be moving on. What he could not know was the full extent of his agony at leaving Fanny Brawne. At Bedhampton Keats had been sorely tempted to return to London.

Off Yarmouth, Isle of Wight, where the *Maria Crowther* was soon becalmed, having been unable to get out of the Solent before the wind dropped, Keats nerved himself for the letter to Brown which he had been delaying in the hope of being able to give his friend some hint of recovery: now he felt that he ought to write while strength was left to him:

I wish to write on subjects that will not agitate me much,—there is one I must mention and have done with it. Even if my body would recover of itself, this would prevent it. The very thing which I want to live most for will be a great occasion of my death. I cannot help it. Who can help it? Were I in health it would make me ill, and how can I bear it in my state? I dare say you will be able to guess on what subject I am harping—you know what was my greatest pain during the first part of my illness at your house. I wish for death every day and night to deliver me from these pains, and then I wish death away, for death would destroy even those pains which are better than nothing. Land and Sea, weakness and decline are great seperators, but death is the great divorcer for ever. When the pang of this thought has passed through my mind, I may say the bitterness of death is passed.

I often wish for you that you might flatter me with the best. I think without my mentioning it for my sake you would be a friend to Miss Brawne when I am dead. You think she has many faults—but, for my sake, think she has not one— —if there is any thing you can do for her by word or deed I know you will do it. I am in a state at present in which woman merely as woman can have no more power over me than stocks and stones, and yet the difference of my sensations with respect to Miss Brawne and my Sister is amazing. The one seems to absorb the other to a degree incredible. I seldom think of my Brother and Sister—in america. The thought of leaving Miss Brawne is beyond every thing horrible—the sense of darkness coming over me—I eternally see her figure eternally vanishing. Some of the phrases she was in the habit of using during my last nursing at Wentworth place ring in my ears. Is there another Life? Shall I awake and find all this a dream? There must be we cannot be created for this sort of suffering. The receiving of this letter is to be one of yours. I will say nothing about our friendship or rather yours to me more than that as you deserve to escape you will never be so unhappy as I am. I should think of—you in my last moments.

I shall endeavour to write to Miss Brawne if possible to day. A sudden stop to my life in the middle of one of these Letters would be no bad thing for it keeps one in a sort of fever awhile. Though fatigued with a Letter longer than any I have written for a long while it would be better to go on for ever than awake to a sense of contrary winds. We expect to put into Portland roads to night. The Captn the Crew and the Passengers are all ill temper'd and weary. I shall write to dilke. I feel as if I was closing my last letter to you.

Hope of a fair start for Italy was defeated the next day by another calm off the Dorsetshire coast. They landed in Lulworth Cove.[1] The unnaturally high spirits of the early days of the voyage had been dropping more frequently into dumb despair and heavy brooding, but now Keats appeared to recover for a few hours his old happy communion with nature. Severn was relieved and delighted; exploring under Keats's guidance the 'caverns and grottoes,' the rock tunnels and fissures of Stair Hole and Durdle Door. Keats, he said, was full of 'a poet's pride' in showing his friends the beauties of a coast already familiar to himself.

We have no record of Keats visiting this part of the country; but perhaps, as Thomas Hardy suggested to Sir Sidney Colvin, he was related to a family of the same name who lived round Dorchester and who bore in face and fire and independence of character a marked resemblance. Keats might have explored the caves in childhood.

On his return to the ship, perhaps reminded by a memory of a careless boyhood's happiness of the joy he had lost, he wrote down the sonnet:

> Bright Star, would I were stedfast as thou art—
>   Not in lone splendor hung aloft the night
> And watching, with eternal lids apart,
>   Like nature's patient, sleepless Eremite,
> The moving waters at their priestlike task
>   Of pure ablution round earth's human shores,
> Or gazing on the new soft-fallen masque
>   Of snow upon the mountains and the moors.
> No—yet still stedfast, still unchangeable,
>   Pillow'd upon my fair love's ripening breast,
> To feel for ever its soft swell, and fall
>   Awake for ever in a sweet unrest,
> Still, still to hear her tender-taken breath,
> And so live ever—or else swoon to death.

[1] Or was it Holworth? See *The Mask of Keats*. Mr. Gittings also amplifies Hardy's suggestion given below. But *see* Appendix XII.

Severn was under the impression that the poem had been composed here: its beauty and power nourished the hope, never absent from his mind, that Keats might recover. He begged for a copy. Keats wrote the sonnet into a volume of Shakespeare's poems Reynolds had given him, on a blank page opposite the heading 'A Lover's Complaint.' He gave to Severn both the volume and the roughly pencilled draft.

Bright Star would I were stedfast as thou art—
Not in lone splendor hung aloft the night
And watching, with eternal lids apart,
Like nature's patient sleepless Eremite,
The moving waters at their priestlike task
Of pure ablution round earth's human shores
Or gazing on the new soft-fallen masque
Of snow upon the mountains and the moors
No — yet still stedfast, still unchangeable
Pillow'd upon my fair love's ripening breast,
To feel for ever its soft swell and fall,
Awake for ever in a sweet unrest,
Still, still to hear her tender taken breath
And so live ever — or else swoon to death

At length, after prowling a fortnight about the Channel like a caged lion, the *Maria Crowther* broke free and sailed past Land's End into the Bay of Biscay. There she encountered squally weather. The passengers were often confined to their bunks with port-holes closed for many hours. Miss Cotterell was getting visibly weaker. The confinement and lack of air, added to fears for the safety of the ship in the heavy seas, must have been a living agony to her. She and Keats reacted on one another, to the detriment of both. They would compare symptoms with a morbidity distressing to Severn. He was up on deck as much as was possible watching with a painter's eye the magnificence of the driving

John Keats on his death-bed
From a drawing by Joseph Severn in the Keats-Shelley Memorial House, Rome

The life mask of John Keats
From an electrotype in the National
Portrait Gallery

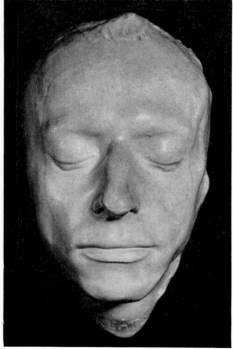

The death mask of John Keats
By permission of the owner.
Copyright strictly reserved

skies and the long curling waves of the sea; cheered at the way in which the gallant little ship met each wave and rode over it diagonally.

Off Cape St. Vincent the wind dropped and a dead calm ensued. On deck and able to converse free from the wind and rain, Keats and Severn read aloud to each other *Don Juan*. When they came to the shipwreck in Canto II Keats flung the book away from him in disgust at the cynicism and flippancy of the treatment.

The sea was smooth with only a gentle undulating movement and glittering bright under a warm sun. They saw in the clarity of the water large and strange fish. Once a whale came up to blow. But the lovely serenity was soon to be broken. The next day they found themselves near to some Portuguese men-of-war.

At first the vessels were an added interest and they leaned on the taffrail admiring a large four-decker, the *San Josef*, heaving gently on the shimmering waves. Suddenly a shot passed close under the cabin window. The *San Josef* had been signalling, but Captain Walsh was below shaving and no one had answered her. The man-of-war drifted nearer and someone shouting through a speaking-trumpet asked, in English, if the *Maria Crowther* had sighted any Spanish or Portuguese privateers, pirate ships sailing away to South America where an attempt was being made to throw off the dominion of Spain and Portugal. Captain Walsh answered no, but was obliged to bring his vessel nearer the *San Josef* for closer enquiry.

The proximity of the immense hulk of the four-decker towering above them, with her decks and rigging swarming with savage, dirty sailors, terrified passengers and captain alike. Captain Walsh had a private reason for fear; vessels in the Bay of Biscay were sometimes plundered. Soon to their relief the *San Josef* sailed away. That afternoon they met with an English naval sloop, a trim, shining contrast to the grim and filthy *San Josef*. When she heard that the *Maria Crowther* had been challenged she turned in pursuit of the Portuguese warships. The admiral commanding them was not chasing privateers, but was himself a rebel trying to prevent vessels going to the help of Spain which was then in the throes of a Carlist rising.

They passed the rock of Gibraltar before dawn and saw the coast of Barbary lit up by the sun's rays in savage beauty. Soon Gibraltar lay behind them, glowing like a vast topaz. Severn made a water-colour sketch while Keats lay quiet under the spell of the scene 'with a look of serene abstraction upon his worn face.'

While passing through the straits (of Gibraltar) Severn 'perceived great changes in Keats for the better—he seem'd recovering—at least looked like it', but this hope was soon dashed when, in some forty-eight hours, Keats was again in a fever, perspiring heavily and coughing up blood. For this sad relapse there was some definite cause which Severn, as he had hastily to finish his letter for despatch, only hinted at in the letter to Haslam quoted above.

They proceeded in lovely weather, and at length, after a voyage of thirty-three days, sailed into the Bay of Naples:

The white houses were lit up with the rising sun, which had just begun to touch them, and being tier above tier upon the hill-slopes, they had a lovely appearance, with so much green verdure and the many vineyards and olive grounds about them. Vesuvius had an immense line of smoke-clouds built up, which every now and then opened and changed with the sun's golden light, edging and composing all kinds of groups and shapes in lengths and masses for miles. Then the mountains of Sorrento to the right seemed like lapis lazuli and gold; the sea between being of a very deep blue such as we had not seen elsewhere, and so rich and beautiful that it gave great splendour to all the objects on shore. . . . Keats was simply entranced with the unsurpassable beauty of the panorama, and looked longingly at the splendid city of Naples and her terraced gardens and vineyards, upon the long range of the Apennines, with majestic Vesuvius emitting strange writhing columns of smoke, golden at their sunlit fringes, and upon the azure foreground covered with ships and all manner of white-sailed small craft.

Severn was always glad when a look of serene enjoyment came to Keats's face, 'for he was often so distraught, with so sad a look in his eyes and with, moreover, a starved, haunting expression that bewildered me.' He had not yet struck at the root of his friend's suffering. Probably he would in regard to Fanny Brawne have echoed Reynolds's opinion that 'Absence from the poor idle Thing of Woman-kind, to whom he has so unaccountably attached himself will not be an ill thing.'

However much they might long to set foot on land again they could not yet escape from the close confinement of the ship. As there was an epidemic of typhus in London, a not uncommon thing in those days of primitive sanitation, the *Maria Crowther* was put in quarantine for ten days. But it was at least a satisfaction to be held in such a lovely place.

The first few hours in the Bay were delightful to Severn. Miss Cotterell was desperately ill, but even she seemed happier now they were in port. Keats, although her suffering added cruelly to his own, was heartening to her in his gaiety. He could not have avoided regarding her somewhat in the light of a patient: perhaps her need helped him to smother down his own hot pain. If he were marching up against a battery so was she, so young and gentle and a woman.

To Severn he talked of that antique world so alive in his mind when 'the Greek galleys and Tyrhenian sloops brought northwards

strange tales of what was happening in Hellas and the mysterious East.'
Ancient and modern Italy were mingling for them. Boatloads of people
passed and repassed in the gay harbour playing upon guitars, laughing,
singing or throwing into the bright air snatches of conversation in their
liquid lovely tongue as they came alongside to barter.

The ship was anchored near the Castell d' Uovo and all day clusters
of richly coloured shouting figures were surrounding her with heaps of
bright fruit—grapes, peaches, figs, melons and new kinds to bring fresh
delight to the palate. This was a keen pleasure to the ill-fed passengers
and especially to Keats who loved ripe fruit. To Severn it seemed as if
he were in Paradise.

The English fleet was in the Bay, and seeing the Union Jack flying
at the masthead of the *Maria Crowther*, the Admiral sent an officer to
make enquiries. Instead of remaining alongside, Lieutenant Sullivan,
with six of his men, came aboard, and as the ship was in quarantine
there they had to remain.

The ship's quarters, already uncomfortably close, were now
horribly congested. However, the cheerfulness of the visitors, and the
luxury of the food and wine that was brought to them, made up at
first in some measure for the discomfort. Charles Cotterell, the brother
of the sick girl, soon appeared alongside and in his gratitude to Keats
and Severn for their care of his sister loaded them with presents. A
bunch of autumn flowers was a joy to Keats, although he would gladly
have given all of them for an English dog-rose.

Soon the rain came down. Discomfort became misery and acute
suffering for the invalids. Severn was now feeling particularly well,
frequent sea-sickness having cleared his liver, but even he felt as if the
foul thick atmosphere of the cabin would kill him: for Miss Cotterell,
with her craving for air, it must have been a living hell.

Not many days passed before Charles Cotterell, anxious about his
sister, came on board, adding one more to their number. With an
English ability to make the best of a situation the little colony were as
merry as they were able. The blunder of the British officers brought,
when the weather was temporarily kind, more of the gay bobbing little
boats filled with people come to mock at them. Mr. Cotterell, who
spoke not only Italian fluently but also the Neapolitan patois, threw
back answers to their gibes much to the taste of the laughing peasants,
translating rapidly for the benefit of those on board. Keats delighted
Severn by the careless gaiety of his manner. His 'golden jokes' and
puns added to the general merriment. But when one of the boatmen
struck up in the presence of the ladies an obscene song, he flared up in
one of his rages, a 'wisp-of-straw' conflagration.

On October 24th he wrote to Mrs. Brawne, 'it looks like a dream

—every man who can row his boat and walk and talk seems a different being from myself. I do not feel in the world.' After telling her of their situation, that he was no better and no worse than when he left England and how the illness of Miss Cotterell had played upon his nerves, he wrote:

I dare not fix my Mind upon Fanny, I have not dared to think of her. The only comfort I have had that way has been in thinking for hours together of having the knife she gave me put in a silver-case—the hair in a Locket—and the Pocket Book in a gold net—Show her this. I dare say no more—Yet you must not believe I am so ill as this Letter may look, for if ever there was a person born without the faculty of hoping, I am he . . . O what an account I could give you of the Bay of Naples if I could once more feel myself a Citizen of this world—I feel a spirit in my Brain would lay it forth pleasantly— O what a misery it is to have an intellect in splints! My Love again to Fanny . . .

In the postscript he wrote: 'Good bye Fanny! God bless you.' In the letter to Brown from Yarmouth he had promised to write to Fanny, but had not done so. This Fanny may not, for her peace of mind, have known; it seems doubtful if that painful letter to Brown were sent at the time. She did not want him to suffer the anguish of writing to her.

Although warned they would be sadly disillusioned with Naples, during ten days of squalid misery the two men looked longingly at the beautiful city. On the 31st they left the ship in chilly rain and mist, taking affectionate leave of the captain who had been more than kind and especially to Keats.

Mr. Cotterell had wanted to invite them to his own house, but had not room for more than his invalid sister. He conducted them to the inn *Villa di Londra* and gave them dinner. They rejoiced in the air and space of large rooms with a fine view of Vesuvius, but had already found out the truth of their friends' disparagement at Naples, being 'quite taken aback by the dirt, the noise, and the smell.' Severn gives a vivid account of the city:

Everything seemed offensive, except the glorious autumnal atmosphere, and the sense of light and joy of the vintage, which was everywhere in evidence. With songs and laughter and cries, and endless coming and going, the whole city seemed in motion . . . The city itself, with its indiscriminate noises and bewildering smells, struck us as one great kitchen, for cooking was going on in every street and at almost every house—*at*, not *in*, for it was all done out-of-doors or upon the thresholds. At every corner was a bare-legged Neapolitan devouring macaroni and roaring for more; mariners in red caps were hawking fish at the tip-top of their voices; and everywhere beggars were strumming guitars or howling ballads. The whole occupation of the citizens seemed to be done in the streets, and never ceased, for, as we soon experienced, it went on all night, so that at first we could not sleep for the continued row.

It will be seen from the above that the wet weather did not last long. The glorious autumnal air warm with the sun was a heady wine away from the stench of the city. The scent and joy of the grape-harvest penetrated even to the heart of Naples: men ran about the streets with heavy-laden baskets of the fruit shouting their wares in a raucous delight.

On the next day Severn wrote to Haslam telling him that Keats was calm and 'thinks favourably of this place for we are meeting with much kind treatment on every side.' Keats himself wrote to Brown:

. . . I am afraid to speak of what I would the fainest dwell upon. As I have gone thus far into it, I must go on a little ;—perhaps it may relieve the load of WRETCHEDNESS which presses upon me. The persuasion that I shall see her no more will kill me. I cannot q— My dear Brown, I should have had her when I was in health, and I should have remained well. I can bear to die— I cannot bear to leave her. O, God! God! God! Everything I have in my trunks that reminds me of her goes through me like a spear. The silk lining she put in my travelling cap scalds my head. My imagination is horribly vivid about her—I see her—I hear her. There is nothing in the world of sufficient interest to divert me from her a moment. This was the case when I was in England; I cannot recollect, without shuddering, the time that I was a prisoner at Hunt's, and used to keep my eyes fixed on Hampstead all day. Then there was a good hope of seeing her again—Now!—O that I could be buried near where she lives! I am afraid to write to her—to receive a letter from her—to see her hand writing would break my heart—even to hear of her any how, to see her name written would be more than I can bear. My dear Brown, what am I to do? Where can I look for consolation or ease? If I had any chance of recovery, this passion would kill me. Indeed, through the whole of my illness, both at your house and at Kentish Town, this fever has never ceased wearing me out. When you write to me, which you will do immediately, write to Rome (poste restante)—if she is well and happy, put a mark thus + ; if—
Remember me to all. I will endeavour to bear my miseries patiently. A person in my state of health should not have such miseries to bear. Write a short note to my sister, saying you have heard from me. Severn is very well. If I were in better health I would urge your coming to Rome. I fear there is no one can give me any comfort. Is there any news of George? O, that something fortunate had ever happened to me or my brothers!—then I might hope,—but despair is forced upon me as a habit. My dear Brown, for my sake, be her advocate for ever. I cannot say a word about Naples; I do not feel at all concerned in the thousand novelties around me. I am afraid to write to her. I should like her to know that I do not forget her. Oh, Brown, I

have coals of fire in my breast. It surprises me that the human heart is capable of containing and bearing so much misery. Was I born for this end? God bless her, and her mother, and my sister, and George, and his wife, and you, and all!

That night misery broke through his resolutely composed mask of cheerfulness. He told Severn much of his grief. His loving emotional friend was at first overwhelmed, but encouraged him to talk in the hope that it might bring relief. Keats went to bed once more outwardly calm.

Having missed the courier they had kept their letters back. The next morning Severn added to his letter to Haslam, telling him how Keats had spoken out and that he felt sure it had relieved him. He ended: 'this Morning he is still very much better—we are in good spirits and I may say hopefull fellows—at least I may say as much for Keats—he made an Italian Pun today—the rain is coming down in torrents.' It is evident that Keats had not told Severn of his inward conviction that he must die.

They remained in Naples four days. Charles Cotterell and other members of the English colony were kind and attentive to them. They drove out into the country-side. Keats admired the flowers growing in abundance and especially the roses, though on being presented with a bouquet of them from a garden he was disappointed to find in them no scent. The story goes that he threw the bunch down in disgust, exclaiming that a rose without scent was a humbug and that he hated humbug both in men and flowers. This, told years later at second hand, was probably an exaggeration. One can hardly imagine Keats, with his love of flowers, handling them roughly or even making a violent remark about a gift procured from an entire stranger by Cotterell who had taken the trouble to descend from the carriage to ask for the roses.

On this ride his old humour gleamed up at the sight of some men by the wayside ravening macaroni in large quantities. He asked that some small coin to buy more macaroni might be thrown to these fellows who scorned 'the humbug of knives and forks.'

If Keats had been in health his native humour and his ability to discern behind 'disagreeables' essential truth would have helped him, in spite of the misery of the people to enjoy the broad Hogarthian scenes in the streets of Naples. We might have had from him sketches as comic and yet as tragically poignant as the 'Duchess of Dunghill.'

The movement and volubility of the crowds were at this time increased by unwonted excitement: there was a revolution in progress. The yoke of a tyrannical king had for a time been thrown off. King Ferdinand had been forced to agree a constitution.[1]

---

[1] Severn (*see* Sharp's *Life*, p. 63), probably in old age, gave a garbled and telescoped account of the political events of the period.

Keats had little faith in the power of the people to maintain their liberty even when he saw the outwardly imposing ranks of the King's army, the backbone of the rebellion. Dire poverty and disease had weakened the Neapolitans to a painful degree. Men and women with faces disfigured and eaten away by a foul disease were a common sight. Professional beggars were an abiding horror to the tourist. This was not the environment for a sick man with nerves on stretch with weakness and sorrow; a man who had in health felt so strongly the misery of the common people. Severn had wanted him to remain in Naples, thinking that the kindness and attention of Cotterell and his friends might be ill exchanged for unknown conditions in Rome, but Keats was anxious to get away.

One evening Keats and Severn went to the San Carlo Theatre, the interior of which was so heavily gilded that it seemed to be built of gold. In common with all Neapolitan theatres it stank abominably. The acting was poor and the singing indifferent, but both men admired the scene-painting and especially the representation of two soldiers on either side of the stage. The audience seemed quiet and dispirited.

When the act came to an end Keats and Severn were amazed to see the soldiers move. They were not painted effigies but flesh-and-blood sentries put upon the stage to secure order; the police (*agenti di Pubblica Sicurezza*), who are still present on the stage at performances in Italian theatres, having the right to call on the army in times of public disturbance. Keats, not realizing such was the custom and looking round at an audience apparently tired and dispirited, was immediately furious. He worked himself up into a frenzy of anger and contempt, declaring he would go at once to Rome; that he could not bear to think he might die and be buried among a people so debased.

The next morning a letter arrived from Shelley repeating his invitation and giving Keats advice how to live in the country; but Keats had already written to Dr. Clark in Rome asking him to obtain lodgings for them, and the letter of credit was with Torlonia, the banker, there. To Rome they would go.

After a farewell dinner given by Cotterell in their honour they set out the next morning in a small carriage. As the *vettura* crawled along Severn was able to keep walking pace beside it, enjoying the air and the exercise. Keats was quiet and listless, though he tried to respond to Severn's enthusiasm for the beauty of the country. In face of an exceptionally fine view, or when they caught sight of the blueness of the sea, he would brighten a little. Severn picked wild flowers to show him and soon the little carriage was filled with fragrance and blossom. Severn found gratification in the strange delight, the almost fanatical ecstasy of Keats over the flowers.

They passed through rich valleys with the hills above them covered for miles and miles with vineyards in which the grape-vines were festooned in natural twists and curves from tree to tree. Severn felt that this land of promise was 'thrown away on these idle beasts of Italians' who 'crawl about like moving logs.' The inns on the road to Rome were notoriously bad: Keats's health was not improved by the poor accommodation and indifferent food. The journey, taking it slowly as they did, seems to have occupied about nine days.

At length they reached the Roman Campagna, the vast uneven wastes of which Keats likened to an inland ocean. Contemporary descriptions of the approach to Rome suggest, in the typical period dislike of wide, solitary spaces, something of the hateful, menacing desolation of Browning's country in 'Childe Roland to the Dark Tower came.' Carcases and skeletons of horses lay about. Ghastly shrivelled arms and legs of highwaymen, the pests of richer travellers, were stuck on posts at intervals on the road. Sometimes there would tower above them a stretch of massy, ruined aqueduct, grim relic of a dead glory.

On the wideness of the plain they saw a shifting spot of bright red, and on approaching, found it to be the crimson cloak of a cardinal. He was shooting small birds which he attracted towards the ground by a small looking-glass attached to an owl tied loosely to a stick. Two liveried footmen were in solemn attendance to load the fowling-pieces.

The bare loneliness of the approach to Rome heightened her ancient beauty. Keats entered her by the Lateran Gate, never to leave her again.

'Land and Sea, weakness and decline are great separators, but death is the great divorcer for ever.'

CHAPTER XXI

The End

DR. CLARK had taken lodgings for them at No. 26, Piazza di Spagna, a house opposite to his own and beside the steps leading up to the church of the Trinità on the Pincian Hill.

The Piazza di Spagna was in the heart of the English quarter of Rome. There were at this time so many English in the city that to the poorer Roman the word 'traveller' was almost synonymous with 'Englishman.' There were many Scotch and English innkeepers and some of the Italian *albergatori* took British names. All the English in Rome were regarded as 'milords' by the people of the tradesmen class and thought to be fabulously rich. Prices were regulated accordingly. The wealthy would enter Rome through the Porto del Popolo and drive through the Via del Babuino into the Piazza di Spagna. Here their high and bulky travelling-carriages, too large to be driven into mews or stables, would stand, much to the inconvenience of both foot-passengers and vehicles.

In the centre of the square is an old fountain called *della Barcaccia* and made in the form of a galley. This commemorates the legend that here the Emperor Domitian had an arena in which he staged mimic sea-fights. The square, called in an old Italian Itinerary 'one of the most beautiful and magnificent in Rome,' was a highway from the fashionable walk on the Pincian Hill to the Corso, the main street of the city, and a lively position for an invalid. Round the fountain brightly coloured chattering groups of peasants would gather, and on the steps leading to the Trinità professional artists' models gathered for hire, a motley collection of Virgins, Josephs and *banditti*.

Dr. James Clark, a Scotsman of thirty-two, was a physician and surgeon who had made a special study of phthisis. Later, becoming Queen Victoria's physician-in-ordinary, he was twice an object of public censure, once with a faulty and scandalous diagnosis in the case of Lady Flora Hastings, a lady-in-waiting, and more seriously when, refusing consultation, he failed to discover until too late that the Prince Consort was suffering from typhus fever. The Queen, however, retained confidence in him: he was created a baronet, became a member of the Senate for the University of London, and ended his days at Bagshot Park, a house lent to him by Queen Victoria. To the end of his long and eminent life (he died in 1870) Sir James Clark probably never suspected his ultimate popular fame would rest upon the fact that, near the beginning of his career, he attended a young dying poet.

From the first Dr. Clark took a vivid interest in Keats, heartily wishing he were wealthy enough to maintain him in Rome at his own expense. He quickly realized that there was on his patient's mind a load which would retard recovery and wrote to England asking that all financial anxiety be removed. He feared that Keats might be painfully conscious of living on the money of friends.

Although he suspected disease of the heart and lungs Clark thought the main seat of the trouble to be the stomach. He found Severn 'very attentive to him, but . . . not best suited for his companion.' It seems likely that poor Severn was affected by illness, and especially the illness of a friend, in the same way as Keats, but with less power of mind or discipline of past sorrow to control the feeling. In quarantine he had once been obliged to creep away into a corner to indulge in a passion of tears. Acute sensibility made his task of nursing Keats harder and his unselfish devotion the finer.

At first Keats's health improved. Rome could not but be a joy to him, although it was a pale shadow of that joy he might have felt in health and with his love beside him. To the young painter Rome was a revelation. The past was reanimated for him in the mind of the poet Keats; that universal mind which could leap the centuries and live freely in time.

Dr. Clark, fearing it might prove too much for him, forbade regular sight-seeing: Keats did, however, go to see one of the notorieties of the day, the new statue by Canova of the Princess Borghese, a sister of Napoleon. The statue is nude to the waist and reclines on a sofa with the body lifted up on one elbow. The other arm rests lightly on the up-curved hip and the hand holds an apple. Keats found it 'in beautiful bad taste' and gave it a name which was to remain, 'The Æolian Harp.' It is told of Princess Pauline that when a friend remonstrated with her for sitting half-naked to the sculptor, she replied: "Oh, there was a very good fire in the room."

This beautiful and notorious lady used to walk on the fashionable promenade, the Pincian Hill. Here Keats and Severn spent much of their time with a consumptive who was alone in Rome, a Lieutenant Elton. Elton, a tall and exceptionally handsome man, attracted the roving eye of the Princess. Her bold and languishing glances so wrought upon Keats's nerves that he declared he could walk on the Pincian Hill no longer. Soon, however, the doctor ordered exercise on horseback and the two young invalids went riding. Severn was now freer. He could study the beauties of Rome and begin to pursue his art again.

Soon after their arrival Keats had insisted that Severn should visit the artists to whom he had introductions. Dr. Clark had given him a further introduction to John Gibson, the sculptor. When Severn arrived at the studio Lord Colchester, a connoisseur and patron of the arts, was present. Severn modestly made a move to retire, but Gibson insisted he should come in and gave him the same attention as to the nobleman. This struck Severn as odd and gratifying: artists must be men of considerably more consequence in Rome than in England where they were treated as a kind of superior tradesmen. He hastened home to tell Keats who was delighted with what he called this first 'treat to humanity.'

In discussing Severn's prospects Keats was not too sure that the coming to Rome would be an advantage in his application for the Scholarship. The touchy Council of the Academy might be offended: here was a man applying for the Rome Scholarship when he was already there. Keats had another reason for believing there would be considerable opposition to the award of the pension of which he now told Severn for the first time. The group of painters round the Academy were prone to sorry jealousies. Keats had been present at a dinner given by De Wint when the award of the gold medal was being discussed. One painter present said it had been given to an old man who had tried for it so many times that the Council felt pity for him.

Keats waited for this absurd lie to be refuted. Hilton, personally acquainted with Severn, was there. No word came. Keats rose in a passion, saying he would no longer sit at table with such traducers and snobs; that they very well knew that Severn was a young man and had never before tried for a prize of any kind. Keats knew him intimately and had seen and admired the picture sent in. He walked out of the house.

Keats urged his friend to begin at once upon sketches for the picture he must submit to the Academy. The subject of it was to be 'The Death of Alcibiades.' While Severn worked he himself read or studied Italian; even contemplated the writing of a long poem on Milton's Sabrina, a project discussed with Severn on the journey out. He tried loyally to remain cheerful in aspect and to employ his restless mind, but one day he opened a volume of Alfieri at the first tragedy in the book, 'Filippo,' and came upon:

> Misera me! sollievo a me non resta
> Altro che'l pianto, ed il pianto è delitto.[1]

He lost his control and threw the book away from him in anguish.

---

[1] Wretched me! there is no solace left for me
Except weeping, and weeping is a crime.

On November 30th Keats wrote with difficulty his last letter. It was to Brown. He said:

... I am afraid to encounter the pro-ing and con-ing of anything interesting to me in England. I have an habitual feeling of my real life having passed, and that I am leading a posthumous existence. God knows how it would have been—but it appears to me—however, I will not speak of that subject. I must have been at Bedhampton nearly at the time you were writing to me from Chichester—how unfortunate—and to pass on the river too! There was my star predominant! I cannot answer anything in your letter, which followed me from Naples to Rome, because I am afraid to look it over again. I am so weak (in mind) that I cannot bear the sight of any handwriting of a friend I love so much as I do you. Yet I ride the little horse, and, at my worst, even in quarantine, summoned up more puns, in a sort of desperation, in one week than in any year of my life. There is one thought enough to kill me; I have been well, healthy, alert, &c., walking with her, and now—the knowledge of contrast, feeling for light and shade, all that information (primitive sense) necessary for a poem, are great enemies to the recovery of the stomach. There, you rogue, I put you to the torture; but you must bring your philosophy to bear, as I do mine, really, or how should I be able to live?

He had not yet written to Reynolds, but delayed week by week in the hope of being able to send better news of his health. He wrote sadly:

If I recover, I will do all in my power to correct the mistakes made during sickness; and if I should not, all my faults will be forgiven.

He asked Brown to write to George and to his sister 'who walks about my imagination like a ghost—she is so like Tom.' He ended: 'I can scarcely bid you good-bye, even in a letter. I always made an awkward bow. God bless you!'

The stomach trouble was not improved by the bad food they had for the first week. It was sent up by a *trattoria* or restaurant situated, Severn told a visitor in old age, on the ground floor of the house, and apparently belonging to the landlady. Complaints to her being of no avail, Keats hit upon a plan to mend matters which he would not reveal to his friend. When next the porter came up with the food Keats went forward smiling roguishly at Severn and saying: "Now, Severn, you'll see it!" Taking the large square tin box which contained the dishes he opened the window 'and thus disappeared a fowl, a rice pudding, cauliflower, a dish of macaroni, etc.' The *padrona* was present but she joined good-naturedly in the shout of laughter which went up from the astonished porter. "Now," said Keats, "you'll see, Severn, that we'll have a decent dinner." In less than half an hour an excellent meal came up and without extra charge.

In future they were well served. Severn appreciated the good fare, and especially the vegetables which were fine, and beautifully cooked. The *padrona*, however, charged them heavily on the general assumption that all Englishmen were 'milords.'

As Keats had expressed a wish for music Severn hired from one Anna Angeletti in the house (almost certainly the landlady) a pianoforte for seven *scudi* (about thirty-two shillings) a month. Dr. Clark lent him some volumes of music and among them Haydn's symphonies. The symphonies gave Keats particular delight. He said: 'This Haydn is like a child for there is no knowing what he will do next!' Severn was able to give his friend many hours of relief from brooding by playing to him.

On Sunday, December 10th, Keats had a severe hæmorrhage followed by others. He was soon in a dangerously high fever. Dr. Clark took eight ounces of blood from his arm. It was thick and black.

When the doctor had left them Keats got out of bed in search of one of the medicines he had asked Severn to buy at the chemists in Gravesend, a 'fore-seen resource,' a bottle of laudanum; but Severn, guessing why this drug was ordered, had put it out of reach. Keats demanded to have the laudanum. Severn refused. Keats raged at him but he remained steady.

When his passion had subsided Keats pleaded in heart-rending words to let him end his life, to let him spare a dear friend the trouble and anguish, the squalid detail of a painful death. Severn spoke gently and firmly, telling him that to end his life would be to wrong his friends; that he himself felt it a privilege to nurse him. Keats then fell into such a paroxysm of rage and despair that Severn feared he would die. When Dr. Clark came again he took the laudanum away.

Severn's convictions as a Christian forbade him to allow his friend this merciful way out. For this modern humanitarian feeling must not blame Severn, but rather pity him for the cruelty he was obliged to inflict and admire him for his strength to do it. Brown might have acted otherwise, but Brown had perhaps unwittingly given Keats far more pain in his last days: with his strongly expressed agnostic views it was probably he who had reft from Keats that hope in an after-life which had lessened in some degree the parting from Tom. Now he was despairingly convinced that Death would divorce him for ever from the woman he loved.

Severn was heavily burdened. Italians had at that time a morbid fear of illness: neither the landlady nor her maid would do anything to help. Severn was obliged to light fires, make beds and prepare light foods for Keats in addition to incessant attendance on him. Keats with his forehead burning, eyes glassy and staring, harrowed him by talking of England, of Brown and of the happy days in Mrs. Brawne's care. Fever had robbed Keats of his habitual reticence and now his misery was more fully brought home to Severn.

All hope of saving his life seemed vain. Dr. Clark would not commit himself but hinted that he could not 'minister to a mind diseased.' He redoubled his kindness and attention and, although a busy man, went all over Rome one day to find a particular sort of fish for Keats. His wife prepared it. In future she cooked any solid food Keats was able or allowed to take.

His diet was kept cruelly low. He seems to have lived mainly on bread-and-milk. In his ravings he cried out that he would die of hunger. Heart-rent by his complaints Severn was moved to give him more than the doctor had allowed, only to be told with severity that he would kill his friend if he exceeded the prescribed diet. Dr. Clark came over to see his patient four or five times a day and said that he was to be called if he were needed any time of the day or night.

In Keats's grief and suffering his sister was not forgotten. He sent a message to Brown asking that Mrs. Brawne and Mrs. Dilke should call upon her at Walthamstow.

There were in the house two other British subjects; one an elderly Englishman and the other a young Irishman, both with men-servants of their own. They seem not to have lifted a finger for Severn. A sculptor living in Rome, William Ewing, came in to relieve Severn from time to time and helped him in various ways.

At home the anxious waiting girl was impatient for news from Rome. She had heard indirectly from Brown and Haslam of the acute discomfort in quarantine, of the arrival of Keats in Rome and his improvement in health, but this good news had not allayed her fears as it was necessarily stale. A letter then took a fortnight to arrive in England. Haslam was not much cheered. He continued to hope sturdily, but regarded the spitting of blood during the voyage as ominous. He exhorted Severn to keep up his diary letters and hoped that 'Doctor Clark will give' to Severn 'what you most stand in need of—a confidence amounting to a faith.' Severn must keep a firm and happy countenance before the invalid.

On December 14th Severn wrote unhappily to Brown. This letter did not reach England until late in the next month: on January 16th we find Fanny Brawne telling Fanny Keats that her brother is exercising on horseback every day. It was from a letter written to Brown on the 17th that the Brawnes heard the mournful news of Keats's relapse.

Christmas, probably the first he had spent away from his family, was to Severn 'the strangest and saddest, yet not altogether the least happy I had ever spent.' Keats, now rid of his fever but weak and suffering, must often from his bed have watched this friend of his who was older in years and yet so much younger at heart. Severn was a man who in many ways never grew old; one who kept to the end youthful enthusiasms and found new ones. He saw life perhaps too rosily, but this gift could bring happiness to others.

Keats must have wondered what future lay before this eager, volatile spirit. One day he turned his large eyes, glowing in the thin face, towards his friend and said:

"Severn, I bequeath to you all the happiness I have ever known."

Severn thought he was wandering again and tried to soothe him, but Keats continued firmly:

"This is the last Christmas I shall ever see but I hope you will see many and be happy. It would be second death for me if I knew that your goodness now was your loss hereafter."

Perhaps it was permitted to him to know that Severn's temporary sacrifice to him was the means of prosperity in the future. It was as the friend of Keats that Severn's reputation first rose in the English colony of Rome, to spread outward over the years until he was a successful painter in oils with a European patronage.

In early January, Severn had a fresh anxiety added to his burden: the *padrona* reported to the police that there was a man in her house dying of consumption. This meant that by Roman law everything in his room, even the paper on the walls, would after his death be destroyed by fire and compensation paid to the owner. As the fever left Keats he slowly improved in health and was moved for a part of the day into the larger, airier sitting-room. If this were known it would mean that the contents of both rooms would be burnt. There was in the sitting-room property to the value of one hundred and fifty pounds apart from the personal loss of books and private possessions. It would be difficult enough to pay for the simple furnishings of the bedroom without this large sum being added.

Severn having no money, well aware that none would come from his friend's estate, had to move Keats without the landlady's knowledge. This was not easy as she lived on the same floor and the servant, when she did trouble to clean the lodgers' apartments, entered from an adjoining room. Severn took the precaution of blocking up the communicating door while he prepared the room for Keats.

Naturally Keats could not be told anything of the matter. Severn was forced to go dinnerless and to tell him that the servant had prepared the room while he took a meal out. Keats did not believe him but, mercifully for Severn, made no further enquiry. No one but Dr. Clark knew of the use of the second room.

By the middle of the month Keats was well enough to go out into the sunshine, but this news could not reach England until the next month. Severn's despairing letter had only reached Brown on January 9th. At Wentworth Place he and the two women were in a state of miserable suspense. It was Mrs. Brawne's painful task, herself agitated, to tell her daughter that Keats was dangerously ill. Fanny received the news with the calmness of despair. She said: "I believe he must soon die and when you hear of his death tell me immediately. I am not a fool." Brown wrote to Severn:

He is present to me everywhere and at all times—he now seems sitting by my side and looking hard in my face, though I have taken the opportunity of writing this in company—for I scarcely believe I could do it alone. Much as I have loved him, I never knew how closely he was wound about my heart.

He expressed again his personal gratitude to Severn. In a letter to Keats of December 21st he had written: 'Do you remember my anagram on your name? How pat it comes now to Severn! My love to him and the said anagram, "Thanks Joe!"'

Severn's letters to his family were as cheerful as he could make them. He laid stress for his mother's benefit on the good food and how he enjoyed it. He told them that 'at the beginning of January all the trees were in blossom here, and in our houses we have roses blowing—when I know you have nothing but your bellows blowing.'

On January 11th he wrote hopefully to Mrs. Brawne; out of a mistaken sense of kindness, too hopefully. Keats, he said, 'had changed to calmness and quietude, as singular as productive of good for his mind was most certainly killing him.' Keats himself had no wish to live and had taken a final leave 'of this world and all its future hopes'; but out of this calm, a putting aside of dreams and ambitions, his friend hoped that new strength would come.

Fanny had withheld the bad news from Fanny Keats, but now when there was 'merely a hope, a chance,' she wrote to tell her of the attack. She could not share with Severn the delusion that the calm which was come upon Keats might herald a recovery. 'He has given up even wishing to live.'

Good God! Is it to be borne that he, formed for everything good, and, I think I dare say, for everything great is to give up his hopes of life and happiness so young too, and to be murdered, for that is the case, by a mere malignity of the world, joined to want of feeling in those who ought above all to have felt for him—I am sure that nothing during his long illness has hurt me so much as to hear he was resigned to die. . . .

Towards the end of January Keats was again seriously ill. This attack he knew to be his last. When the hæmorrhages were over he lay with eyes closed in a sunken state bordering on death.

Severn, sitting by him far into the night, felt it dangerous to fall asleep. Often he had kept himself awake by writing letters, but to-night as, weeping silently, he looked at the wan, thin face on the pillow, he had not the heart for writing. Suddenly he thought of a way in which he could both keep himself awake and give to Keats's friends a memorial of these last days. He made a tender and lovely drawing[1] of Keats's head with the light of the candle upon it, writing underneath, '28th Jan. 3 o'clock Mg. Drawn to keep me awake—a deadly sweat was on him all this night.'

Severn, scarcely ever able to leave Keats, no longer had, perhaps from motives of economy, his meals sent up from the *trattoria* below and often depended for food on the kindly ministrations of Mrs. Clark who constantly sent in small delicacies, both for invalid and nurse.

That nervous irritability which makes the attendance on consumptives peculiarly hard now increased to an almost unbearable degree: by day and night Keats was making demands on him. He would ask for a hot drink and when it was given him no longer want it. Once Severn made coffee for him twice and each time he threw it away without drinking it. When Severn patiently made a third cup Keats, touched into his old consideration and love for his friend, broke down, crying out against the fate which made him inflict so much suffering on one so devoted. He wondered, knowing his friend's uneven temperament, that he could remain so steadfast. Severn, an earnest Christian, must be supported now by a higher power.

Severn, who had inwardly lamented Keats's lack of faith, that in his last moments he could not have the consolation of religion, procured a copy of Jeremy Taylor's *Holy Living and Dying* and tried to prepare Keats's mind for death. Keats listened with patience, eager to grasp at a hope of a life to come. He allowed Severn to pray beside him.

Keats's bright falcon eyes were large and of an unearthly brightness. When Dr. Clark came in he would look up at him and say: "How long is this posthumous existence of mine to last?" The good doctor, although accustomed to pain and death, was so moved that often he could not speak.

There was added to Severn's anxieties the possibility of money difficulties. On coming to Rome Keats had, on the advice of Torlonia,

[1] Original is in the Keats-Shelley Memorial House, Rome.

the banker, drawn one hundred and twenty pounds on his first draft and placed it in the bank. This had put Taylor in an awkward position; he had been expecting that the credit would be drawn upon in small sums and that in the meantime he could make up the balance with money sent over by George. Not a penny had come from America: Taylor found himself unable to meet the credit. Dr. Clark wrote to England urging that the matter be set right at once as no word of money difficulties must come to the ear of his patient.

Taylor immediately set to work to collect some money. Rice, Hilton and other friends subscribed ten pounds each and Taylor took fifty from a sum entrusted to him by Lord Fitzwilliam for the benefit of the peasant poet Clare and John Keats. This was done as rapidly as possible, but the matter could not be arranged with Torlonia in faraway Italy before the harassed Severn was reduced to his last crown, and that owing for rent. He could have earned money by painting miniatures for the wealthy English in Rome, but was unable to leave the house. Keats could not bear him out of his sight.

This heavy anxiety, added to the ever-present inward grief that his friend was dying 'without the common spiritual comforts that many a rogue and fool has in his last moments,' made Severn's burden almost intolerable. But he went on day after day by the death-bed, tending, soothing and humouring his friend and sitting up far into the night.

Sometimes, however hard he might try to fight against it, fatigue would overcome him. He would awake in the dark and have to fumble with flint and steel to get a light again. One night Keats awoke just as the candle was guttering to the finish and, as Severn was dozing, did not like to rouse him. Suddenly a second candle lit up as if by magic. Keats, charmed, called out: "Severn! Severn! here's a little fairy lamplighter actually lit up the second candle!" Severn had fixed a thread from the base of one candle to the wick of the other.

These days were dark and long. Keats lay in his bed in painful longing for kindly death. Anxious letters came from friends, but he had no wish to see them. He was too far now from life. His sister and his beloved wrote. Their letters remained unopened. Fanny Brawne's letters were only to be given to him if he expressed a wish to hear from her. He never did. Once when Severn inadvertently gave him a letter from her the painful agitation it aroused threw him into a fever. He could not open it.

At home the poor girl was waiting for the end which must come. From time to time her nerves would betray her into fits of boisterous gaiety painful to her anxious mother and to Brown. Mrs. Brawne had kept from her the worst of the news. Brown did not agree with this course, thinking it better she should know the exact state of affairs. She wrote to Fanny Keats: 'All I do is to persuade myself, I shall never see him again.'

Dr. Clark, afraid that Severn might break down, arranged for an English nurse to relieve him. Keats liked her. Severn was able to get out into the air and sunshine.

Keats asked him to visit his future resting-place, the open burial-ground of the non-Catholics at the foot of Monte Testaccio within the ancient walls of the city. There were daisies and anemones there and sweet-scented violets overspreading the graves. Keats loved violets. He said: "I can already feel the flowers growing over me."

Sheep grazed on the open field and flocks of goats were brought there. A few ilex-trees threw a dark and grateful shade and an ancient tomb, the pyramid of Caius Cestius, pointed upwards to the sky linking the old with the new, a silent memory of antique time. It was a scene in part familiar to Keats: Poussin, Claude and Salvator Rosa had painted there. 'It might make one in love with death, to think that one should be buried in so sweet a place.'

Unfortunately the nurse was taken ill,[1] so after a few brief hours of leisure Severn was again kept by the bedside. As Keats neared the grave he became calmer; talking a good deal, but so peacefully that Severn could not even now entirely suppress a tiny flame of hope. But all hope must have been at an end when at night, on the 12th, Keats pronounced those poignant words to be written on his tomb; a tomb which, with its broken-stringed lyre, Severn had already designed at his particular request some time before they left England.

As he lay now 'very calm and resigned', his only anxiety was a fear that Severn might contract the disease. "You must not," he said, "look at me in my dying gasp nor breathe my passing breath—not even breathe on me." The risk to Severn's health was greater than Keats in his generation could have guessed: Severn was not a robust man and years of sedentary work must have robbed him of much of the resilience of youth. But mercifully the tragic story of John Keats was not further darkened by the death of his devoted friend. By some miracle Severn escaped infection, living on to a great age.

Three days before Keats's death he was visited by a Spanish gentleman, Señor Valentin Maria Llanos y Gutierrez, who, if Keats could have looked into the future, would have been of singular interest to him. With an introduction probably from Severn, Señor Llanos visited the Brawnes in September, 1821, and soon after called on Miss Fanny Keats at Walthamstow. In March, 1826, she became Señora Llanos.

---

[1] She was, however, again in attendance the day Keats died. *See* Severn's letter to Taylor, March 6th, 1821, *The Keats Circle*, p. 225.

From time to time in these last days Keats gave to Severn clear directions as to what he wished to be done after his death. As he lay quietly waiting for the end he held tightly in his hand a white cornelian, 'the gift of his widowing love.' This seemed to be his only consolation, the only thing tangible in a shadowy world.

As he grew weaker he would lie for hours as if asleep: when he opened his eyes there was in them a look of doubt and horror until he saw the familiar figure of his friend sitting patiently by him. It was these 'bright falcon eyes' which alone remained to bring to Severn's memory those happy hours in wood and meadow when the light and colour, the small rustlings of nature had brought to them quick attention and a rapt joy. Now they had a steady piercing, an unearthly look hardly to be borne.

At half-past four in the afternoon of Friday, February 23rd, he whispered: "Severn, lift me up, for I am dying. I shall die easy." Looking up into the face of his friend he added: "Don't be frightened. Thank God it has come."

Severn took him in his arms. The phlegm was boiling and tearing in his chest and throat. The grim fight for breath lasted seven hours. He held fast to Severn's hand. At eleven o'clock the breathing was easier: he might have been sleeping. But life was ebbing away. Before midnight Keats was dead.

The next day his body was opened. The lungs were found to be almost entirely destroyed. The marvel was that he had lived so long. A cast was taken of the face, hand and foot.[1] Unopened letters from the two girls he loved were placed in the coffin, together with a purse and some hair. The letter from Fanny Brawne, the receipt of which had so torn his spirit, was laid on his heart.

He was buried on the 26th. There followed Severn, Dr. Clark and a Dr. Luby, Dr. Wolff (the English Chaplain), William Ewing, Richard Westmacott, Henry Parke and Ambrose Poynter. Because of the hostility of the Romans to non-Catholics it was necessary for interments in the Protestant cemetery to take place at night or in the early morning. It was dark when the carriage left the Piazza di Spagna but dawn was breaking as they reached the foot of the pyramid of Caius Cestius.

Severn, exhausted and grief-stricken, had to be supported at the graveside by William Ewing. After the men had filled in the earth Dr. Clark made them plant some tufts of daisies on the mound. He thought Keats would have wished it.

The news of Keats's death did not reach England until the middle of

[1] *See* Appendix XIV.

March. Fanny Brawne took it quietly. To his sister she wrote: 'you do not, you never can know how much he suffered. So much that I do believe were it in my power I would not bring him back.' She wasted with inward grief, lost her fine colour and was for years painfully thin. It was twelve years before she married. She never spoke willingly of him and wore the ring he had given her to the day of her death.

For weeks after Keats's death Severn lay ill at the last sad home in the Piazza di Spagna. As painter, and later as British Consul, he spent in Rome many years of his long life always remembering Keats, watching with pride a growing poetic fame and valuing more and more the privilege of having been his friend. To pass through the Piazza di Spagna was ever pain to him.

He would spend quiet hours alone in the burial-ground at the foot of Mount Testaccio where the tomb of old Caius Cestius threw for a space of each day a pointing shadow, the shadow of antique time, over the grave of Keats. By early summer the red-rimmed daisies had over-spread the grave and soon the violets crept up. When in 1861, Severn, an old man, returned to Rome after an absence of twenty years, the custodian of the cemetery complained that he could not keep the violets on the grave; they were so constantly plucked as remembrances. Severn answered him rejoicing: "Sow and plant twice as much."

Sixty-one years after Keats's death Severn's body was laid there beside the honoured grave of his friend; the nameless grave on which are written those words immortal:

Here lies One
Whose Name was writ in Water.

APPENDICES

I

(i) The story of Keats's financial embarrassments begins with the will of his grandfather, John Jennings, dated 1st February, 1805, five weeks before his death when from the shaky signature one may judge he was already a dying man. He employed, not a lawyer but a land surveyor, Joseph Pearson of Edmonton, to whose amateur drafting the uncertainty of the terms of the bequest to his son, Midgley, and the consequent Chancery proceedings, were due. The executors of the will were Alice Jennings, Midgley John Jennings and Charles Danvers of Upper Thames Street, City of London.

When the terms of a will were uncertain, by the law of that time action had to be brought before the Court of Chancery. Mr. Gittings has asserted that the action Rawlings v. Jennings was unfriendly, but 'before the Judicature Act (1873) the *form* of all such actions had to be undoubtedly contentious —one had to assert a wrong or an injury in order to claim a remedy, or indeed to obtain a ruling' (quoted from Mr. John Rutherford's review of *The Keats Inheritance*, Keats-Shelley *Journal*, vol. XV, 1966). Alexander Popham, a Master in Chancery, on March 6th, 1806, said: 'I have been attended by the Solicitor for all Parties.' This in itself refutes Mr. Gittings' assertion that the action was litigious.

Terms of the Will and Court of Chancery decisions

To his wife, Alice Jennings, 'two hundred pounds per year being part of the monies I now have in Bank Security entirely for her own Use and disposal—together with all my household furniture and effects of what nature or kind soever that I may be possessed of at the time of my decease.'

On May 22nd, 1806, observing "this will is very obscure," the Master of the Rolls directed that 'so much capital stock' should be paid to Mrs. Jennings 'as will produce her £200 a year.' Mrs. Jennings claimed the whole residue of the personal estate, viz., that a surplus undisposed by the terms of the will should be regarded as 'effects,' but this claim was not sustained: the surplus went into the general estate to be divided—according to the law at that time—between the executors. Charles Danvers disclaiming, it was divided between Alice and Midgley John.

To his son, Midgley John, three thousand nine hundred pounds 'for his use during his Natural life and if he shall die without issue I then give and bequeath to his widow if living at the time of his decease the sum of £500—and the remaining part to return to my family.'

Owing to the figure of £3,900 being incorrect, it was found that John

Jennings had in fact left only £2,900 of Government stock to his son (see *The Keats Inheritance*, p. 11). In 1806 Midgley enquired of the Court 'whether the capital will, upon his death without issue, sink into the residue of the testator's personal estate or not: and whether on his death leaving issue, the said capital will or will not belong, and become payable to, and divisible between such issue.' The Court postponed a decision until such a situation should arise.

In July 1811 the Lord High Chancellor directed that the widow of Midgley Jennings (died on November 21st, 1808) should retain half of the money left to him for life and half of the surplus mentioned above, and in 1815, after the death of Mary Sweetingburgh, half of the capital of the latter's annuity.

> To his daughter, Frances Rawlings, 'Fifty Pounds per year during her natural Life and after her Decease the same to be equally divided amongst my Grand Children Sons and Daughter of the said Frances Rawlings, children of the late Thomas Keats.'

The amount of £1,666.13.4. was set aside by the Court for this purpose. Because the Keats children were not informed of its existence, this money remained in Chancery untouched until 1825 when Fanny obtained administration of her brothers' estates.

£200 which should have been paid to Frances Rawlings as arrears on her annuity and maintenance for her children allowed up to her death from interest on the £1,000 legacy mentioned below (after her death the property of William Rawlings but not claimed by him) lay in Chancery unclaimed until 1888 when (no trace of Rawlings' descendants being found) Ralph Thomas, a solicitor examining the Keats's money affairs for the information of Sir Sidney Colvin, claimed it for Mdme. Llanos (Fanny Keats) and, it is thought, obtained it for her. This however is not certain: the fact remains that there is still, 165 years after Jennings's death, in the list of 'Unclaimed Balances' in the Court of Chancery a sum of £260.3.10 'to the credit of Rawlings v. Jennings'.

In 1806 Frances Rawlings (Rawlings *v.* Jennings) had claimed a share of the unwilled residue as next of kin but as she was not an executor the claim was disallowed.

> To the Keats grandchildren 'One thousand pounds to be equally divided amongst them as they became of age with the accumulating interest thereon' and in case either of them should die before they came of age 'the sum to be equally divided among survivors.'

This was also dealt with in 1825. See the full accounts for all the children given in *The Keats Inheritance*, Ap. 7.

> To Mary Sweetingburgh (his sister) thirty pounds a year for life.

After Mrs. Sweetingburgh died in 1813 the capital, £1,000, was divided equally between the executors of Midgley Jennings and the trustees for the Keats children, Abbey and Sandell. We do not know whether Keats received the benefit of this.

Sums of £5 to Charles Sweetingburgh, Betsy Cousins and Sarah Boswell, children of Mrs. Sweetingburgh, and to Thomas Baxter of Kensington, to his wife, and to Henry Nash of Penn Street, Bucks.

In view of the fact that it was on leasehold premises, with a lease ending on Lady Day, 1805, the 'Swan and Hoop' was not bequeathed. It is perhaps here of interest to trace the course of John Jennings' career from 1774, when he married, became a Freeman of the City and an Innholder. His address was given as the 'Swan and Hoop' but it was not until November 27th, 1776 that he leased from the Corporation of London a messuage adjoining the 'Swan and Hoop' Ale House, together with the stable yard, for eight years from the previous Lady Day. In 1784 he acquired the 'Swan and Hoop' Ale House on the south side of the stables, up to then occupied by one James Hood. After his death in 1805 there are signs in pencillings on the lease that it was about to be transferred to Frances Keats, widow, but, owing one supposes to Frances' speedy remarriage, when it would pass to her second husband the property was again split; William Turk owning and running the ale house and Joshua Vevers, assignee of William Rawlings, the stables. As Rawlings' name appears in the Triennial Directory as occupier, probably Vevers was in fact a manager, since livery stable keepers had, by the law of that time, also to be Innholders, which Rawlings was not.

In regard to Rawlings as a bank clerk, the clerks at this time were poorly paid (£75 a year if they did not 'live in' with annual increments of £5 to an average maximum of £100) and with little chance of advancement: security of tenure seems to have been the only advantage to these men who were little more than scribes. Abbey's statement that he would eventually have drawn a salary of £700 may suggest some wild boasting on Rawlings' part.

The only other property in which Jennings appears to have had an interest was at Knightsbridge, a mortgage of £1,200 to Charles Hammond.

(ii) In regard to Abbey as trustee Mr. Gittings has endeavoured to represent him as an honest man (at least up to the period of his final financial difficulties), asserting that he was entirely ignorant of the existence of the Chancery funds. But how could this be? Would any responsible person take over a trust without acquainting himself with every detail; and in this case detail readily available from Walton, the family lawyer? Also it is noticeable that no word of these funds was apparently spoken by him until George, safely in America, could be induced to sign a power of attorney.

A trustee before the *Fraudulent Trustees Act*, 1857, had large powers: it was not difficult for an ingenious man, accountable to no one, to do away with funds. Only a relation or friend could approach the Court of Chancery with a request to investigate the trust, but in the case of the young Keatses there was no one. Otherwise only his victims could question the trusteeship as they came of age—by which time there remained probably little or no means with which to prosecute. In Fanny's case, it will be remembered, Mrs. Abbey tried to put back the date of majority by misrepresenting her age. Fortunately her marriage and Dilke's vigorous aid saved her money, or part of it. In a joint will made with her husband in 1842 (see *K-S.M. Bulletin* XVIII 'Evidence in Spain' by Fernando Paradinas) Fanny declared that Abbey had robbed her of £1,500. To George in a letter dated May 31st, 1826 she forthrightly dubbed her guardian 'a consummate villain'. That George, who earlier had been hoodwinked, came to take a similar view is clear from a letter to Dilke of March 10th, 1826 (unpublished, in the Keats Memorial House) in which he writes: 'On a further examination of Mr. Abbey's behaviour I am convinced of your Opinion of him.' It is not known how much George lost through Abbey's defalcation, but it was probably a good bit more than in Fanny's case.

II

There is a small operating theatre which, by the accident of its being above a church, survived the destruction of St. Thomas's Hospital when it had to make way for a railway line in 1862. The theatre, originally a herb garret, was not set up until 1821, so Keats could not have attended operations here; but, reconstructed on an inventory found in the Hospital archives, it is of major interest as the only early nineteenth century operating theatre existing in this country. It can be seen on application to the Secretary, Guy's Hospital.

III

There were four Kirkman brothers of an age to be friendly with Keats and their cousin Mathew, born in 1794, 1795, 1797 and 1798; Edward James, Henry Richard, George Buchanan, Charles Felton. George was eventually a member of the firm of Renshaw & Kirkman, wholesale stationers, London. This information was given to Keats House by the late Dr. T. G. Crump whose wife was a Mathew.

IV

James Rice died, aged forty, on December 1st, 1832 and was buried at St Mary's Church, Putney. In 'The Reynolds–Hood Commonplace Book,' *Keats–Shelley Journal*, Vol. X, 1961 Mr. Paul Kaufman gives us two more poems by Rice which appear to show more than a warm regard for Jane Reynolds, one of which I think well worth quoting:

> Were those the Tablets of thy Heart,
> Or this a leaf of
>   Memory's tree,
> I should rejoice that even a part
> So small as this were filled by me.

2
Yet if to see and love thy worth
Might win a niche in that
pure shrine,
Believe me Jane, there's not on Earth
The Friend whose claim surpasses mine.

Rice
12 February 1816

Was he related to the Rev. Edward Rice, afterwards Head Master of Christ's Hospital?

V

p. 125, notes 1 & 2. A careful examination of available evidence by Mr. Leonidas M. Jones (Keats–Shelley *Journal* vol. III, 1954) strongly suggests that this notice was not by Keats, but Reynolds. 2. Is this a misprint for facets?

VI

Of the sonnet written at Burns's tomb we have no holograph, only a copy made by Jeffrey, Georgiana's second husband, a proved inaccurate transcriber. I think it of interest to read the transcript and compare it with the accepted edited version given in the text:

—On visiting the Tomb of Burns—
The Town, the churchyard, & the setting sun,
The Clouds, the trees, the rounded hills all seem
Though beautiful, Cold—strange—as in a dream,
I dreamed long ago, now new begun
The shortlived, paly summer is but won
From winters ague, for one hours gleam:
Through saphire warm, their stars do never beam,
All is cold Beauty; pain is never done.
For who has mind to relish Minos-wise,
The real of Beauty, free from that dead hue
Fickly imagination & sick pride
    * wan upon it! Burns! with honor due
I have oft honoured thee. Great shadow; hide
Thy face, I sin against thy native skies.
    * Note. An illegible word occurs here.

Readers will note the principal variants, 1.7, Through. 1.11. Fickly, and the word omitted guessed at as Cast. Fickly is perhaps the most interesting. Mr. J. C. Maxwell has commented in the Keats-Shelley *Journal*, vol. IV, 1955 that, although the Quarto gives fickle, the First Folio has Fickly. The Folio owned in facsimile by Keats has many markings on the page on which this occurs, *King Lear*, II, iv, 188, and pride appears in the previous line. l.12. Cast was inserted by Lord Houghton.

Mr. Maxwell also gives Middleton Murry's interpretation of this difficult poem, together with his own.

VII

In her *Fanny Brawne* Miss Joanna Richardson suggested that the Lady from Hastings might be Isabella Jones (see p. 312 here). This Mr. Gittings took up, working out an identity between the two with a good deal of circumstantial evidence cleverly presented.

In itself a linking of Mrs. Jones and the Lady, though of interest, would be relatively unimportant; but Mr. Gittings has given it importance by building up an emotional superstructure which involves the exploiting of great poems to illustrate and develop an alleged intrigue for which there is no factual basis in Keats's life (and few poets have been so well documented). All this, surprisingly enough, has been accepted, or partially accepted by some scholars in spite of the fact that Keats himself specifically stated that he had 'no libidinous thought' about the Lady, and equating her with Georgiana, the cherished and admired young sister-in-law.

Over here at least one voice has been raised in strong protest. Middleton Murry, although he accepted Isabella as the Lady, categorically declared: 'There is no evidence at all that Keats was passionately in love with Isabella Jones' (*Keats*, 1953). In America Miss Aileen Ward, following on Clarence D. Thorpe's critical review of *The Mask of Keats* in the Keats-Shelley *Journal*, vol. VI, 1957, has in vol. X, 1961, skilfully refuted the poetic 'evidence' pointing to 'the verbal parallels which Gittings offers as proof of his theory' as 'not merely remote and unconvincing . . . they are for the most part irrelevant.' As for the trifling 'Hush, hush' which Mr. Gittings uses as a sort of love manifesto, someone, probably C. W. Dilke, in the *Athenaeum* of October, 1859 suggested that the music to which Keats wrote this lyric was not, as Charlotte Reynolds stated in old age (see p. 92 here) a Spanish but a German air by one Daniel Stiebelt. Making a difficult research among the Stiebelt songs Miss Ward discovered one in 6/8 measure which admirably fits the words though she admits there may be others in the same rhythm equally possible. But whether a Spanish or a German air, it seems sensible to accept Charlotte's statement rather than Mr. Gittings' conjecture and, with Miss Ward, to date it in early 1818 when Keats was still on good terms with the Reynolds women.

In regard to Isabella Jones, Mr. Roger Ellis, of the Historical Manuscripts Commission, a collatoral descendant of Taylor, tells me of 'a persistent family tradition that Mrs. Jones was Taylor's mistress.' In the Royal Academy Exhibition, 1819, a miniature portrait of Mrs. Jones by A. E. Chalon, R.A. was exhibited. Where is it now?

VIII

Mr. Gittings has identified the elder Dilke's house in Chichester as 11, Eastgate Square. It now bears a plaque.

After four or five days there Keats and Brown walked the thirteen miles to Bedhampton to stay with Dilke's sister, Mrs. Snook, at the Mill House, a building first identified by Guy Murchie (see Keats-Shelley *Journal*, vol. III, 1954). In 1964 the Keats-Shelley Memorial Association erected a plaque, unveiled by the Earl of Bessborough, of Stansted, bearing the words: 'In this house in 1819 John Keats finished his poem "The Eve of St. Agnes" and here in 1820 he spent his last night in England.'

It is Mr. Gittings' opinion that Keats gathered material for 'The Eve of St. Mark' in Chichester: that he did so at Stansted Chapel in certain. The illuminated manuscript over which Bertha pores contains images which have previously baffled readers; images which are not Christian symbols. Mr. Gittings points out that in the stained glass above the altar Keats saw, besides stars, angels' wings and a fiery blaze, a seven-branched candlestick and the Ark of the Covenant with its attendant Cherubim. Keats may also have drawn inspiration for stanzas XXIV and XXV of 'The Eve of St. Agnes' from the side windows in the Chapel.

IX

The Astronomer Royal informs me that in 1819 the planet Venus was visible up to the end of June over the sea as a morning star before sunrise: surely Keats, in some early vigil, grieving over the parting from Fanny and watching it from that 'little coffin' of a bedroom was here inspired to write the sonnet so poignant, so intimately personal, 'Bright Star, would I were stedfast as thou art.' In this connection see Horace, Odes, I, iii. 'Venus is appealed to because having sprung from the foam of the sea she was supposed to influence the waves.' T. E. Page.

X

'The Cap and Bells'.

It is not possible to disentangle the threads of this unfinished poem. Although the two main themes (or what we conceive them to be) appear contemporary, the story is set remotely 'In midmost Ind'; recalling in the person of Elfinan the cruel tyrant Tipu Sultan, ruler of Mysore and, until routed and killed at Seringapatam in 1799, arch-enemy of the East India Company. This, though unfamiliar to us, was recent history to Keats's generation; and as constant reminder there stood in the Leadenhall headquarters of the Company for all Londoners to see (and to play with, extorting weird music and horrid groans) Tipu's Man-Tiger-Organ (see sts. XXXVII-XXXVIII) an instrument set in a wooden tiger, the Sultan's emblem, devouring a hapless European. See 'Keats's Indian Allegory' by Phyllis Mann,

Keats-Shelley *Journal*, VI, 1957. The Tiger Organ is now in the Victoria and Albert Museum.

For further suggestions as to sources etc. see *The Mask of Keats*.

XI

In *Homes and Haunts of the Most Eminent British Poets* (1847) William Howitt wrote (p. 299): 'Mr. Hunt accompanied Keats and the young lady [Fanny Brawne] to the place of embarkation in a coach, and saw them part. It was a most trying moment. Neither of them entertained a hope to see each other again in life, yet each endeavoured to subdue the feelings of such a moment, to the retention of outward composure.'

Without further evidence I have hesitated to accept this statement.

XII

Publications before 1846

Apart from separate poems printed in magazines, the first publication of Keats's works was the Paris *Galignani* in 1829 which included the works of Coleridge and Shelley. There was no English edition until 1840. In America, however, there were nine issues copying the Galignani and one which presented his work together with that of Howitt and Milman.

Over here in 1840 Keats's poems appeared in *Smith's Standard Library*, issued by William Smith and Bradbury and Evans, in a paper-backed edition at two shillings. In 1841 and 1844 this was repeated with the addition in 1841 of a frontispiece portrait by Hilton.

Mr. MacGillivray in his Bibliography warns us against laying an undue emphasis on the number of foreign editions since they were all pirated; but surely they must give a fairly strong indication that Keats was more highly valued outside his own country. After all, even if they are gathering easy profits through a pirated edition, publishers want to sell their books.

XIII

Investigation has revealed that there were numbers of Keatses in Dorset, particularly in the region of Corfe and in Poole.

From recent information, however, independently received from Dr. Paradinas, a descendant of Fanny Keats, and by Mr. Robert A. J. Jennings, great-great-grandson of Midgley John, it now appears practically certain that both the Keatses and Jennings were in early 18th century domiciled in Cornwall, at or around Madron near Penzance. See Keats-Shelley Memorial *Bulletins* XVIII and XX, 'Evidence in Spain' by Fernando Paradinas and 'The Jennings Family' by William A. W. Jarvis. Dr. Paradinas states that Fanny Llanos, in a daughter's birth certificate, registered the child's grandfather, Thomas Keats, as from Landsend.

It is also of interest to note that in the 1730's Rawlings was a common name in the Penzance district.

XIV

The death mask, which it has been conjectured was taken by Gherardi, mask-maker to Canova, was apparently sent by Severn to Taylor. After Taylor's death it was bought, in 1865 by Lord Houghton, together with a bust of Keats and a medallion, for £1 14s. I cannot trace its subsequent history.

At some time a plaster cast was taken from this matrix and sold, up to 1921 and perhaps later, first at 2s. 6d. and then 5s., by C. Smith of London. In spite of this by some curious oversight all record of the death mask (beyond the information given above) was lost to Keats scholars until 1947 when the cast photographed here came to light. I only know of two other examples one of which, belonging to Mr. Vivian Meynell, is on loan to the National Portrait Gallery. A cast catalogued in the Browning Sale, 1913 at Sotheby's (item 1394) I suspect to have been the life mask so often misdescribed.

As there can be no comparison with the matrix a remote doubt as to authenticity must be acknowledged; though the strong likeness to the later portraits is marked. Further evidence is given by measurements taken of both life and death mask by Professor F. Wood Jones, F.R.S., Fellow of the Royal College of Surgeons who, together with Mr. T. B. Layton, D.S.O., M.S. of Guy's, examined the cast. They agree that 'there is nothing incompatible with both masks being of the same man, living or dead.'

The casts of the hand and foot seem completely to have disappeared.

BIBLIOGRAPHY

Life, Letters and Literary Remains of John Keats, Richard Monckton Milnes, Moxon, 1848.

Keats's Poetical Works, with memoir by Lord Houghton, Moxon, 1866.

The Complete Works of John Keats, edited by Harry Buxton Forman, Gowans and Gray, 1901.

John Keats, Sir Sidney Colvin, Macmillan and Co. Ltd., 1920.

The Letters of John Keats, Maurice Buxton Forman, Oxford University Press, 1952.

Keats's Letters, Marginalia, Edmund Blunden, Studies in English Literature, Tokyo, 1931.

The Keats Circle and *More Letters*, ed. by Hyder E. Rollins and W. J. Bate, Harvard and Oxford University Presses, 1965.

Life of Keats, Charles Brown, edited by Dorothy Hyde Bodurtha and Willard Bissell Pope, Oxford University Press, 1937.

Recollections of Keats, by Charles Cowden Clarke, *The Atlantic Monthly*, January, 1861.

Life and Letters of Joseph Severn, William Sharp, Sampson Low, 1892.

John Keats, Letters of Joseph Severn to H. Buxton Forman, edited by Maurice Buxton Forman. Printed for private circulation, Oxford, 1933.

The Poems of John Keats, edited by H. W. Garrod, Clarendon Press, 1939.

Keats-Shelley Memorial Bulletin I–XX, edited by Rennell Rodd, Nelson Gay and Dorothy Hewlett.

Keats-Shelley *Journal* I–XVIII.

Essays in Criticism, Matthew Arnold, Macmillan and Co., 1888.

Keats's Craftsmanship, M. R. Ridley, Clarendon Press, 1933.

Poetical Works of John Keats, H. W. Garrod, Clarendon Press, 1955.

Collected Essays, No. 4, Dr. Robert Bridges, A Critical Introduction to Keats, Oxford University Press, 1929.

Studies in Keats, and *Keats*, J. Middleton Murry, Oxford University Press, 1930 and 1955.

The Living Year and *The Mask of Keats*, Robert Gittings, 1954, 1956.

The Mind of John Keats, Clarence Dewitt Thorpe, Oxford University Press, 1926.

The Evolution of Keats's Poetry, Claude Lee Finney, Sir Humphrey Milford, 1936.

Keats and Shakespeare, J. Middleton Murry, Oxford University Press, 1935.

Keats's Shakespeare, Caroline F. E. Spurgeon, Oxford University Press, 1928.

Keats and the Dæmon King, by Werner W. Beyer, New York, Oxford University Press, 1947.

The Consecrated Urn, Bernard Blackstone, Longmans, Green, 1959.

Shelley and Keats as they struck their Contemporaries, Edmund Blunden, Beaumont, 75 Charing Cross Road, 1925.

Memorials of John Flint South, C. Feltoe, John Murray, 1884.
Keats as Medical Student, Sir William Hale-White, Guy's Hospital Report, 1925.
Keats as doctor and patient, Sir William Hale-White, K.B.E., Oxford University Press, 1938.
John Keats, Apothecary and Poet, Sir George Newman, T. Booth, Sheffield, 1921.
Disciples of Æsculapius, Sir Benjamin Ward Richardson, Hutchinson, 1900.
John Keats and Joshua Waddington, by George A. R. Winston, Guy's Hospital Reports, Vol. 92, reprint, 1943.

Letters of Fanny Brawne to Fanny Keats, edited by Fred Edgcumbe, Oxford University Press, 1936.
Fanny Brawne, Joanna Richardson, Thames & Hudson, 1952.
Fanny Keats and her Letters, Marie Adami, *Cornhill Magazine*, October, 1935.
Recollections of Writers, Charles and Mary Cowden Clarke, Sampson Low, 1892.
The Diary of B. R. Haydon, edited by Willard B. Pope, Harvard University Press, 1960–63.
Imagination and Fancy, Leigh Hunt, Smith Elder and Co., 1845.
Leigh Hunt, Edmund Blunden, Cobden-Sanderson, 1930.
Shelley, Edmund Blunden, Collins, 1946.
John Hamilton Reynolds, Poetry and Prose, George L. Marsh, Sir Humphrey Milford, 1928.
Some Letters and Miscellanea of Charles Brown, edited by Maurice Buxton Forman, Oxford University Press, 1937.
The Papers of a Critic, Charles Wentworth Dilke, John Murray, 1875.
Keats's Publisher, Edmund Blunden, Jonathan Cape, 1936.
James and Horace Smith, A. H. Beavan, Hurst and Blackett, 1899.
My Long Life, Mary Cowden Clarke, T. Fisher Unwin, 1896.
The Cowden Clarkes, Richard Altick, Oxford University Press, Geoffrey Cumberlege, 1948.
Barry Cornwall, B. W. Procter, *An Autobiographical Fragment*, Bell, 1877.
Leigh Hunt's "Examiner" Examined, Edmund Blunden, Cobden-Sanderson, 1928.
Keats and the Periodicals of his Time, Modern Philology, Vol. 32, pp. 37–53. George L. Marsh and Newman I. White.
Keats, Bibliography, J. R. MacGillivray, Toronto University Press, 1949.

INDEX

A

B